HORI-san and
MIYamura-KUN

HORIMIYA

O × DAISUKE HAGIWARA

3

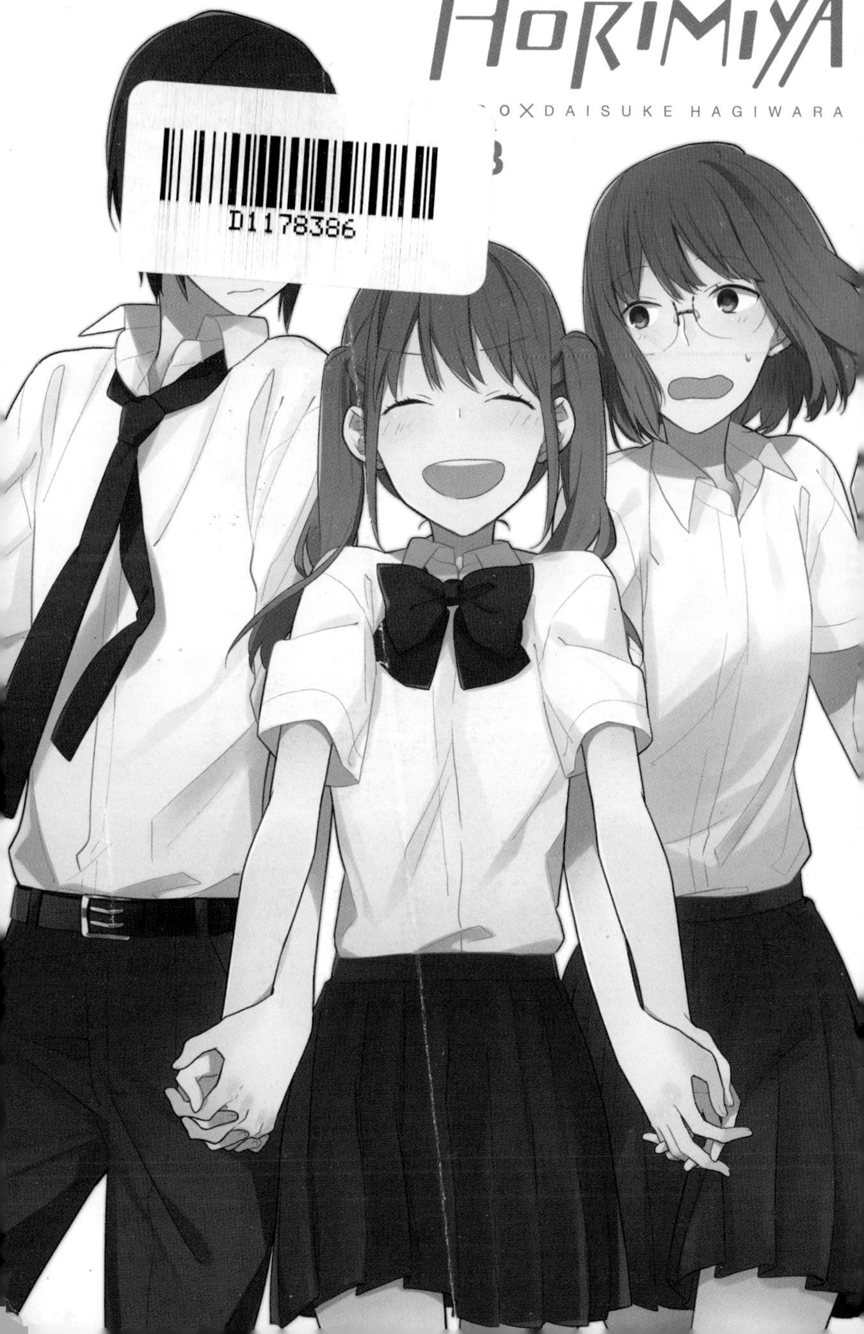

HORI-san and
MIYAMURA-kun

HORIMIYA

03

CONTENTS ★

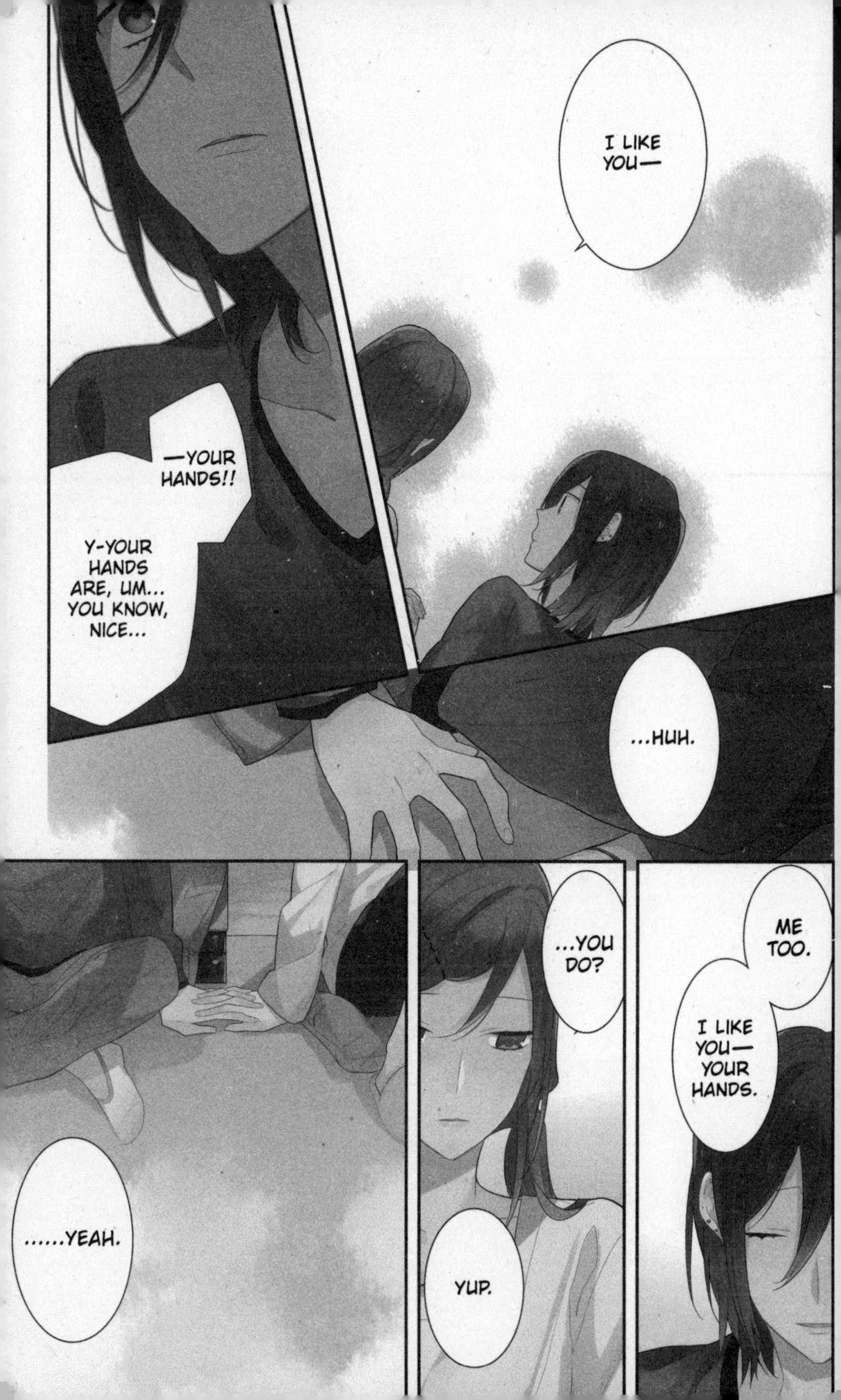
I LIKE YOU—
—YOUR HANDS!!
Y-YOUR HANDS ARE, UM... YOU KNOW, NICE...
...HUH.
ME TOO.
I LIKE YOU— YOUR HANDS.
...YOU DO?
YUP.
......YEAH.

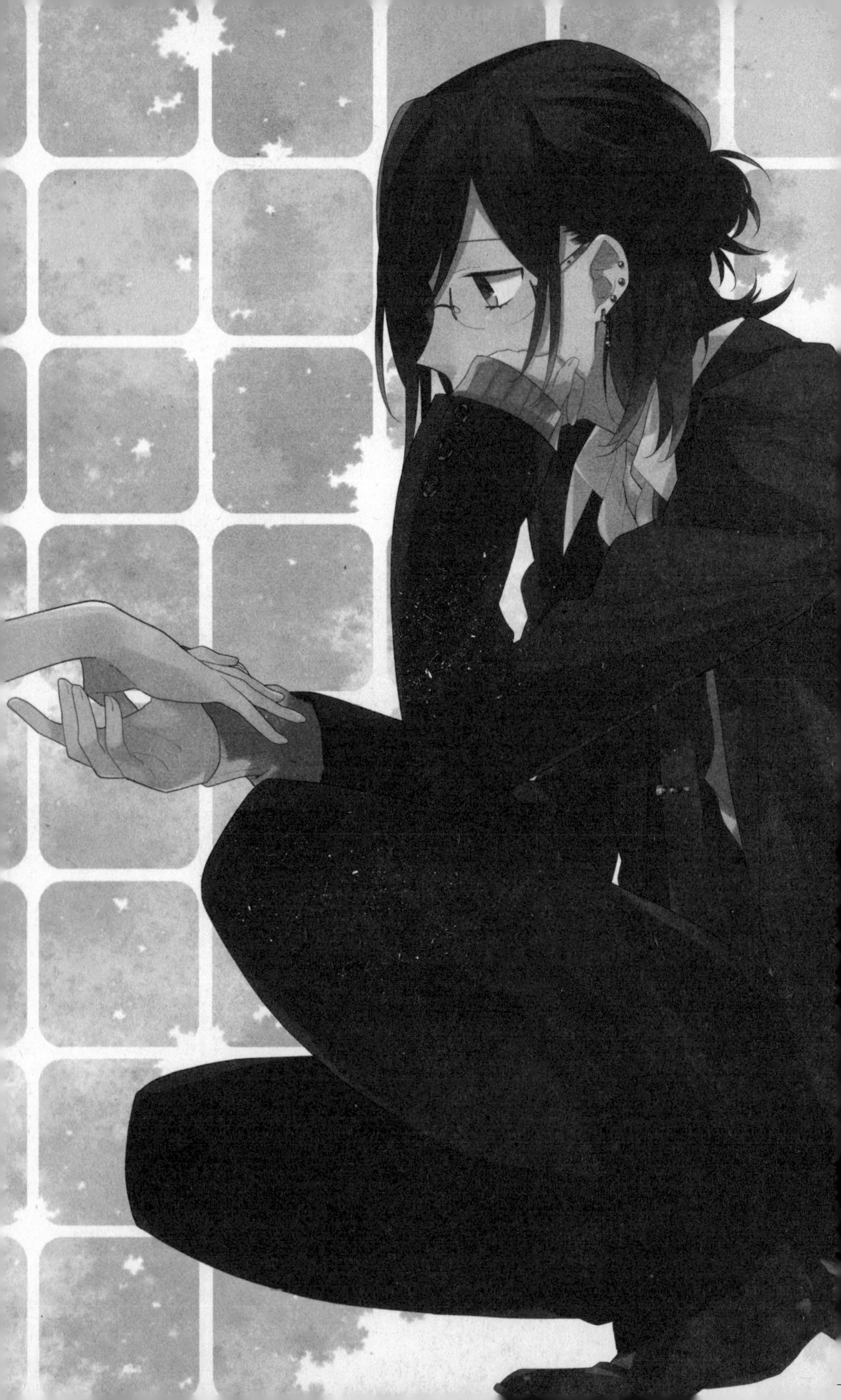

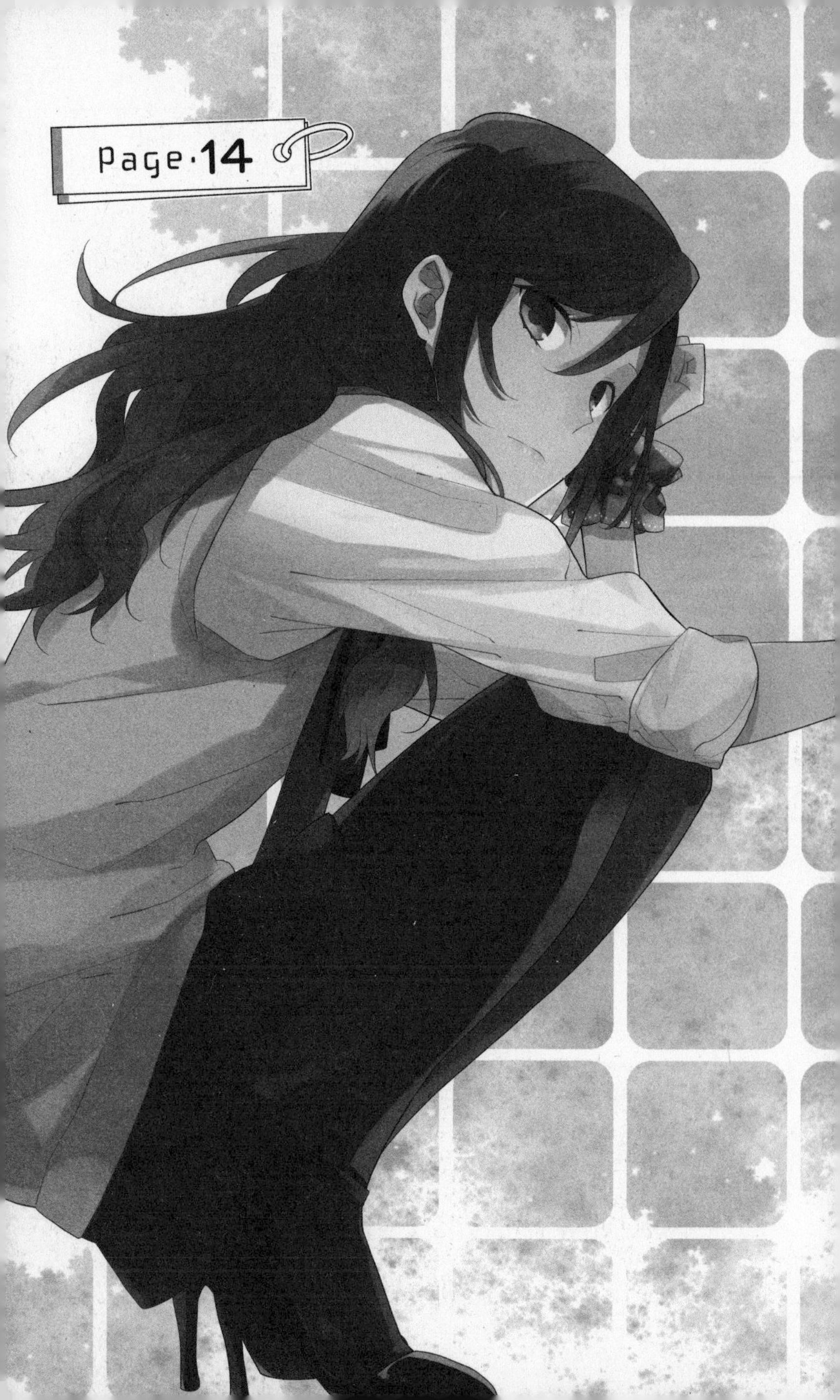
page·14

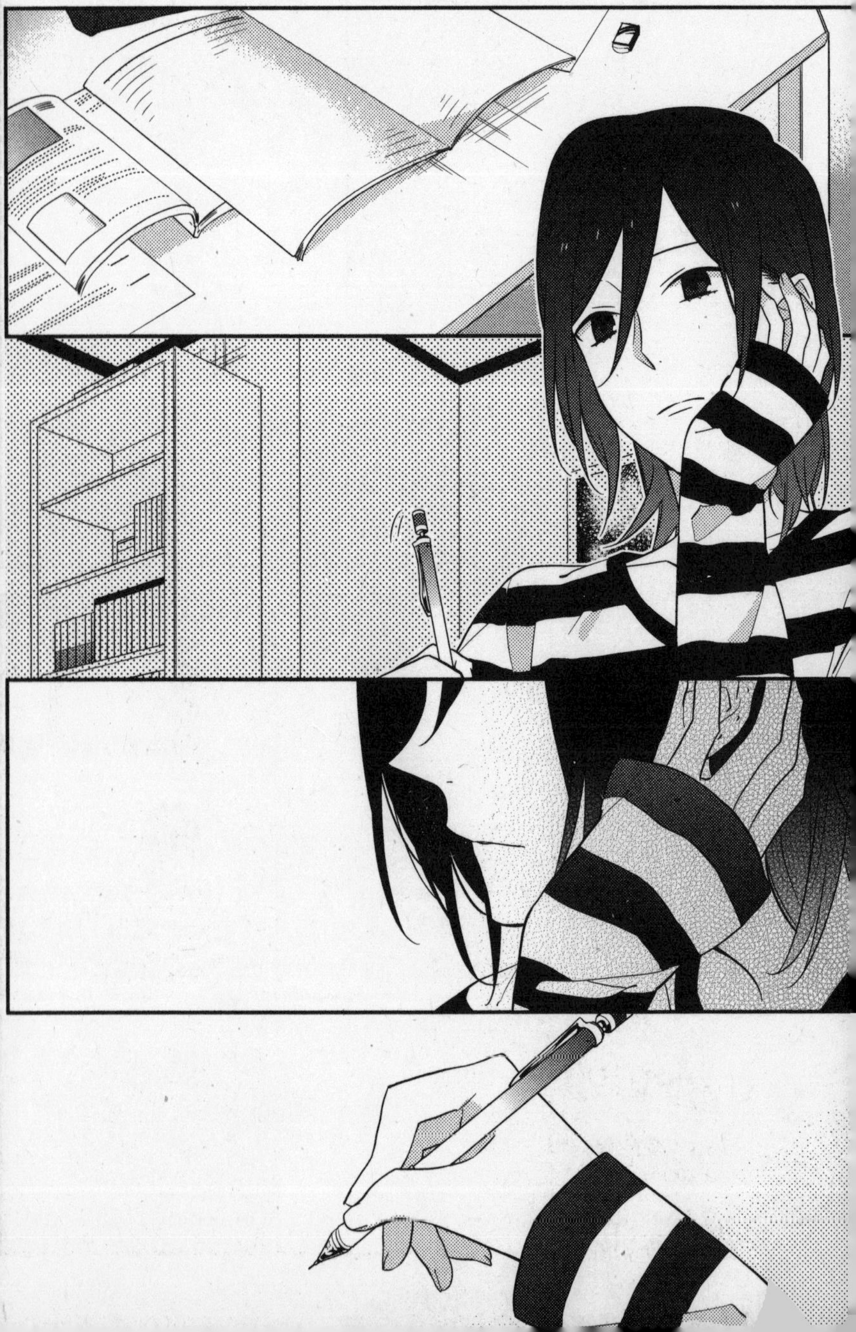

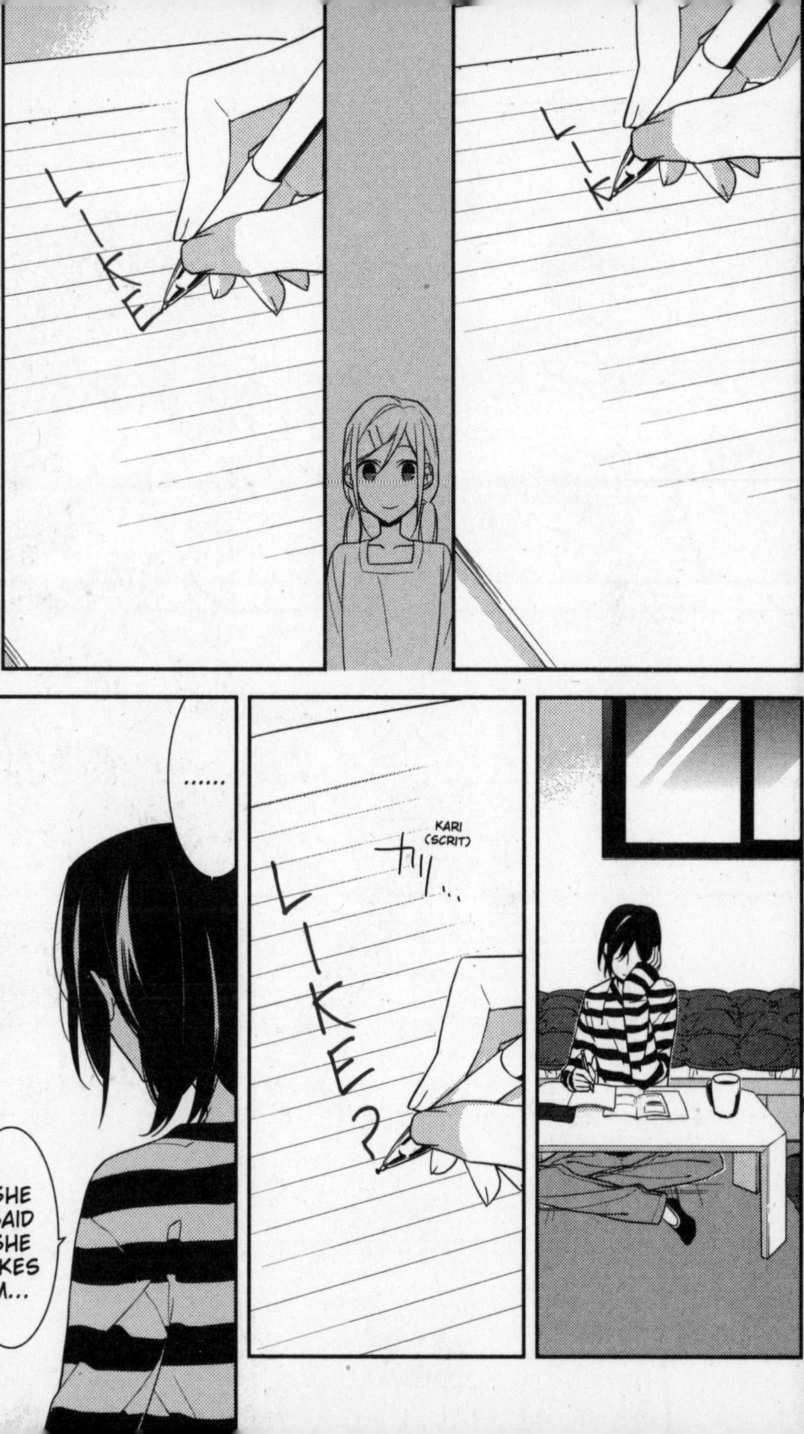
LIK
LIKE
カリ…
KARI (SCRIT)
LIKE?
......
SHE SAID SHE LIKES M...

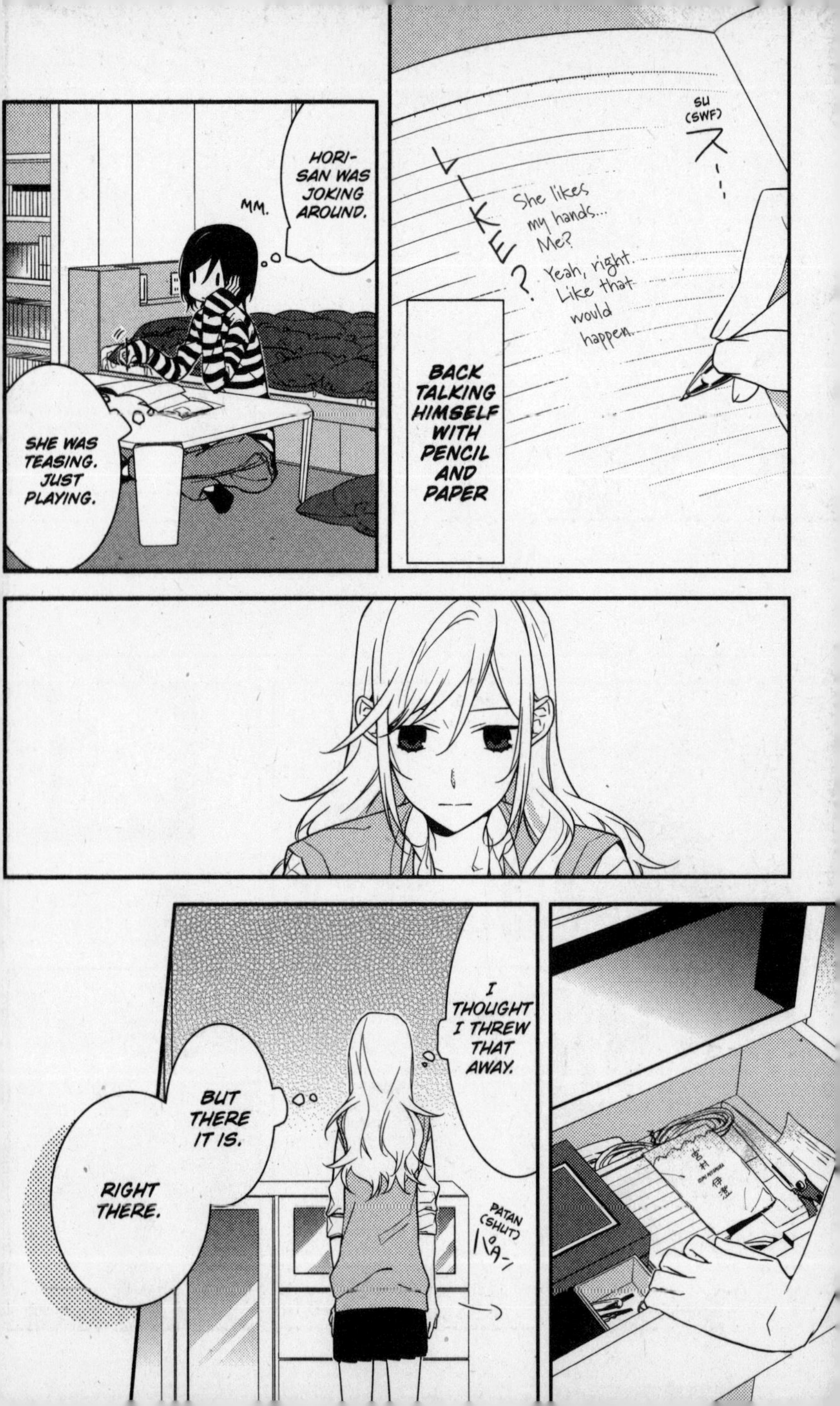
SU (SWF)
LIKE?
She likes my hands... Me?
Yeah, right. Like that would happen.
BACK TALKING HIMSELF WITH PENCIL AND PAPER
HORI-SAN WAS JOKING AROUND.
MM.
SHE WAS TEASING. JUST PLAYING.
I THOUGHT I THREW THAT AWAY.
BUT THERE IT IS.
RIGHT THERE.
PATAN (SHUT)

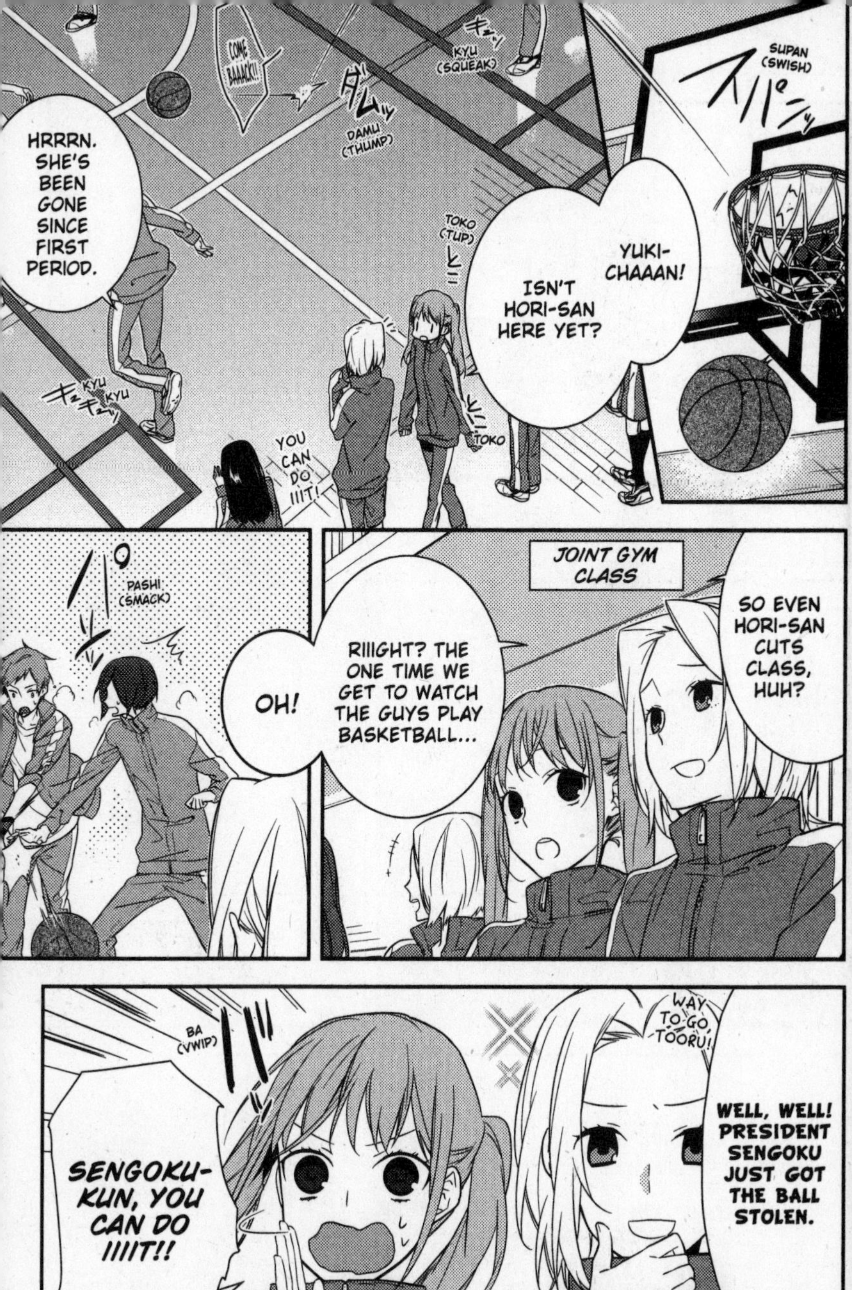
SUPAN (SWISH)
YUKI-CHAAAN!
ISN'T HORI-SAN HERE YET?
TOKO (TUP)
TOKO
KYU (SQUEAK)
COME BAAACK!!
DAMU (THUMP)
YOU CAN DO IIIIT!
HRRRN. SHE'S BEEN GONE SINCE FIRST PERIOD.
KYU KYU
JOINT GYM CLASS
SO EVEN HORI-SAN CUTS CLASS, HUH?
RIIIGHT? THE ONE TIME WE GET TO WATCH THE GUYS PLAY BASKETBALL...
OH!
PASHI (SMACK)
WAY TO GO, TOORU!
WELL, WELL! PRESIDENT SENGOKU JUST GOT THE BALL STOLEN.
BA (VWIP)
SENGOKU-KUN, YOU CAN DO IIIIT!!

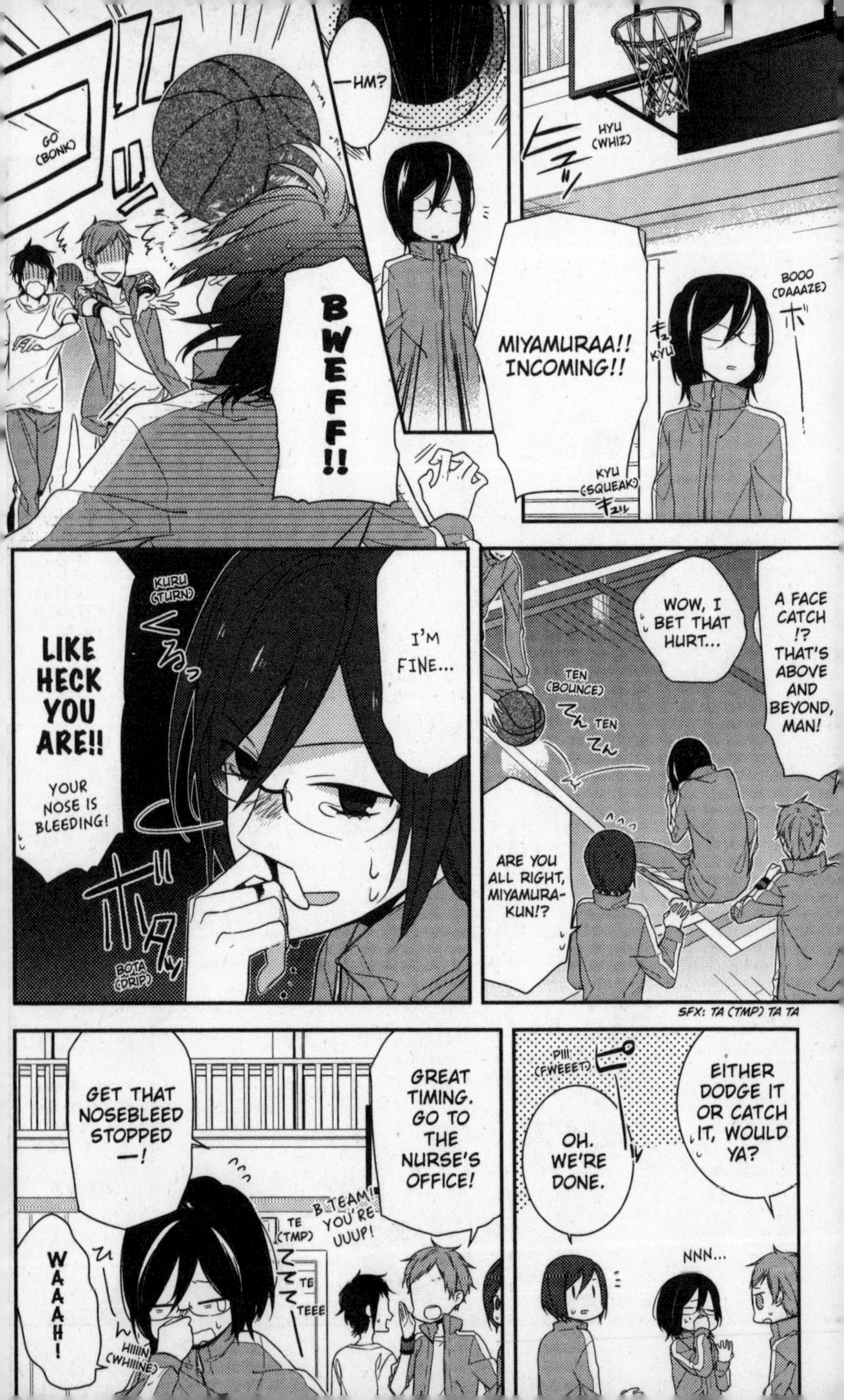
HYU (WHIZ)
MIYAMURAA!! INCOMING!!
BOOO (DAAAZE)
KYU
KYU (SQUEAK)
—HM?
GO (BONK)
BWEFF!!
A FACE CATCH!? THAT'S ABOVE AND BEYOND, MAN!
WOW, I BET THAT HURT...
TEN (BOUNCE) TEN
ARE YOU ALL RIGHT, MIYAMURA-KUN!?
I'M FINE...
KURU (TURN)
LIKE HECK YOU ARE!!
YOUR NOSE IS BLEEDING!
BOTA (DRIP)
SFX: TA (TMP) TA TA
PIII (FWEEEET)
EITHER DODGE IT OR CATCH IT, WOULD YA?
OH. WE'RE DONE.
NNN...
GREAT TIMING. GO TO THE NURSE'S OFFICE!
GET THAT NOSEBLEED STOPPED—!
B TEAM! YOU'RE UUUP!
TE (TMP) TE TEEE
WAAAAH!
HIIIN (WHIIINE)

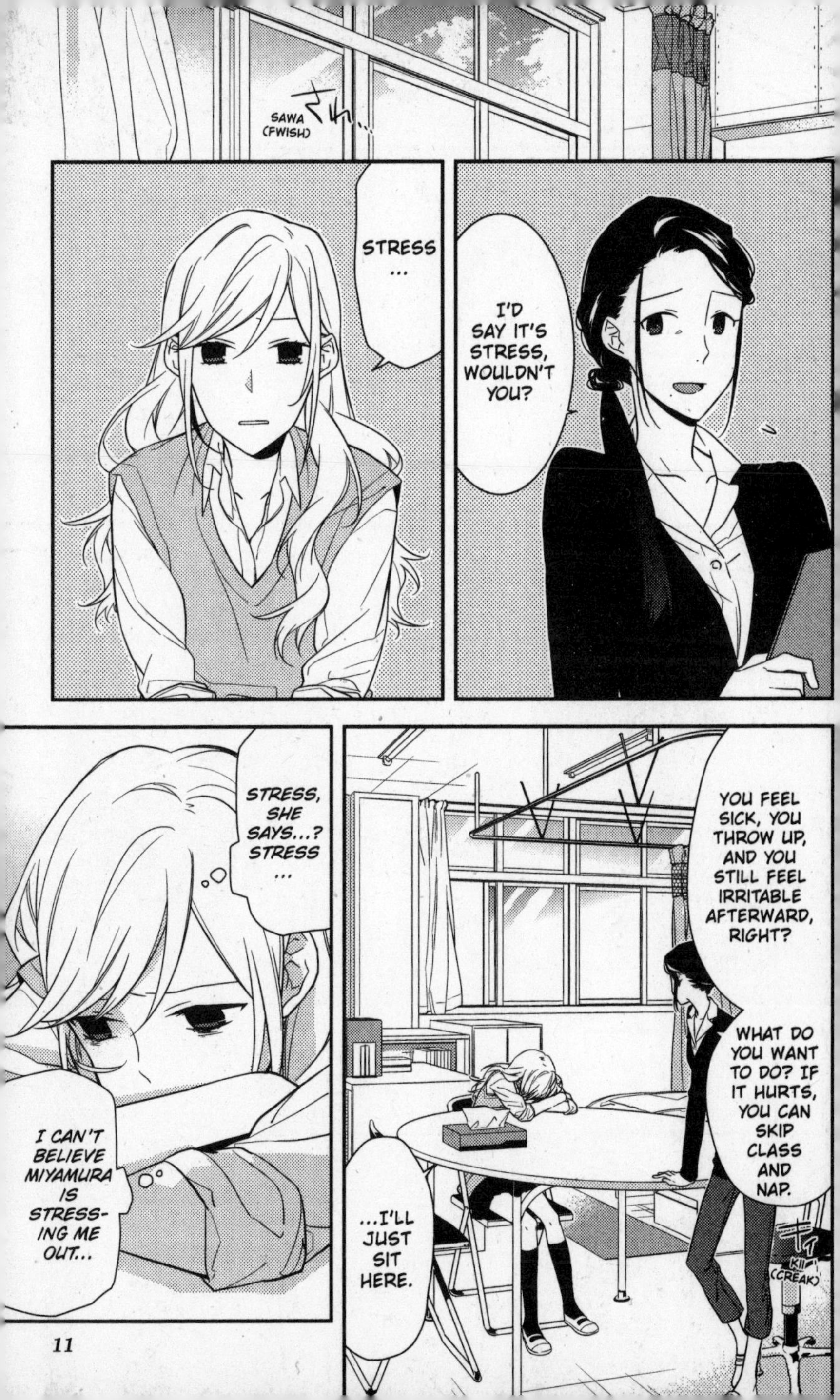
SAWA (FWISH)
I'D SAY IT'S STRESS, WOULDN'T YOU?
STRESS ...
YOU FEEL SICK, YOU THROW UP, AND YOU STILL FEEL IRRITABLE AFTERWARD, RIGHT?
WHAT DO YOU WANT TO DO? IF IT HURTS, YOU CAN SKIP CLASS AND NAP.
KII (CREAK)
...I'LL JUST SIT HERE.
STRESS, SHE SAYS...? STRESS ...
I CAN'T BELIEVE MIYAMURA IS STRESSING ME OUT...

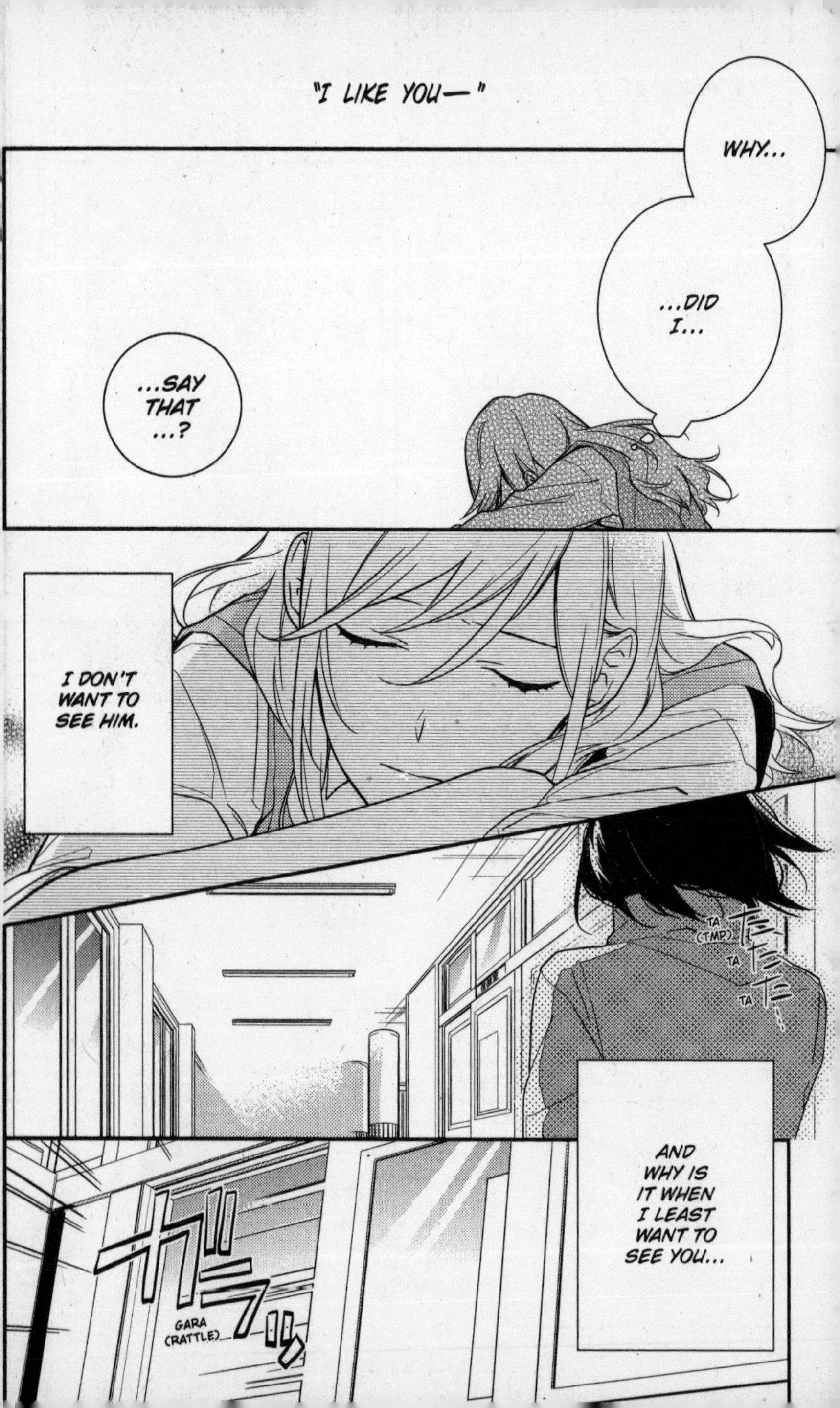
"I LIKE YOU—"
WHY...
...DID I...
...SAY THAT ...?
I DON'T WANT TO SEE HIM.
TA (TMP) TA TA
AND WHY IS IT WHEN I LEAST WANT TO SEE YOU...
GARA (RATTLE)

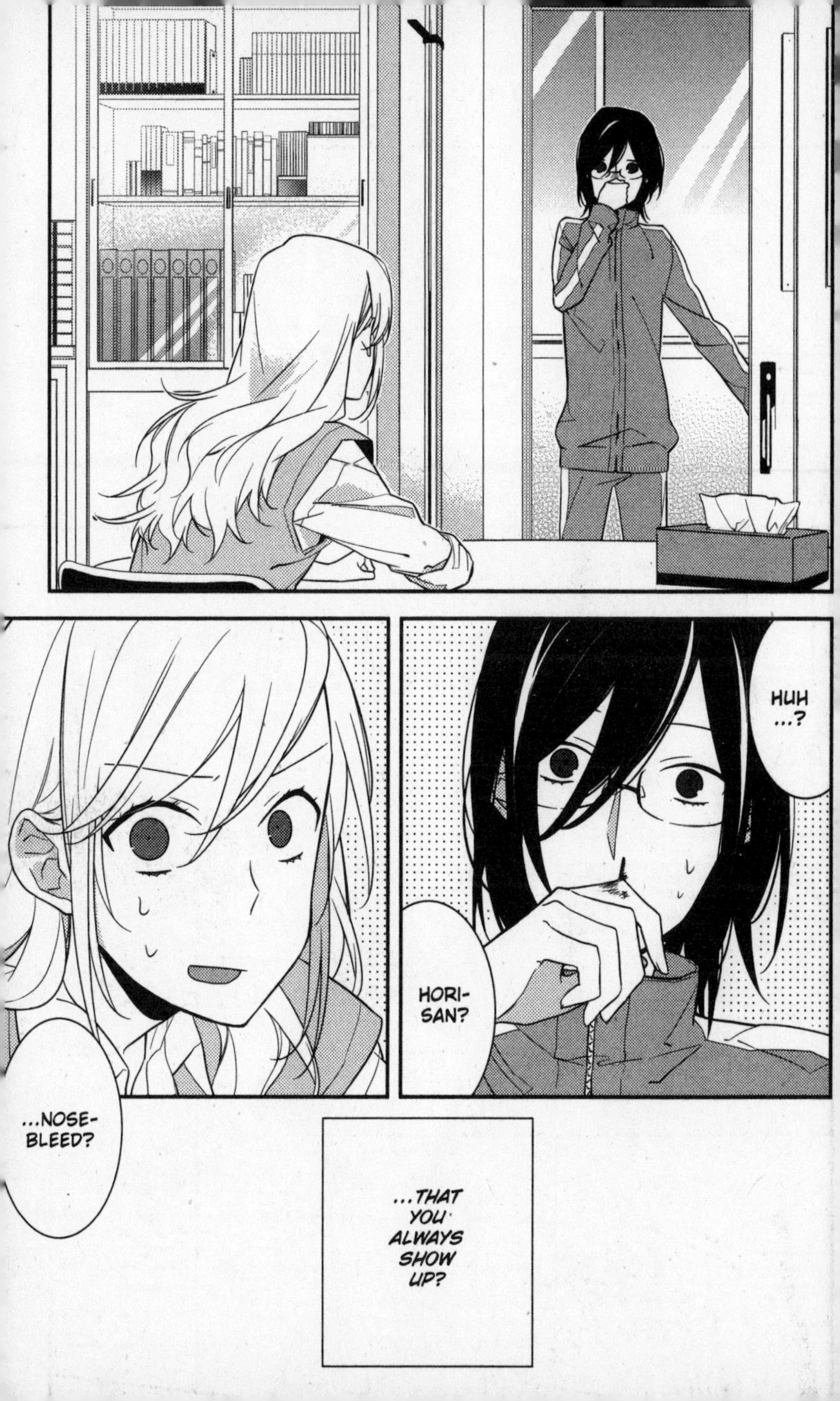
HUH ...?
HORI-SAN?
...NOSE-BLEED?
...THAT YOU ALWAYS SHOW UP?

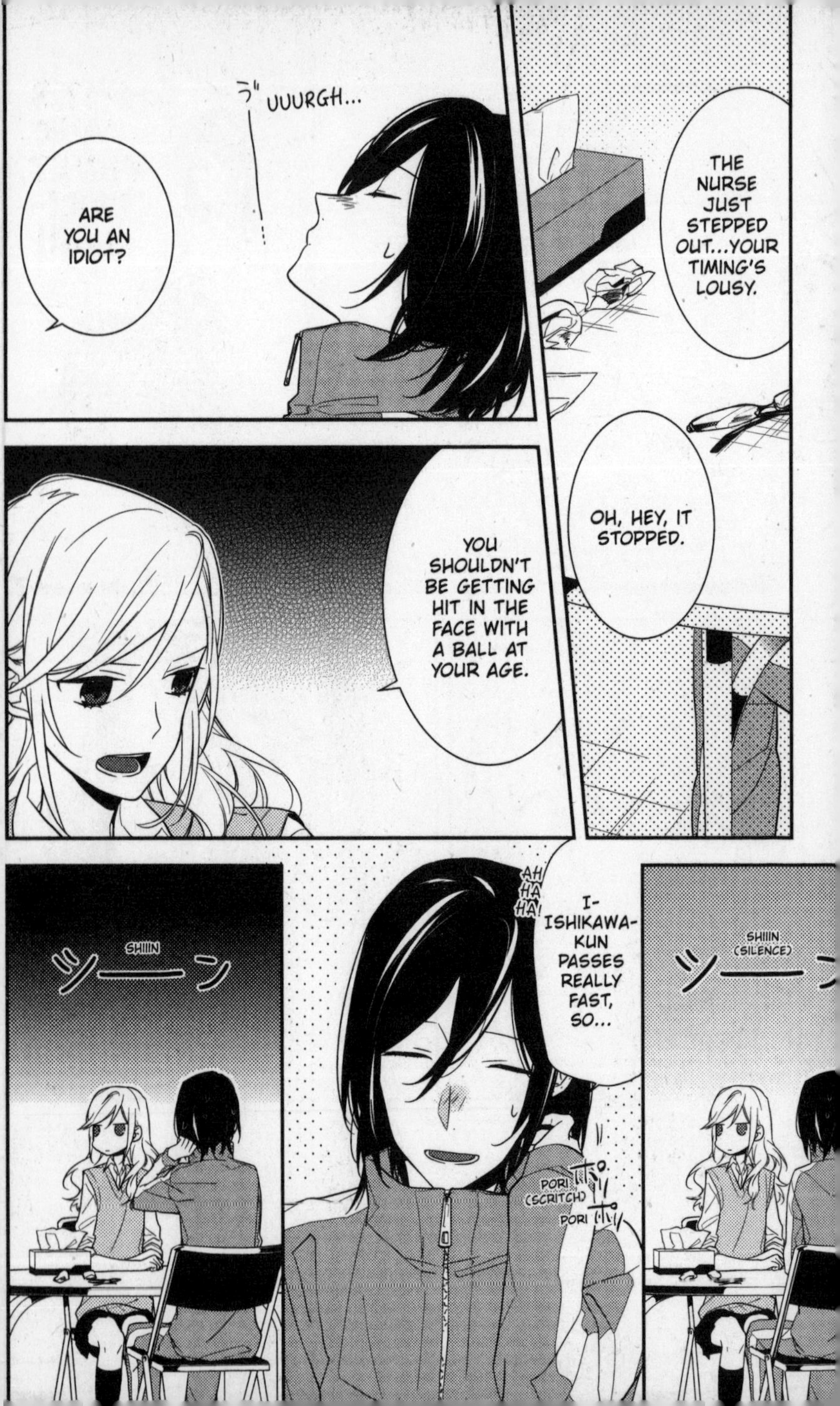
THE NURSE JUST STEPPED OUT...YOUR TIMING'S LOUSY.
OH, HEY, IT STOPPED.
う゛ UUURGH...
ARE YOU AN IDIOT?
YOU SHOULDN'T BE GETTING HIT IN THE FACE WITH A BALL AT YOUR AGE.
ツーン
SHIIN (SILENCE)
AH HA HA!
I- ISHIKAWA-KUN PASSES REALLY FAST, SO...
ポリ PORI (SCRITCH)
ポリ PORI
ツーン
SHIIN

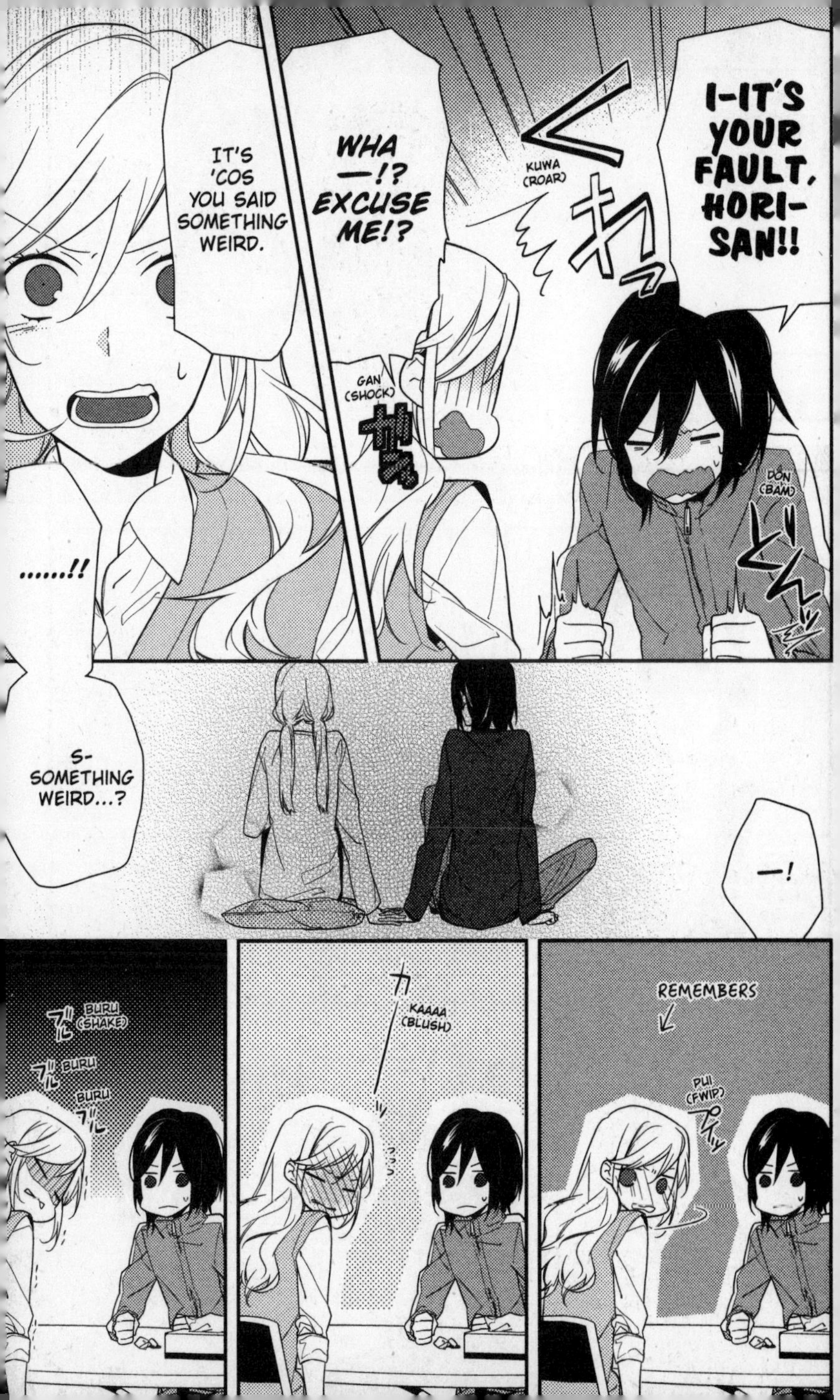

I-IT'S YOUR FAULT, HORI-SAN!!
KUWA (ROAR)
DON (BAM)
WHA—!? EXCUSE ME!?
GAN (SHOCK)
IT'S 'COS YOU SAID SOMETHING WEIRD.
......!!
—!
S- SOMETHING WEIRD...?
REMEMBERS
PUI (FWIP)
KAAAA (BLUSH)
BURU (SHAKE)
BURU
BURU

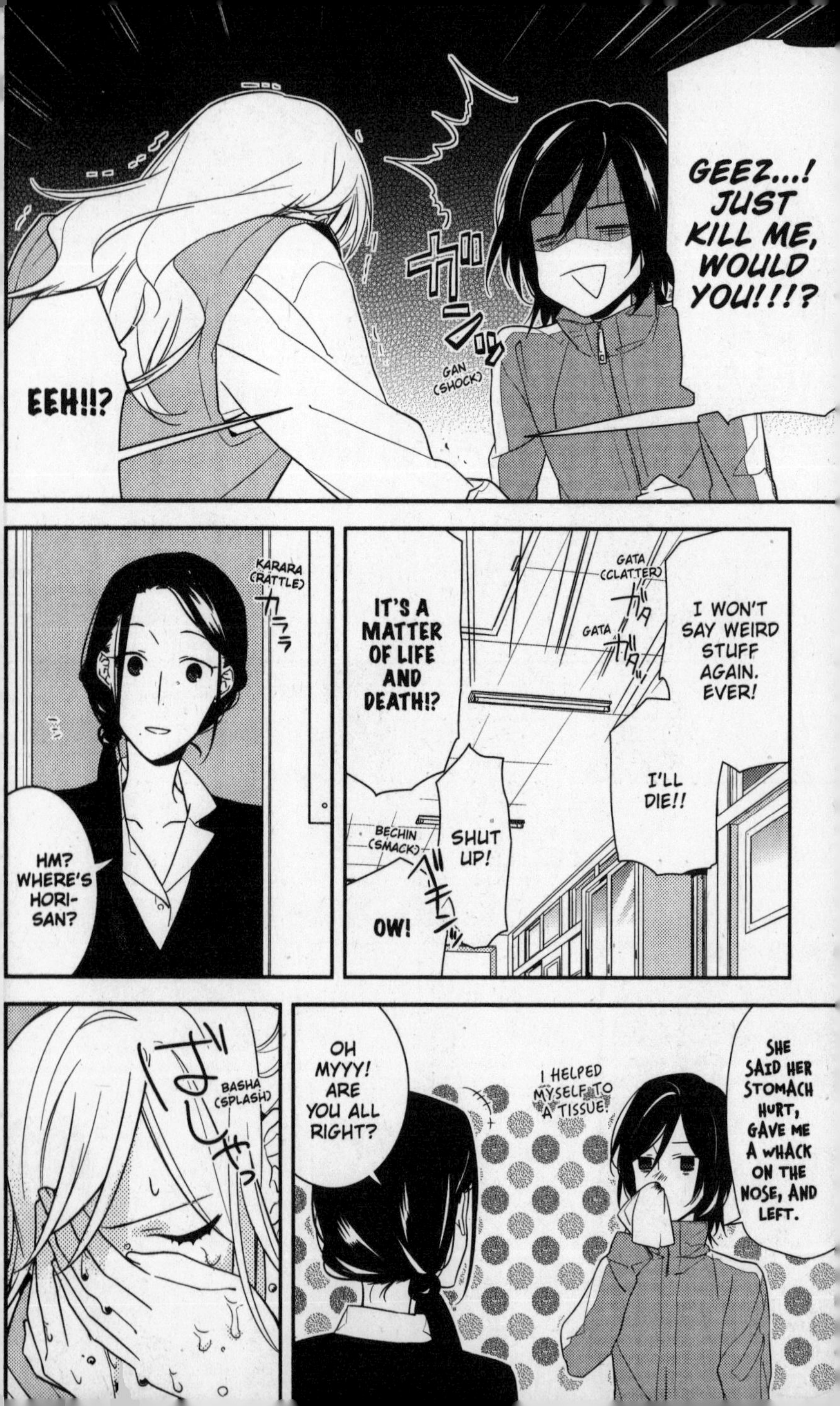
GEEZ...! JUST KILL ME, WOULD YOU!!!?
GAN (SHOCK)
EEH!!?
I WON'T SAY WEIRD STUFF AGAIN. EVER!
GATA (CLATTER)
GATA
I'LL DIE!!
IT'S A MATTER OF LIFE AND DEATH!?
SHUT UP!
BECHIN (SMACK)
OW!
KARARA (RATTLE)
HM? WHERE'S HORI-SAN?
SHE SAID HER STOMACH HURT, GAVE ME A WHACK ON THE NOSE, AND LEFT.
I HELPED MYSELF TO A TISSUE.
OH MYYY! ARE YOU ALL RIGHT?
BASHA (SPLASH)

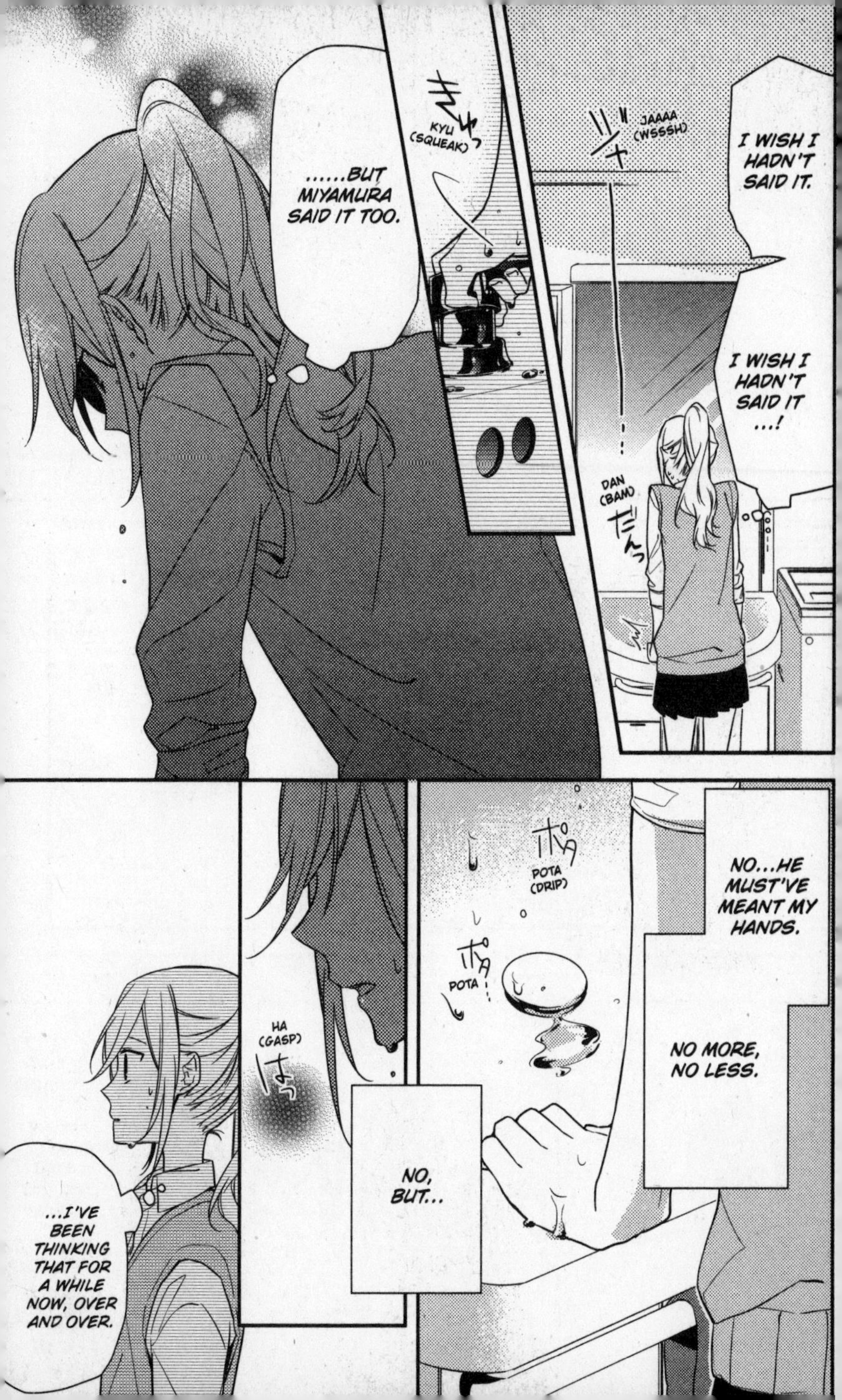
JAAAA (WSSSH)
I WISH I HADN'T SAID IT.
I WISH I HADN'T SAID IT ...!
DAN (BAM)
だんっ
KYU (SQUEAK)
......BUT MIYAMURA SAID IT TOO.
NO...HE MUST'VE MEANT MY HANDS.
ポタ
POTA (DRIP)
ポタ
POTA
NO MORE, NO LESS.
NO, BUT...
HA (GASP)
はっ
...I'VE BEEN THINKING THAT FOR A WHILE NOW, OVER AND OVER.

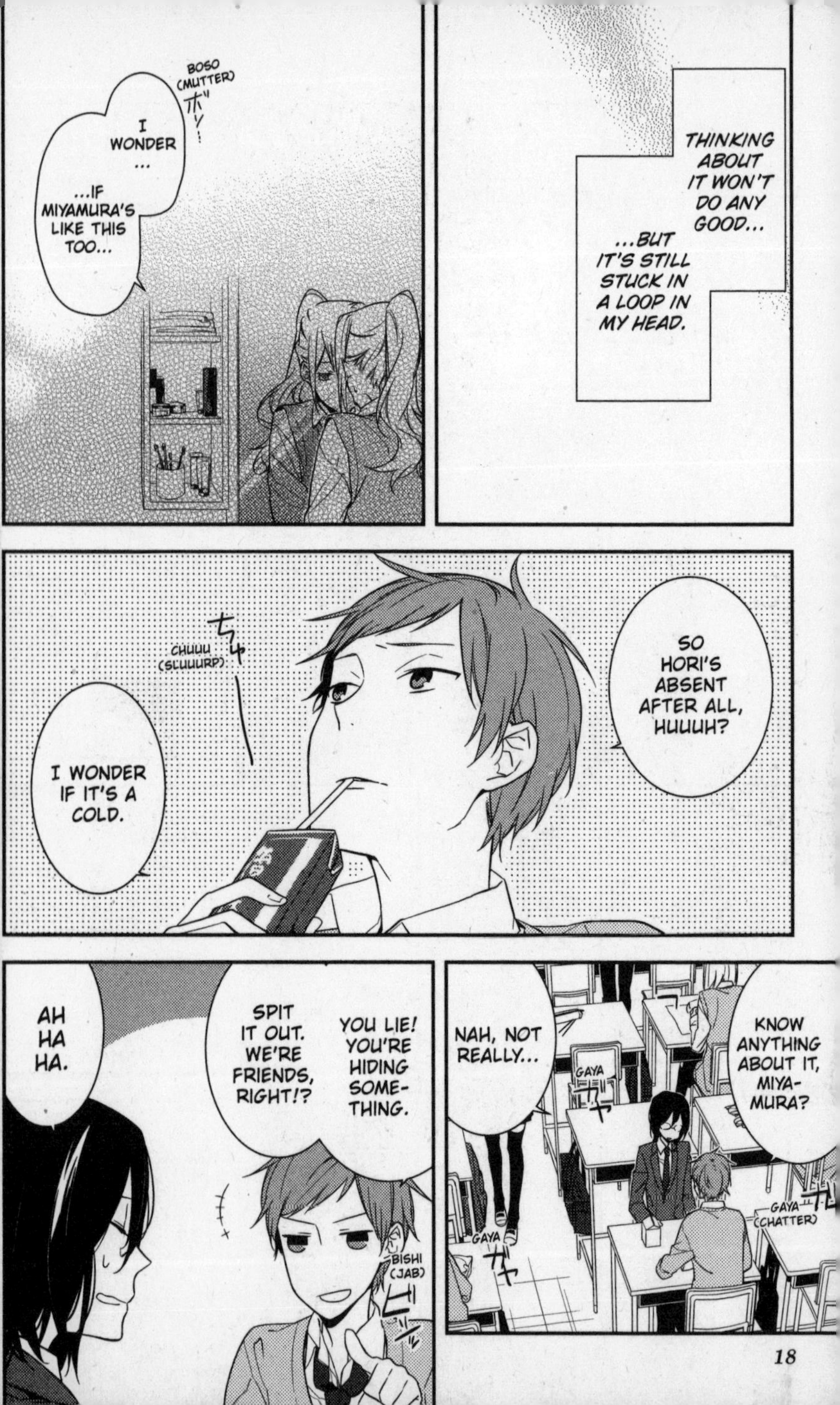

THINKING ABOUT IT WON'T DO ANY GOOD...
...BUT IT'S STILL STUCK IN A LOOP IN MY HEAD.
BOSO (MUTTER)
I WONDER... ...IF MIYAMURA'S LIKE THIS TOO...
SO HORI'S ABSENT AFTER ALL, HUUUH?
CHUUU (SLUUURP)
I WONDER IF IT'S A COLD.
KNOW ANYTHING ABOUT IT, MIYA-MURA?
GAYA (CHATTER)
GAYA
NAH, NOT REALLY...
GAYA
YOU LIE! YOU'RE HIDING SOME-THING.
SPIT IT OUT. WE'RE FRIENDS, RIGHT!?
BISHI (JAB)
AH HA HA.

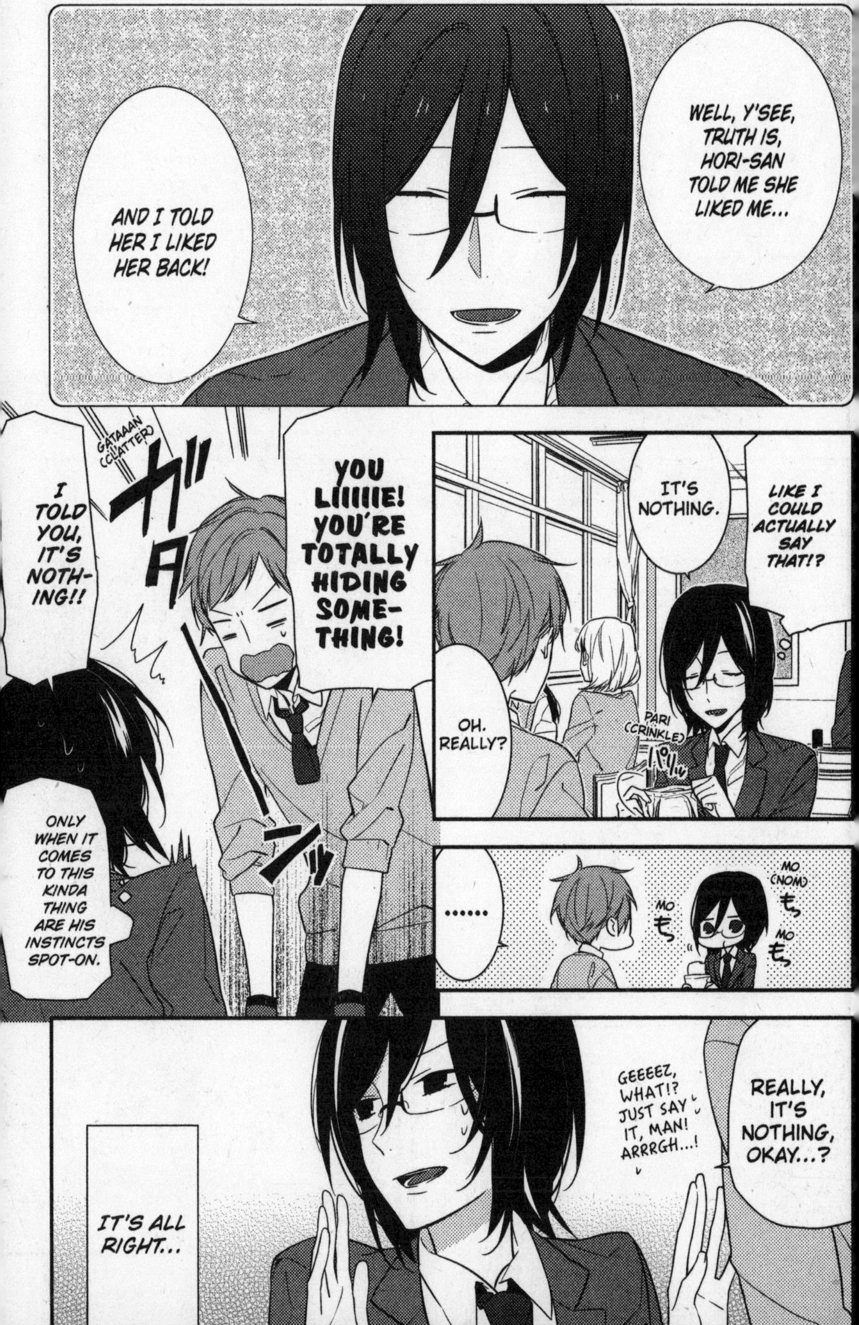
WELL, Y'SEE, TRUTH IS, HORI-SAN TOLD ME SHE LIKED ME...
AND I TOLD HER I LIKED HER BACK!
LIKE I COULD ACTUALLY SAY THAT!?
IT'S NOTHING.
PARI (CRINKLE)
OH. REALLY?
MO (NOM)
MO
MO
......
GATAAAN (CLATTER)
YOU LIIIIIIE! YOU'RE TOTALLY HIDING SOME-THING!
I TOLD YOU, IT'S NOTH-ING!!
ONLY WHEN IT COMES TO THIS KINDA THING ARE HIS INSTINCTS SPOT-ON.
REALLY, IT'S NOTHING, OKAY...?
GEEEEZ, WHAT!? JUST SAY IT, MAN! ARRRGH...!
IT'S ALL RIGHT...

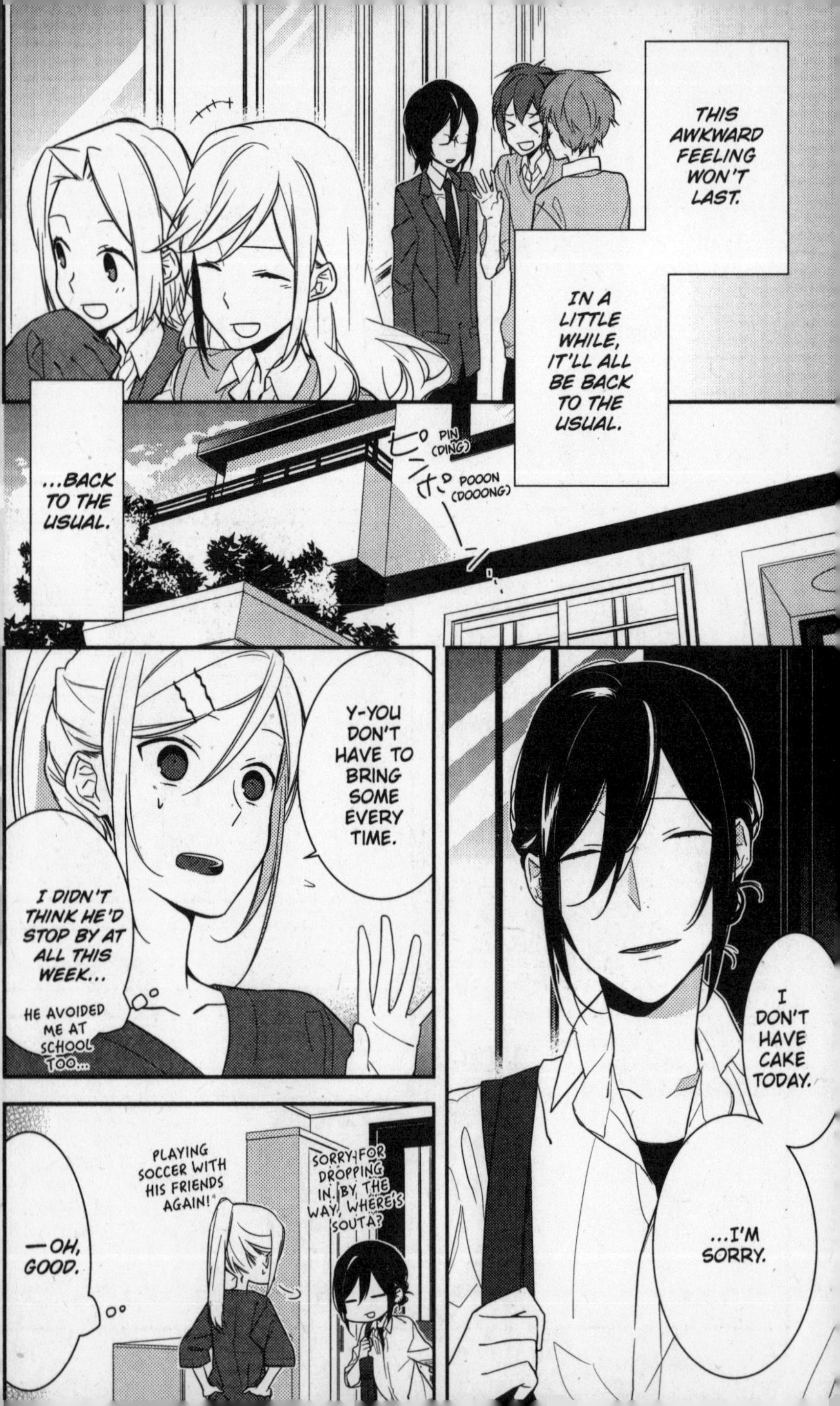

THIS AWKWARD FEELING WON'T LAST.
IN A LITTLE WHILE, IT'LL ALL BE BACK TO THE USUAL.
PIN (DING)
POOON (DOOONG)
...BACK TO THE USUAL.
I DON'T HAVE CAKE TODAY.
...I'M SORRY.
Y-YOU DON'T HAVE TO BRING SOME EVERY TIME.
I DIDN'T THINK HE'D STOP BY AT ALL THIS WEEK...
HE AVOIDED ME AT SCHOOL TOO...
SORRY FOR DROPPING IN. BY THE WAY, WHERE'S SOUTA?
PLAYING SOCCER WITH HIS FRIENDS AGAIN!
—OH, GOOD.

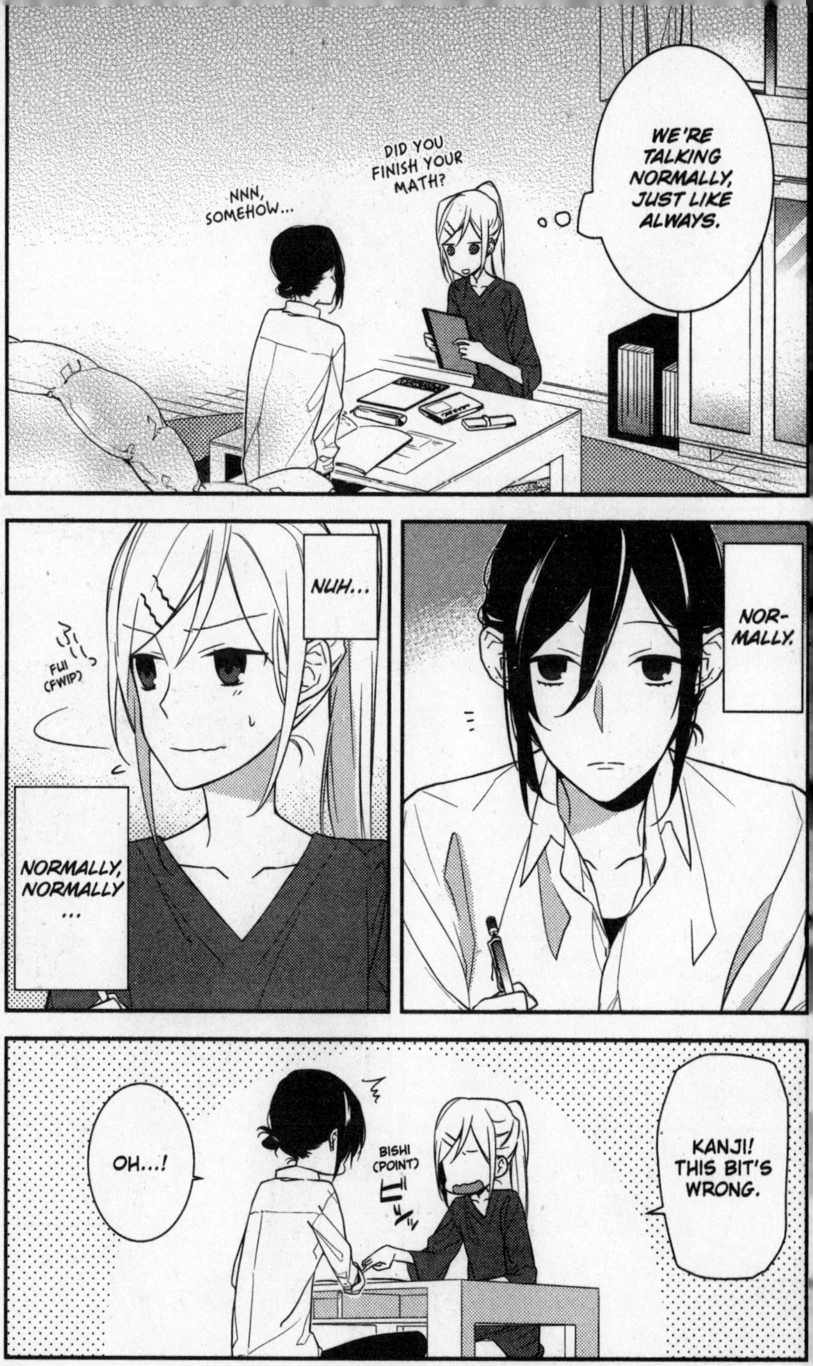
WE'RE TALKING NORMALLY, JUST LIKE ALWAYS.
DID YOU FINISH YOUR MATH?
NNN, SOMEHOW...
NOR-MALLY.
NUH...
ふいっ
FUI (FWIP)
NORMALLY, NORMALLY ...
KANJI! THIS BIT'S WRONG.
ビシッ
BISHI (POINT)
OH...!

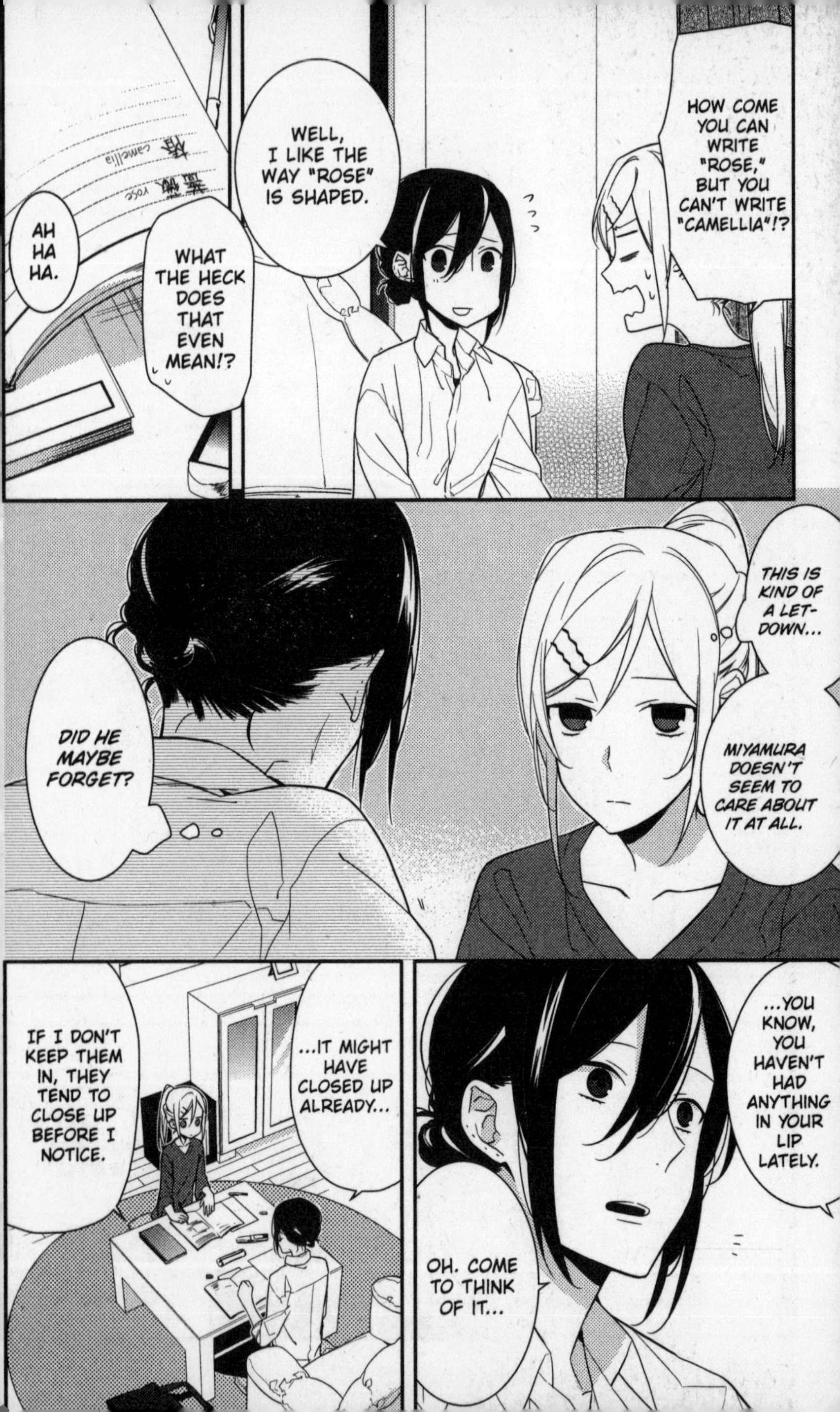

HOW COME YOU CAN WRITE "ROSE," BUT YOU CAN'T WRITE "CAMELLIA"!?
WELL, I LIKE THE WAY "ROSE" IS SHAPED.
WHAT THE HECK DOES THAT EVEN MEAN!?
AH HA HA.
THIS IS KIND OF A LET-DOWN...
MIYAMURA DOESN'T SEEM TO CARE ABOUT IT AT ALL.
DID HE MAYBE FORGET?
...YOU KNOW, YOU HAVEN'T HAD ANYTHING IN YOUR LIP LATELY.
OH. COME TO THINK OF IT...
...IT MIGHT HAVE CLOSED UP ALREADY...
IF I DON'T KEEP THEM IN, THEY TEND TO CLOSE UP BEFORE I NOTICE.

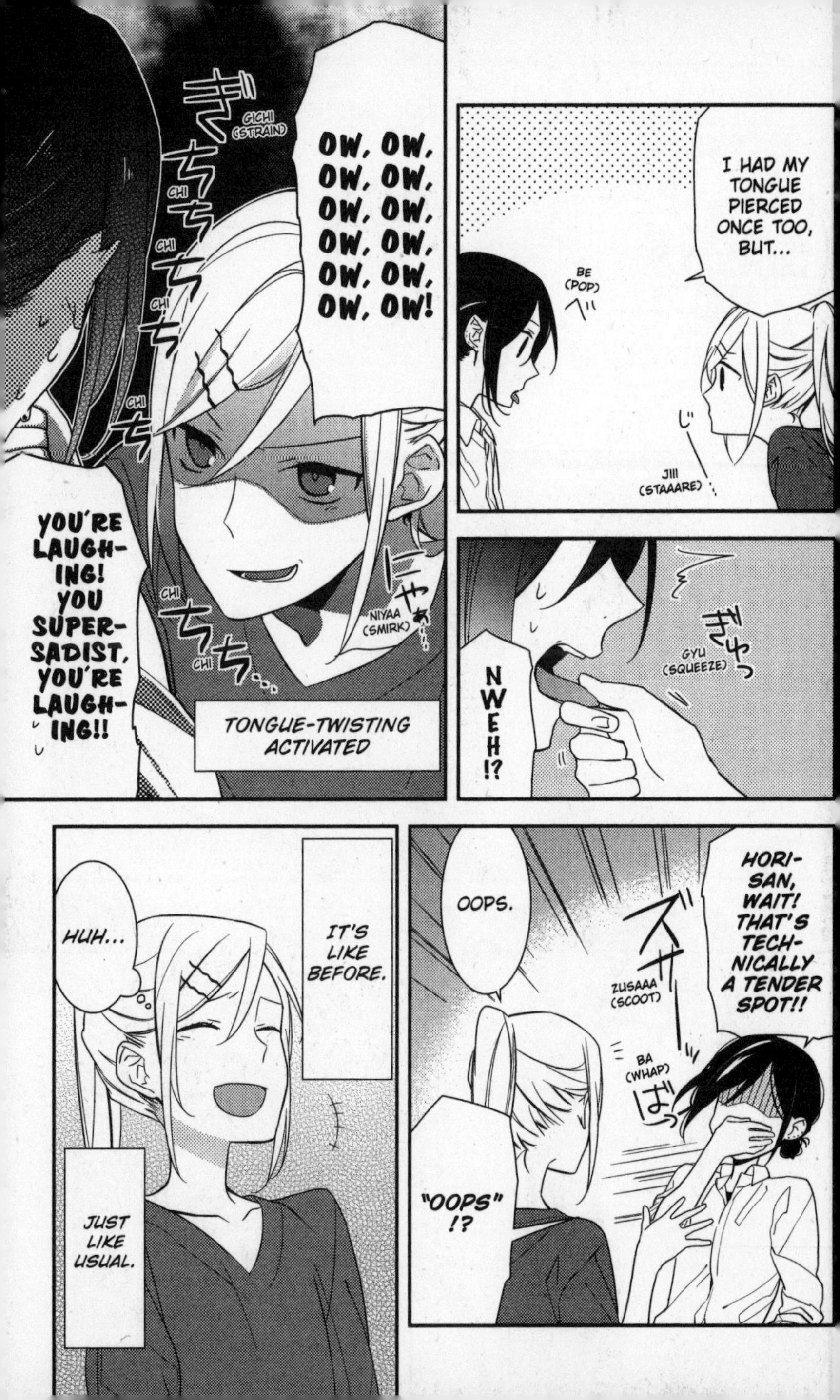
I HAD MY TONGUE PIERCED ONCE TOO, BUT...
BE (POP)
JIII (STAAARE)
GYU (SQUEEZE)
NWEH!?
GICHI (STRAIN)
OW, OW, OW, OW, OW, OW, OW, OW, OW, OW, OW, OW!
CHI
CHI
CHI
CHI
CHI
CHI
NIYAA (SMIRK)
YOU'RE LAUGHING! YOU SUPER-SADIST, YOU'RE LAUGHING!!
TONGUE-TWISTING ACTIVATED
HORI-SAN, WAIT! THAT'S TECHNICALLY A TENDER SPOT!!
OOPS.
ZUSAAA (SCOOT)
BA (WHAP)
"OOPS" !?
IT'S LIKE BEFORE.
HUH...
JUST LIKE USUAL.

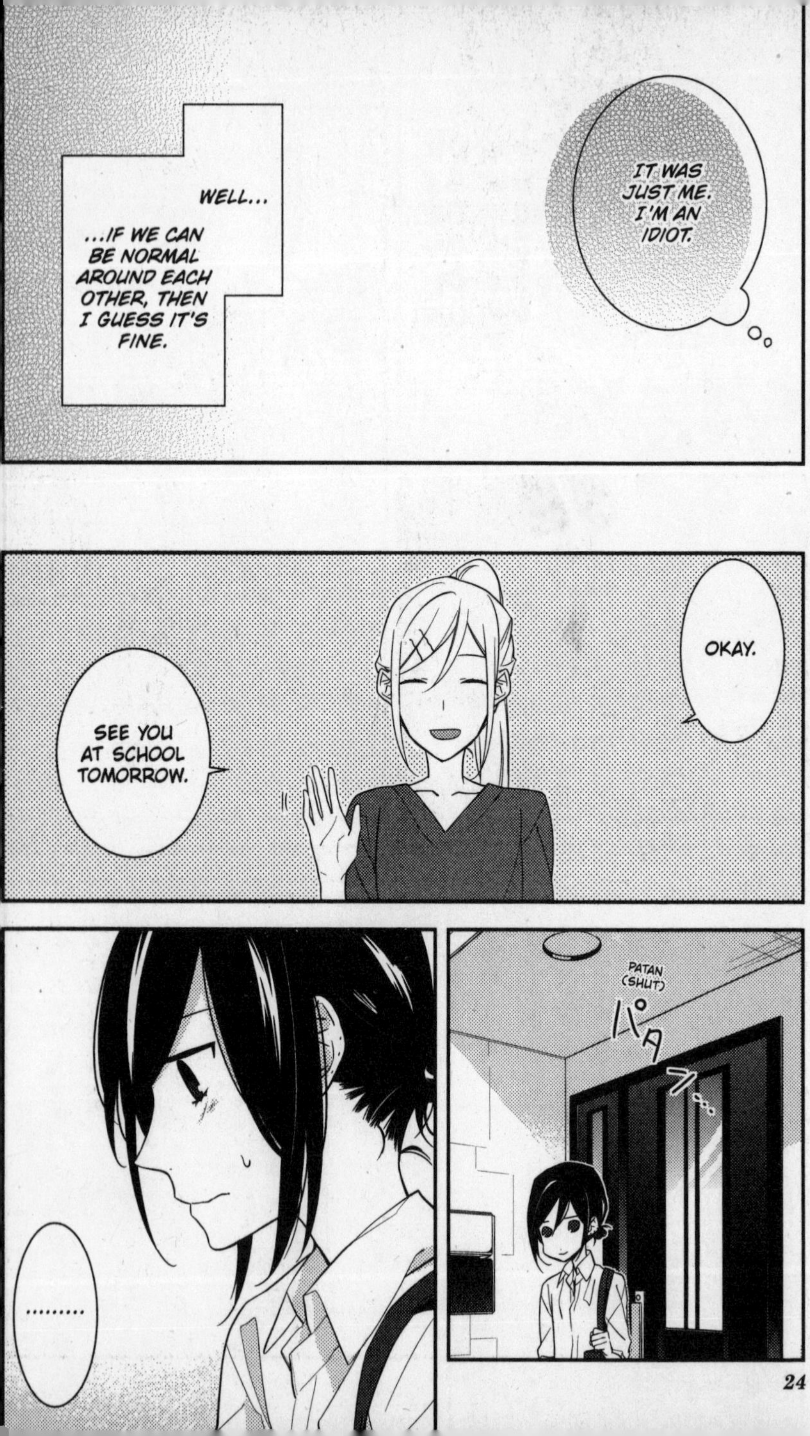
IT WAS JUST ME. I'M AN IDIOT.
WELL...
...IF WE CAN BE NORMAL AROUND EACH OTHER, THEN I GUESS IT'S FINE.
OKAY.
SEE YOU AT SCHOOL TOMORROW.
PATAN (SHUT)
....

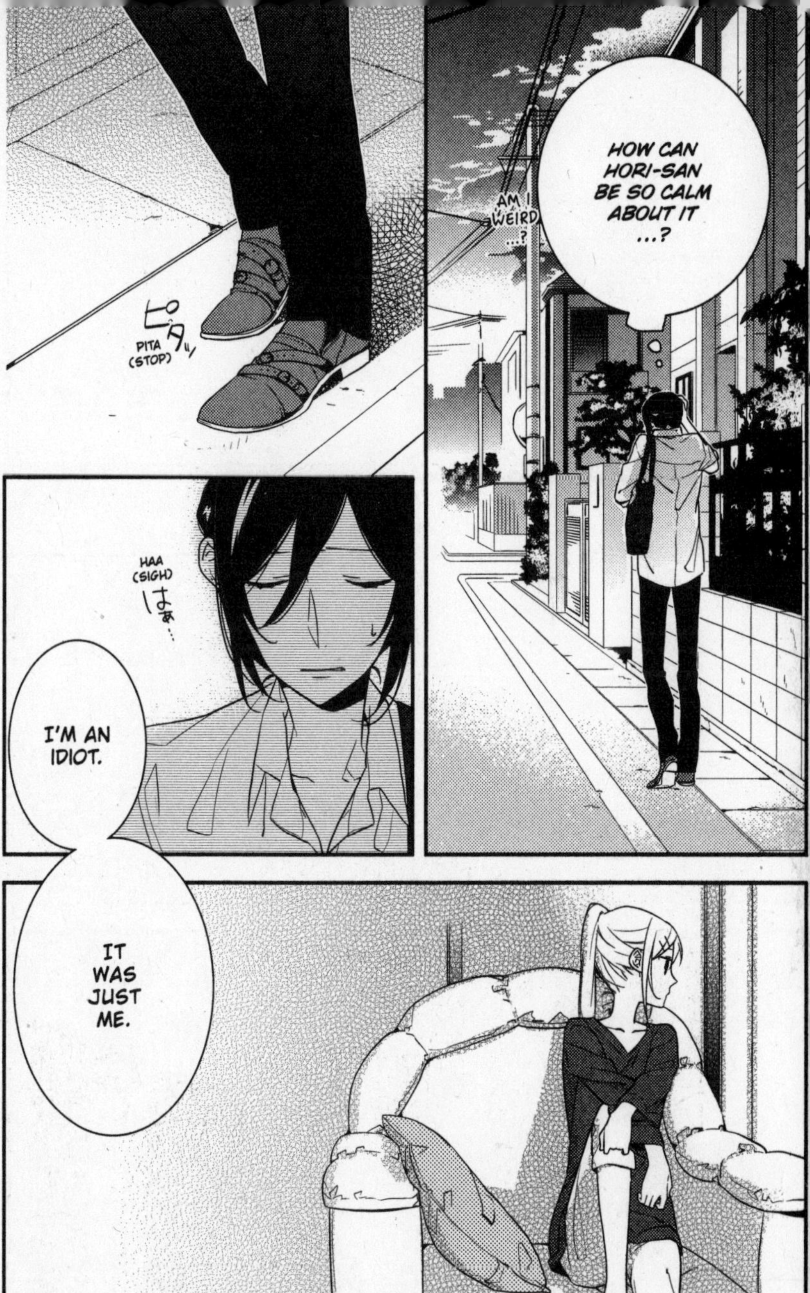
HOW CAN HORI-SAN BE SO CALM ABOUT IT ...?
AM I WEIRD ...?
ピタッ
PITA (STOP)
HAA (SIGH)
はぁ…
I'M AN IDIOT.
IT WAS JUST ME.

HORIMIYA

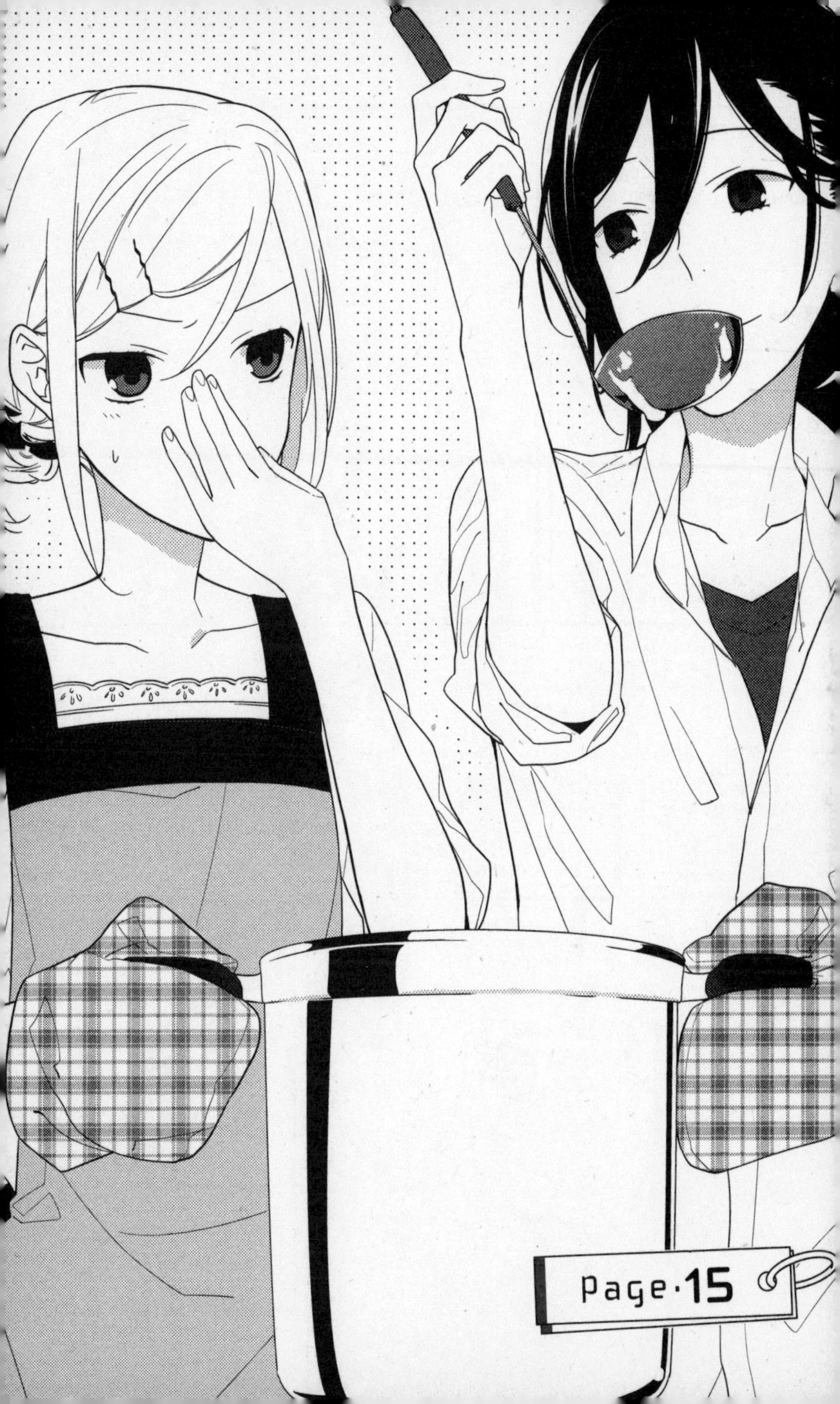

page·15

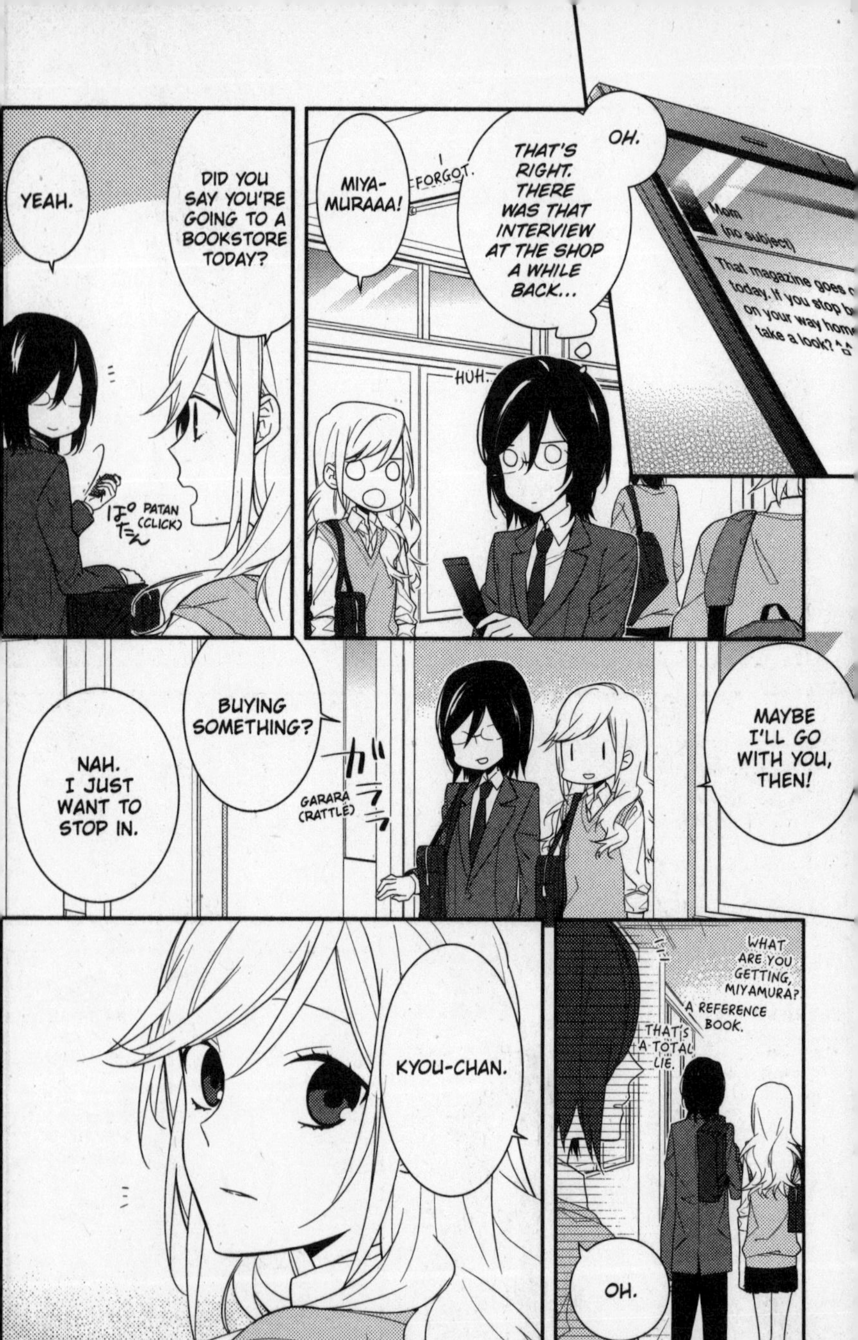
Mom
(no subject)
That magazine goes o
today. If you stop b
on your way hom
take a look? ^_^
OH.
THAT'S RIGHT. THERE WAS THAT INTERVIEW AT THE SHOP A WHILE BACK...
MIYA-MURAAA!
I FORGOT.
HUH.
DID YOU SAY YOU'RE GOING TO A BOOKSTORE TODAY?
YEAH.
ぱたん PATAN (CLICK)
MAYBE I'LL GO WITH YOU, THEN!
BUYING SOMETHING?
NAH. I JUST WANT TO STOP IN.
ガラ GARARA (RATTLE)
WHAT ARE YOU GETTING, MIYAMURA?
A REFERENCE BOOK.
THAT'S A TOTAL LIE.
OH.
KYOU-CHAN.

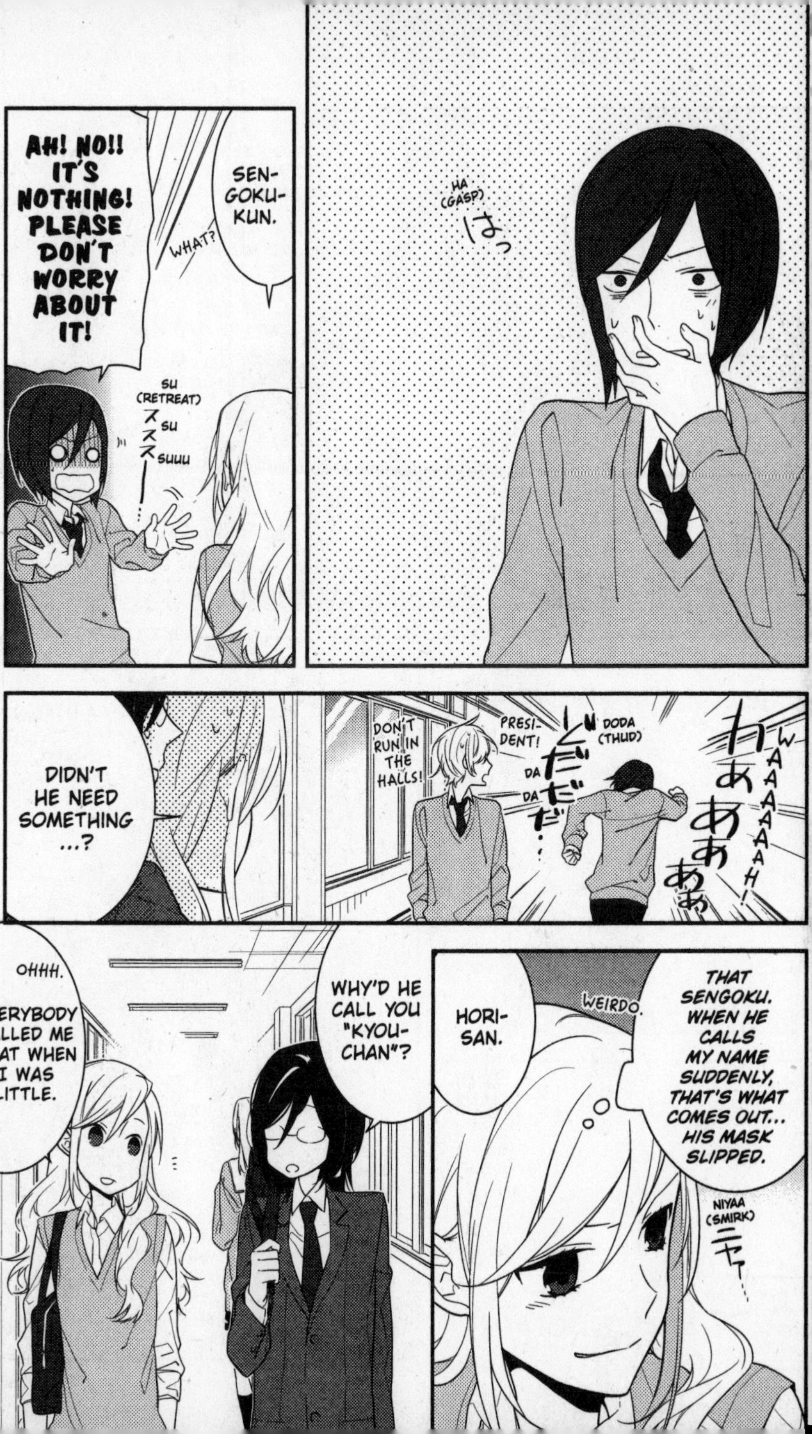
HA (GASP)
はっ
SEN-GOKU-KUN.
WHAT?
AH! NO!! IT'S NOTHING! PLEASE DON'T WORRY ABOUT IT!
SU (RETREAT)
SU
SUUU
WAAAAAAH!
DODA (THUD)
DA
DA
PRESI-DENT!
DON'T RUN IN THE HALLS!
DIDN'T HE NEED SOMETHING ...?
HORI-SAN.
THAT SENGOKU. WHEN HE CALLS MY NAME SUDDENLY, THAT'S WHAT COMES OUT... HIS MASK SLIPPED.
WEIRDO.
NIYAA (SMIRK)
WHY'D HE CALL YOU "KYOU-CHAN"?
OHHH.
EVERYBODY CALLED ME THAT WHEN I WAS LITTLE.

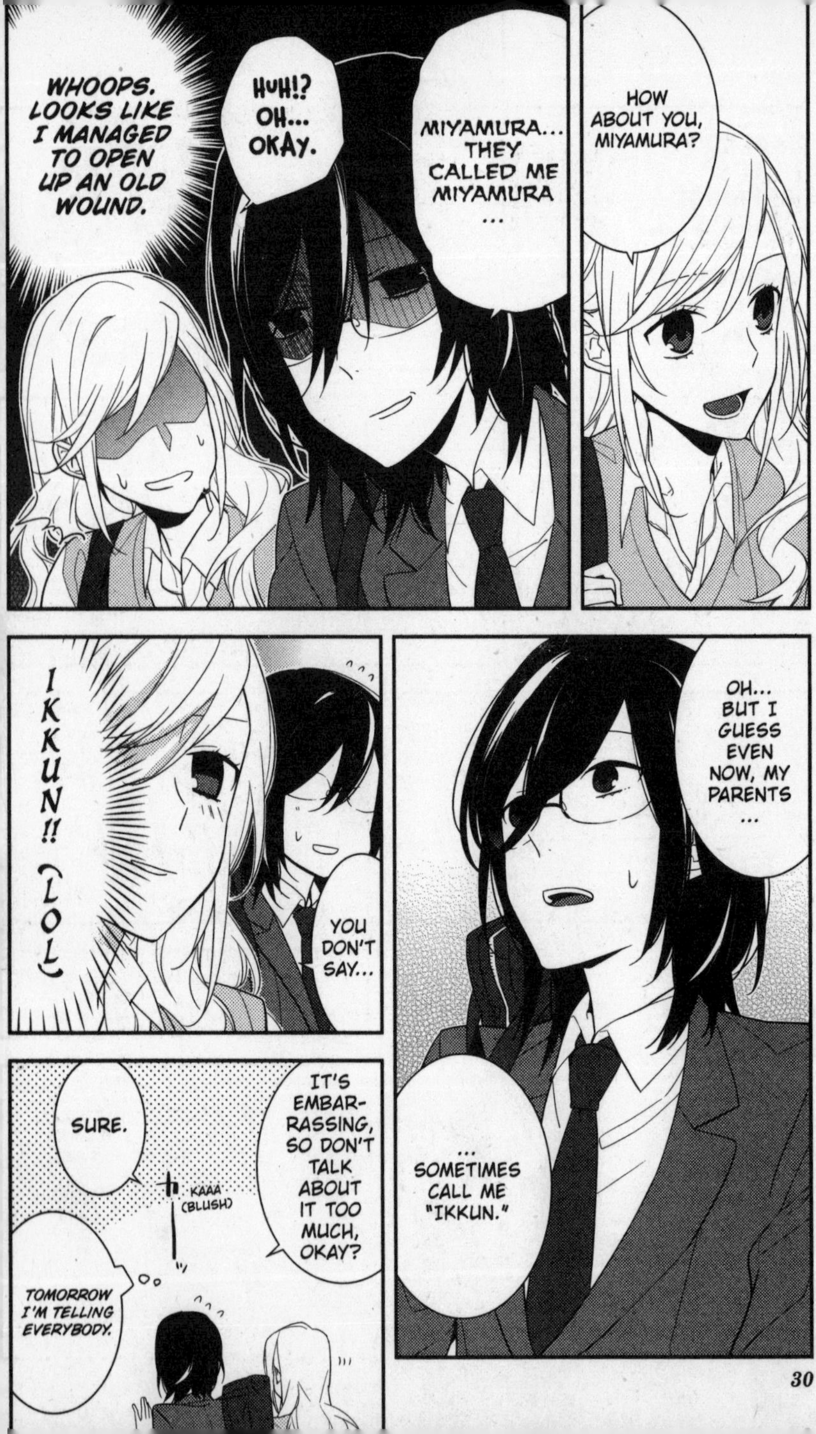
HOW ABOUT YOU, MIYAMURA?
MIYAMURA... THEY CALLED ME MIYAMURA ...
HUH!? OH... OKAY.
WHOOPS. LOOKS LIKE I MANAGED TO OPEN UP AN OLD WOUND.
OH... BUT I GUESS EVEN NOW, MY PARENTS ...
... SOMETIMES CALL ME "IKKUN."
YOU DON'T SAY...
IKKUN!! (LOL)
IT'S EMBARRASSING, SO DON'T TALK ABOUT IT TOO MUCH, OKAY?
SURE.
KAAA (BLUSH)
TOMORROW I'M TELLING EVERYBODY.

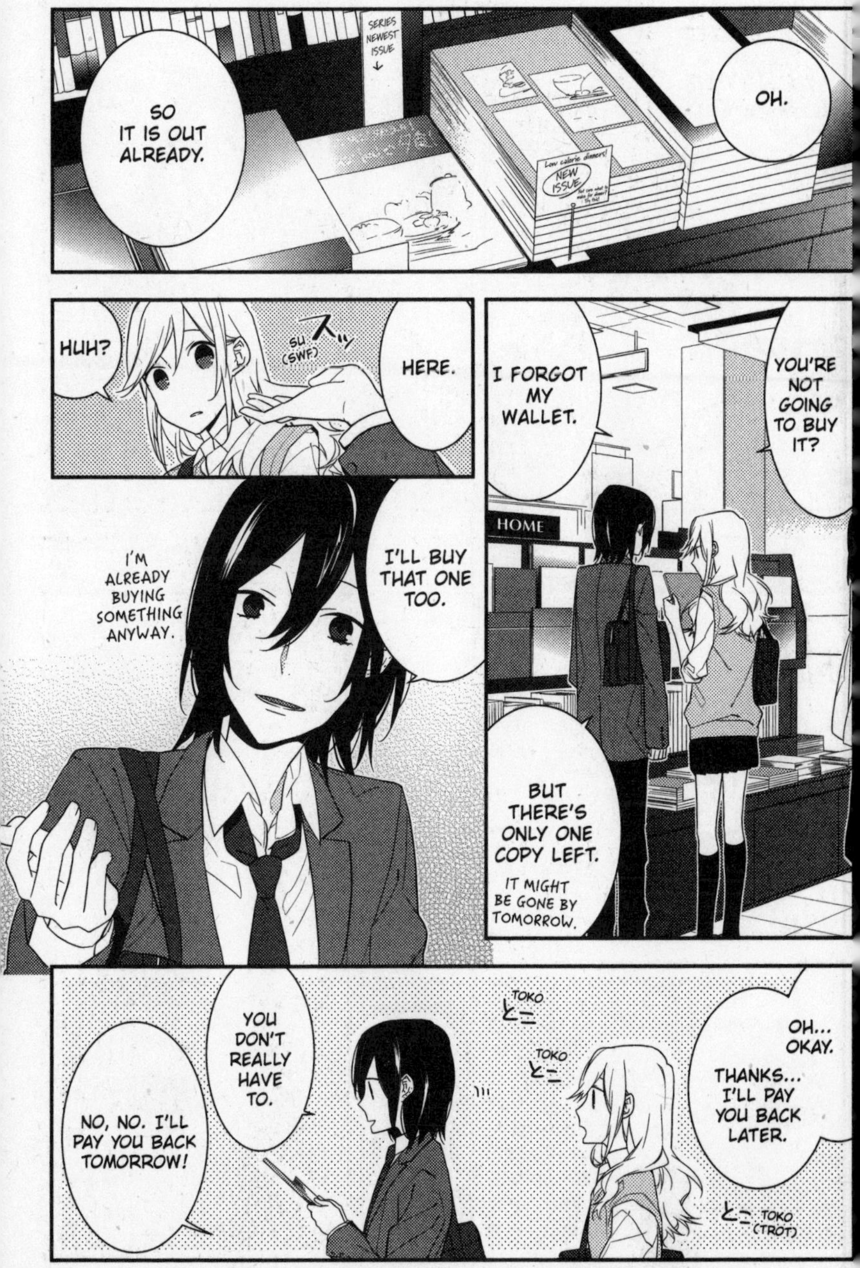
OH.
SERIES NEWEST ISSUE ↓
SO IT IS OUT ALREADY.
Low calorie dinners!
NEW ISSUE
YOU'RE NOT GOING TO BUY IT?
I FORGOT MY WALLET.
HOME
BUT THERE'S ONLY ONE COPY LEFT.
IT MIGHT BE GONE BY TOMORROW.
HERE.
スッ SU (SWF)
HUH?
I'LL BUY THAT ONE TOO.
I'M ALREADY BUYING SOMETHING ANYWAY.
OH... OKAY.
THANKS... I'LL PAY YOU BACK LATER.
とこ TOKO
とこ TOKO
とこ TOKO (TROT)
YOU DON'T REALLY HAVE TO.
NO, NO. I'LL PAY YOU BACK TOMORROW!

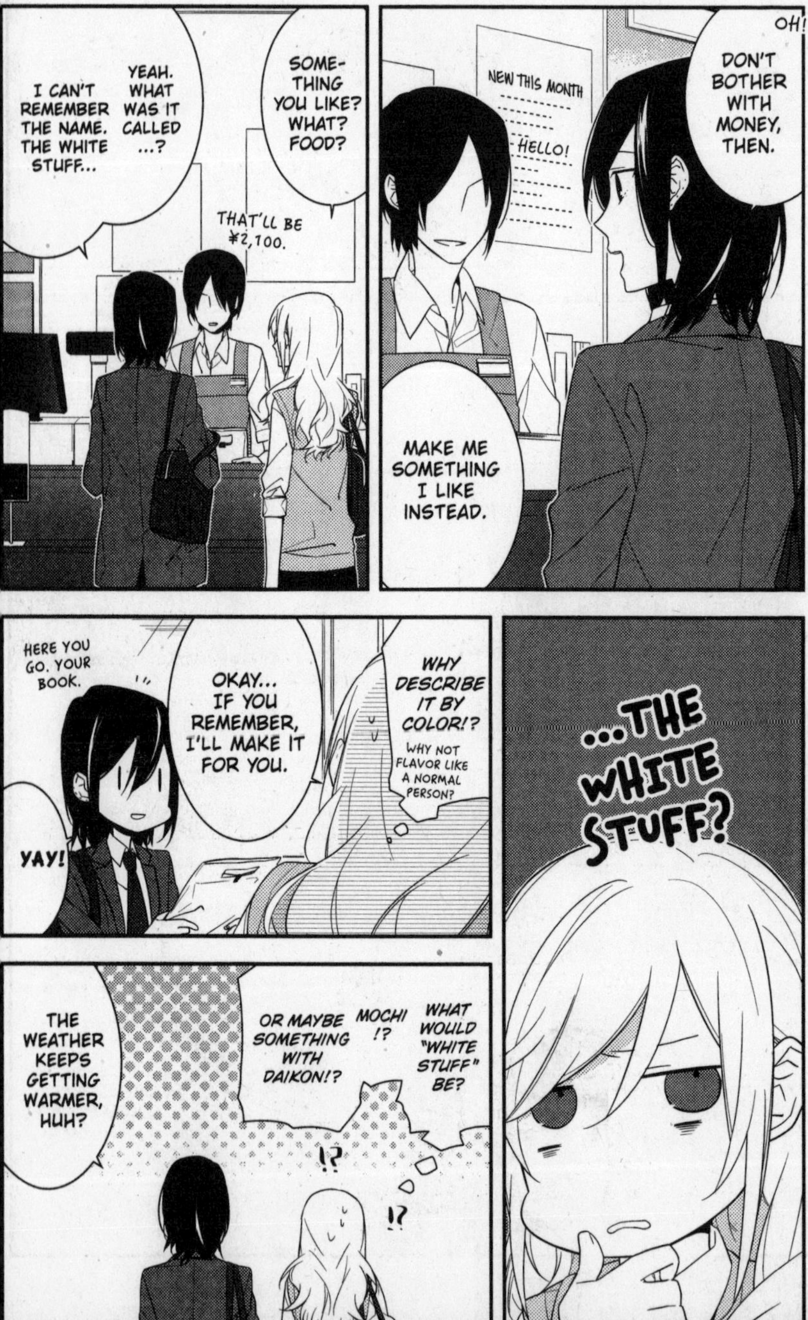

OH!
DON'T BOTHER WITH MONEY, THEN.
NEW THIS MONTH
HELLO!
MAKE ME SOMETHING I LIKE INSTEAD.
SOME-THING YOU LIKE? WHAT? FOOD?
YEAH. WHAT WAS IT CALLED ...?
I CAN'T REMEMBER THE NAME. THE WHITE STUFF...
THAT'LL BE ¥2,100.
...THE WHITE STUFF?
WHY DESCRIBE IT BY COLOR!?
WHY NOT FLAVOR LIKE A NORMAL PERSON?
OKAY... IF YOU REMEMBER, I'LL MAKE IT FOR YOU.
HERE YOU GO. YOUR BOOK.
YAY!
WHAT WOULD "WHITE STUFF" BE?
MOCHI !?
OR MAYBE SOMETHING WITH DAIKON!?
THE WEATHER KEEPS GETTING WARMER, HUH?
!?
!?

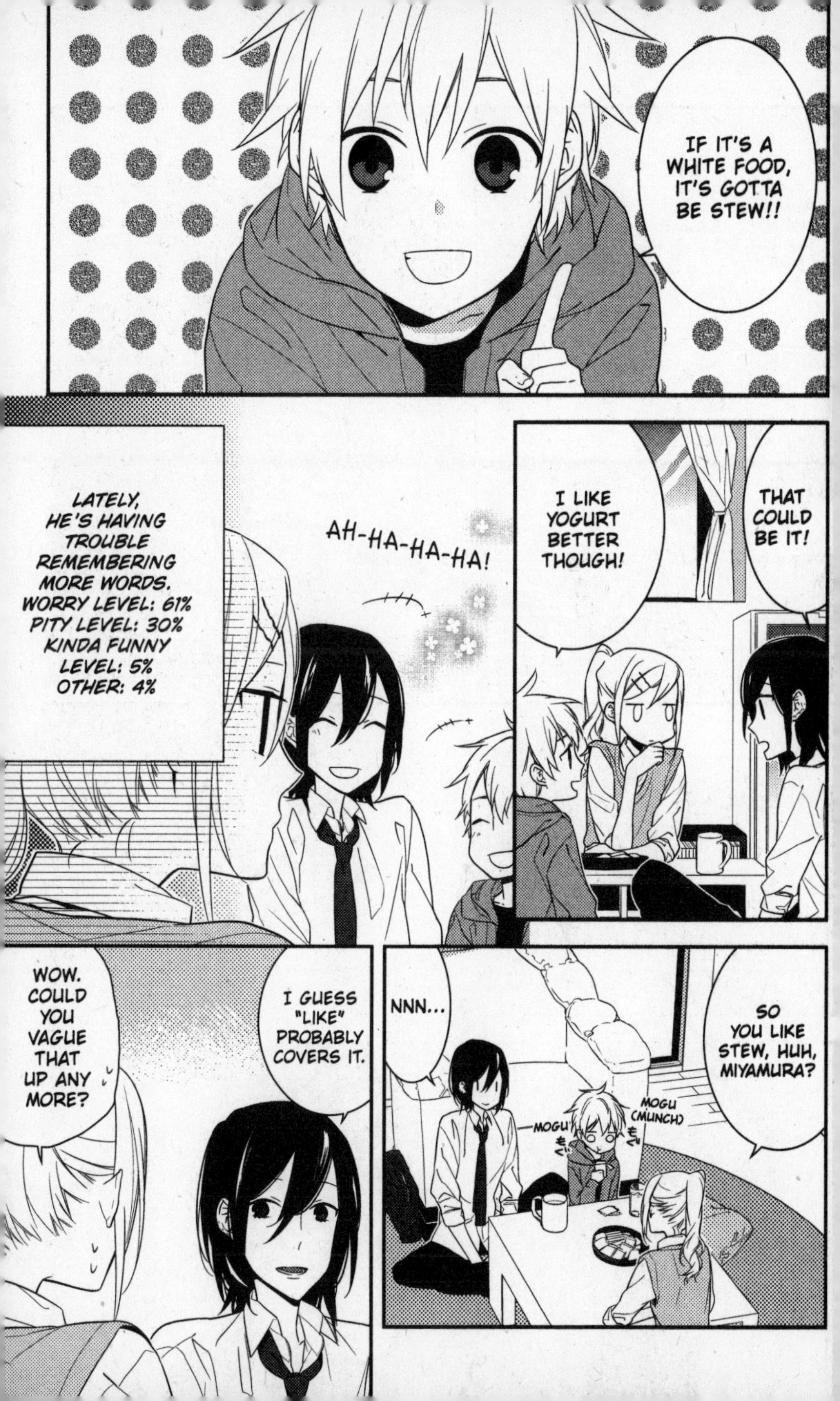
IF IT'S A WHITE FOOD, IT'S GOTTA BE STEW!!
THAT COULD BE IT!
I LIKE YOGURT BETTER THOUGH!
AH-HA-HA-HA!
LATELY, HE'S HAVING TROUBLE REMEMBERING MORE WORDS. WORRY LEVEL: 61% PITY LEVEL: 30% KINDA FUNNY LEVEL: 5% OTHER: 4%
SO YOU LIKE STEW, HUH, MIYAMURA?
MOGU (MUNCH)
もぐ
MOGU
もぐ
NNN...
I GUESS "LIKE" PROBABLY COVERS IT.
WOW. COULD YOU VAGUE THAT UP ANY MORE?

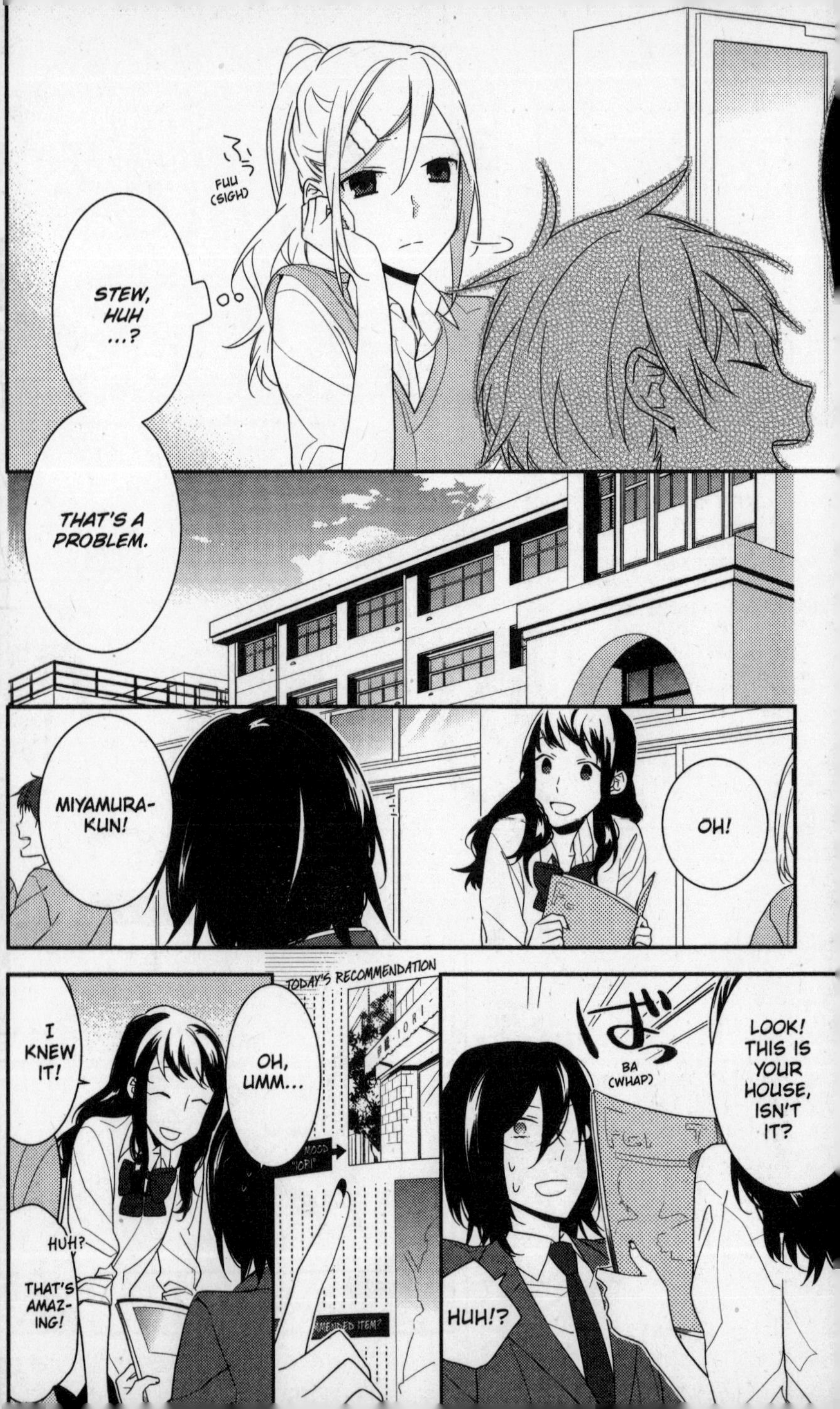

FUU (SIGH)
STEW, HUH ...?
THAT'S A PROBLEM.
OH!
MIYAMURA-KUN!
LOOK! THIS IS YOUR HOUSE, ISN'T IT?
BA (WHAP)
HUH!?
TODAY'S RECOMMENDATION
MOOD "IORI"
OH, UMM...
I KNEW IT!
HUH?
THAT'S AMAZ-ING!

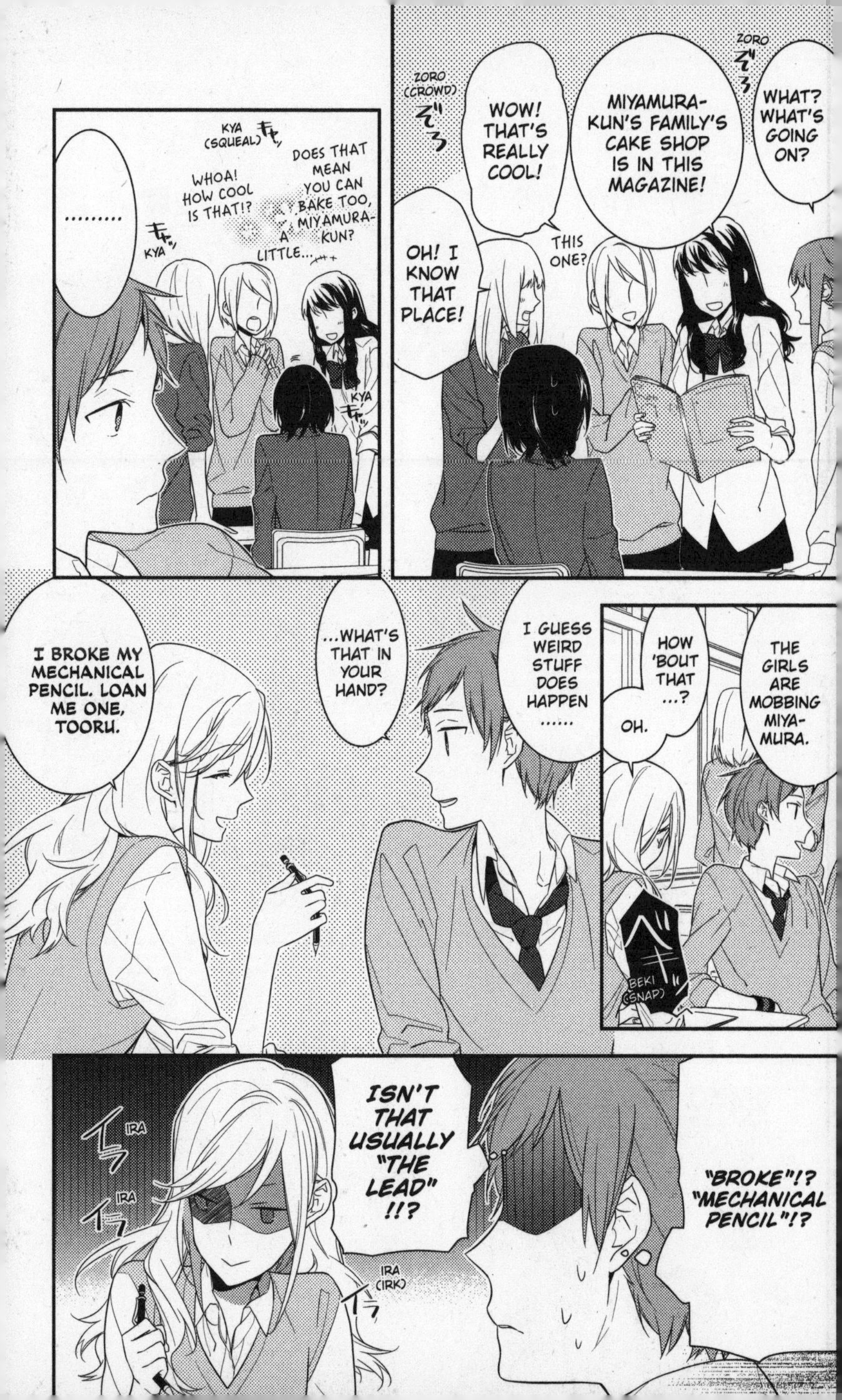
ZORO
WHAT? WHAT'S GOING ON?
MIYAMURA-KUN'S FAMILY'S CAKE SHOP IS IN THIS MAGAZINE!
WOW! THAT'S REALLY COOL!
ZORO (CROWD)
THIS ONE?
OH! I KNOW THAT PLACE!
DOES THAT MEAN YOU CAN BAKE TOO, MIYAMURA-KUN?
KYA (SQUEAL)
WHOA! HOW COOL IS THAT!?
A LITTLE...
KYA
KYA
....
THE GIRLS ARE MOBBING MIYAMURA.
HOW 'BOUT THAT...?
OH.
BEKI (SNAP)
I GUESS WEIRD STUFF DOES HAPPEN......
...WHAT'S THAT IN YOUR HAND?
I BROKE MY MECHANICAL PENCIL. LOAN ME ONE, TOORU.
"BROKE"!? "MECHANICAL PENCIL"!?
ISN'T THAT USUALLY "THE LEAD"!!?
IRA
IRA
IRA (IRK)

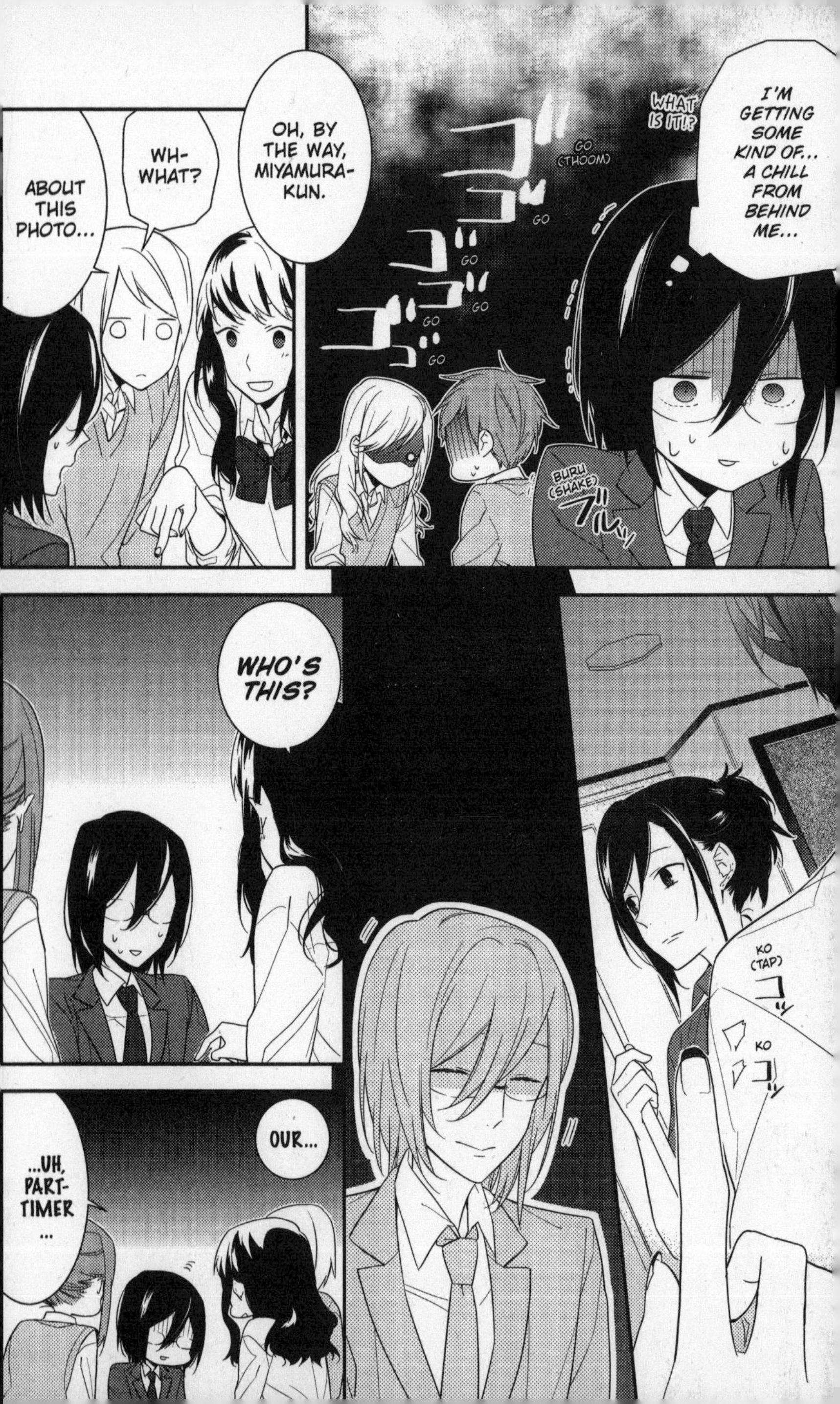
I'M GETTING SOME KIND OF... A CHILL FROM BEHIND ME...
WHAT IS IT!?
GO (THOOM)
GO
GO
GO
GO
GO
BURU (SHAKE)
OH, BY THE WAY, MIYAMURA-KUN.
WH-WHAT?
ABOUT THIS PHOTO...
KO (TAP)
KO
WHO'S THIS?
OUR...
...UH, PART-TIMER ...

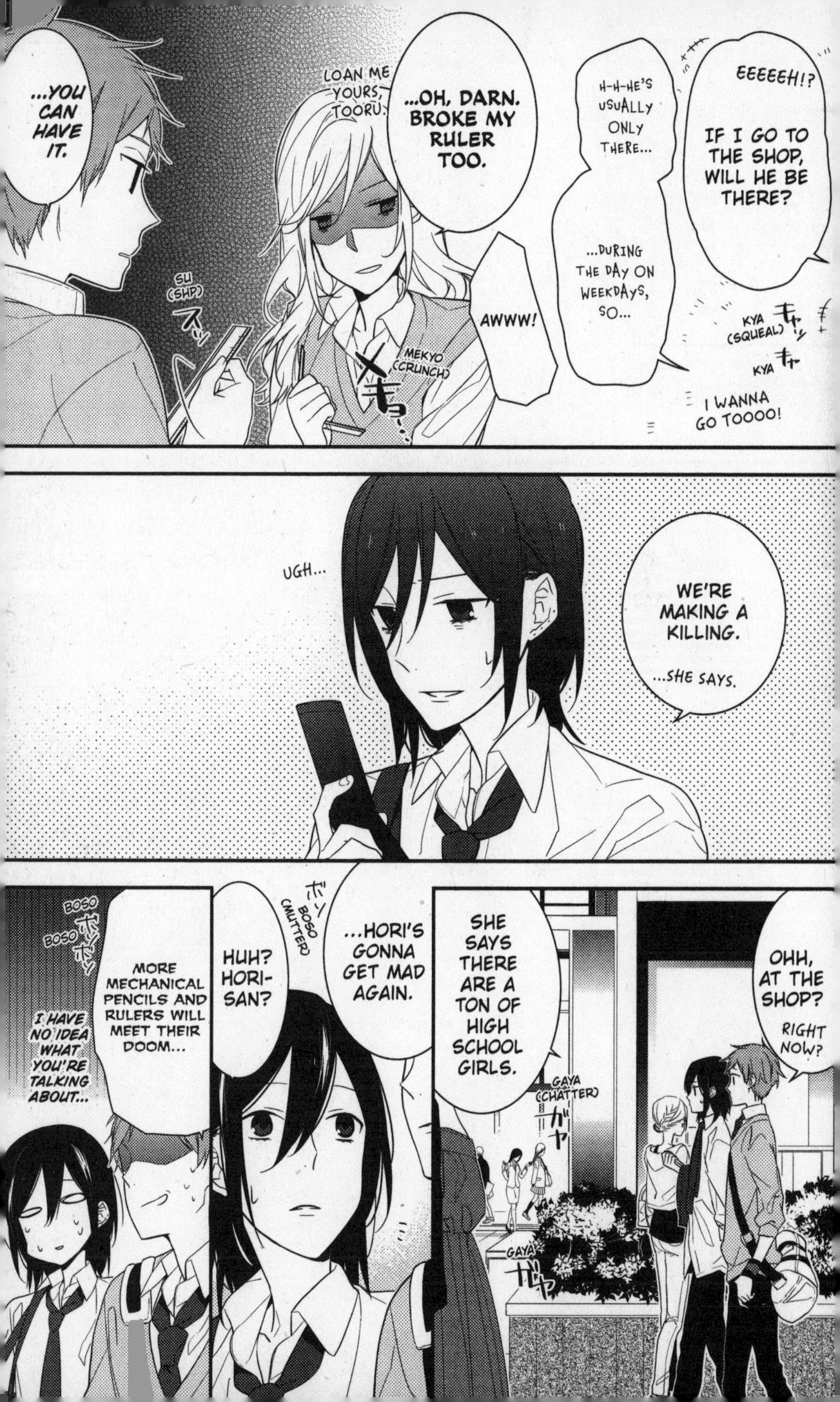
EEEEEH!?
IF I GO TO THE SHOP, WILL HE BE THERE?
H-H-HE'S USUALLY ONLY THERE...
...DURING THE DAY ON WEEKDAYS, SO...
KYA (SQUEAL)
KYA
I WANNA GO TOOOO!
AWWW!
...OH, DARN. BROKE MY RULER TOO.
LOAN ME YOURS, TOORU.
MEKYO (CRUNCH)
SU (SHP)
...YOU CAN HAVE IT.
WE'RE MAKING A KILLING.
...SHE SAYS.
UGH...
OHH, AT THE SHOP?
RIGHT NOW?
SHE SAYS THERE ARE A TON OF HIGH SCHOOL GIRLS.
GAYA (CHATTER)
GAYA
BOSO (MUTTER)
...HORI'S GONNA GET MAD AGAIN.
HUH? HORI-SAN?
BOSO BOSO
MORE MECHANICAL PENCILS AND RULERS WILL MEET THEIR DOOM...
I HAVE NO IDEA WHAT YOU'RE TALKING ABOUT...

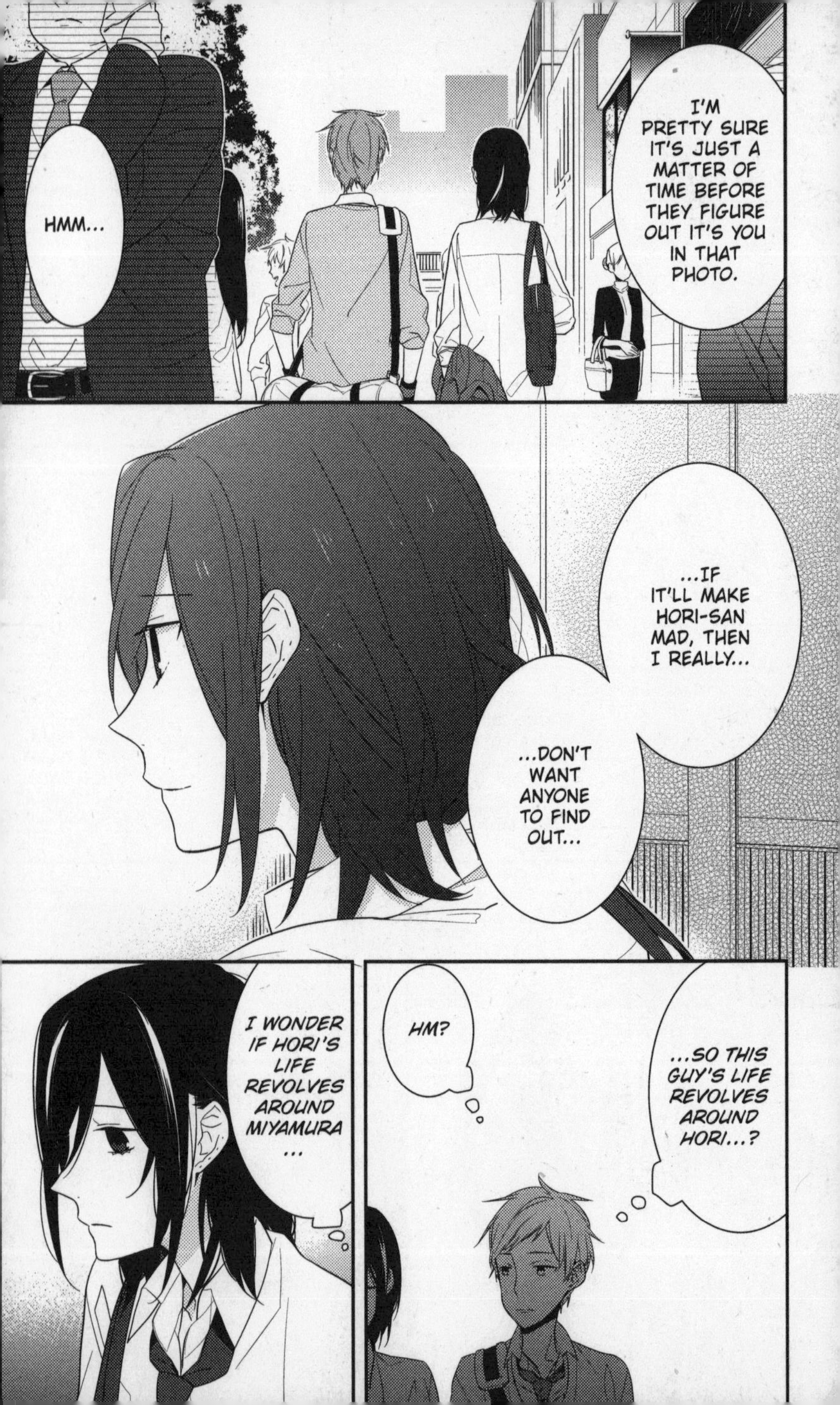
I'M PRETTY SURE IT'S JUST A MATTER OF TIME BEFORE THEY FIGURE OUT IT'S YOU IN THAT PHOTO.
HMM...
...IF IT'LL MAKE HORI-SAN MAD, THEN I REALLY...
...DON'T WANT ANYONE TO FIND OUT...
...SO THIS GUY'S LIFE REVOLVES AROUND HORI...?
HM?
I WONDER IF HORI'S LIFE REVOLVES AROUND MIYAMURA...

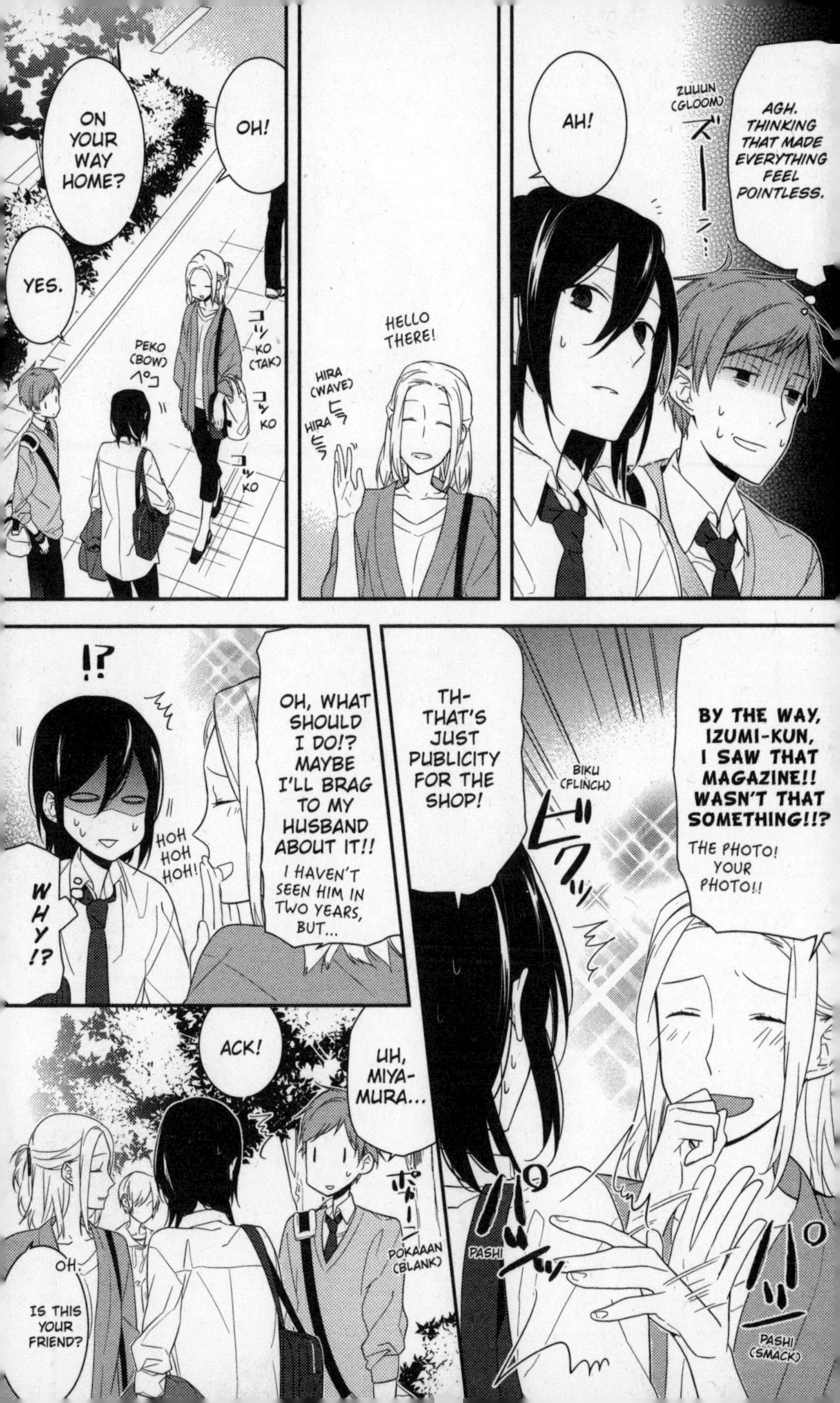

AGH. THINKING THAT MADE EVERYTHING FEEL POINTLESS.
ZUUUN (GLOOM)
AH!
HELLO THERE!
HIRA (WAVE)
HIRA
OH!
ON YOUR WAY HOME?
YES.
KO (TAK)
KO
KO
PEKO (BOW)
BY THE WAY, IZUMI-KUN, I SAW THAT MAGAZINE!! WASN'T THAT SOMETHING!!?
THE PHOTO! YOUR PHOTO!!
BIKU (FLINCH)
TH- THAT'S JUST PUBLICITY FOR THE SHOP!
PASHI (SMACK)
PASHI
OH, WHAT SHOULD I DO!? MAYBE I'LL BRAG TO MY HUSBAND ABOUT IT!!
I HAVEN'T SEEN HIM IN TWO YEARS, BUT...
HOH HOH HOH!
!?
WHY!?
UH, MIYA-MURA...
ACK!
POKAAAN (BLANK)
OH.
IS THIS YOUR FRIEND?

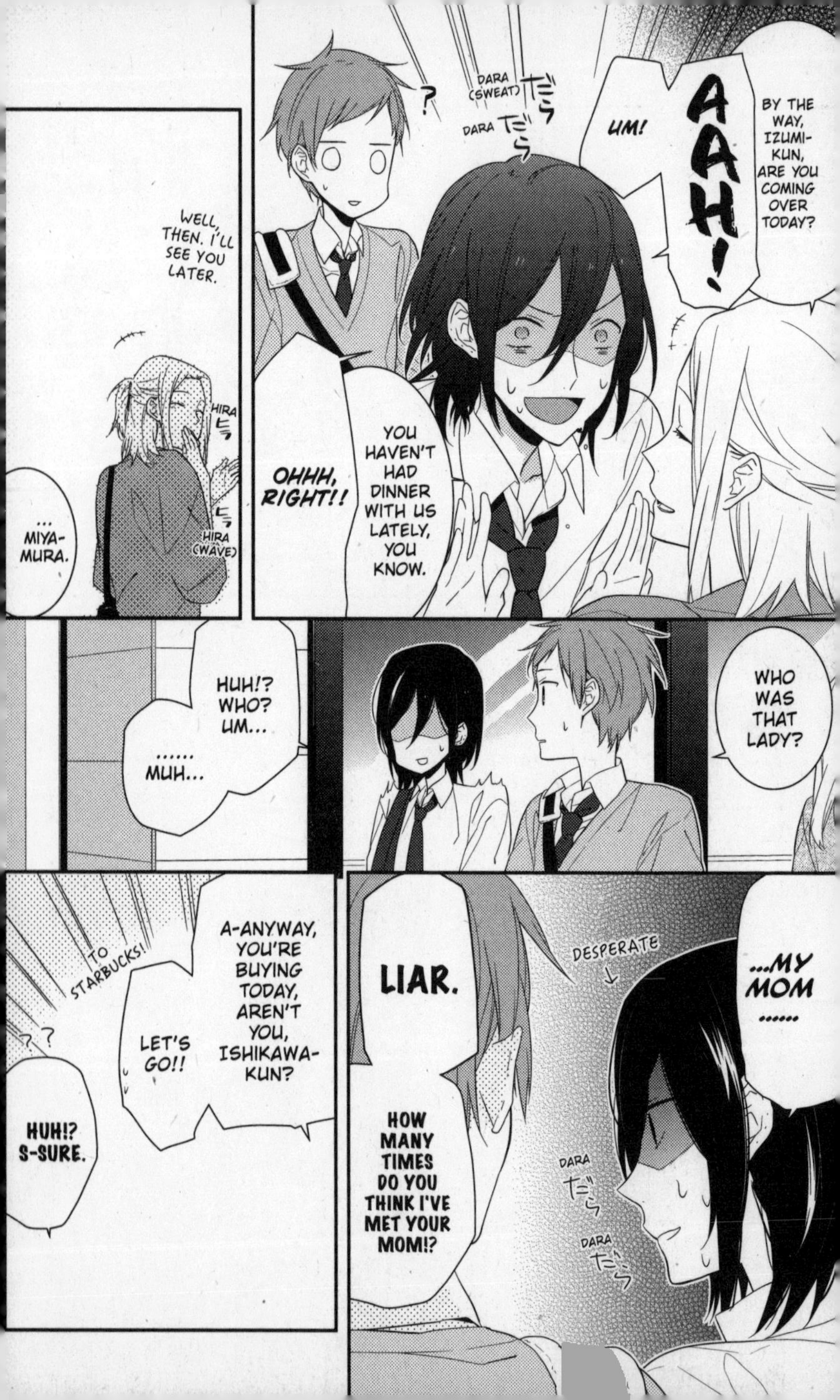
BY THE WAY, IZUMI-KUN, ARE YOU COMING OVER TODAY?
AAH!
UM!
DARA (SWEAT) だら
DARA だら
?
YOU HAVEN'T HAD DINNER WITH US LATELY, YOU KNOW.
OHHH, RIGHT!!
WELL, THEN. I'LL SEE YOU LATER.
HIRA ヒラ
HIRA (WAVE) ヒラ
... MIYA-MURA.
WHO WAS THAT LADY?
HUH!? WHO? UM...
...... MUH...
...MY MOM ......
DESPERATE
LIAR.
HOW MANY TIMES DO YOU THINK I'VE MET YOUR MOM!?
DARA だら
DARA だら
A-ANYWAY, YOU'RE BUYING TODAY, AREN'T YOU, ISHIKAWA-KUN?
LET'S GO!!
TO STARBUCKS!
??
HUH!? S-SURE.

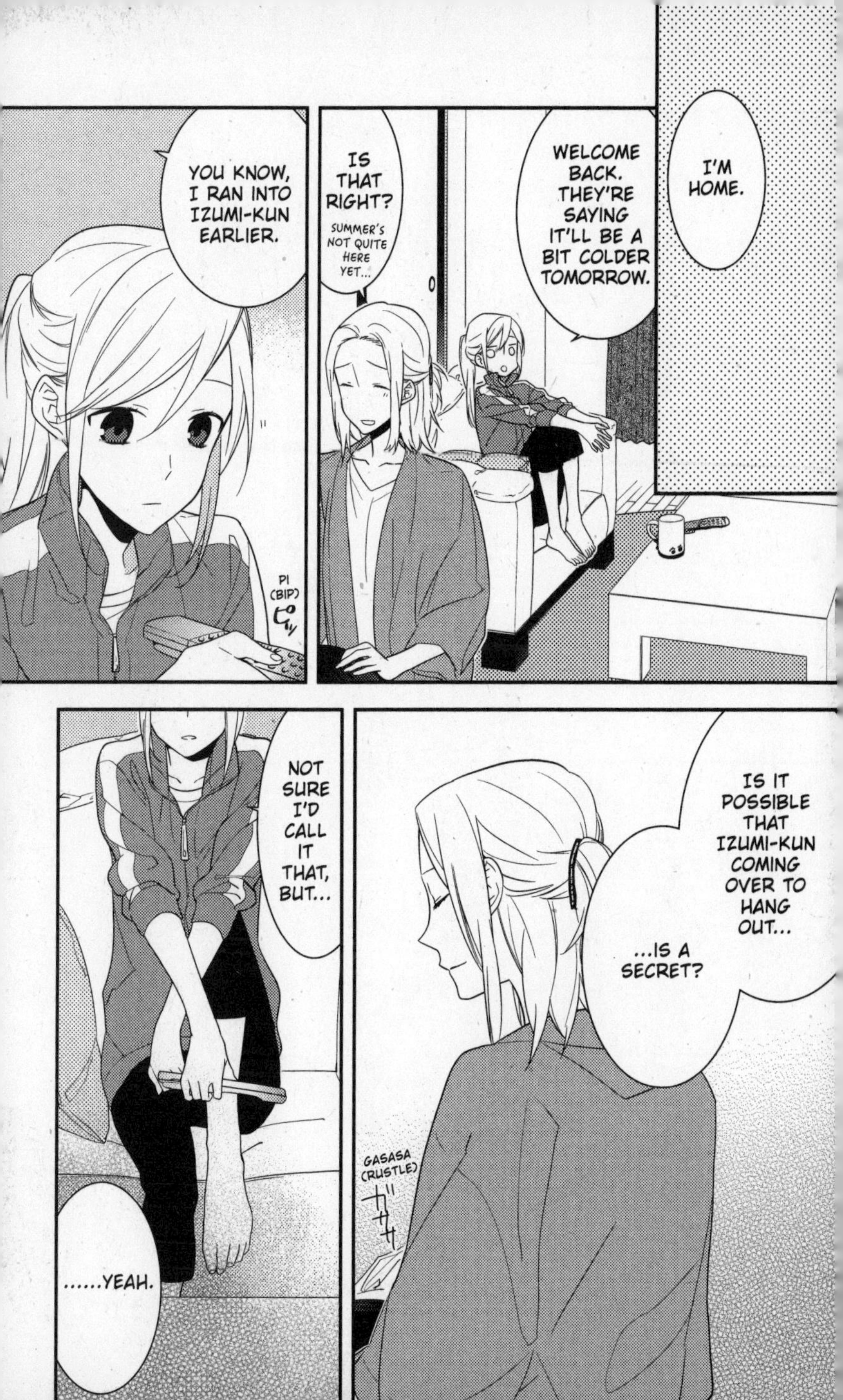
I'M HOME.
WELCOME BACK. THEY'RE SAYING IT'LL BE A BIT COLDER TOMORROW.
IS THAT RIGHT?
SUMMER'S NOT QUITE HERE YET...
YOU KNOW, I RAN INTO IZUMI-KUN EARLIER.
PI (BIP)
IS IT POSSIBLE THAT IZUMI-KUN COMING OVER TO HANG OUT...
...IS A SECRET?
GASASA (RUSTLE)
NOT SURE I'D CALL IT THAT, BUT...
......YEAH.

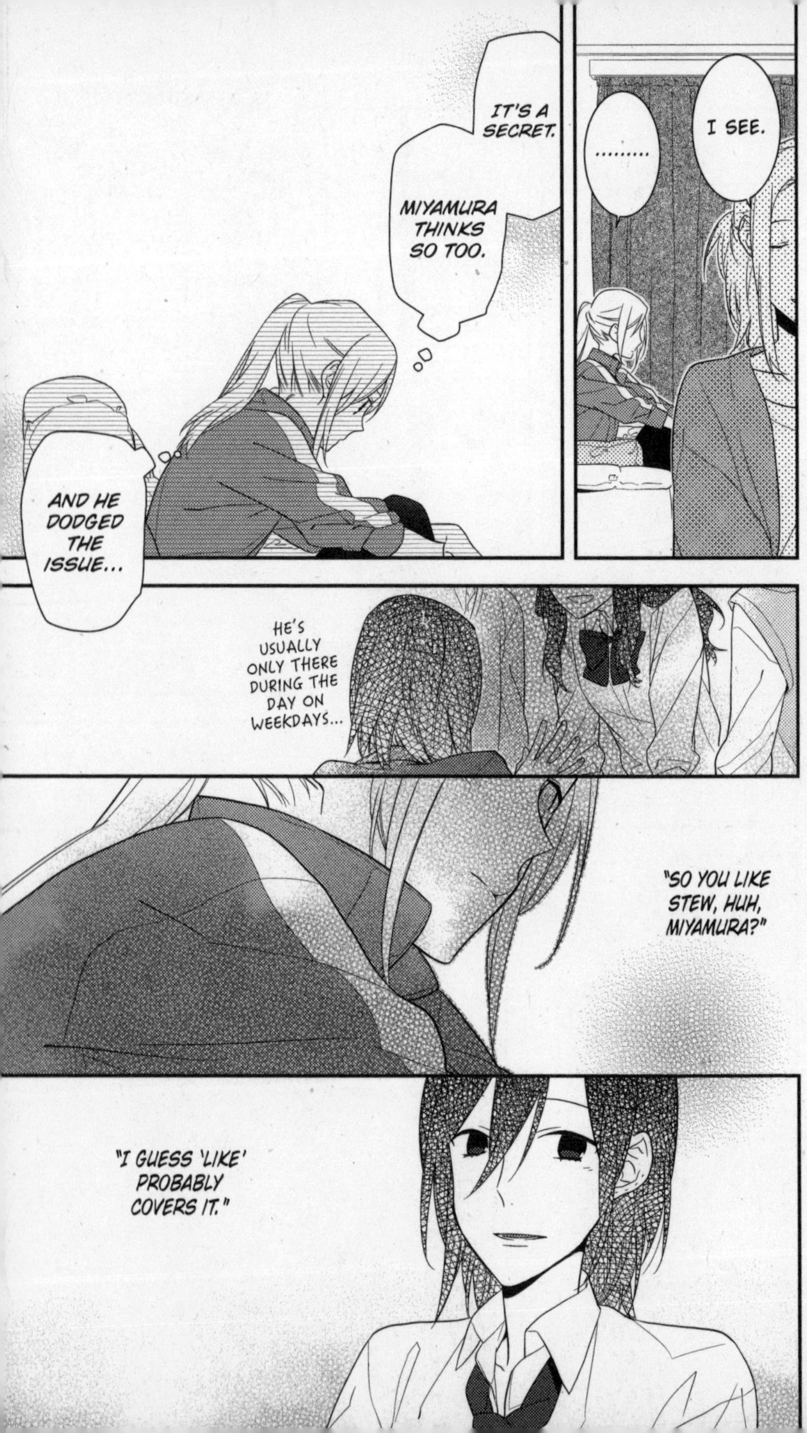
I SEE.
....
IT'S A SECRET.
MIYAMURA THINKS SO TOO.
AND HE DODGED THE ISSUE...
HE'S USUALLY ONLY THERE DURING THE DAY ON WEEKDAYS...
"SO YOU LIKE STEW, HUH, MIYAMURA?"
"I GUESS 'LIKE' PROBABLY COVERS IT."

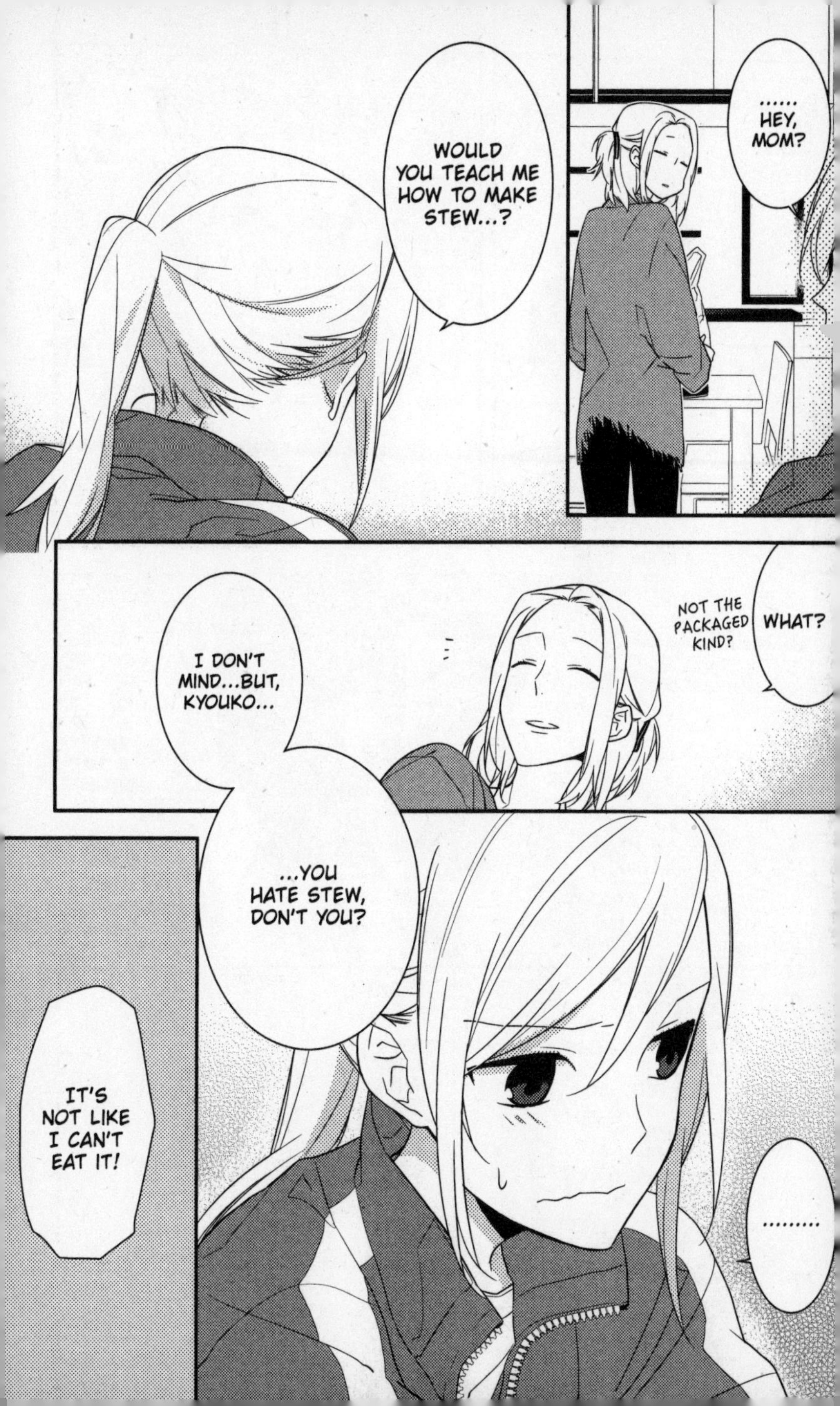
......HEY, MOM?
WOULD YOU TEACH ME HOW TO MAKE STEW...?
WHAT?
NOT THE PACKAGED KIND?
I DON'T MIND...BUT, KYOUKO...
...YOU HATE STEW, DON'T YOU?
....
IT'S NOT LIKE I CAN'T EAT IT!

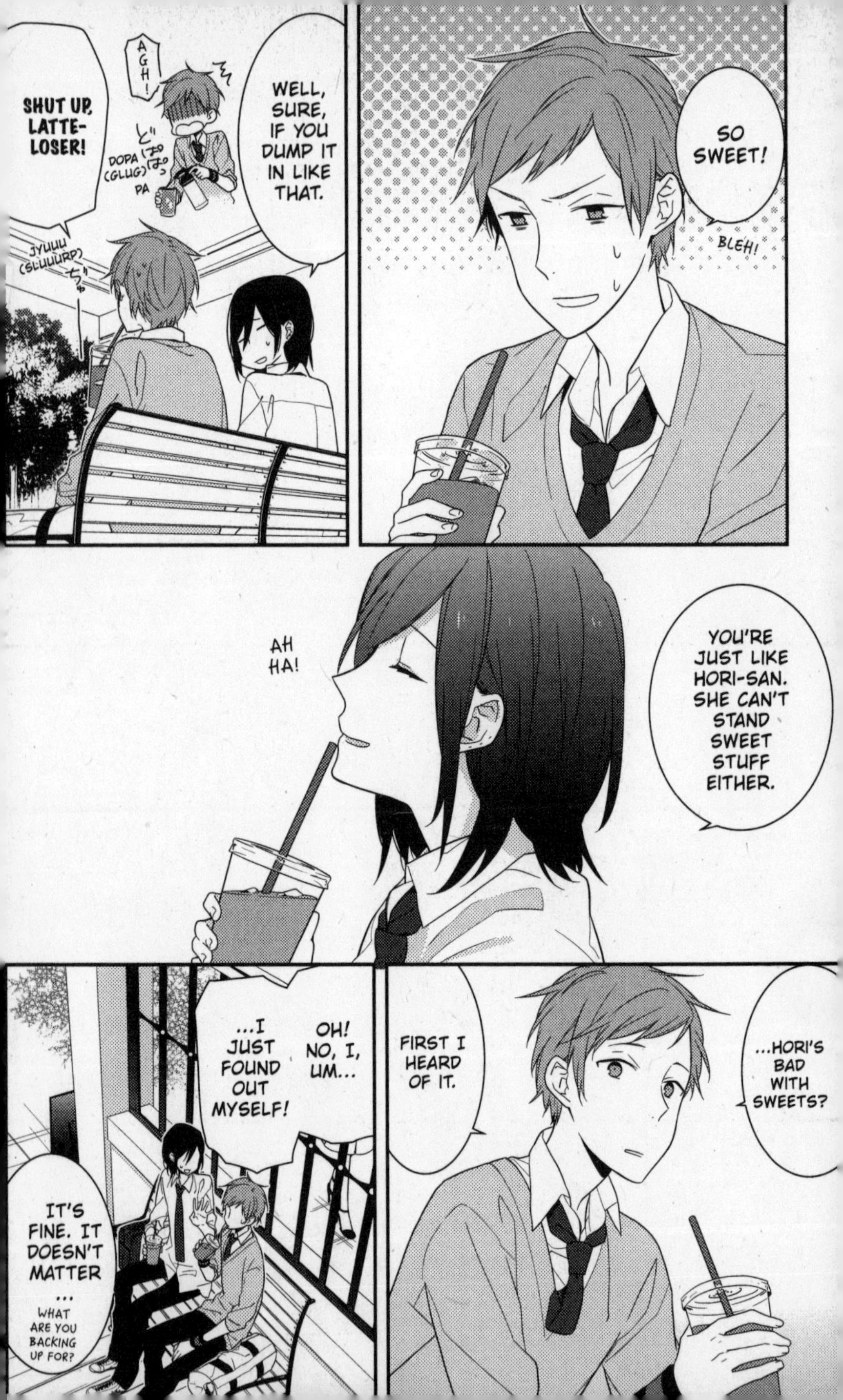
SO SWEET!
BLEH!
WELL, SURE, IF YOU DUMP IT IN LIKE THAT.
AGH!
どぼぼぼっ
DOPA (GLUG) PA
SHUT UP, LATTE-LOSER!
JYUUU (SLUUURP)
ぢゅ
YOU'RE JUST LIKE HORI-SAN. SHE CAN'T STAND SWEET STUFF EITHER.
AH HA!
...HORI'S BAD WITH SWEETS?
FIRST I HEARD OF IT.
OH! NO, I, UM...
...I JUST FOUND OUT MYSELF!
IT'S FINE. IT DOESN'T MATTER...
WHAT ARE YOU BACKING UP FOR?

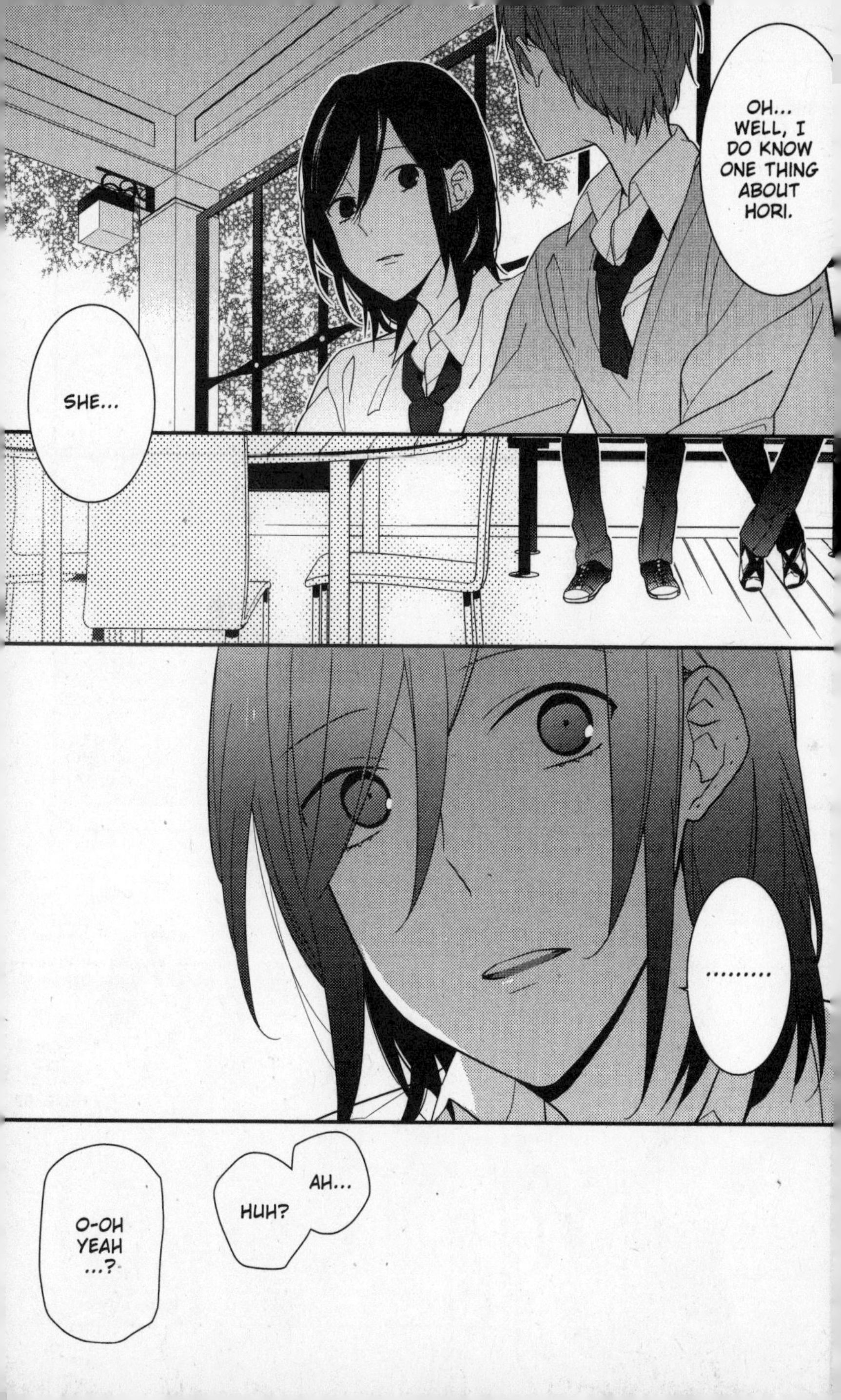
OH... WELL, I DO KNOW ONE THING ABOUT HORI.
SHE...
....
AH... HUH?
O-OH YEAH ...?

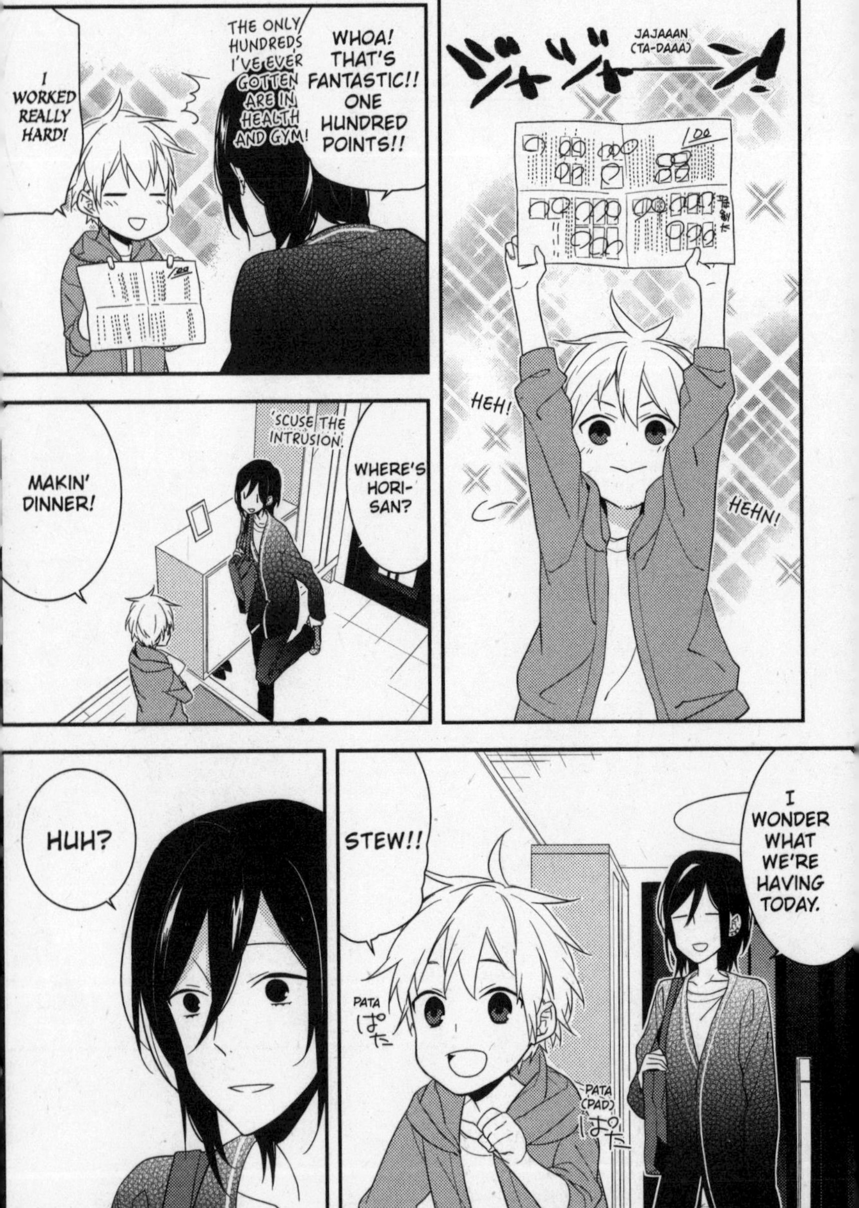
JAJAAAN (TA-DAAA)
ジャジャーン!
100
HEH!
HEHN!
WHOA! THAT'S FANTASTIC!! ONE HUNDRED POINTS!!
THE ONLY HUNDREDS I'VE EVER GOTTEN ARE IN HEALTH AND GYM!
I WORKED REALLY HARD!
'SCUSE THE INTRUSION!
WHERE'S HORI-SAN?
MAKIN' DINNER!
I WONDER WHAT WE'RE HAVING TODAY.
PATA (PAD)
ぱた
STEW!!
PATA
ぱた
HUH?

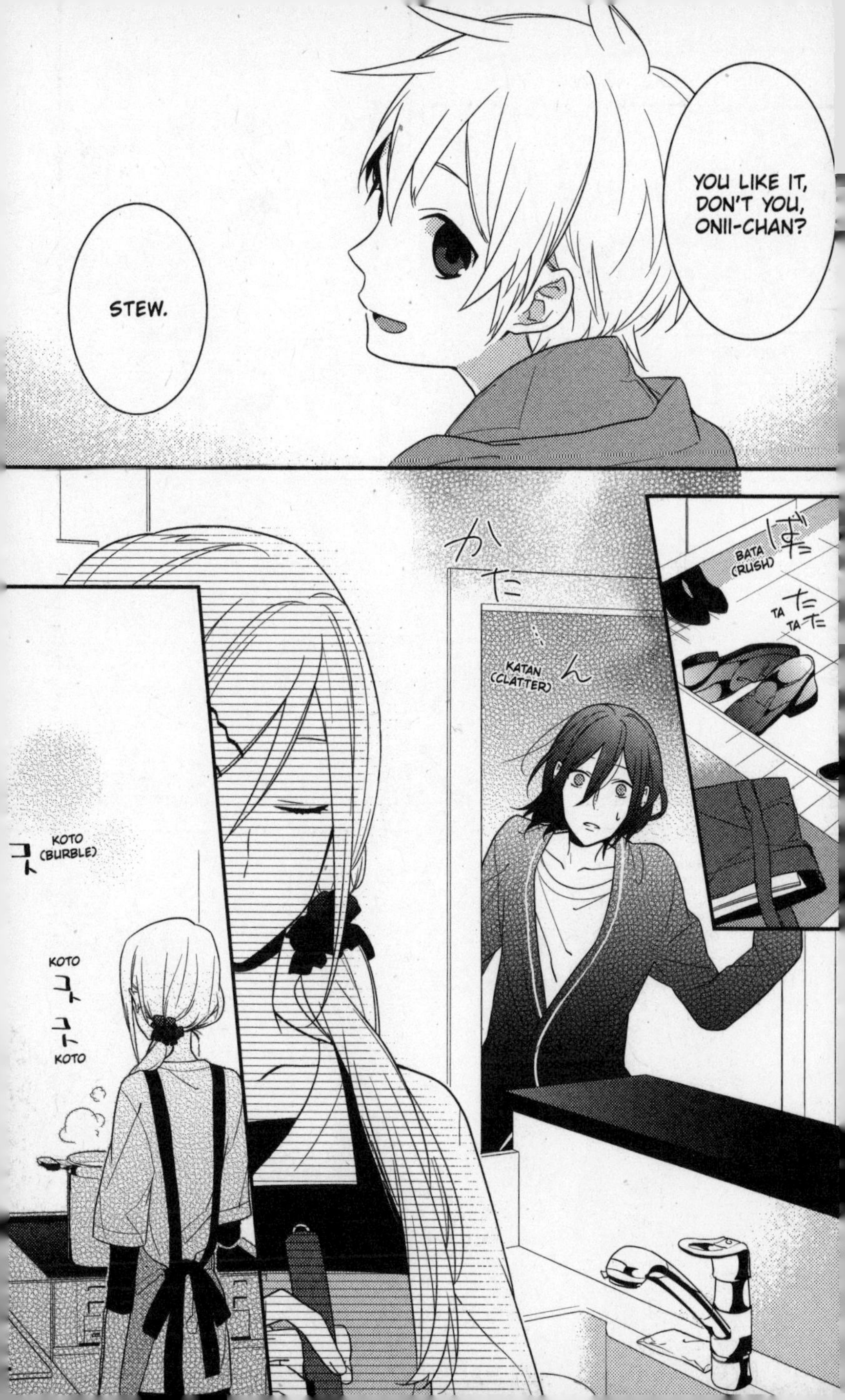
YOU LIKE IT, DON'T YOU, ONII-CHAN?
STEW.
BATA (RUSH)
TA TA
TA TA
KATAN (CLATTER)
KOTO (BURBLE)
KOTO
KOTO

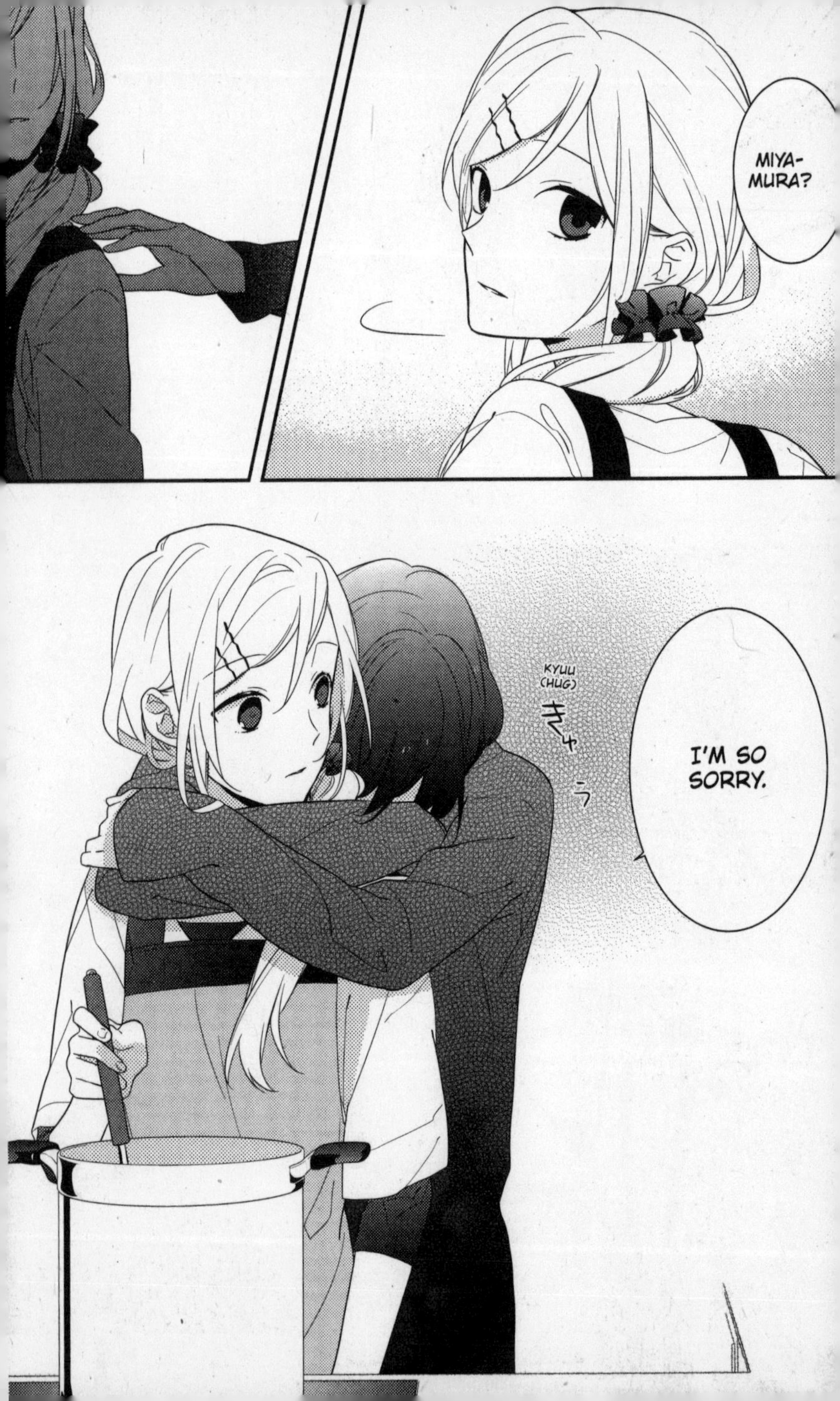
MIYA-MURA?
I'M SO SORRY.
KYUU (HUG)
きゅっ

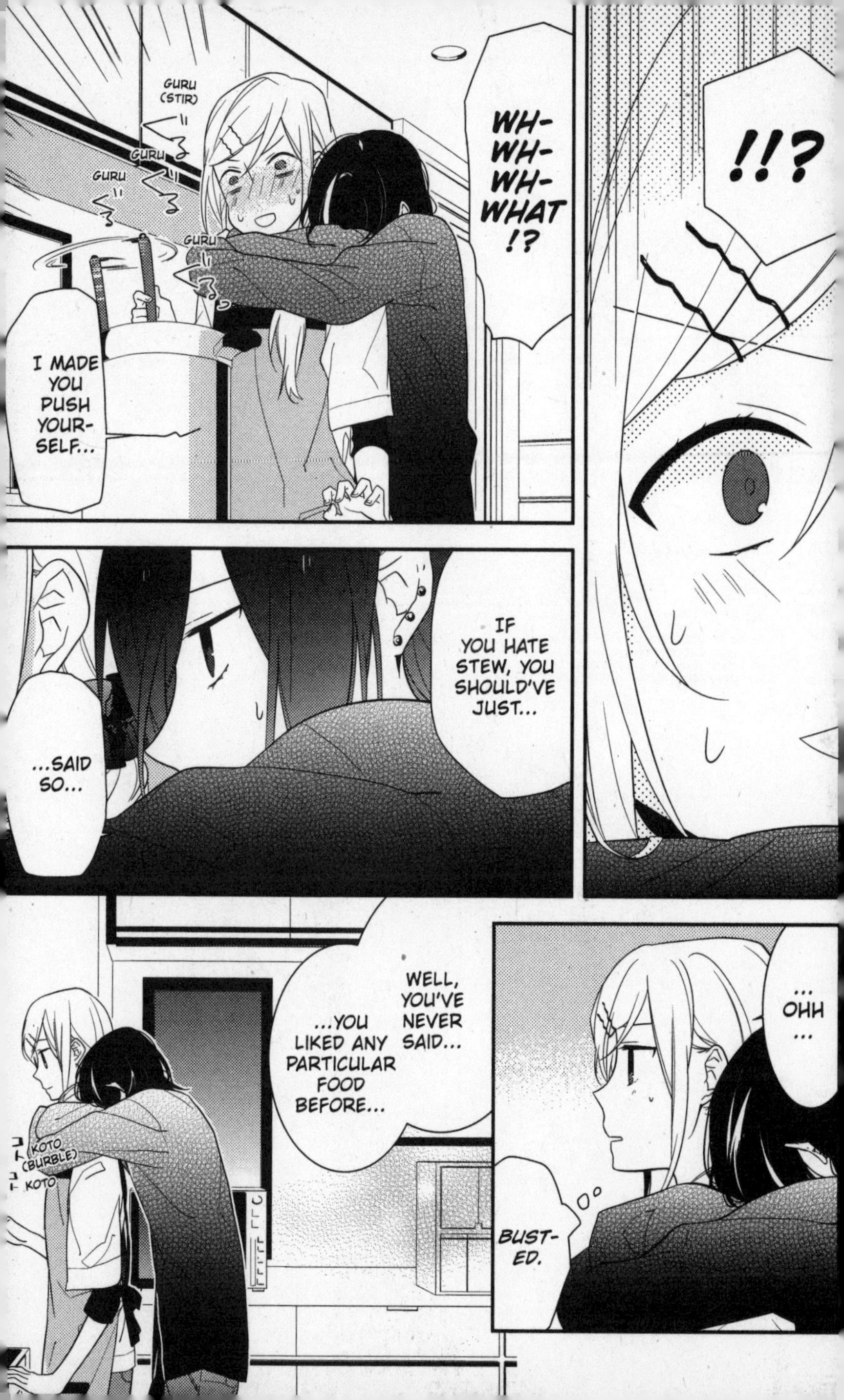
!!?
WH-WH-WH-WHAT!?
GURU (STIR)
GURU
GURU
GURU
I MADE YOU PUSH YOURSELF...
IF YOU HATE STEW, YOU SHOULD'VE JUST...
...SAID SO...
...OHH...
BUSTED.
WELL, YOU'VE NEVER SAID...
...YOU LIKED ANY PARTICULAR FOOD BEFORE...
KOTO (BURBLE)
KOTO

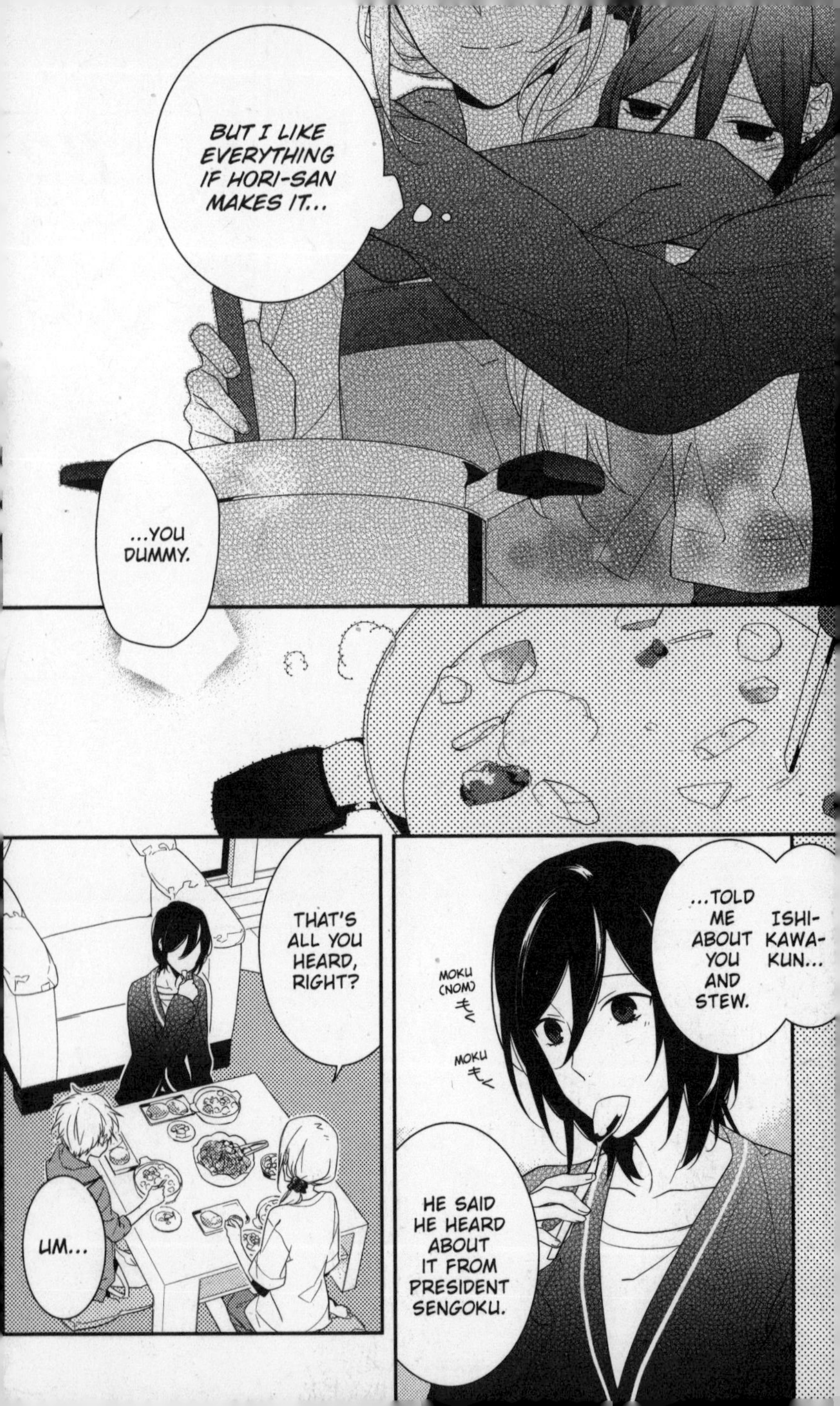
BUT I LIKE EVERYTHING IF HORI-SAN MAKES IT...
...YOU DUMMY.
ISHI-KAWA-KUN...
...TOLD ME ABOUT YOU AND STEW.
MOKU (NOM) もく
MOKU もく
HE SAID HE HEARD ABOUT IT FROM PRESIDENT SENGOKU.
THAT'S ALL YOU HEARD, RIGHT?
UM...

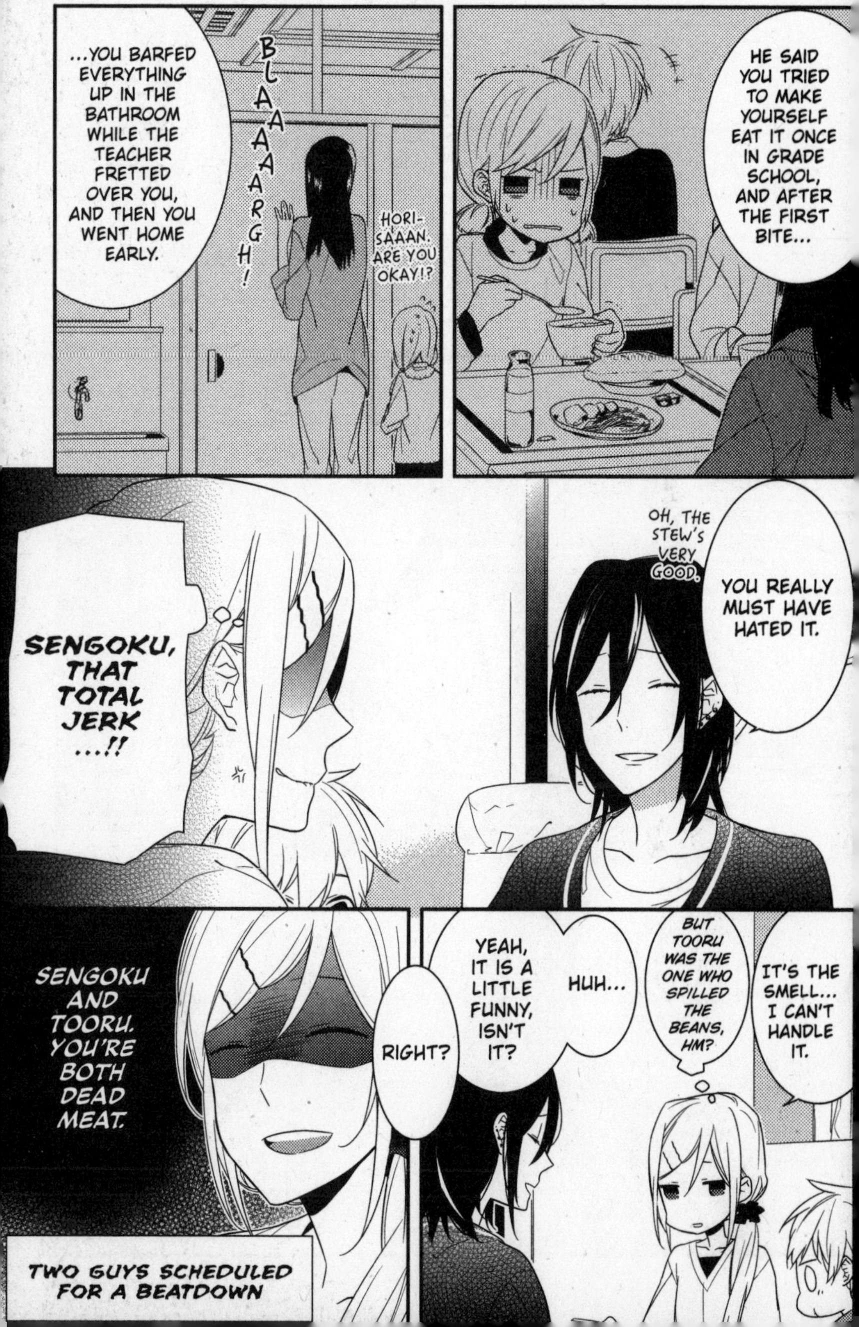
HE SAID YOU TRIED TO MAKE YOURSELF EAT IT ONCE IN GRADE SCHOOL, AND AFTER THE FIRST BITE...
...YOU BARFED EVERYTHING UP IN THE BATHROOM WHILE THE TEACHER FRETTED OVER YOU, AND THEN YOU WENT HOME EARLY.
BLAAAAARGH!
HORI-SAAAN. ARE YOU OKAY!?
OH, THE STEW'S VERY GOOD.
YOU REALLY MUST HAVE HATED IT.
SENGOKU, THAT TOTAL JERK ...!!
IT'S THE SMELL... I CAN'T HANDLE IT.
BUT TOORU WAS THE ONE WHO SPILLED THE BEANS, HM?
HUH...
YEAH, IT IS A LITTLE FUNNY, ISN'T IT?
RIGHT?
SENGOKU AND TOORU. YOU'RE BOTH DEAD MEAT.
TWO GUYS SCHEDULED FOR A BEATDOWN

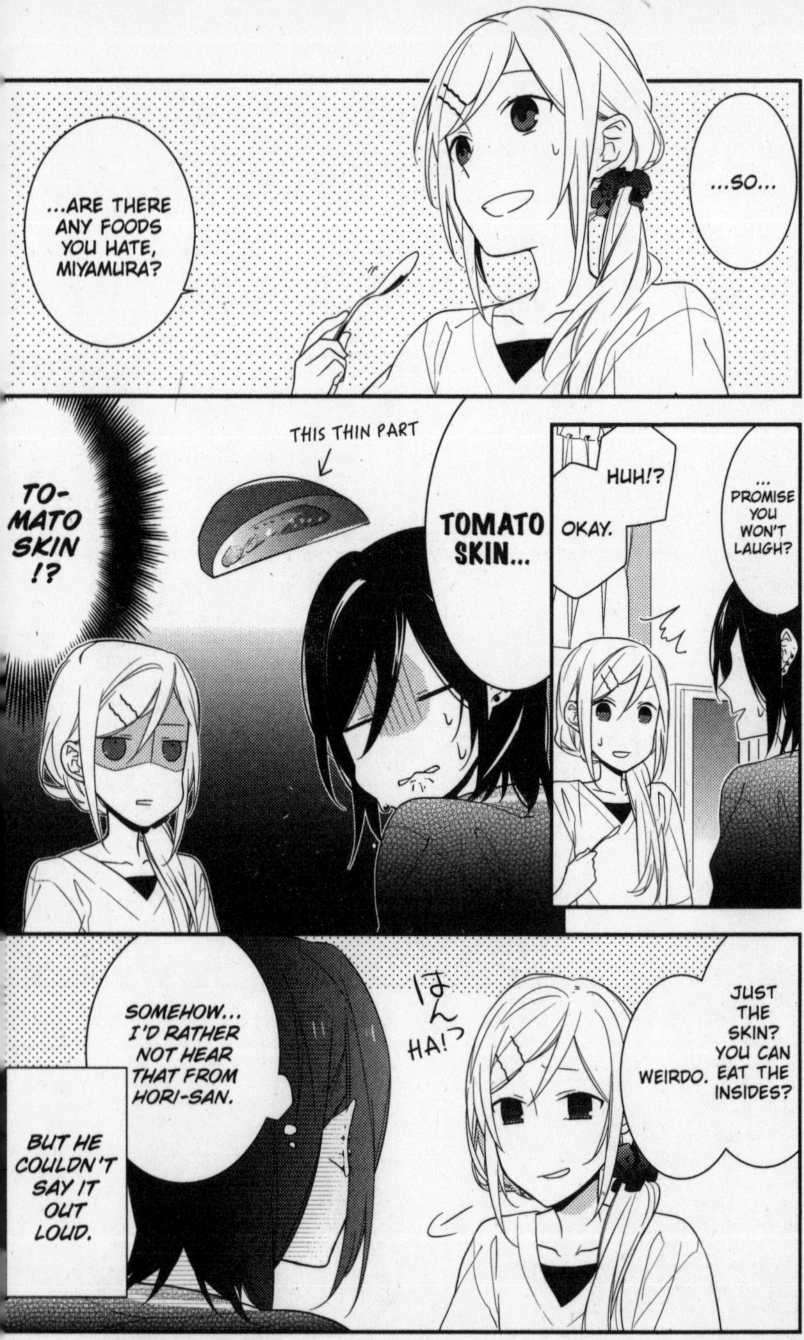
...SO...
...ARE THERE ANY FOODS YOU HATE, MIYAMURA?
...PROMISE YOU WON'T LAUGH?
HUH!?
OKAY.
TOMATO SKIN...
THIS THIN PART
TO-MATO SKIN!?
JUST THE SKIN? YOU CAN EAT THE INSIDES?
WEIRDO.
はん
HA!?
SOMEHOW... I'D RATHER NOT HEAR THAT FROM HORI-SAN.
BUT HE COULDN'T SAY IT OUT LOUD.

HORIMIYA

HORIMIYA

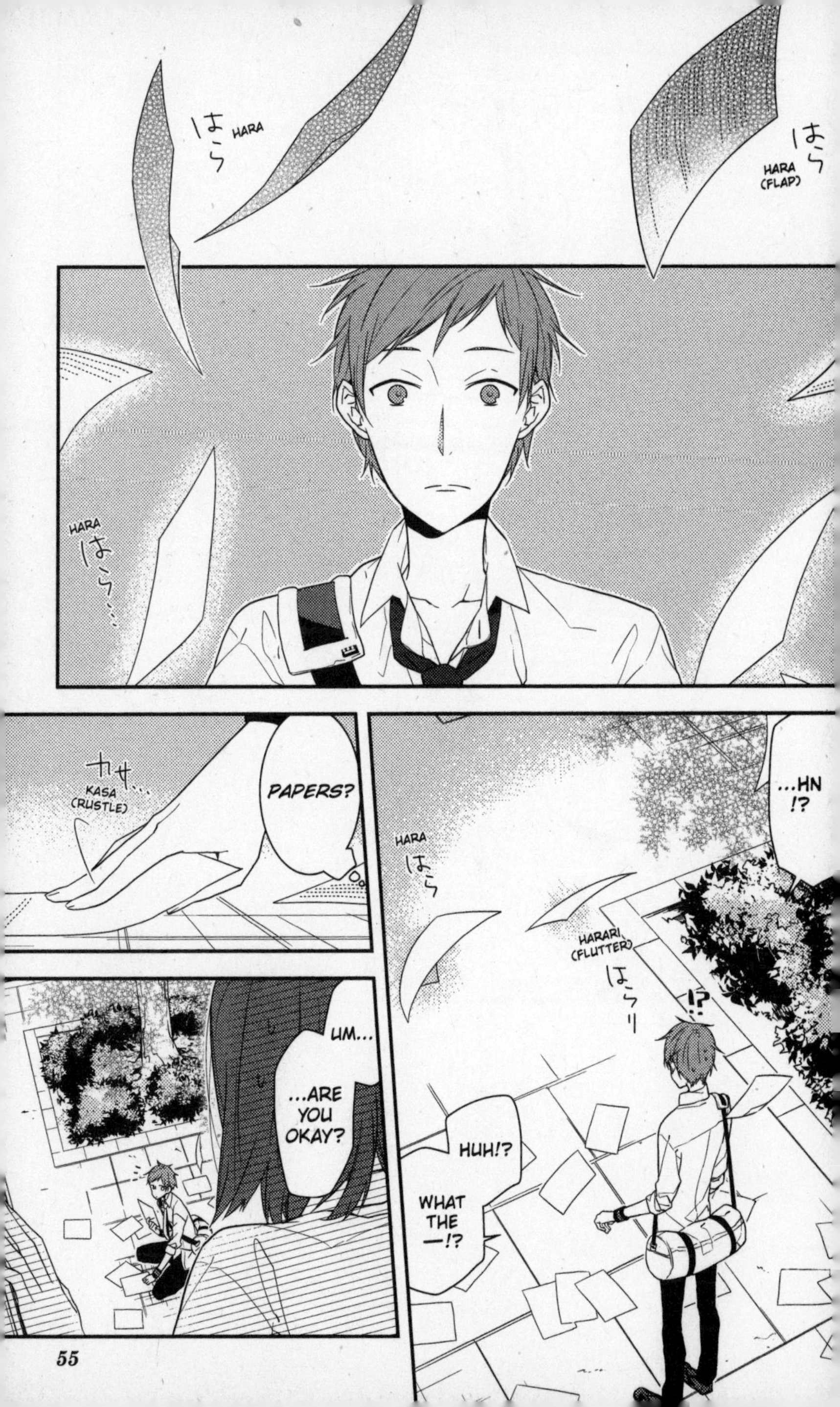

はら
HARA (FLAP)
はら
HARA
HARA
はら…
…HN !?
HARA
はら
HARARI (FLUTTER)
はらり
!?
HUH!?
WHAT THE —!?
カサ…
KASA (RUSTLE)
PAPERS?
UM…
…ARE YOU OKAY?

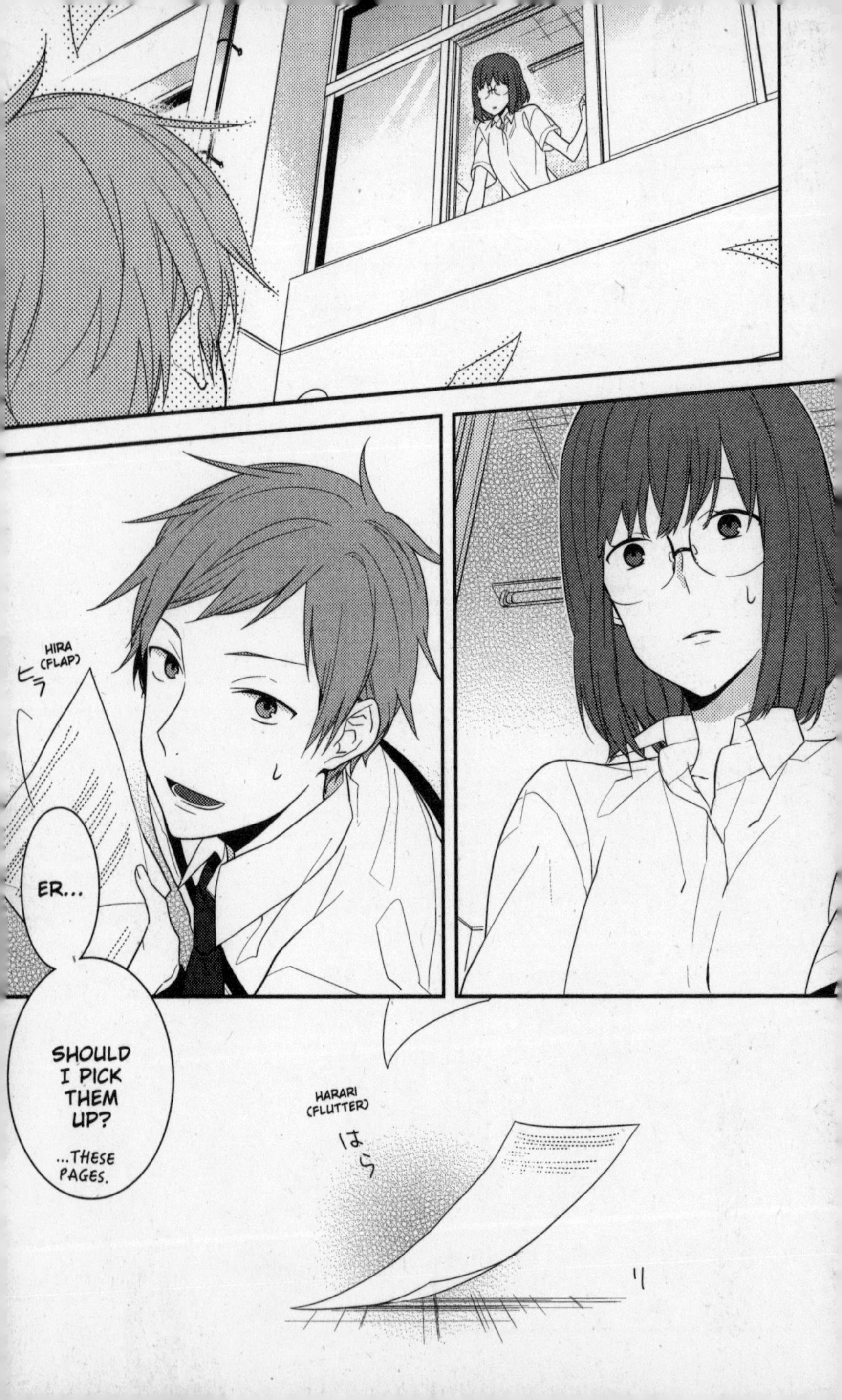
HIRA (FLAP)
ヒラ
ER...
SHOULD I PICK THEM UP?
...THESE PAGES.
HARARI (FLUTTER)
はら
り

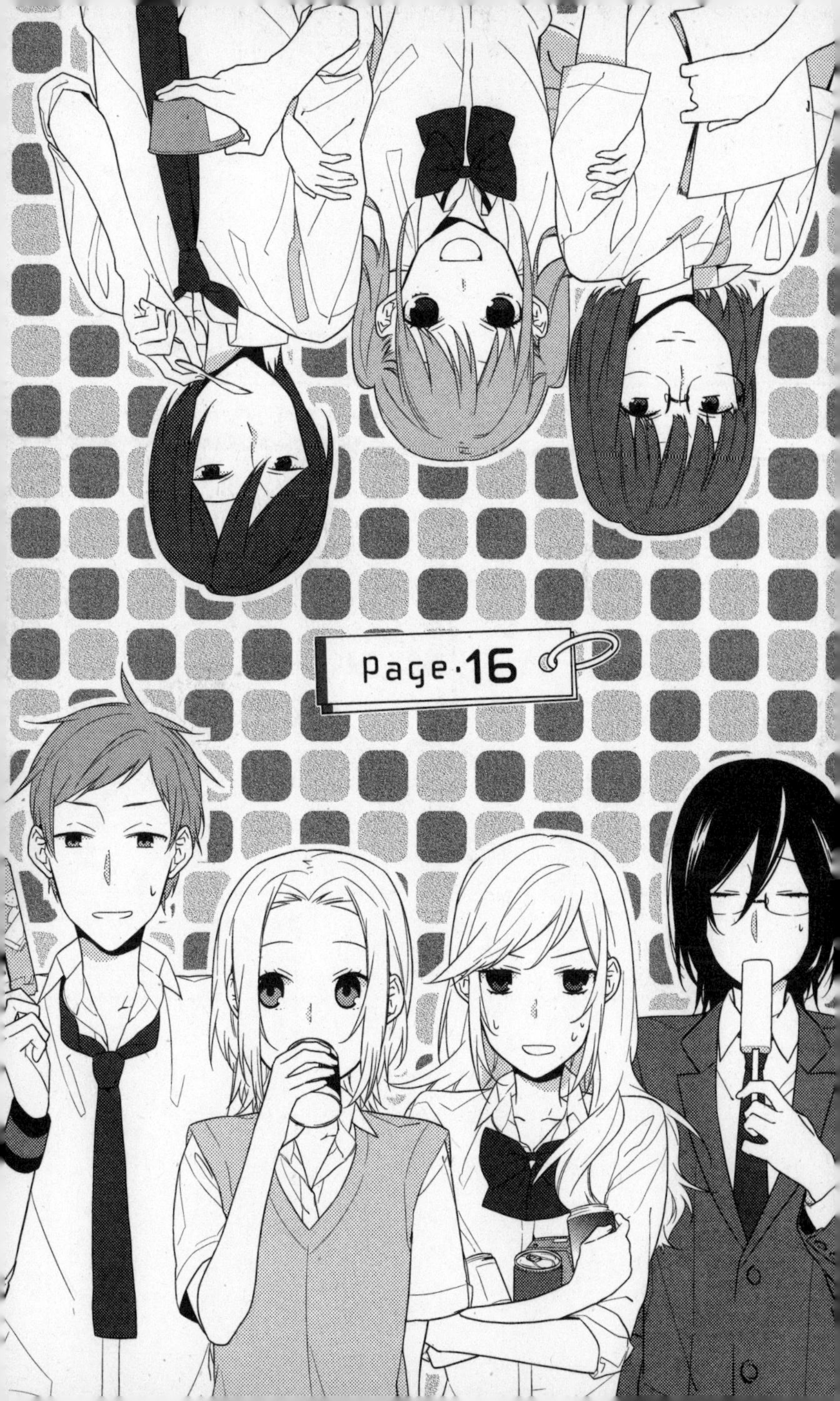
Page·16

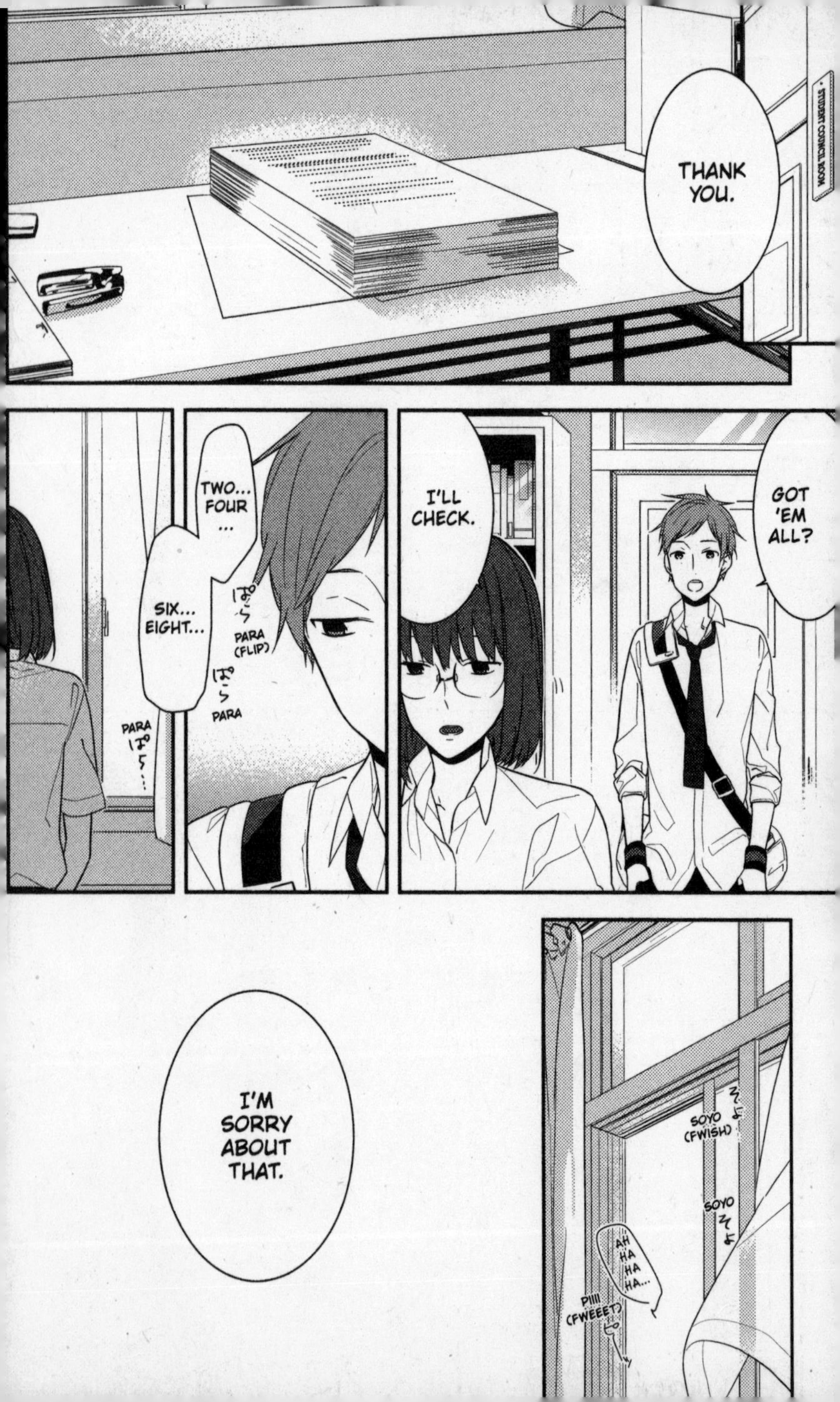
STUDENT COUNCIL ROOM
THANK YOU.
GOT 'EM ALL?
I'LL CHECK.
TWO... FOUR ...
SIX... EIGHT...
ぱら PARA (FLIP)
ぱら PARA
PARA ぱら...
SOYO (FWISH) そよ
SOYO そよ
AH HA HA HA...
PIIII (FWEEET) ピー
I'M SORRY ABOUT THAT.

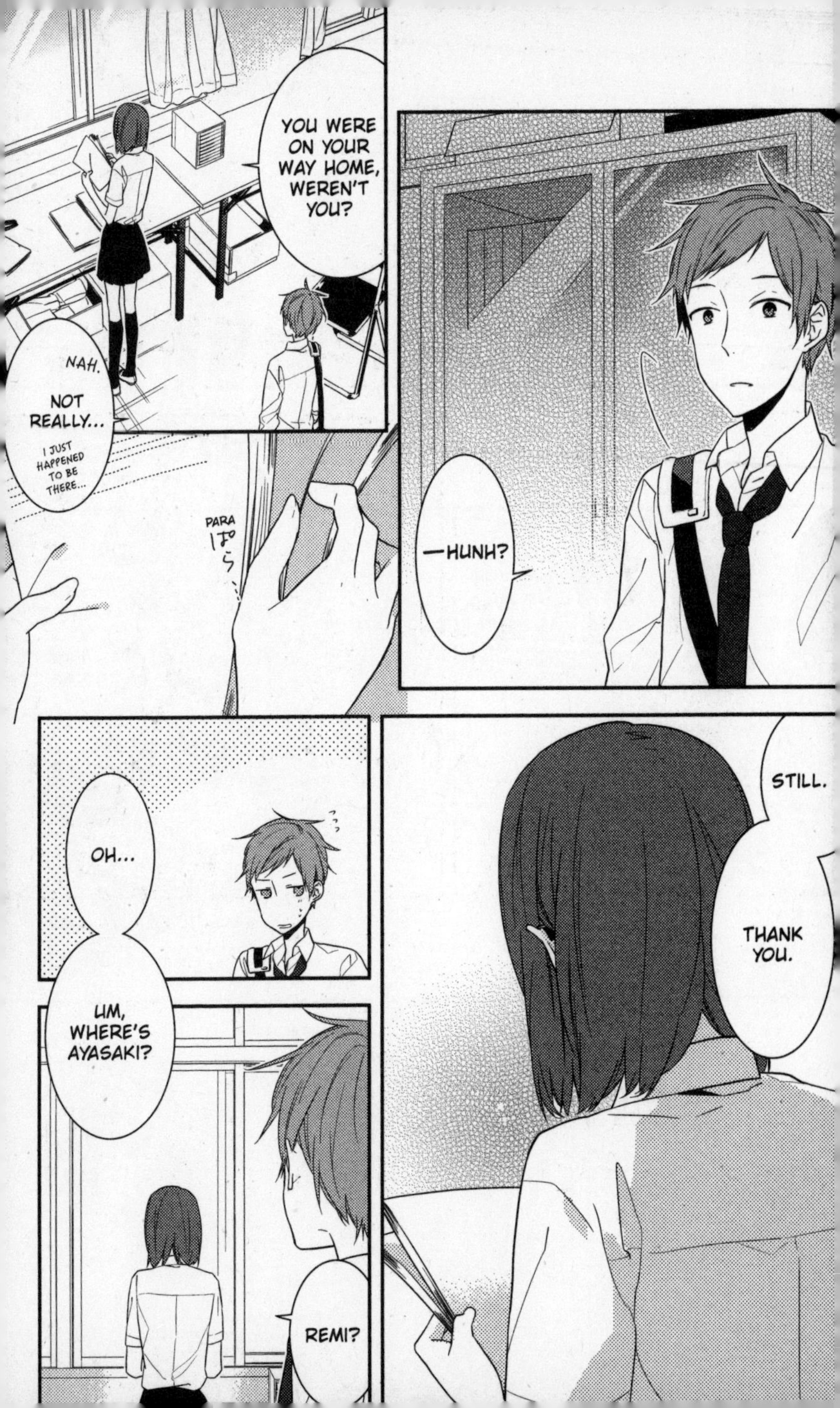
YOU WERE ON YOUR WAY HOME, WEREN'T YOU?
—HUNH?
NAH.
NOT REALLY...
I JUST HAPPENED TO BE THERE...
PARA
ぱら
STILL.
THANK YOU.
OH...
UM, WHERE'S AYASAKI?
REMI?

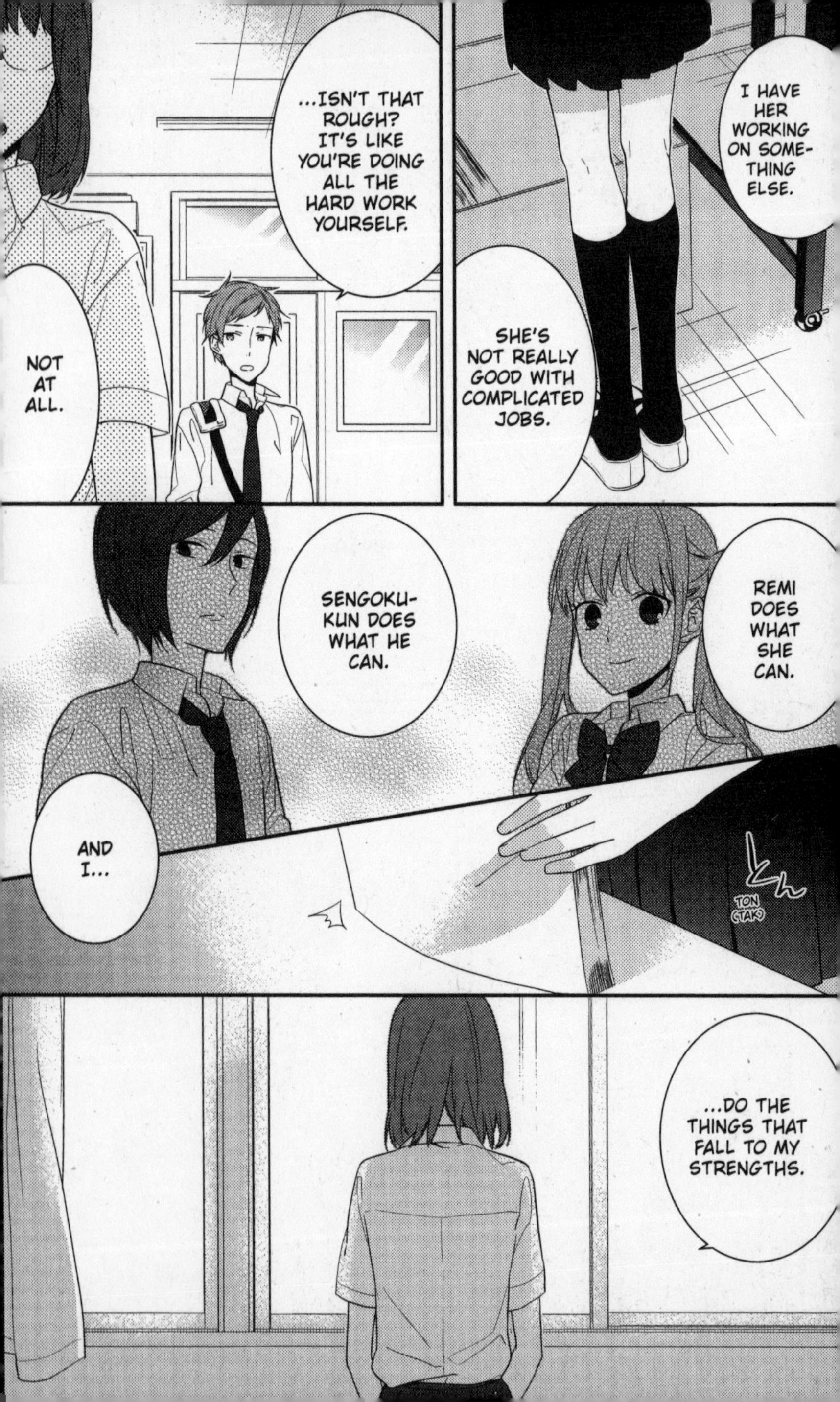
I HAVE HER WORKING ON SOME-THING ELSE.
SHE'S NOT REALLY GOOD WITH COMPLICATED JOBS.
...ISN'T THAT ROUGH? IT'S LIKE YOU'RE DOING ALL THE HARD WORK YOURSELF.
NOT AT ALL.
REMI DOES WHAT SHE CAN.
SENGOKU-KUN DOES WHAT HE CAN.
とん
TON (TAK)
AND I...
...DO THE THINGS THAT FALL TO MY STRENGTHS.

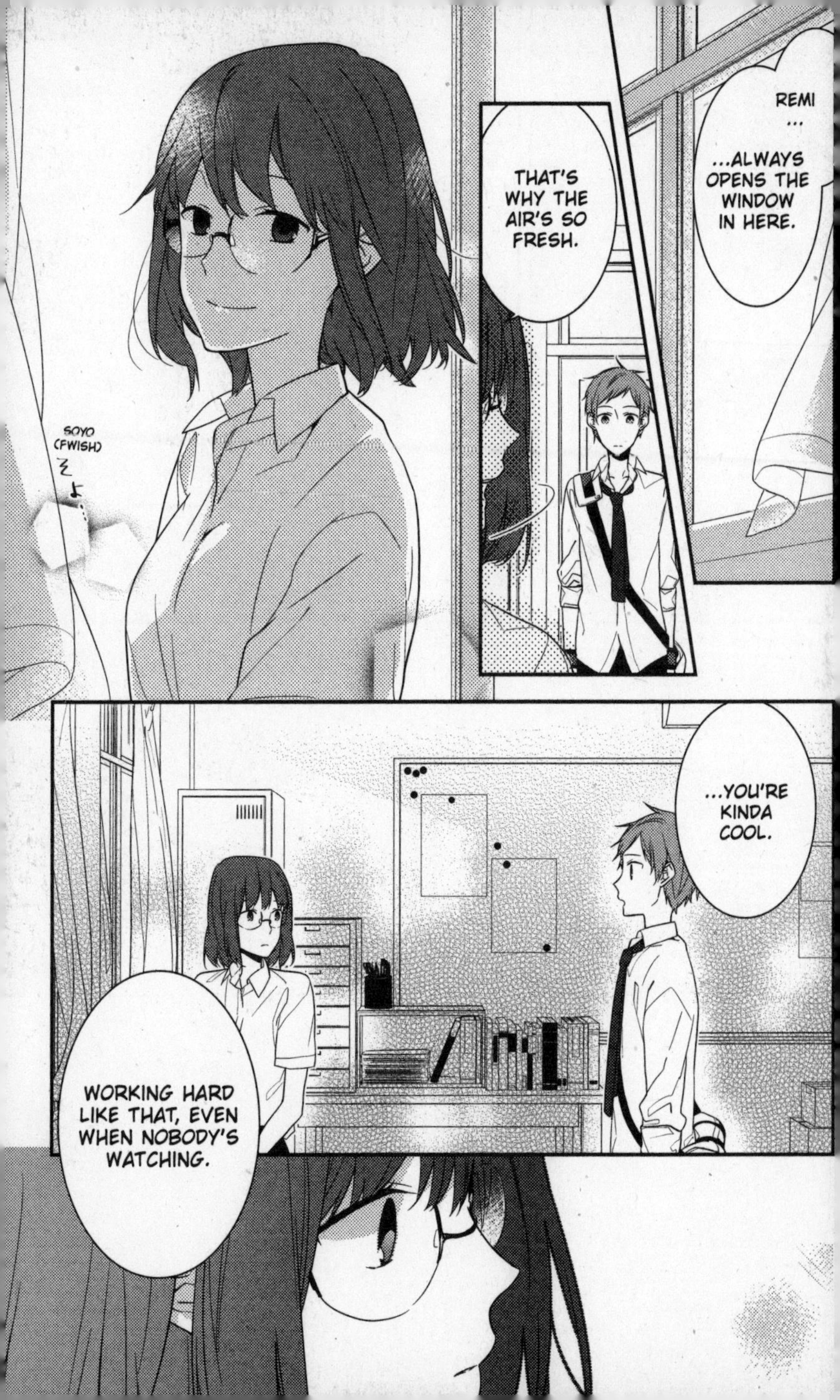
REMI ...
...ALWAYS OPENS THE WINDOW IN HERE.
THAT'S WHY THE AIR'S SO FRESH.
SOYO (FWISH)
そよ
...YOU'RE KINDA COOL.
WORKING HARD LIKE THAT, EVEN WHEN NOBODY'S WATCHING.

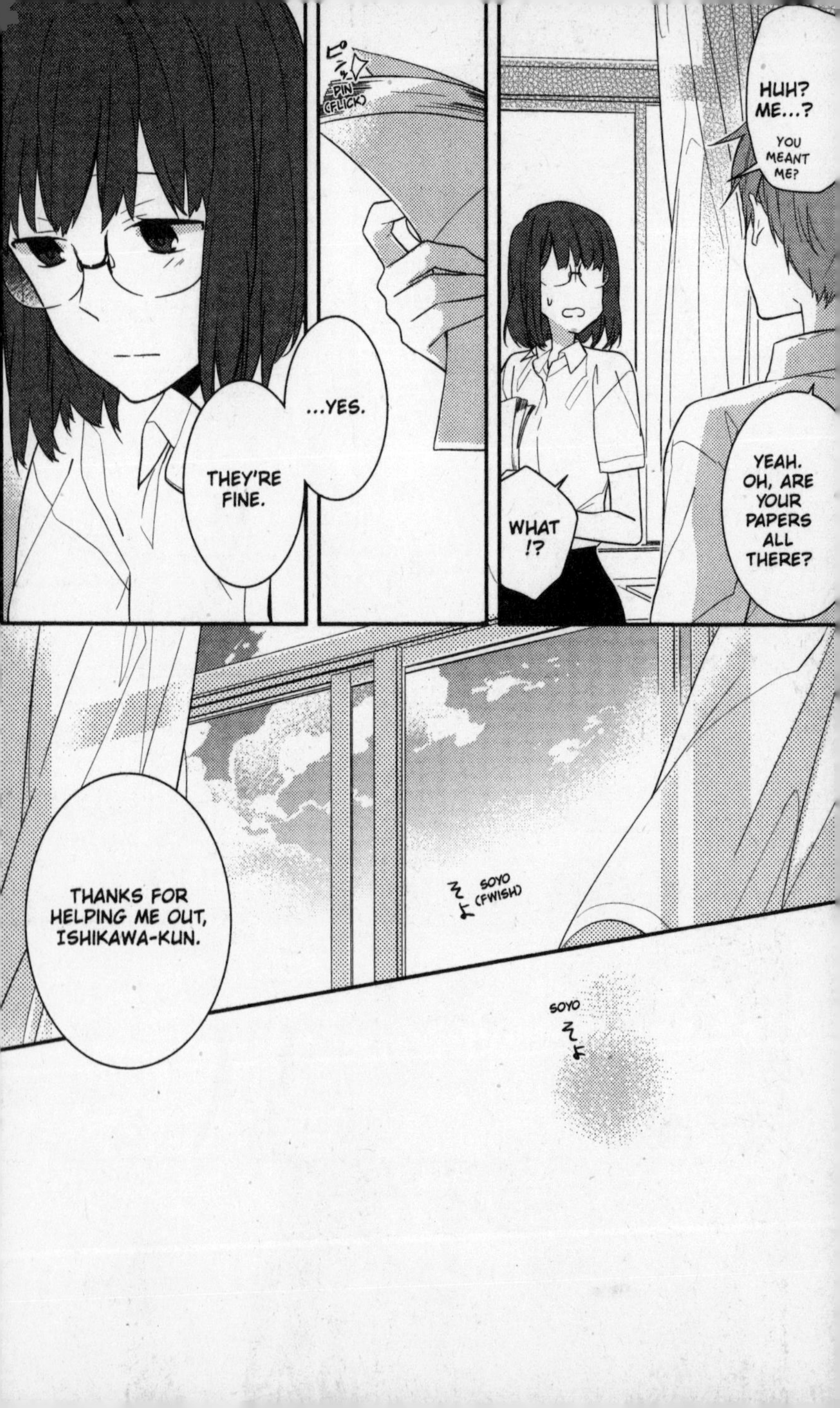
HUH? ME...?
YOU MEANT ME?
YEAH. OH, ARE YOUR PAPERS ALL THERE?
WHAT!?
PIN (FLICK)
...YES.
THEY'RE FINE.
SOYO (FWISH)
THANKS FOR HELPING ME OUT, ISHIKAWA-KUN.
SOYO

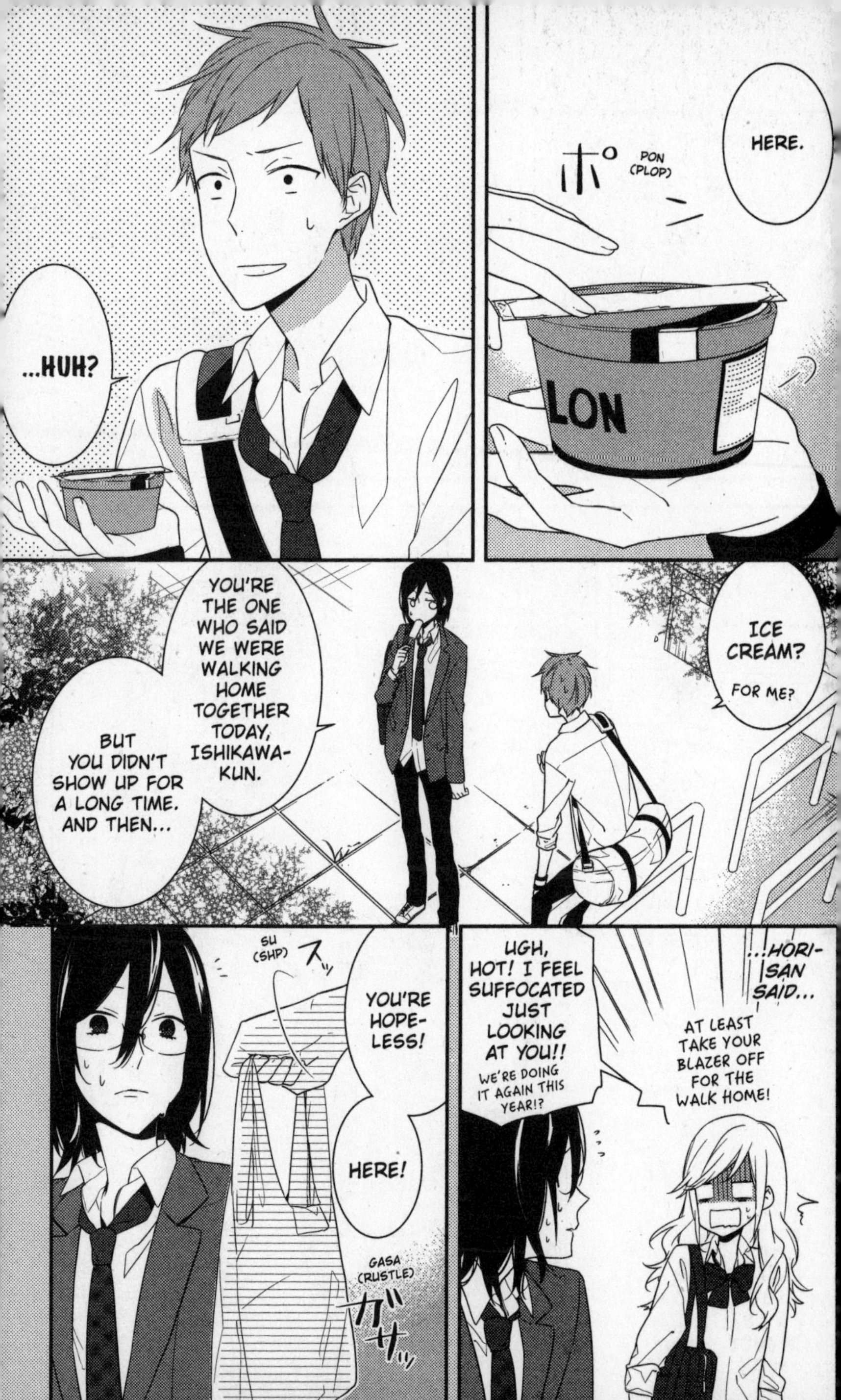
HERE.
ポ
PON (PLOP)
LON
...HUH?
ICE CREAM?
FOR ME?
YOU'RE THE ONE WHO SAID WE WERE WALKING HOME TOGETHER TODAY, ISHIKAWA-KUN.
BUT YOU DIDN'T SHOW UP FOR A LONG TIME. AND THEN...
...HORI-SAN SAID...
AT LEAST TAKE YOUR BLAZER OFF FOR THE WALK HOME!
UGH, HOT! I FEEL SUFFOCATED JUST LOOKING AT YOU!!
WE'RE DOING IT AGAIN THIS YEAR!?
YOU'RE HOPE-LESS!
SU (SHP)
スッ
HERE!
GASA (RUSTLE)
ガサッ

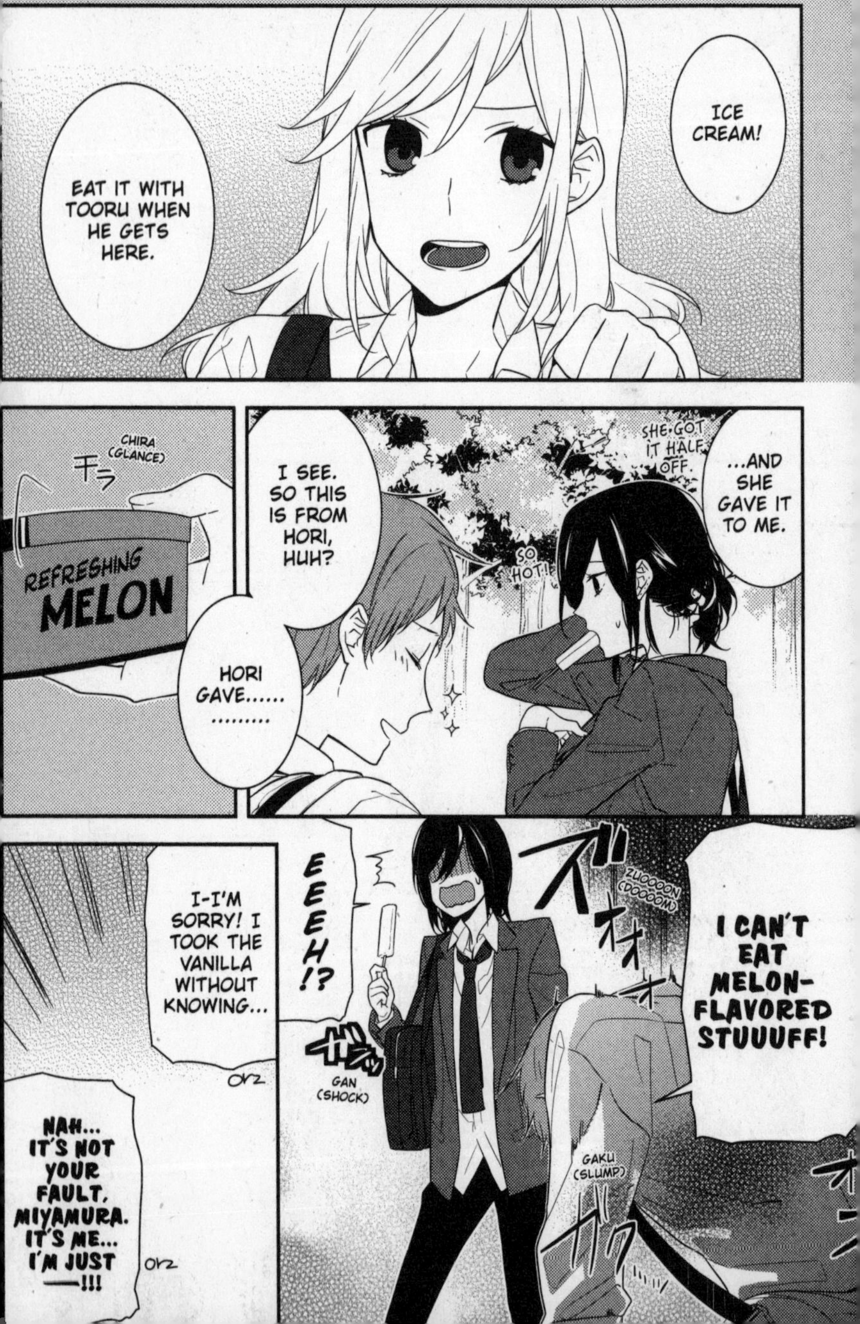
ICE CREAM!
EAT IT WITH TOORU WHEN HE GETS HERE.
...AND SHE GAVE IT TO ME.
SHE GOT IT HALF OFF.
SO HOT!
I SEE. SO THIS IS FROM HORI, HUH?
HORI GAVE...... ....
チラ
CHIRA (GLANCE)
REFRESHING MELON
ZUOOOON (DOOOOM)
I CAN'T EAT MELON-FLAVORED STUUUFF!
EEEEH!?
GAN (SHOCK)
GAKU (SLUMP)
I-I'M SORRY! I TOOK THE VANILLA WITHOUT KNOWING...
orz
NAH... IT'S NOT YOUR FAULT, MIYAMURA. IT'S ME... I'M JUST—!!!
orz

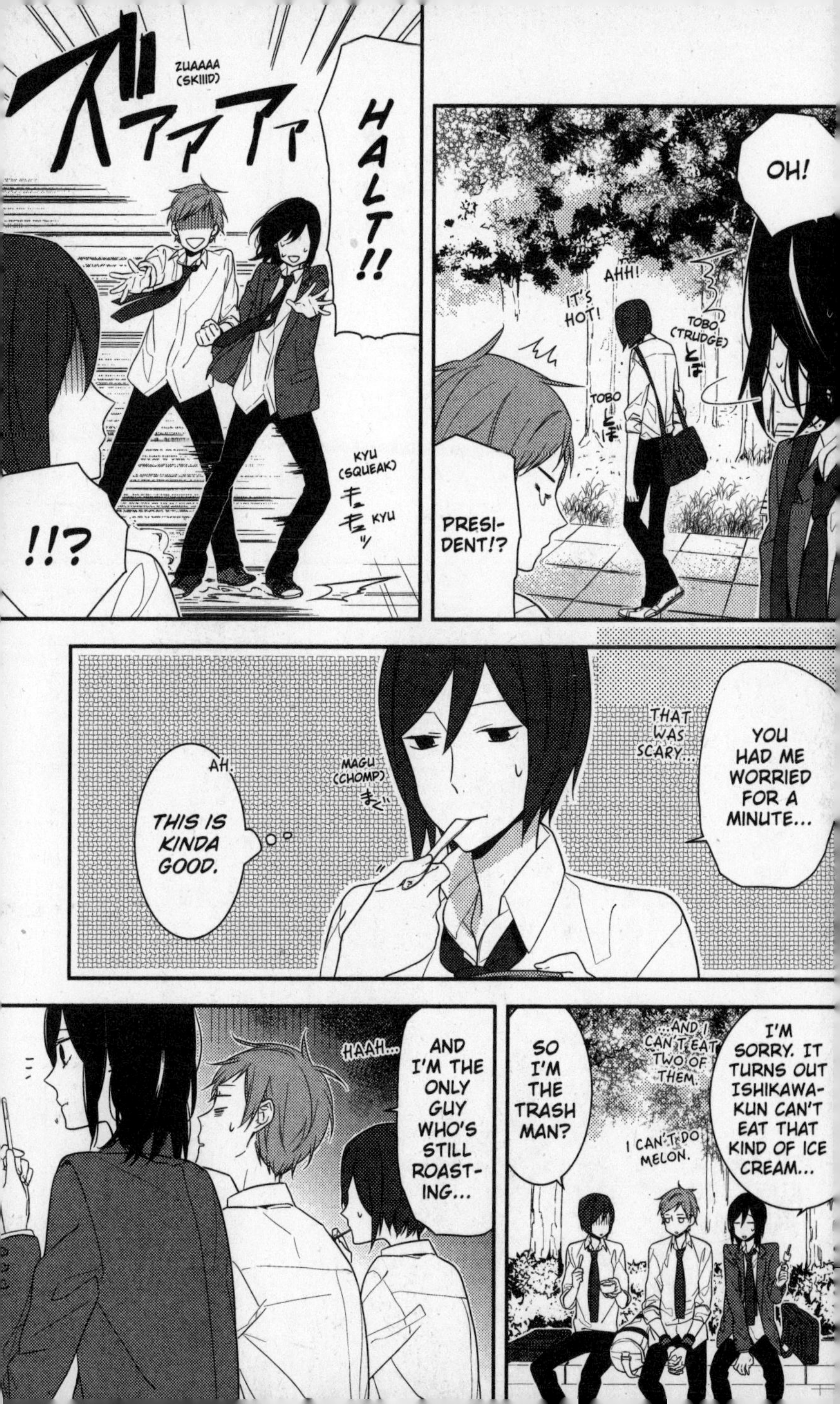
OH!
TOBO (TRUDGE) とぼ
AHH!
IT'S HOT!
TOBO とぼ
PRESI-DENT!?
HALT!!
ZUAAAA (SKIIID)
ズァアアァ
KYU (SQUEAK) キュ
KYU キュッ
!!?
YOU HAD ME WORRIED FOR A MINUTE...
THAT WAS SCARY...
MAGU (CHOMP) まぐ
AH.
THIS IS KINDA GOOD.
I'M SORRY. IT TURNS OUT ISHIKAWA-KUN CAN'T EAT THAT KIND OF ICE CREAM...
...AND I CAN'T EAT TWO OF THEM.
I CAN'T DO MELON.
SO I'M THE TRASH MAN?
AND I'M THE ONLY GUY WHO'S STILL ROASTING...
HAAH...

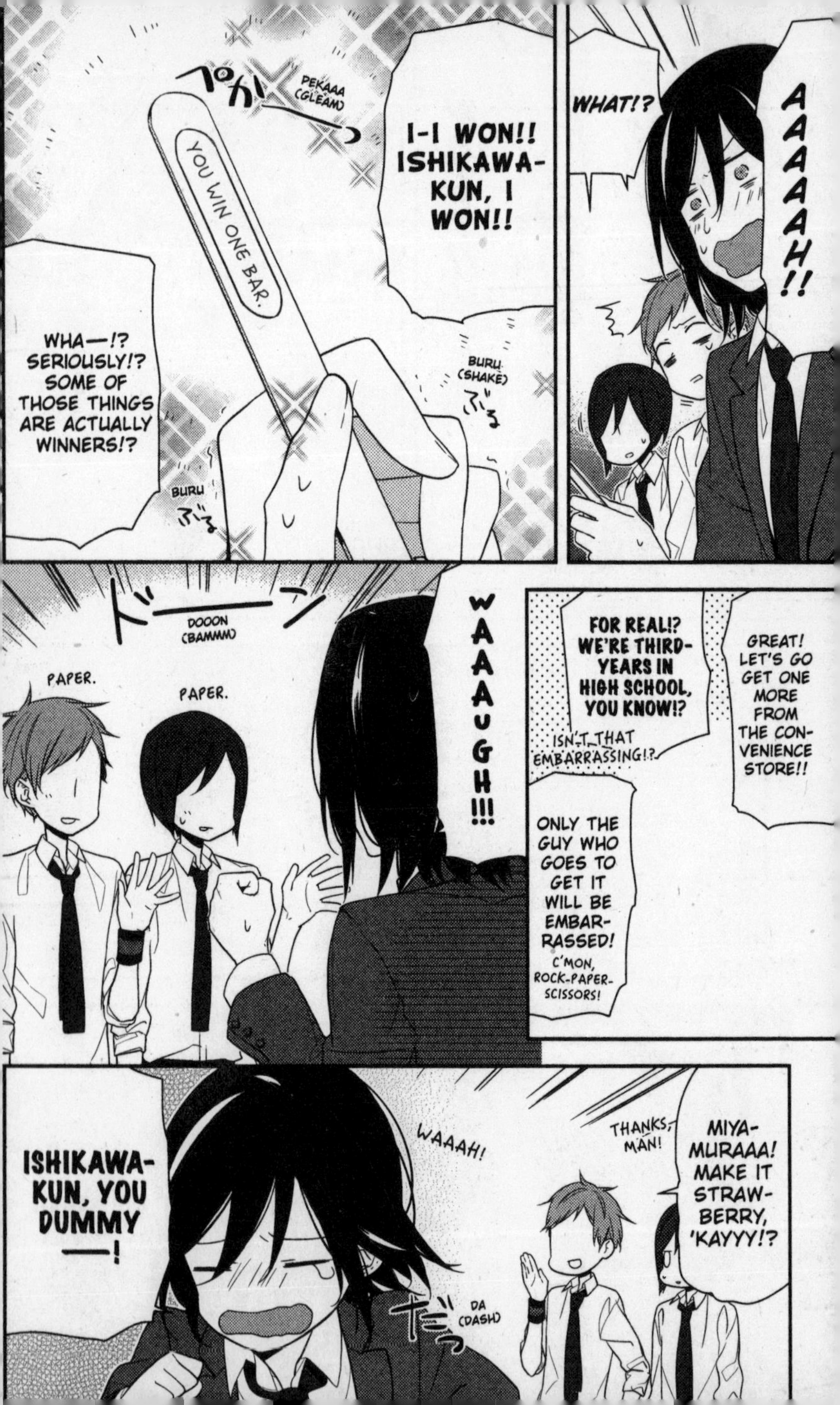

WHAT!?
AAAAAAH!!
I-I WON!! ISHIKAWA-KUN, I WON!!
PEKAAA (GLEAM)
YOU WIN ONE BAR.
BURU (SHAKE)
ぶる
WHA—!? SERIOUSLY!? SOME OF THOSE THINGS ARE ACTUALLY WINNERS!?
BURU
ぶる
GREAT! LET'S GO GET ONE MORE FROM THE CONVENIENCE STORE!!
FOR REAL!? WE'RE THIRD-YEARS IN HIGH SCHOOL, YOU KNOW!?
ISN'T THAT EMBARRASSING!?
ONLY THE GUY WHO GOES TO GET IT WILL BE EMBARRASSED!
C'MON, ROCK-PAPER-SCISSORS!
WAAAAUGH!!!
DOOON (BAMMM)
PAPER.
PAPER.
MIYA-MURAAA! MAKE IT STRAW-BERRY, 'KAYYY!?
THANKS, MAN!
WAAAH!
ISHIKAWA-KUN, YOU DUMMY—!
DA (DASH)

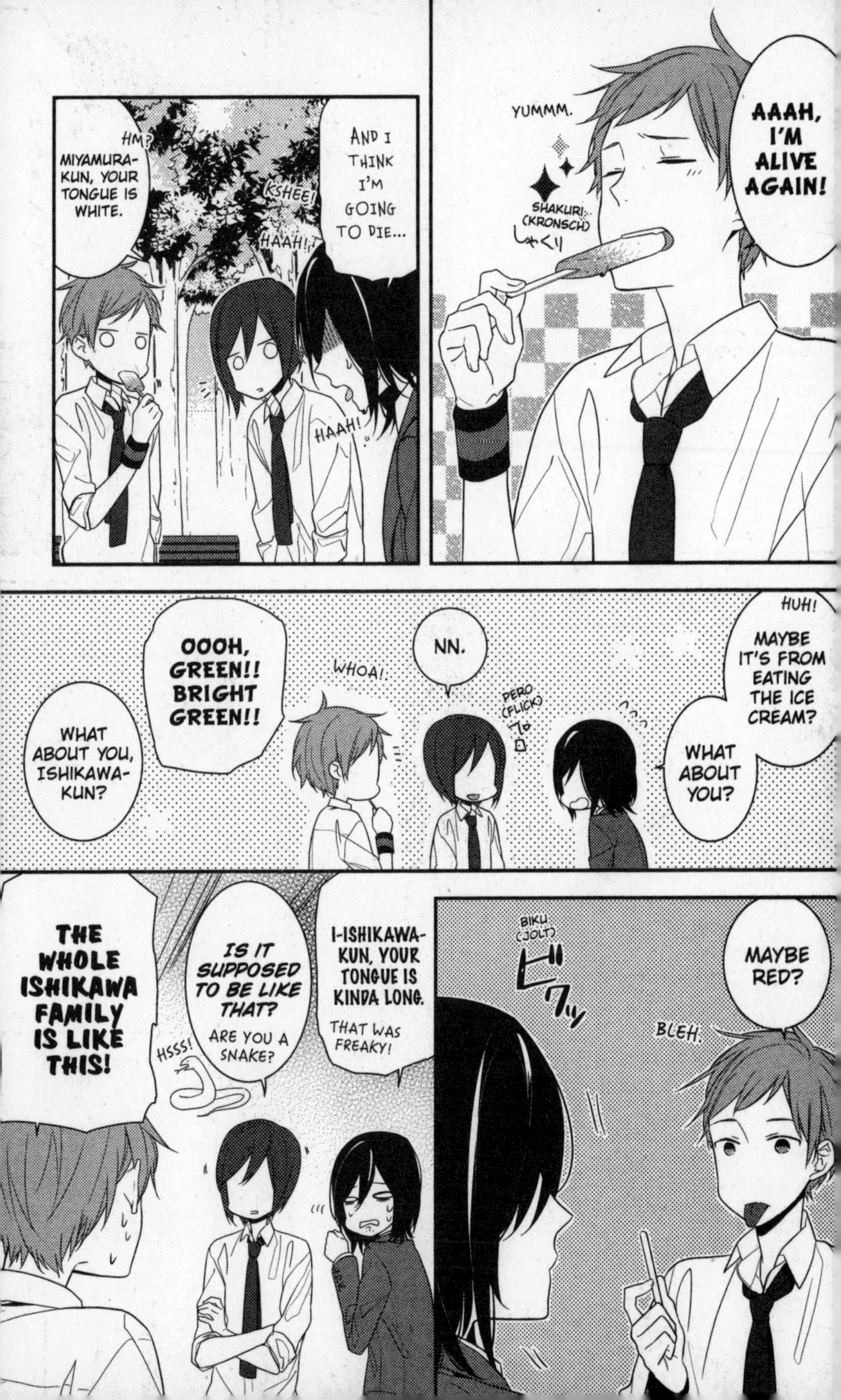
AAAH, I'M ALIVE AGAIN!
YUMMM.
SHAKURI (KRONSCH)
しゃくり
AND I THINK I'M GOING TO DIE...
HM? MIYAMURA-KUN, YOUR TONGUE IS WHITE.
KSHEE!
HAAH!
HAAH!
HUH! MAYBE IT'S FROM EATING THE ICE CREAM?
WHAT ABOUT YOU?
NN.
PERO (FLICK)
ペロ
WHOA!
OOOH, GREEN!! BRIGHT GREEN!!
WHAT ABOUT YOU, ISHIKAWA-KUN?
MAYBE RED?
BLEH.
BIKU (JOLT)
ビクッ
I-ISHIKAWA-KUN, YOUR TONGUE IS KINDA LONG.
THAT WAS FREAKY!
IS IT SUPPOSED TO BE LIKE THAT?
ARE YOU A SNAKE?
HSSS!
THE WHOLE ISHIKAWA FAMILY IS LIKE THIS!

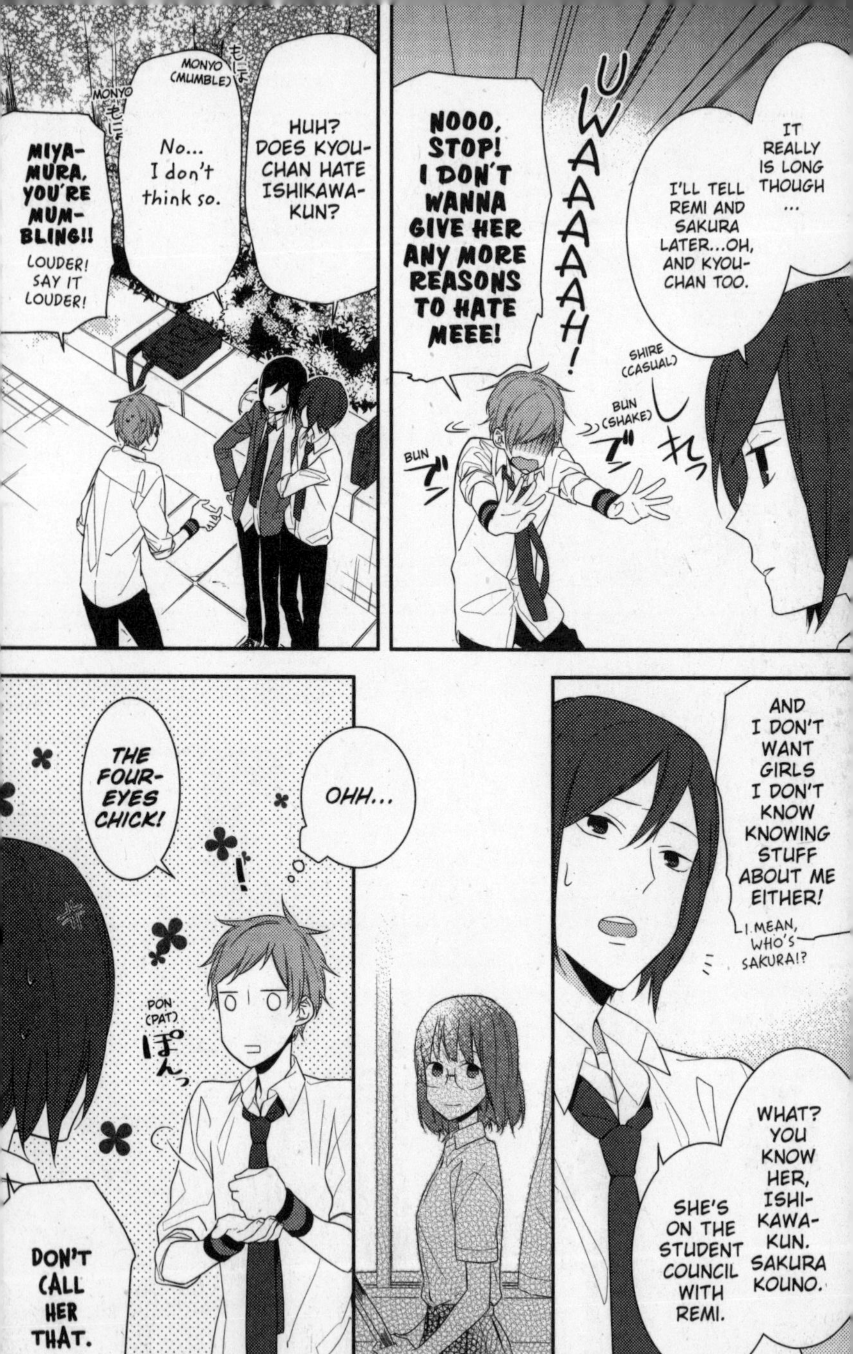
IT REALLY IS LONG THOUGH...
I'LL TELL REMI AND SAKURA LATER...OH, AND KYOU-CHAN TOO.
UWAAAAAAAH!
NOOO, STOP! I DON'T WANNA GIVE HER ANY MORE REASONS TO HATE MEEE!
SHIRE (CASUAL)
BUN (SHAKE)
BUN
HUH? DOES KYOU-CHAN HATE ISHIKAWA-KUN?
MONYO (MUMBLE)
No... I don't think so.
MONYO
MIYAMURA, YOU'RE MUMBLING!!
LOUDER! SAY IT LOUDER!
AND I DON'T WANT GIRLS I DON'T KNOW KNOWING STUFF ABOUT ME EITHER!
I MEAN, WHO'S SAKURA!?
WHAT? YOU KNOW HER, ISHIKAWA-KUN. SAKURA KOUNO.
SHE'S ON THE STUDENT COUNCIL WITH REMI.
OHH...
THE FOUR-EYES CHICK!
PON (PAT)
DON'T CALL HER THAT.

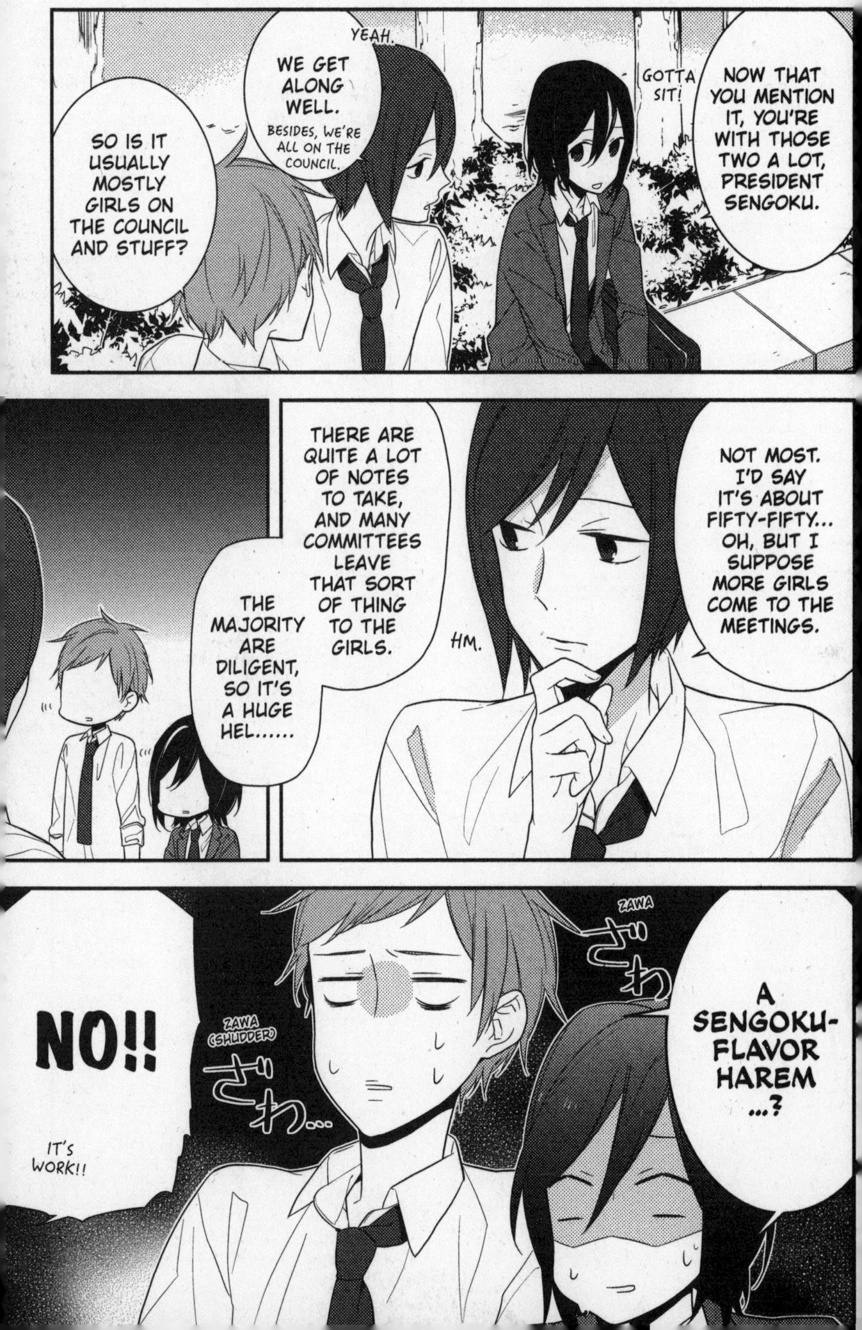

NOW THAT YOU MENTION IT, YOU'RE WITH THOSE TWO A LOT, PRESIDENT SENGOKU.
GOTTA SIT!
YEAH.
WE GET ALONG WELL.
BESIDES, WE'RE ALL ON THE COUNCIL.
SO IS IT USUALLY MOSTLY GIRLS ON THE COUNCIL AND STUFF?
NOT MOST. I'D SAY IT'S ABOUT FIFTY-FIFTY... OH, BUT I SUPPOSE MORE GIRLS COME TO THE MEETINGS.
HM.
THERE ARE QUITE A LOT OF NOTES TO TAKE, AND MANY COMMITTEES LEAVE THAT SORT OF THING TO THE GIRLS.
THE MAJORITY ARE DILIGENT, SO IT'S A HUGE HEL......
ZAWA
ざわ
A SENGOKU-FLAVOR HAREM ...?
ZAWA (SHUDDER)
ざわ...
NO!!
IT'S WORK!!

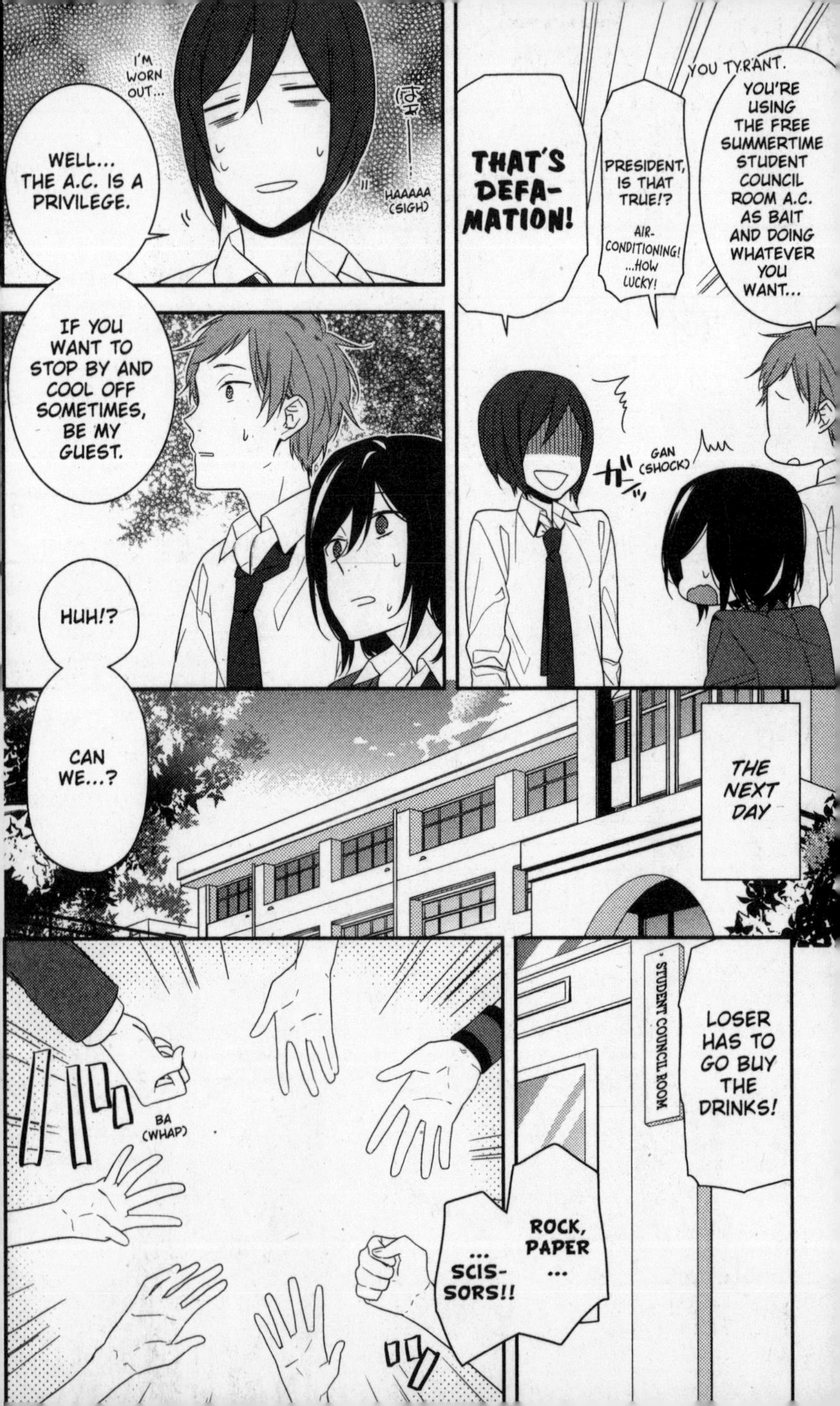
YOU TYRANT.
YOU'RE USING THE FREE SUMMERTIME STUDENT COUNCIL ROOM A.C. AS BAIT AND DOING WHATEVER YOU WANT...
PRESIDENT, IS THAT TRUE!?
AIR-CONDITIONING! ...HOW LUCKY!
THAT'S DEFA-MATION!
GAN (SHOCK)
I'M WORN OUT...
HAAAAA (SIGH)
WELL... THE A.C. IS A PRIVILEGE.
IF YOU WANT TO STOP BY AND COOL OFF SOMETIMES, BE MY GUEST.
HUH!?
CAN WE...?
THE NEXT DAY
STUDENT COUNCIL ROOM
LOSER HAS TO GO BUY THE DRINKS!
ROCK, PAPER ...
... SCIS-SORS!!
BA (WHAP)

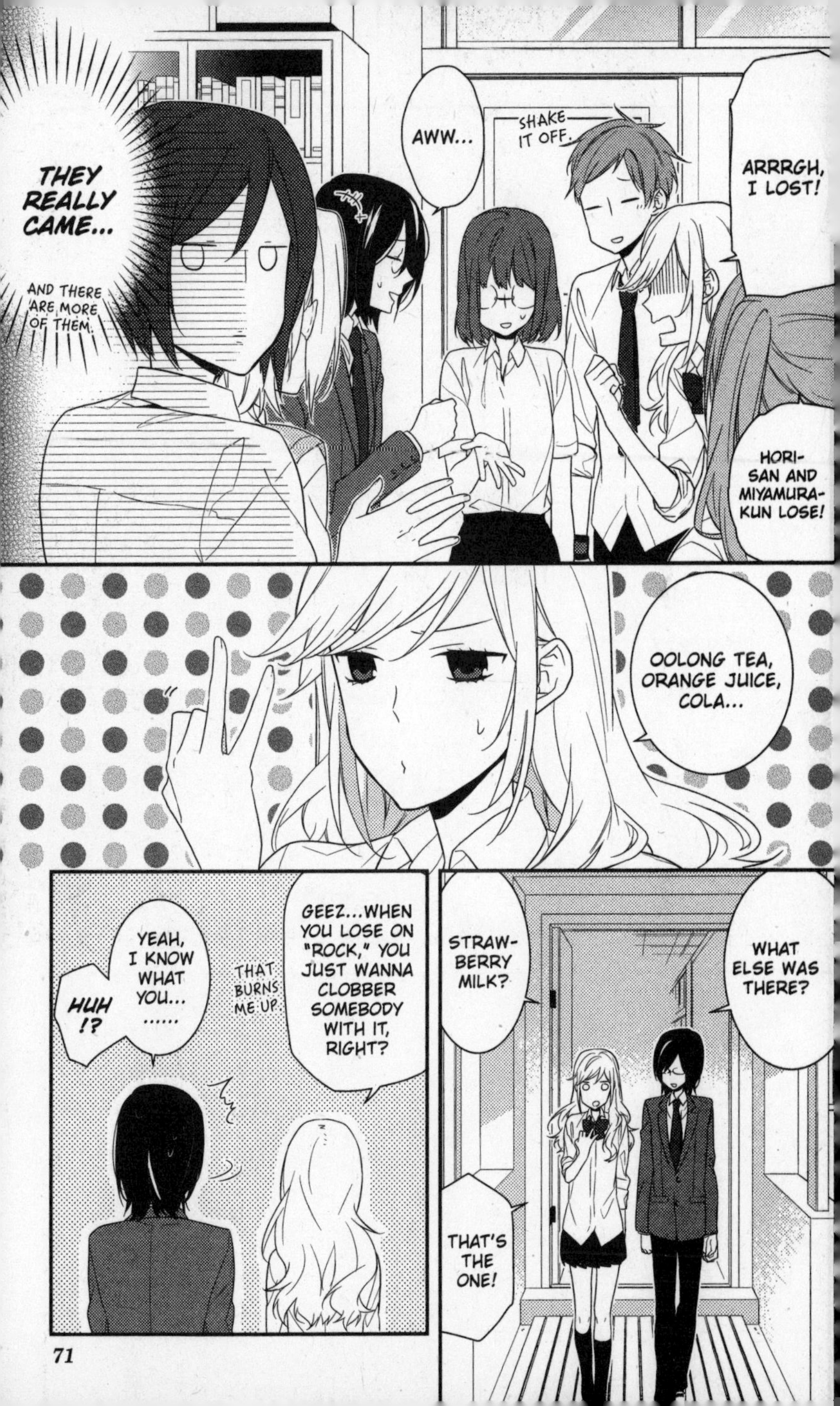
ARRRGH, I LOST!
HORI-SAN AND MIYAMURA-KUN LOSE!
SHAKE IT OFF.
AWW...
THEY REALLY CAME...
AND THERE ARE MORE OF THEM.
OOLONG TEA, ORANGE JUICE, COLA...
WHAT ELSE WAS THERE?
STRAW-BERRY MILK?
THAT'S THE ONE!
GEEZ...WHEN YOU LOSE ON "ROCK," YOU JUST WANNA CLOBBER SOMEBODY WITH IT, RIGHT?
THAT BURNS ME UP.
YEAH, I KNOW WHAT YOU... ......
HUH!?

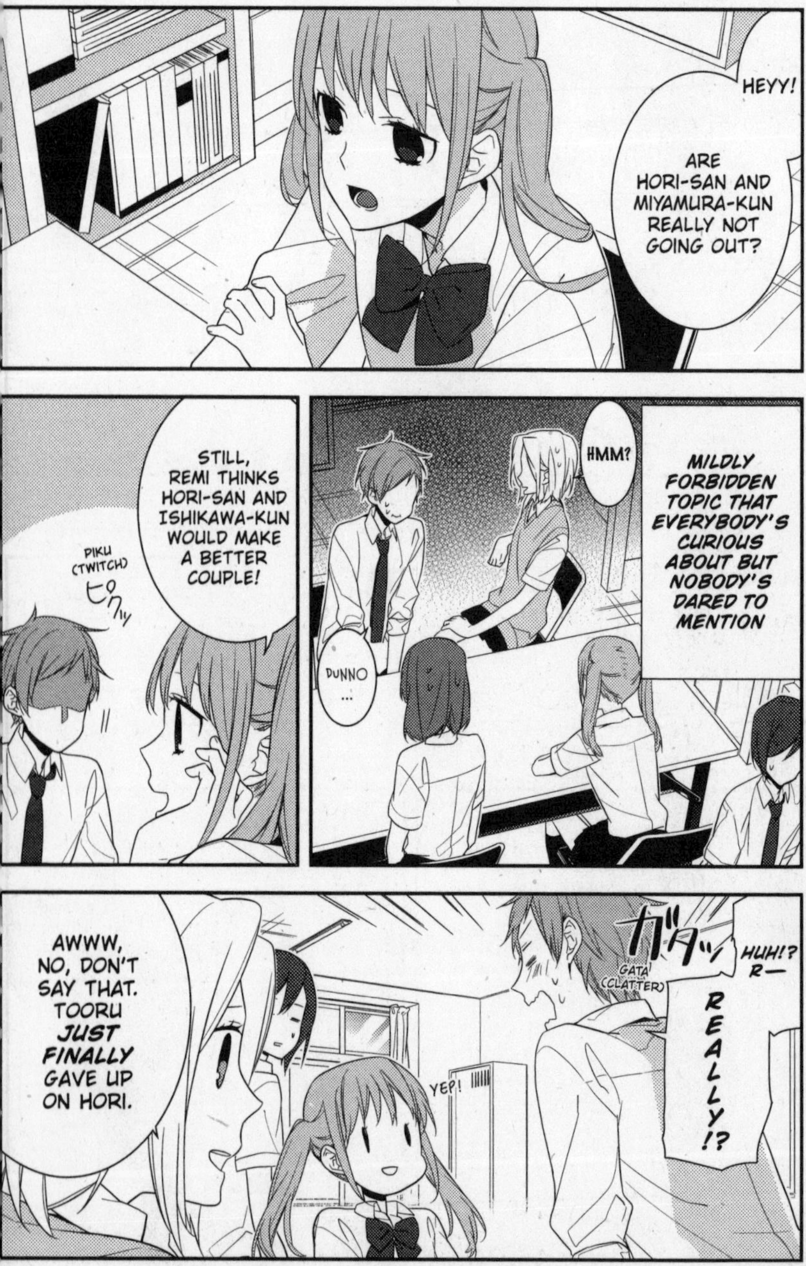
HEYY!
ARE HORI-SAN AND MIYAMURA-KUN REALLY NOT GOING OUT?
MILDLY FORBIDDEN TOPIC THAT EVERYBODY'S CURIOUS ABOUT BUT NOBODY'S DARED TO MENTION
HMM?
DUNNO ...
STILL, REMI THINKS HORI-SAN AND ISHIKAWA-KUN WOULD MAKE A BETTER COUPLE!
PIKU (TWITCH)
ピクッ
HUH!? R—
REALLY!?
ガタッ
GATA (CLATTER)
YEP!
AWWW, NO, DON'T SAY THAT. TOORU JUST FINALLY GAVE UP ON HORI.

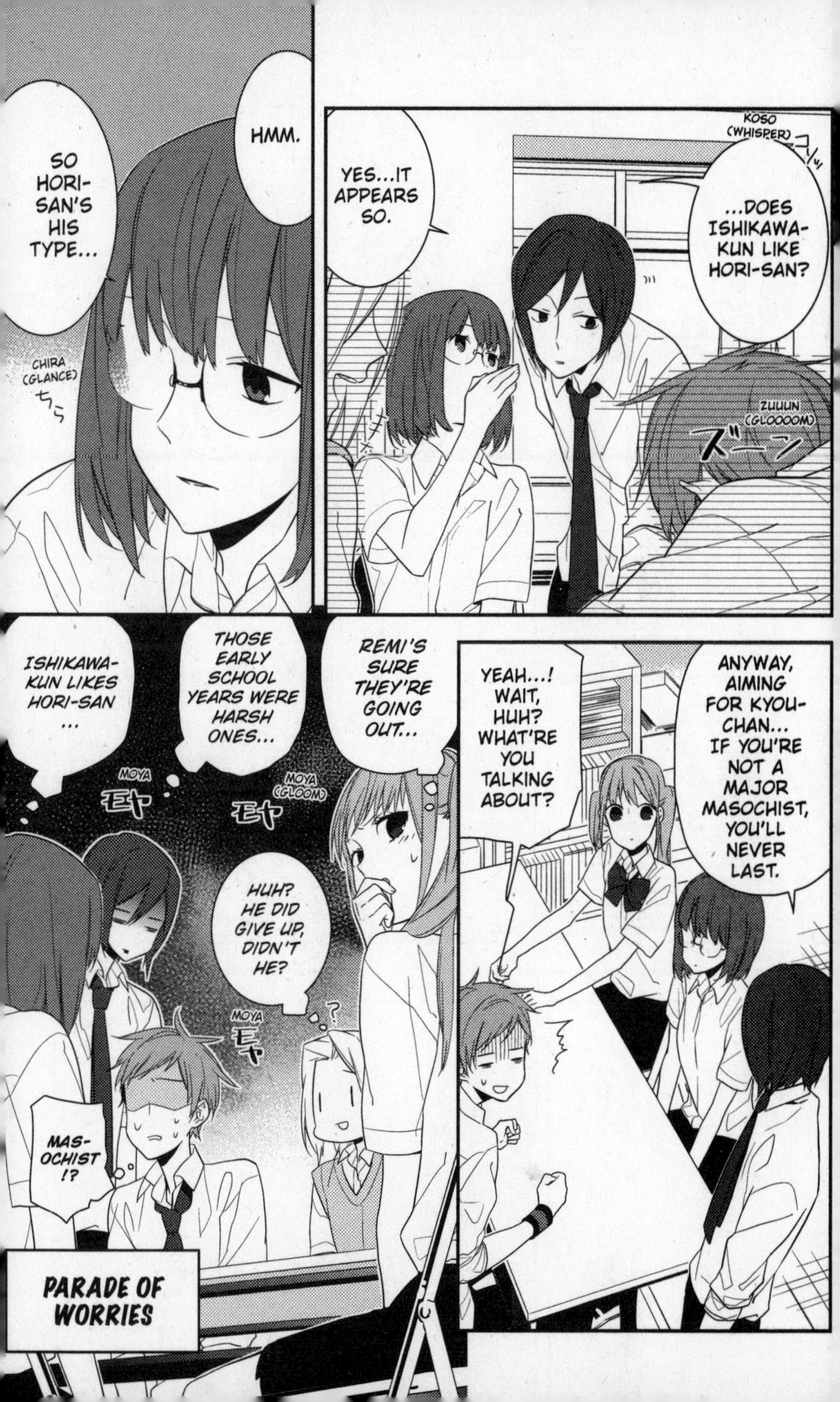
KOSO (WHISPER)
...DOES ISHIKAWA-KUN LIKE HORI-SAN?
YES...IT APPEARS SO.
ZUUUN (GLOOOOM)
HMM.
SO HORI-SAN'S HIS TYPE...
CHIRA (GLANCE)
ANYWAY, AIMING FOR KYOU-CHAN... IF YOU'RE NOT A MAJOR MASOCHIST, YOU'LL NEVER LAST.
YEAH...! WAIT, HUH? WHAT'RE YOU TALKING ABOUT?
REMI'S SURE THEY'RE GOING OUT...
THOSE EARLY SCHOOL YEARS WERE HARSH ONES...
ISHIKAWA-KUN LIKES HORI-SAN...
MOYA (GLOOM)
MOYA
HUH? HE DID GIVE UP, DIDN'T HE?
MOYA
MAS-OCHIST!?
PARADE OF WORRIES

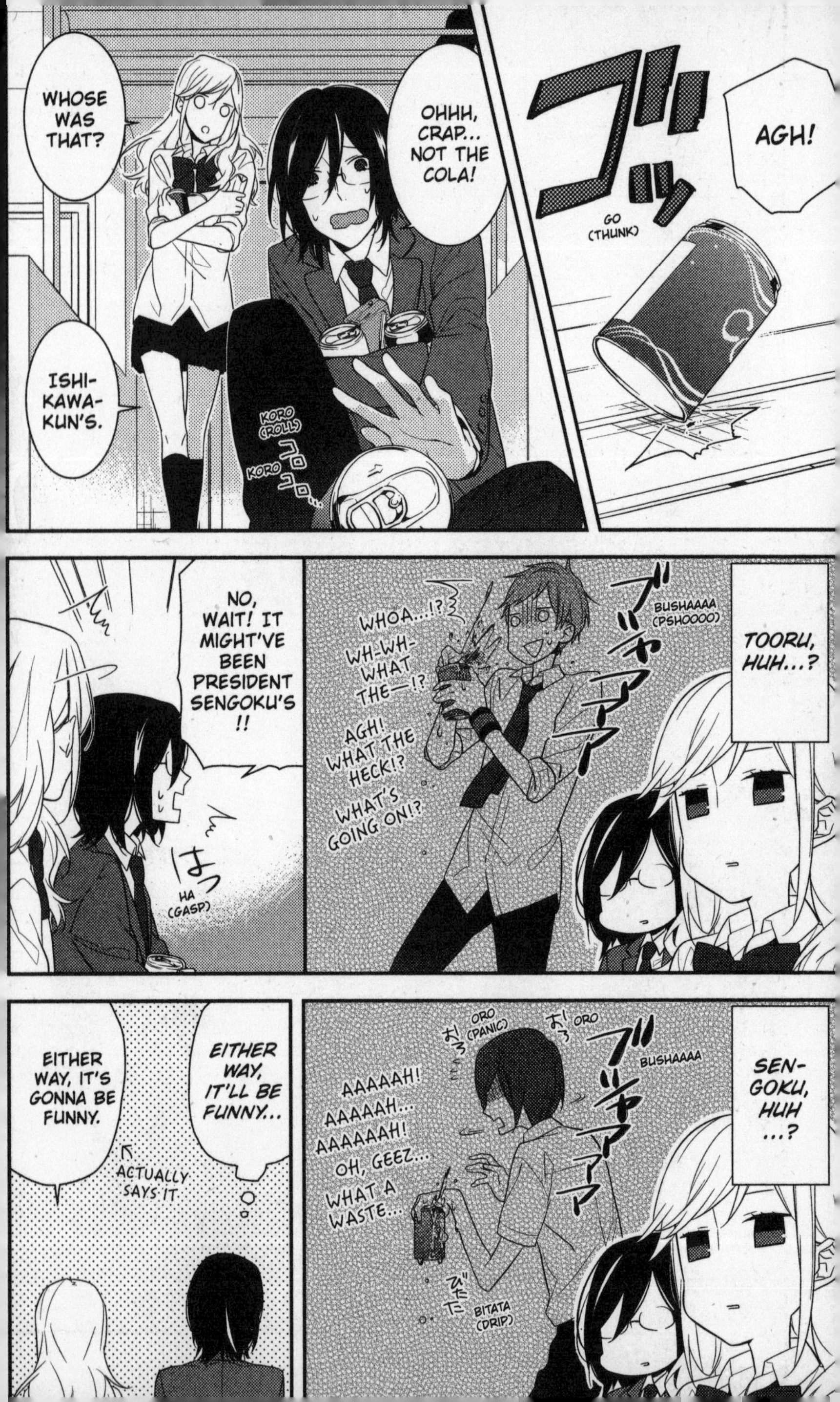
AGH!
GO (THUNK)
OHHH, CRAP... NOT THE COLA!
WHOSE WAS THAT?
ISHI-KAWA-KUN'S.
KORO (ROLL) KORO
TOORU, HUH...?
BUSHAAAA (PSHOOOO)
WHOA...!?
WH-WH-WHAT THE—!?
AGH! WHAT THE HECK!?
WHAT'S GOING ON!?
NO, WAIT! IT MIGHT'VE BEEN PRESIDENT SENGOKU'S!!
HA (GASP)
SEN-GOKU, HUH...?
BUSHAAAA
ORO (PANIC) ORO
AAAAAH! AAAAAH... AAAAAAH!
OH, GEEZ... WHAT A WASTE...
BITATA (DRIP)
EITHER WAY, IT'LL BE FUNNY...
EITHER WAY, IT'S GONNA BE FUNNY.
ACTUALLY SAYS IT

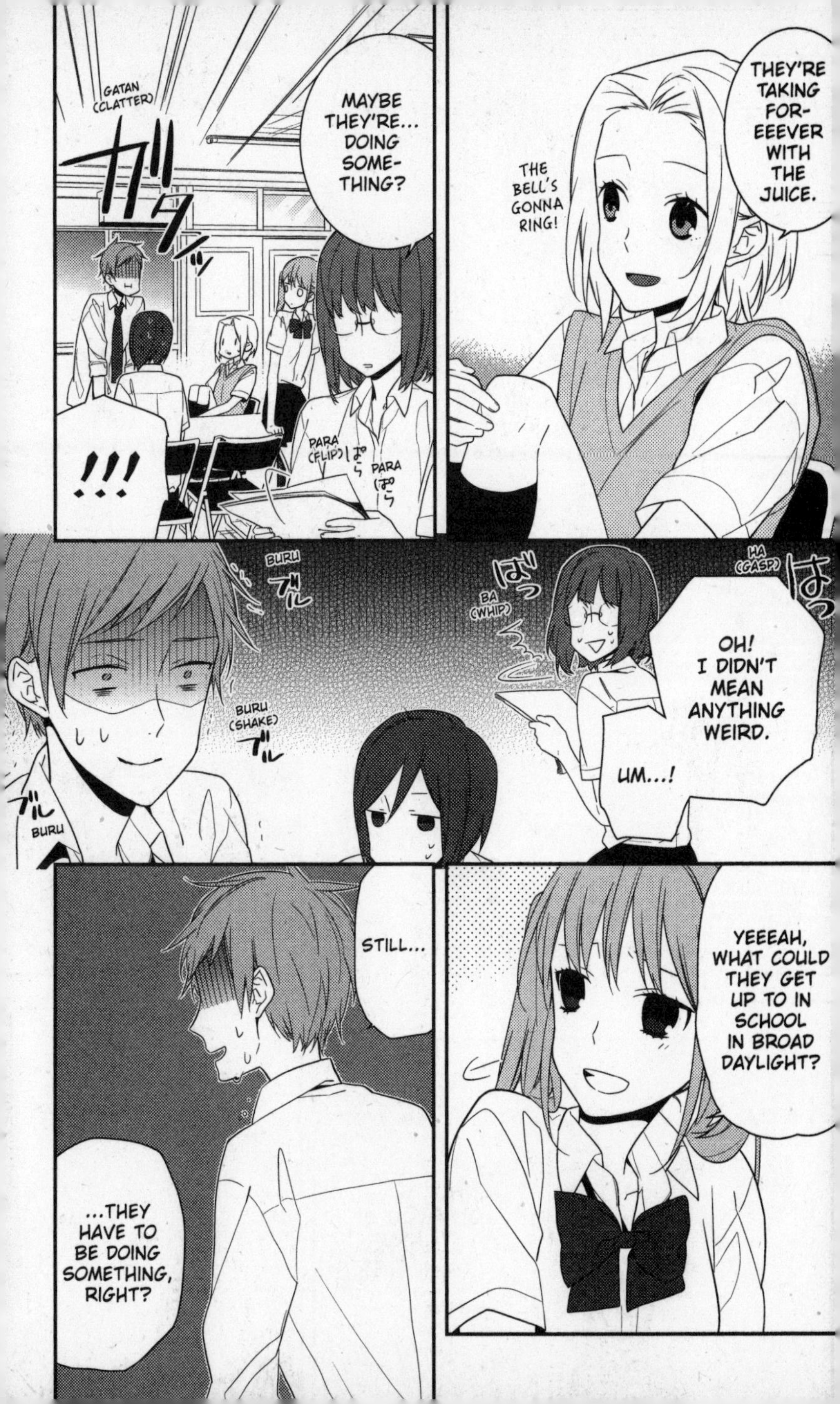
THEY'RE TAKING FOR-EEEVER WITH THE JUICE.
THE BELL'S GONNA RING!
MAYBE THEY'RE... DOING SOME-THING?
PARA (FLIP) ぱら PARA ぱら
GATAN (CLATTER)
ガタッ
!!!
HA (GASP) はっ
OH! I DIDN'T MEAN ANYTHING WEIRD.
UM...!
BA (WHIP) ばっ
BURU ブル
BURU (SHAKE) ブル
ブル BURU
YEEEAH, WHAT COULD THEY GET UP TO IN SCHOOL IN BROAD DAYLIGHT?
STILL...
...THEY HAVE TO BE DOING SOMETHING, RIGHT?

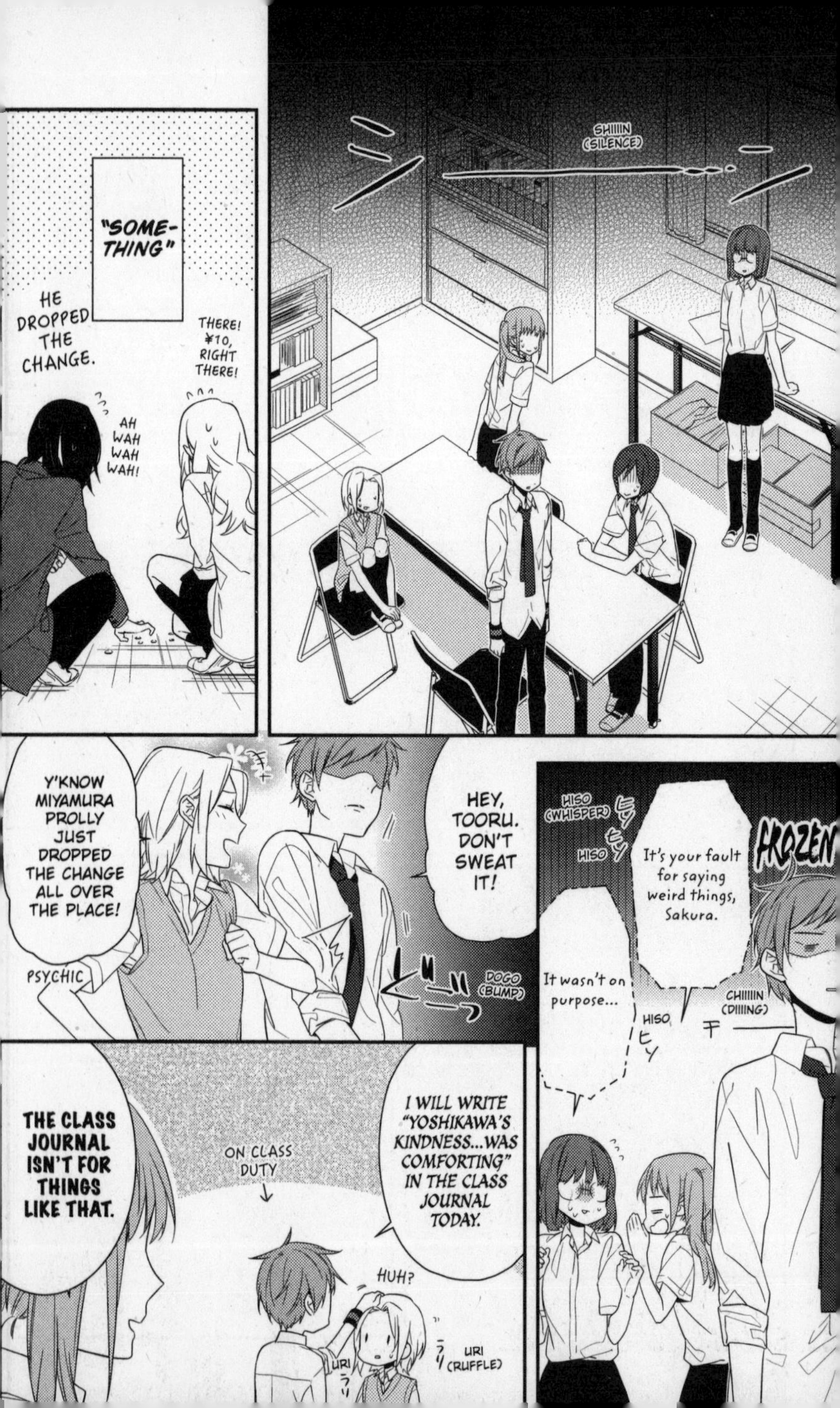
SHIIIN (SILENCE)
"SOME-THING"
HE DROPPED THE CHANGE.
THERE! ¥10, RIGHT THERE!
AH WAH WAH WAH!
FROZEN
HISO (WHISPER)
HISO
It's your fault for saying weird things, Sakura.
It wasn't on purpose...
HISO
CHIIIIN (DIIIING)
HEY, TOORU. DON'T SWEAT IT!
DOGO (BUMP)
Y'KNOW MIYAMURA PROLLY JUST DROPPED THE CHANGE ALL OVER THE PLACE!
PSYCHIC
I WILL WRITE "YOSHIKAWA'S KINDNESS...WAS COMFORTING" IN THE CLASS JOURNAL TODAY.
ON CLASS DUTY
HUH?
URI (RUFFLE)
URI
THE CLASS JOURNAL ISN'T FOR THINGS LIKE THAT.

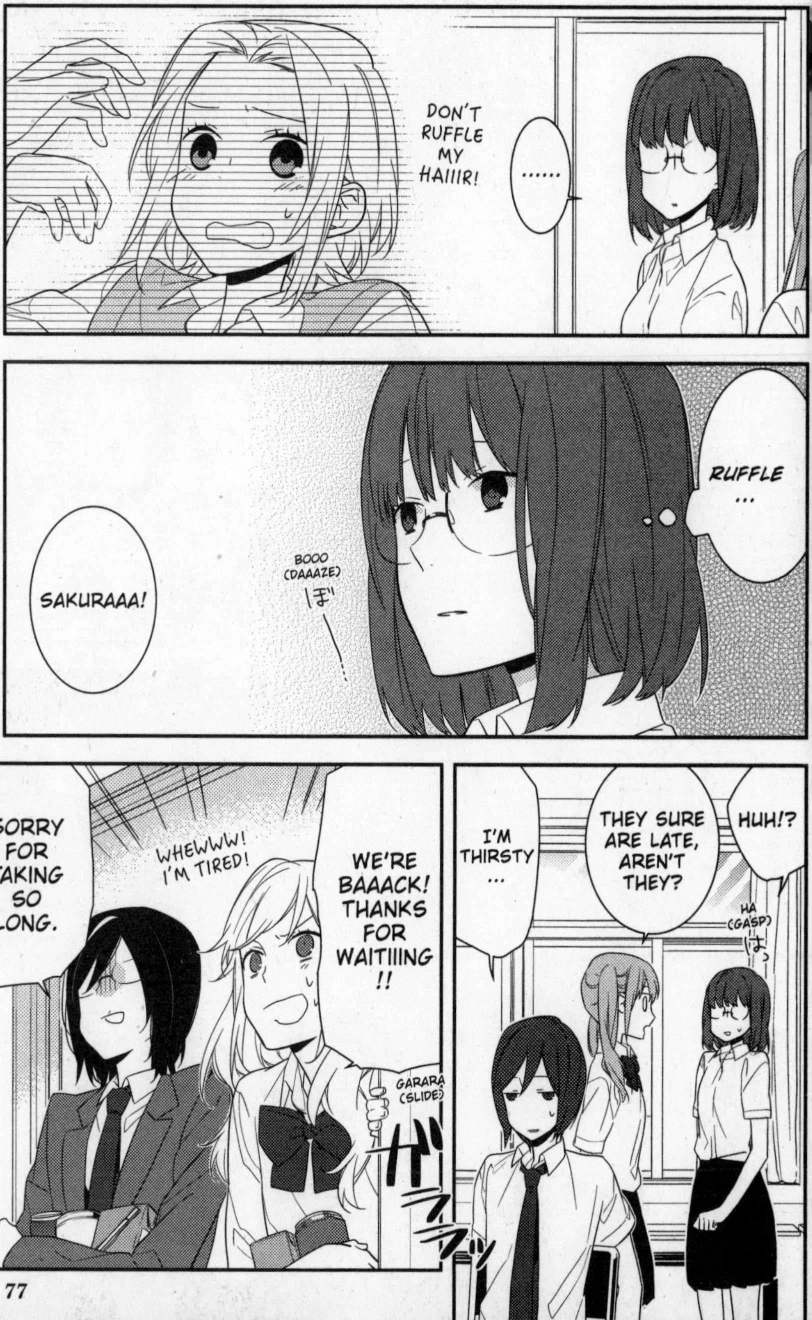

......
DON'T RUFFLE MY HAIIIR!
RUFFLE ...
BOOO (DAAAZE)
ぼ
SAKURAAA!
HUH!?
THEY SURE ARE LATE, AREN'T THEY?
I'M THIRSTY ...
HA (GASP)
は
WE'RE BAAACK! THANKS FOR WAITIIING!!
WHEWWW! I'M TIRED!
SORRY FOR TAKING SO LONG.
GARARA (SLIDE)
ガラ

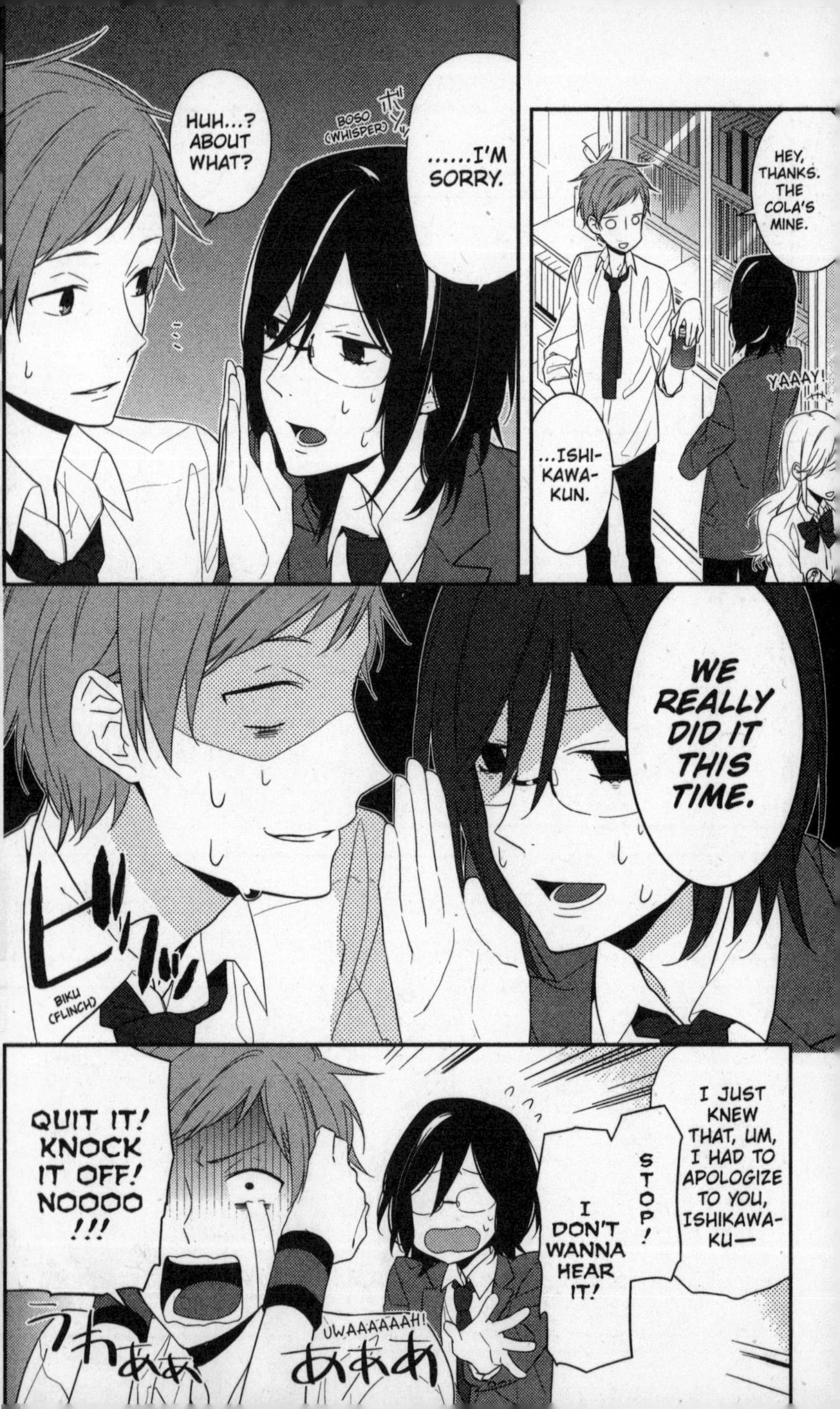
HEY, THANKS. THE COLA'S MINE.
YAAAY!
...ISHI-KAWA-KUN.
......I'M SORRY.
BOSO (WHISPER)
HUH...? ABOUT WHAT?
WE REALLY DID IT THIS TIME.
BIKU (FLINCH)
I JUST KNEW THAT, UM, I HAD TO APOLOGIZE TO YOU, ISHIKAWA-KU—
STOP!
I DON'T WANNA HEAR IT!
QUIT IT! KNOCK IT OFF! NOOOO!!!
UWAAAAAAH!

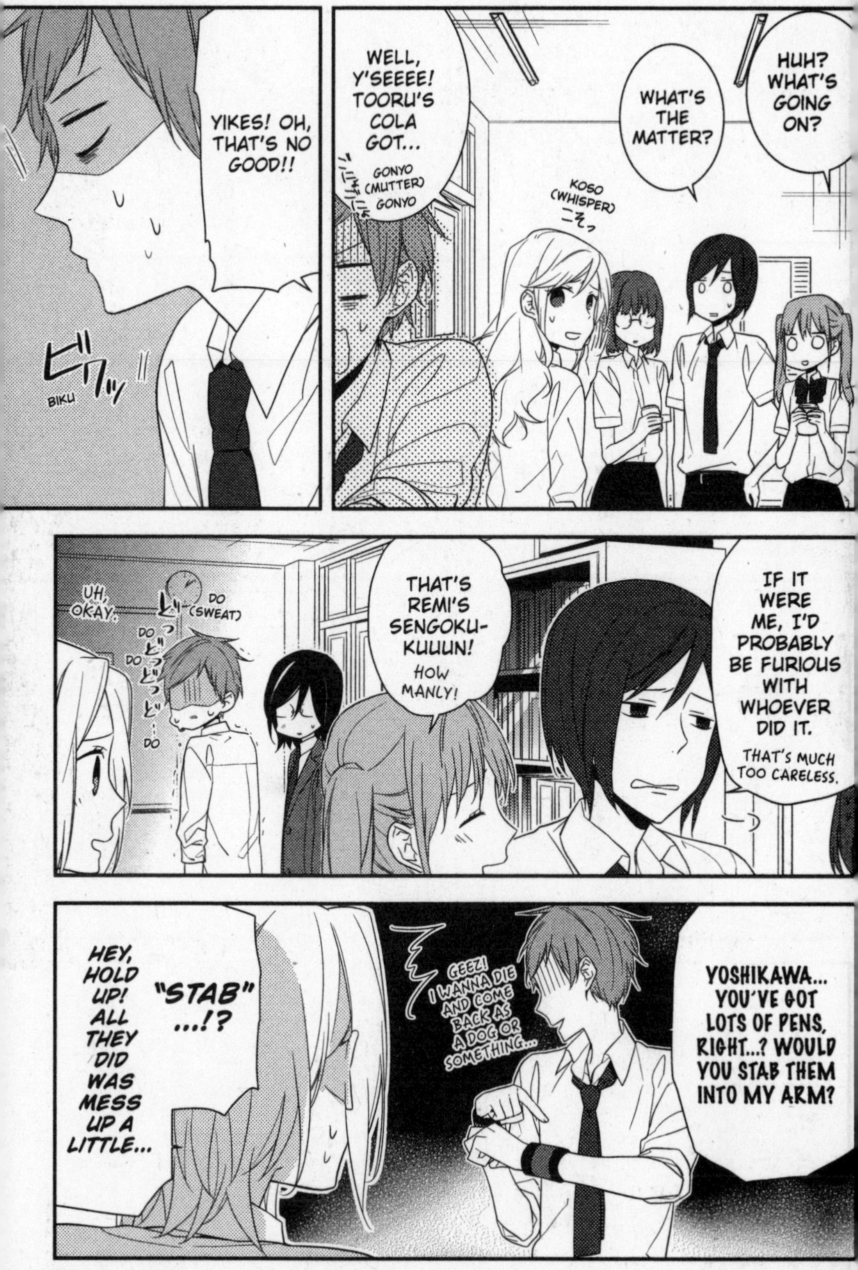

HUH? WHAT'S GOING ON?
WHAT'S THE MATTER?
KOSO (WHISPER) こそっ
WELL, Y'SEEEE! TOORU'S COLA GOT...
GONYO (MUTTER) GONYO
YIKES! OH, THAT'S NO GOOD!!
ビクッ BIKU
IF IT WERE ME, I'D PROBABLY BE FURIOUS WITH WHOEVER DID IT.
THAT'S MUCH TOO CARELESS.
THAT'S REMI'S SENGOKU-KUUUN!
HOW MANLY!
DO (SWEAT)
UH, OKAY..
DO DO DO
YOSHIKAWA... YOU'VE GOT LOTS OF PENS, RIGHT...? WOULD YOU STAB THEM INTO MY ARM?
GEEZ! I WANNA DIE AND COME BACK AS A DOG OR SOMETHING...
"STAB" ...!?
HEY, HOLD UP! ALL THEY DID WAS MESS UP A LITTLE...

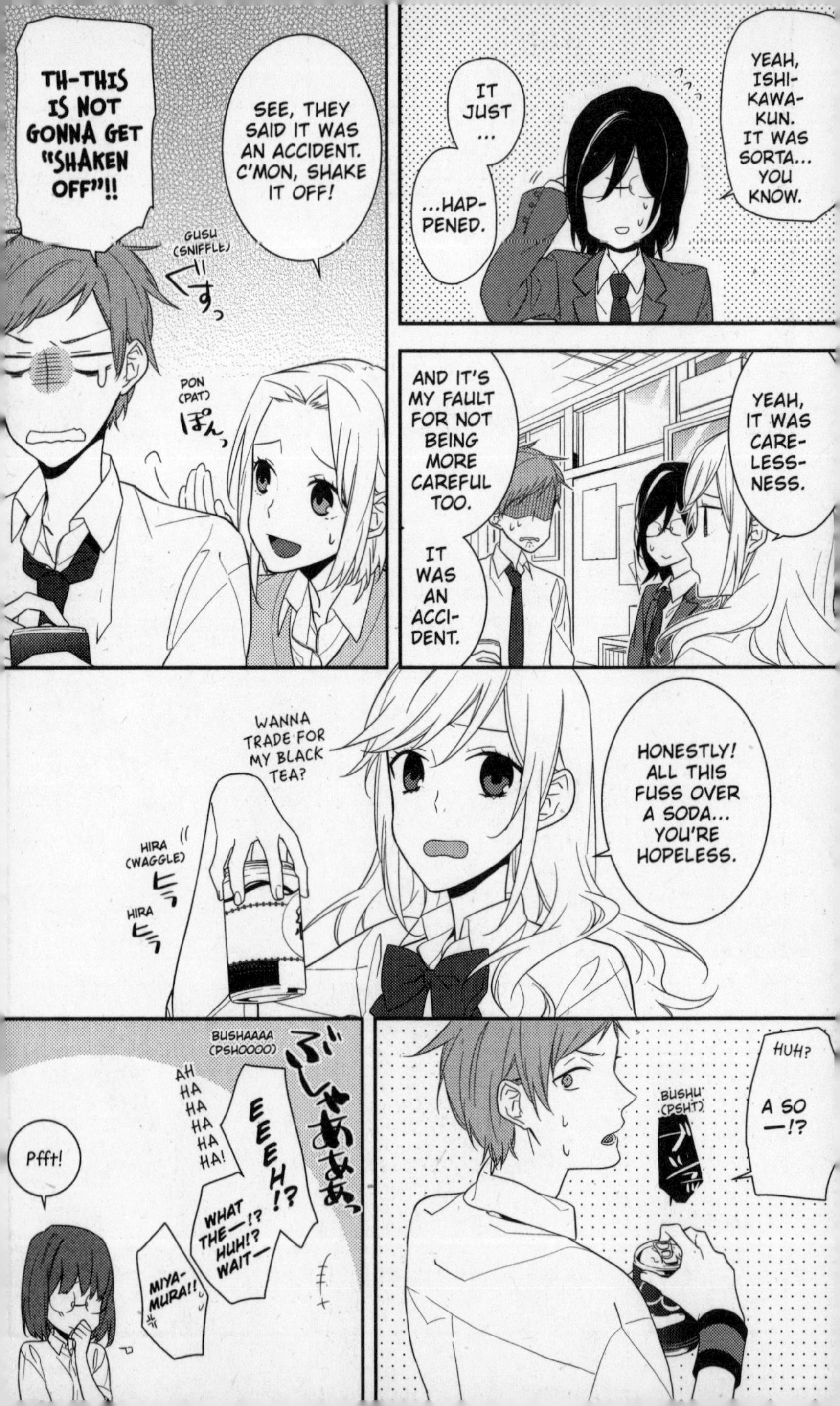
YEAH, ISHIKAWA-KUN. IT WAS SORTA... YOU KNOW.
IT JUST ...
...HAPPENED.
YEAH, IT WAS CARELESSNESS.
AND IT'S MY FAULT FOR NOT BEING MORE CAREFUL TOO.
IT WAS AN ACCIDENT.
SEE, THEY SAID IT WAS AN ACCIDENT. C'MON, SHAKE IT OFF!
TH-THIS IS NOT GONNA GET "SHAKEN OFF"!!
GUSU (SNIFFLE)
ぐすっ
PON (PAT)
ぽんっ
HONESTLY! ALL THIS FUSS OVER A SODA... YOU'RE HOPELESS.
WANNA TRADE FOR MY BLACK TEA?
HIRA (WAGGLE)
ヒラ
HIRA
ヒラ
HUH?
A SO—!?
BUSHU (PSHT)
ブシュ
BUSHAAAA (PSHOOOO)
ぶしゃあああっ
EEEEH!?
AH HA HA HA HA HA!
WHAT THE—!? HUH!? WAIT—
MIYAMURA!!
Pfft!

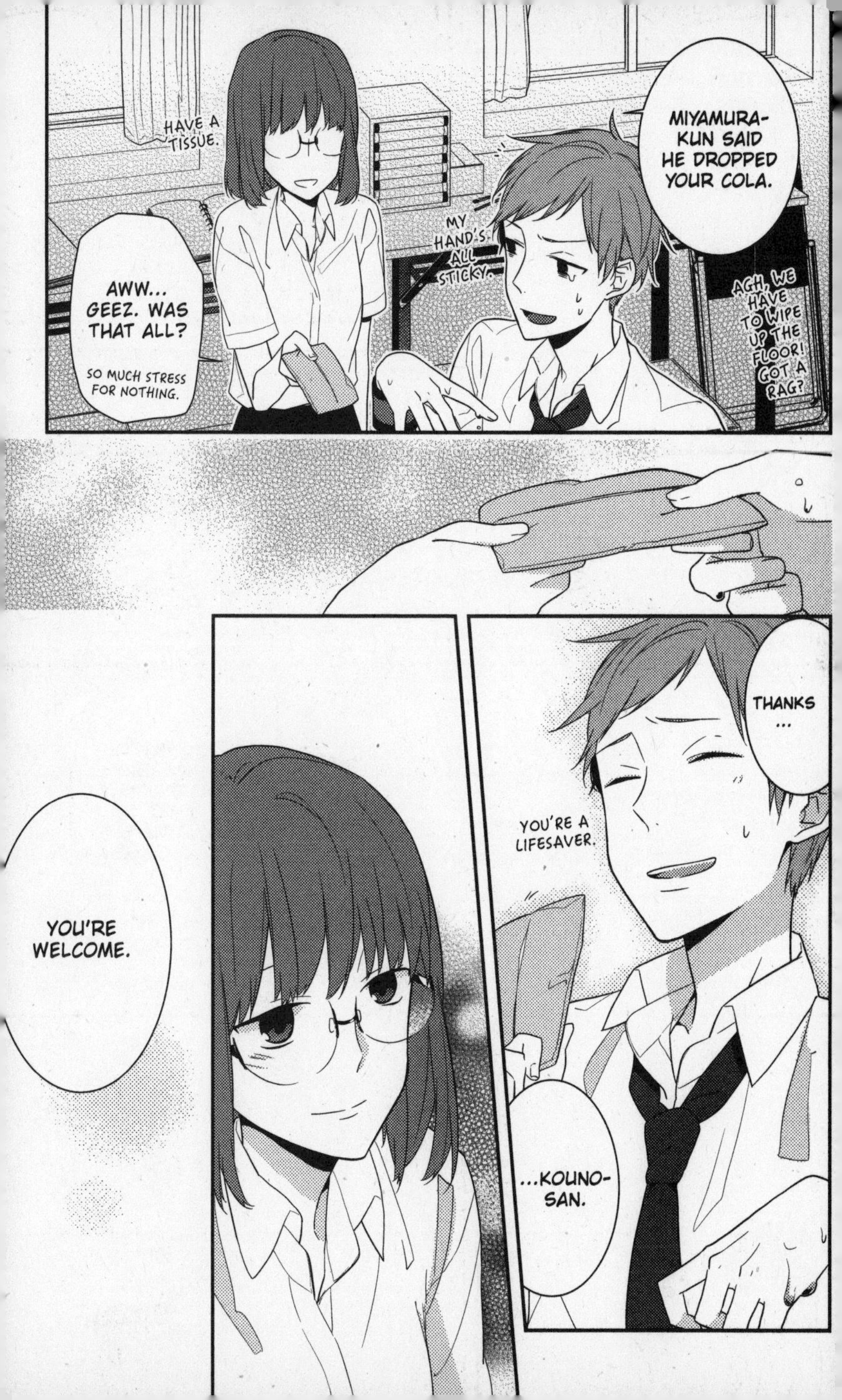
MIYAMURA-KUN SAID HE DROPPED YOUR COLA.
AGH, WE HAVE TO WIPE UP THE FLOOR! GOT A RAG?
MY HAND'S ALL STICKY.
HAVE A TISSUE.
AWW... GEEZ. WAS THAT ALL?
SO MUCH STRESS FOR NOTHING.
THANKS...
YOU'RE A LIFESAVER.
...KOUNO-SAN.
YOU'RE WELCOME.

HORIMIYA

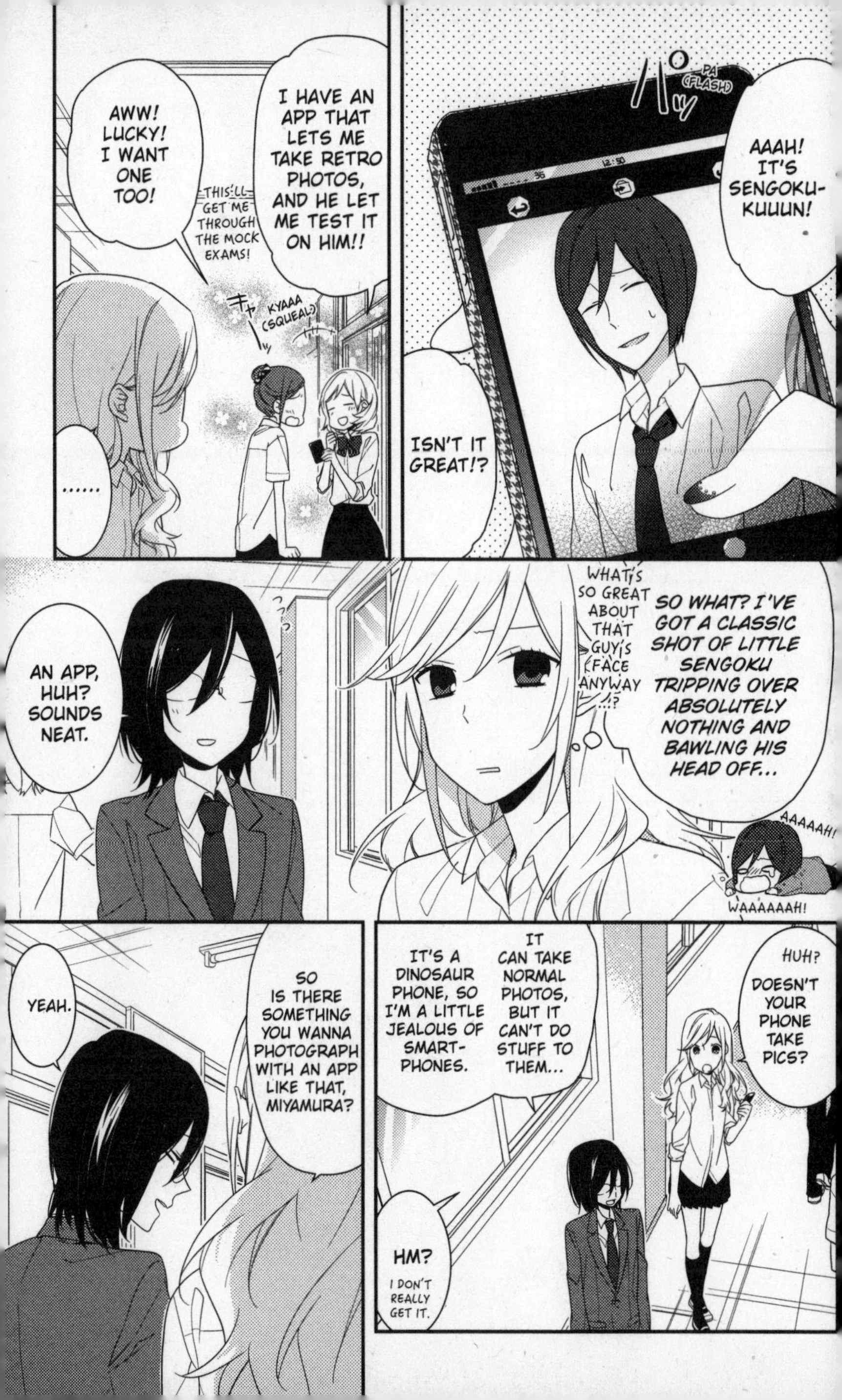
PA (FLASH)
AAAH! IT'S SENGOKU-KUUUN!
ISN'T IT GREAT!?
I HAVE AN APP THAT LETS ME TAKE RETRO PHOTOS, AND HE LET ME TEST IT ON HIM!!
KYAAA (SQUEAL)
AWW! LUCKY! I WANT ONE TOO!
THIS'LL GET ME THROUGH THE MOCK EXAMS!
......
SO WHAT? I'VE GOT A CLASSIC SHOT OF LITTLE SENGOKU TRIPPING OVER ABSOLUTELY NOTHING AND BAWLING HIS HEAD OFF...
AAAAAH!
WAAAAAAH!
WHAT'S SO GREAT ABOUT THAT GUY'S FACE ANYWAY...?
AN APP, HUH? SOUNDS NEAT.
HUH? DOESN'T YOUR PHONE TAKE PICS?
IT CAN TAKE NORMAL PHOTOS, BUT IT CAN'T DO STUFF TO THEM...
IT'S A DINOSAUR PHONE, SO I'M A LITTLE JEALOUS OF SMART-PHONES.
HM?
I DON'T REALLY GET IT.
SO IS THERE SOMETHING YOU WANNA PHOTOGRAPH WITH AN APP LIKE THAT, MIYAMURA?
YEAH.

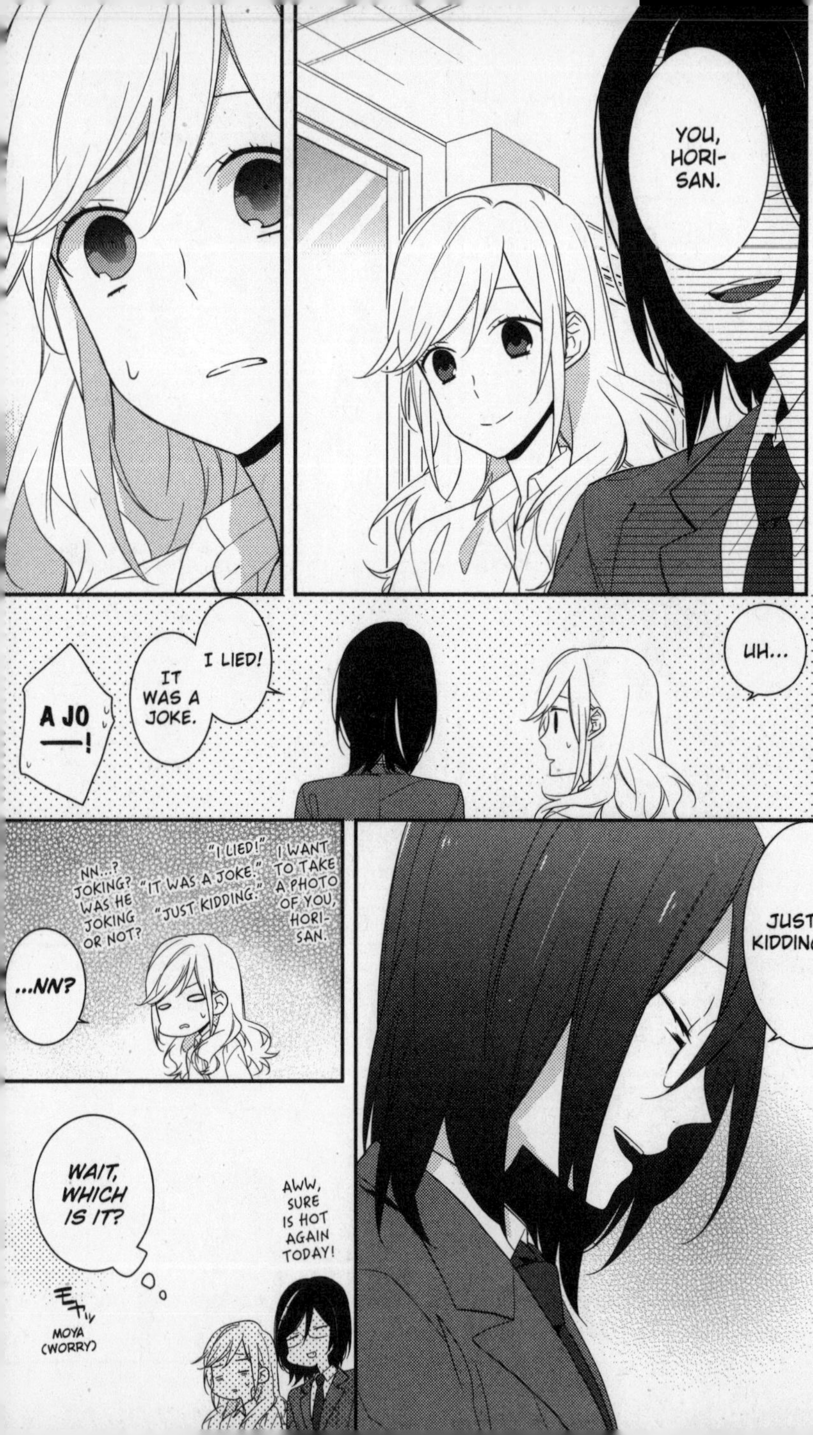
YOU, HORI-SAN.
UH...
I LIED!
IT WAS A JOKE.
A JO—!
JUST KIDDING.
I WANT TO TAKE A PHOTO OF YOU, HORI-SAN.
"I LIED!"
"IT WAS A JOKE."
"JUST KIDDING."
NN...? JOKING? WAS HE JOKING OR NOT?
...NN?
AWW, SURE IS HOT AGAIN TODAY!
WAIT, WHICH IS IT?
MOYA (WORRY)

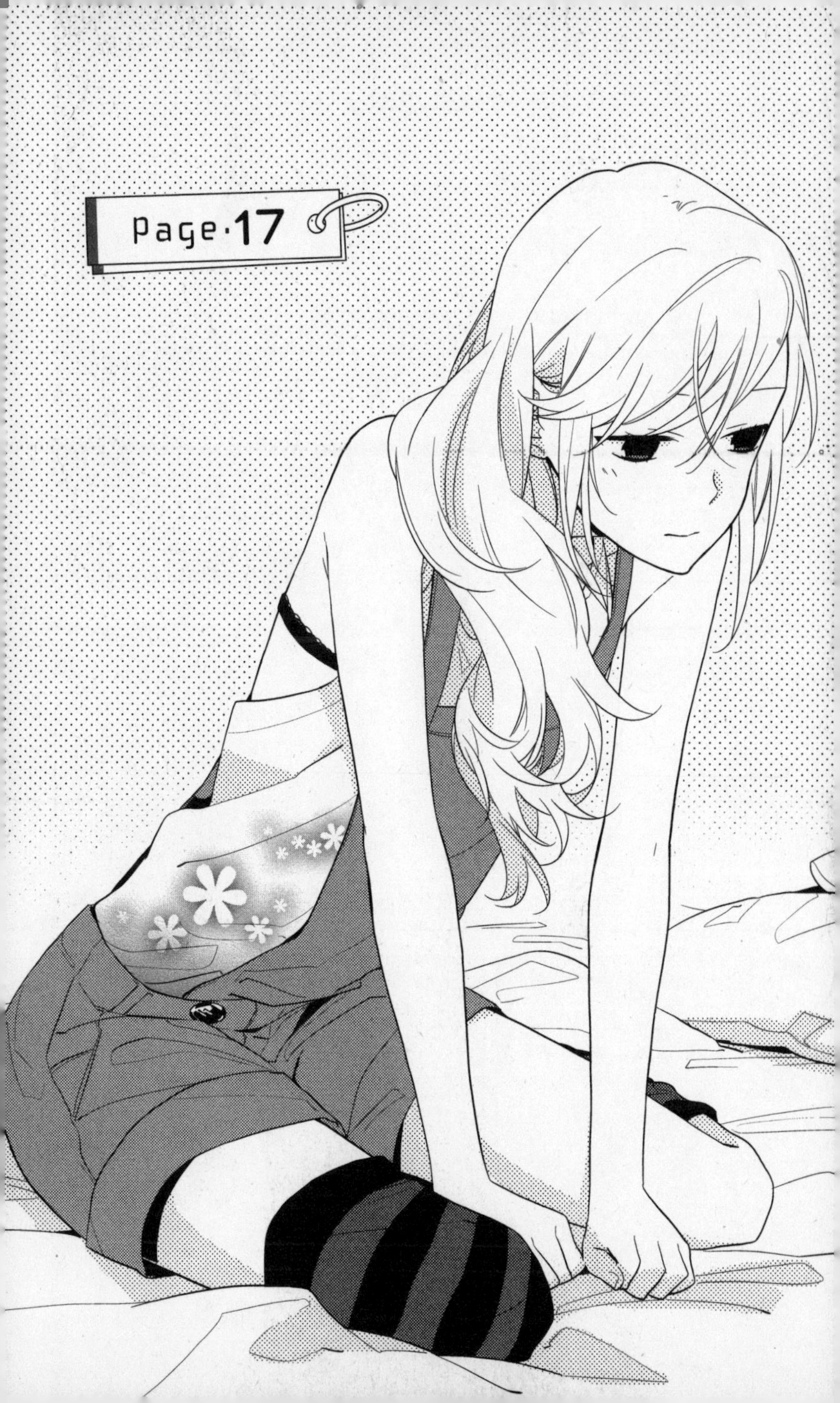
Page·17

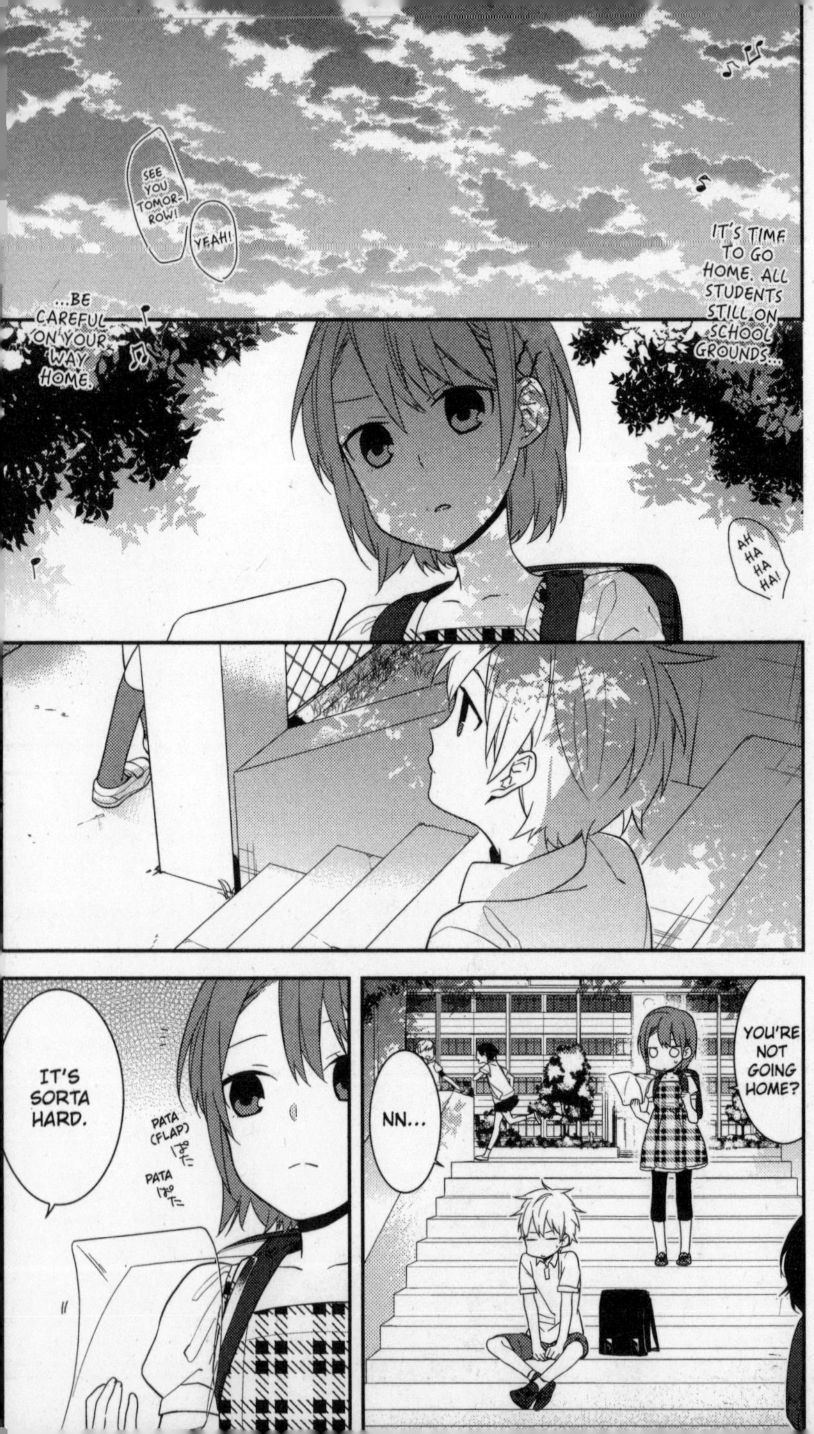

IT'S TIME TO GO HOME. ALL STUDENTS STILL ON SCHOOL GROUNDS...
SEE YOU TOMOR-ROW!
YEAH!
...BE CAREFUL ON YOUR WAY HOME.
AH HA HA HA!
YOU'RE NOT GOING HOME?
NN...
IT'S SORTA HARD.
PATA (FLAP) ぱた
PATA ぱた

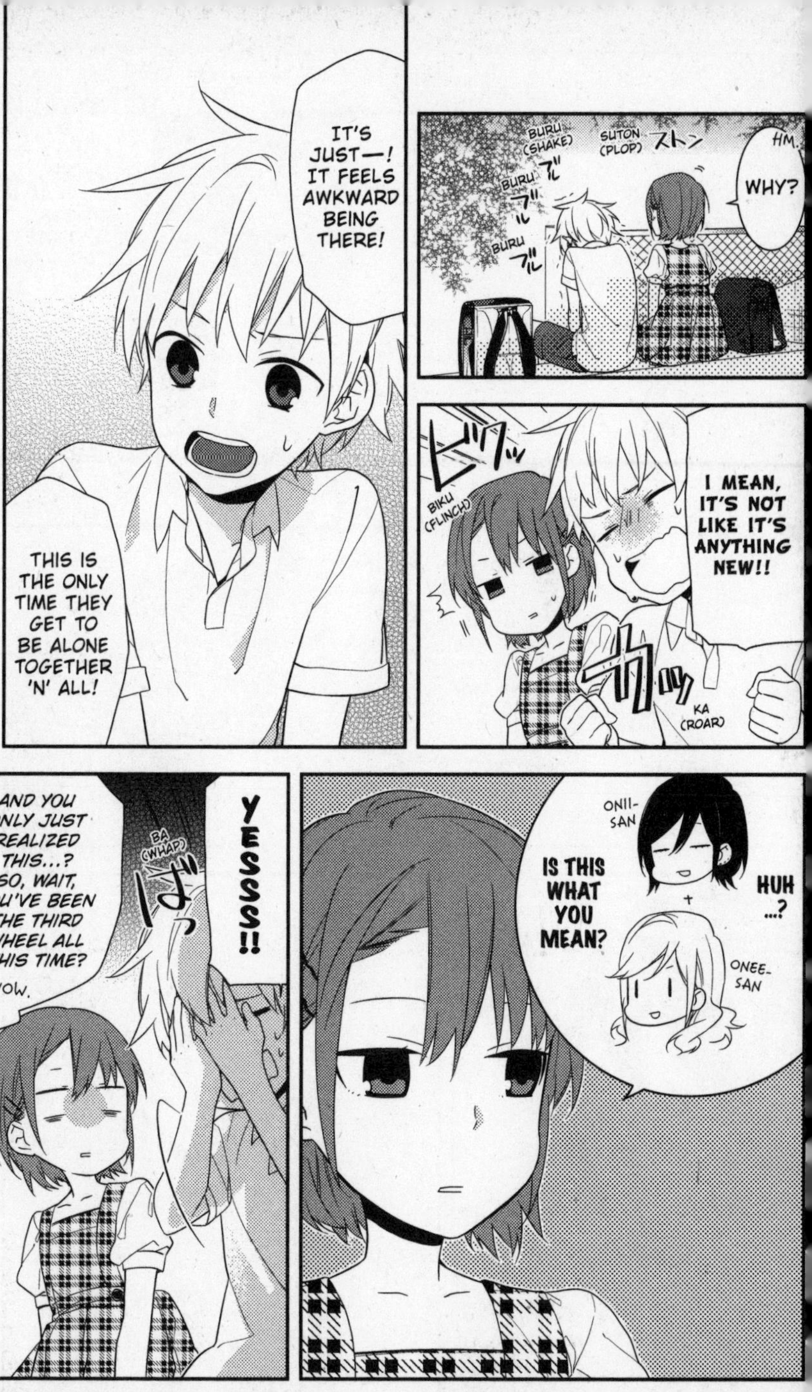
BURU (SHAKE) ブル
BURU ブル
BURU ブル
SUTON (PLOP) ストン
HM. WHY?
ビクッ BIKU (FLINCH)
I MEAN, IT'S NOT LIKE IT'S ANYTHING NEW!!
カッ KA (ROAR)
IT'S JUST—! IT FEELS AWKWARD BEING THERE!
THIS IS THE ONLY TIME THEY GET TO BE ALONE TOGETHER 'N' ALL!
ONII-SAN
IS THIS WHAT YOU MEAN?
HUH ...?
ONEE-SAN
YESSS!!
ばっ BA (WHAP)
AND YOU ONLY JUST REALIZED THIS...? SO, WAIT, YOU'VE BEEN THE THIRD WHEEL ALL THIS TIME?
WOW.

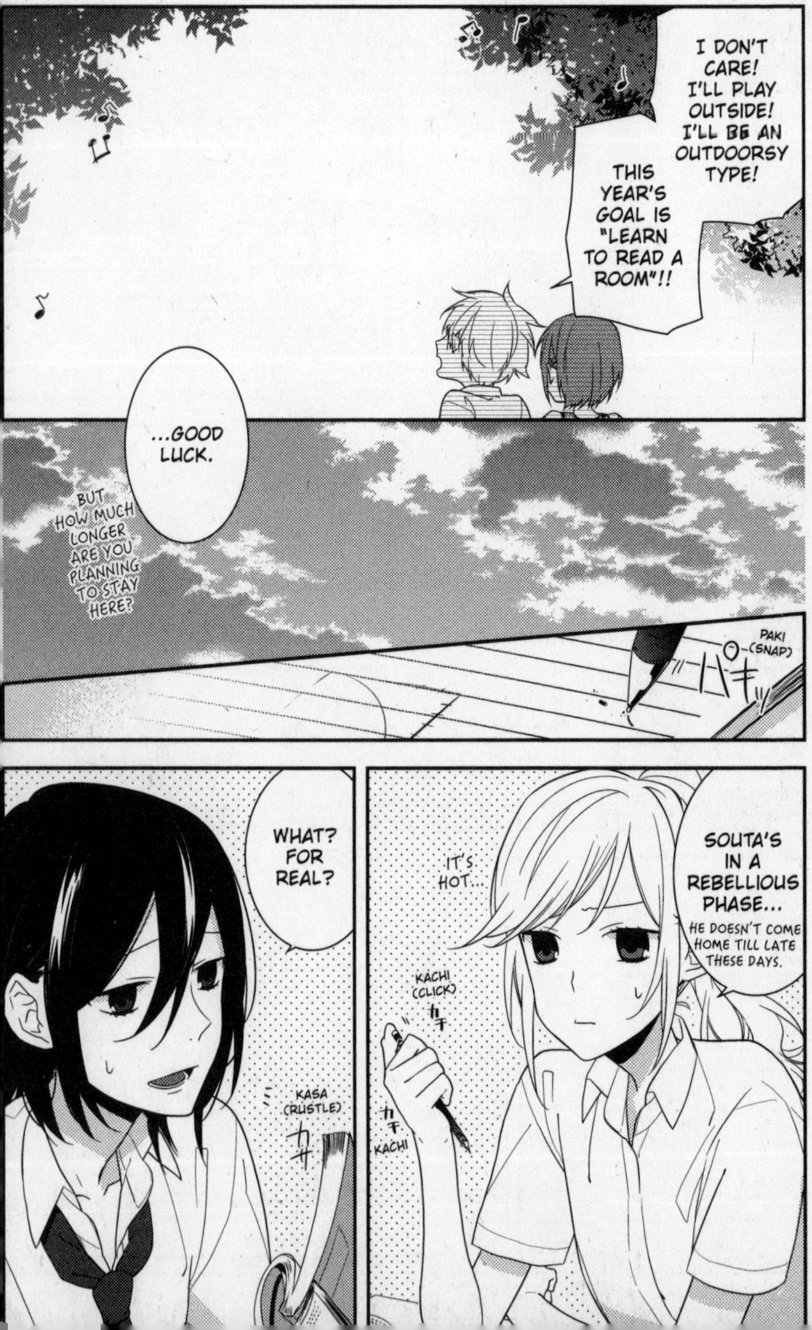
I DON'T CARE! I'LL PLAY OUTSIDE! I'LL BE AN OUTDOORSY TYPE!
THIS YEAR'S GOAL IS "LEARN TO READ A ROOM"!!
...GOOD LUCK.
BUT HOW MUCH LONGER ARE YOU PLANNING TO STAY HERE?
PAKI (SNAP)
SOUTA'S IN A REBELLIOUS PHASE...
HE DOESN'T COME HOME TILL LATE THESE DAYS.
IT'S HOT...
KACHI (CLICK)
KACHI
WHAT? FOR REAL?
KASA (RUSTLE)

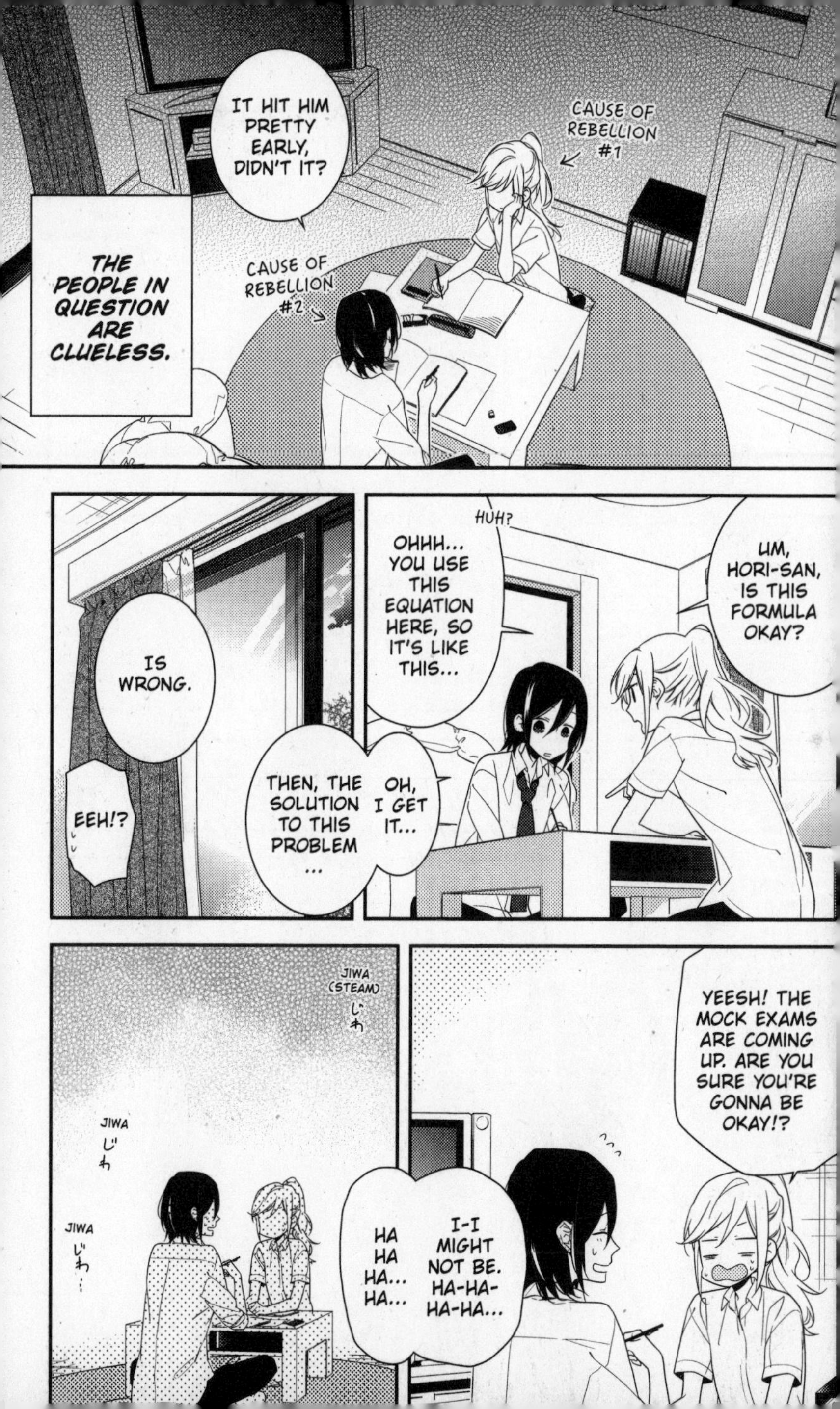
CAUSE OF REBELLION #1
IT HIT HIM PRETTY EARLY, DIDN'T IT?
CAUSE OF REBELLION #2
THE PEOPLE IN QUESTION ARE CLUELESS.
UM, HORI-SAN, IS THIS FORMULA OKAY?
HUH?
OHHH... YOU USE THIS EQUATION HERE, SO IT'S LIKE THIS...
OH, I GET IT...
THEN, THE SOLUTION TO THIS PROBLEM ...
IS WRONG.
EEH!?
YEESH! THE MOCK EXAMS ARE COMING UP. ARE YOU SURE YOU'RE GONNA BE OKAY!?
I-I MIGHT NOT BE. HA-HA-HA-HA...
HA HA HA... HA...
JIWA (STEAM)
じわ
JIWA
じわ
JIWA
じわ・・・

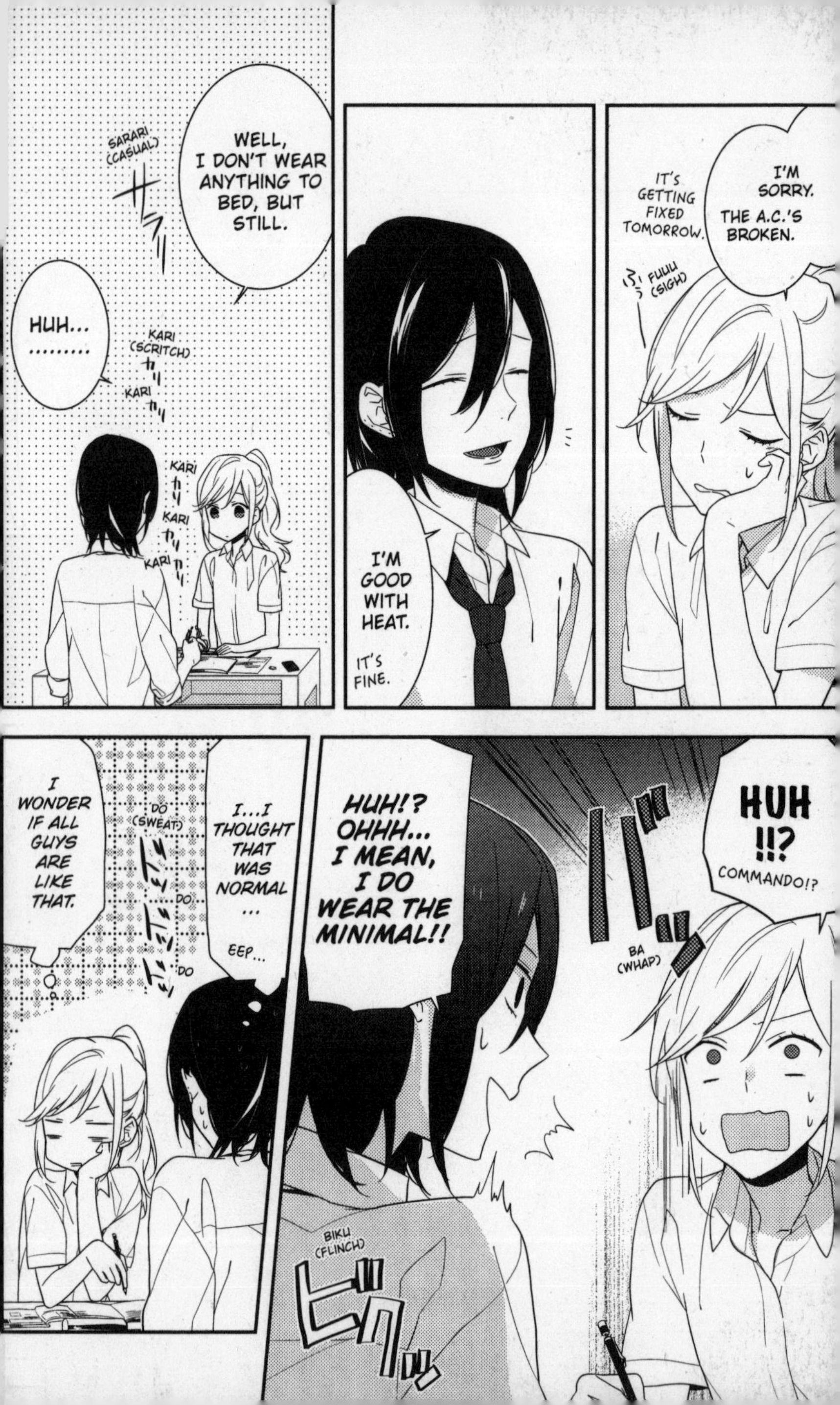
I'M SORRY.
THE A.C.'S BROKEN.
IT'S GETTING FIXED TOMORROW.
FUUU (SIGH)
I'M GOOD WITH HEAT.
IT'S FINE.
WELL, I DON'T WEAR ANYTHING TO BED, BUT STILL.
SARARI (CASUAL)
HUH... ....
KARI (SCRITCH)
KARI
KARI
KARI
KARI
HUH !!?
COMMANDO!?
BA (WHAP)
HUH!? OHHH... I MEAN, I DO WEAR THE MINIMAL!!
BIKU (FLINCH)
I...I THOUGHT THAT WAS NORMAL ...
EEP...
DO (SWEAT)
DO
DO
I WONDER IF ALL GUYS ARE LIKE THAT.

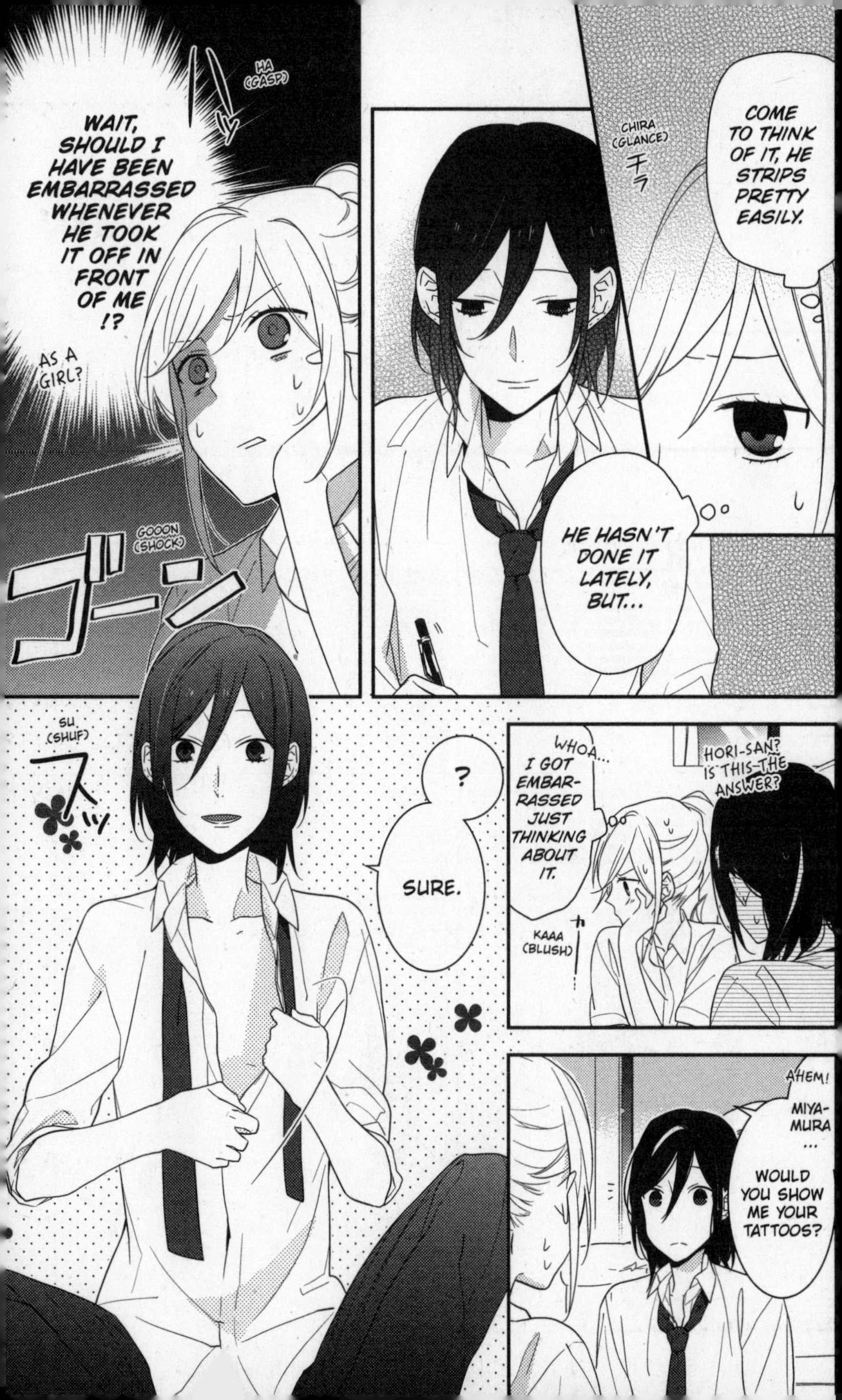

COME TO THINK OF IT, HE STRIPS PRETTY EASILY.
CHIRA (GLANCE)
HE HASN'T DONE IT LATELY, BUT...
HA (GASP)
WAIT, SHOULD I HAVE BEEN EMBARRASSED WHENEVER HE TOOK IT OFF IN FRONT OF ME !?
AS A GIRL?
GOOON (SHOCK)
HORI-SAN? IS THIS THE ANSWER?
WHOA... I GOT EMBARRASSED JUST THINKING ABOUT IT.
KAAA (BLUSH)
AHEM!
MIYAMURA...
WOULD YOU SHOW ME YOUR TATTOOS?
?
SURE.
SU (SHUF)

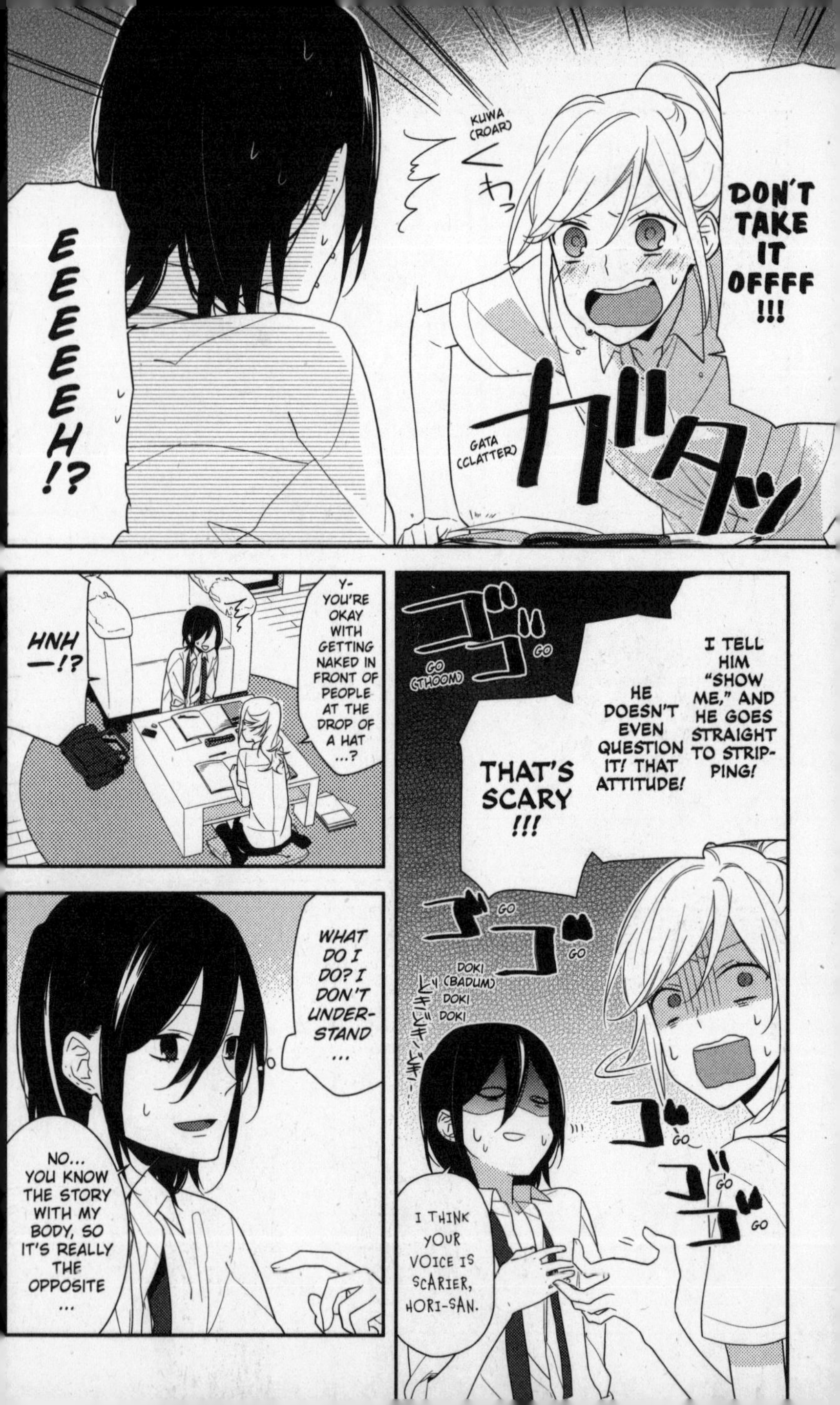
DON'T TAKE IT OFFFF!!!
KUWA (ROAR)
GATA (CLATTER)
EEEEEEH!?
GO GO (THOOM)
I TELL HIM "SHOW ME," AND HE GOES STRAIGHT TO STRIP-PING!
HE DOESN'T EVEN QUESTION IT! THAT ATTITUDE!
THAT'S SCARY!!!
GO GO
DOKI (BADUM) DOKI DOKI
GO GO GO
I THINK YOUR VOICE IS SCARIER, HORI-SAN.
Y-YOU'RE OKAY WITH GETTING NAKED IN FRONT OF PEOPLE AT THE DROP OF A HAT...?
HNH—!?
WHAT DO I DO? I DON'T UNDER-STAND...
NO... YOU KNOW THE STORY WITH MY BODY, SO IT'S REALLY THE OPPOSITE...

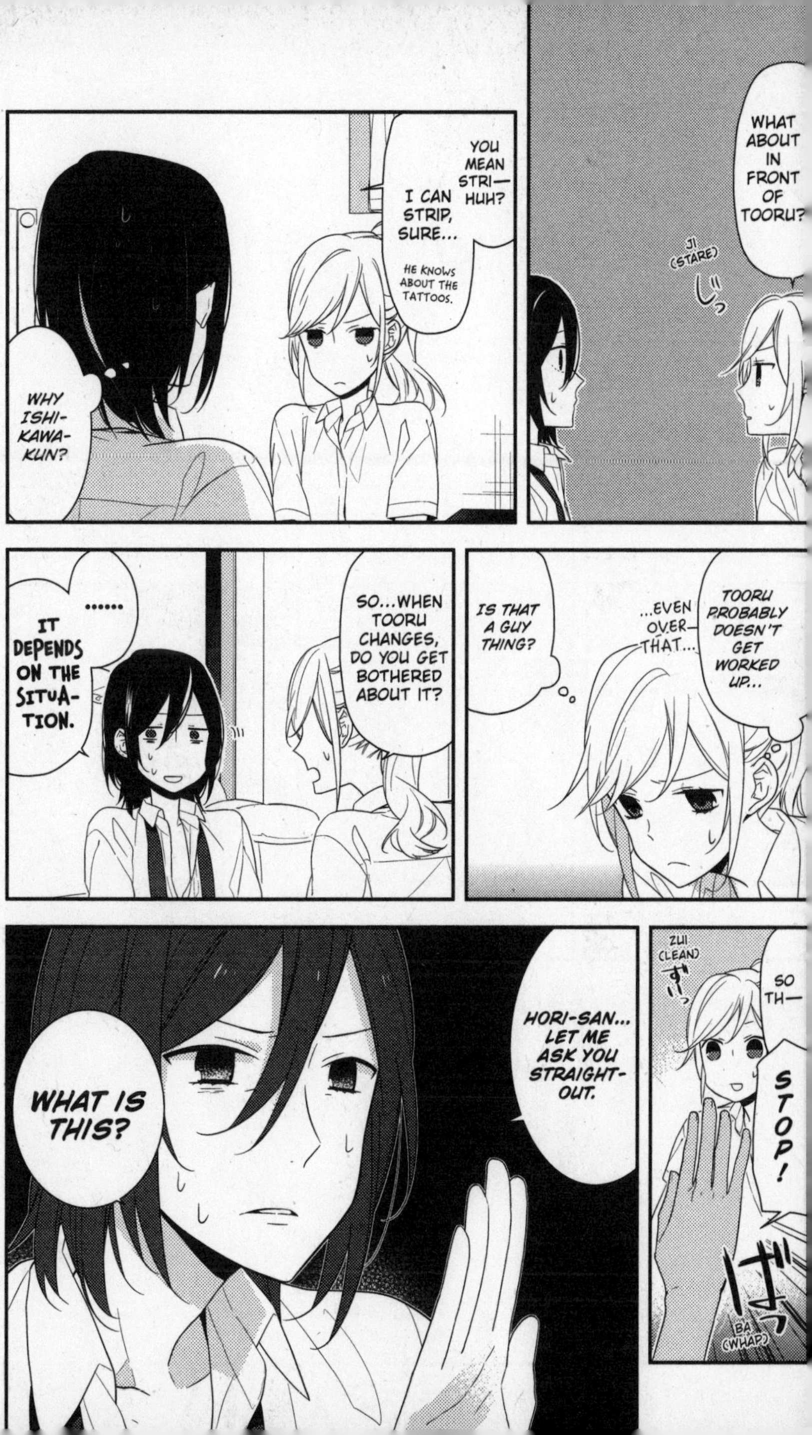
WHAT ABOUT IN FRONT OF TOORU?
JI (STARE)
じっ
YOU MEAN STRI— HUH?
I CAN STRIP, SURE...
HE KNOWS ABOUT THE TATTOOS.
WHY ISHI-KAWA-KUN?
TOORU PROBABLY DOESN'T GET WORKED UP...
...EVEN OVER THAT...
IS THAT A GUY THING?
SO...WHEN TOORU CHANGES, DO YOU GET BOTHERED ABOUT IT?
......
IT DEPENDS ON THE SITUA-TION.
ZUI (CLEAN)
ずいっ
SO TH—
STOP!
ばっ
BA (WHAP)
HORI-SAN... LET ME ASK YOU STRAIGHT-OUT.
WHAT IS THIS?

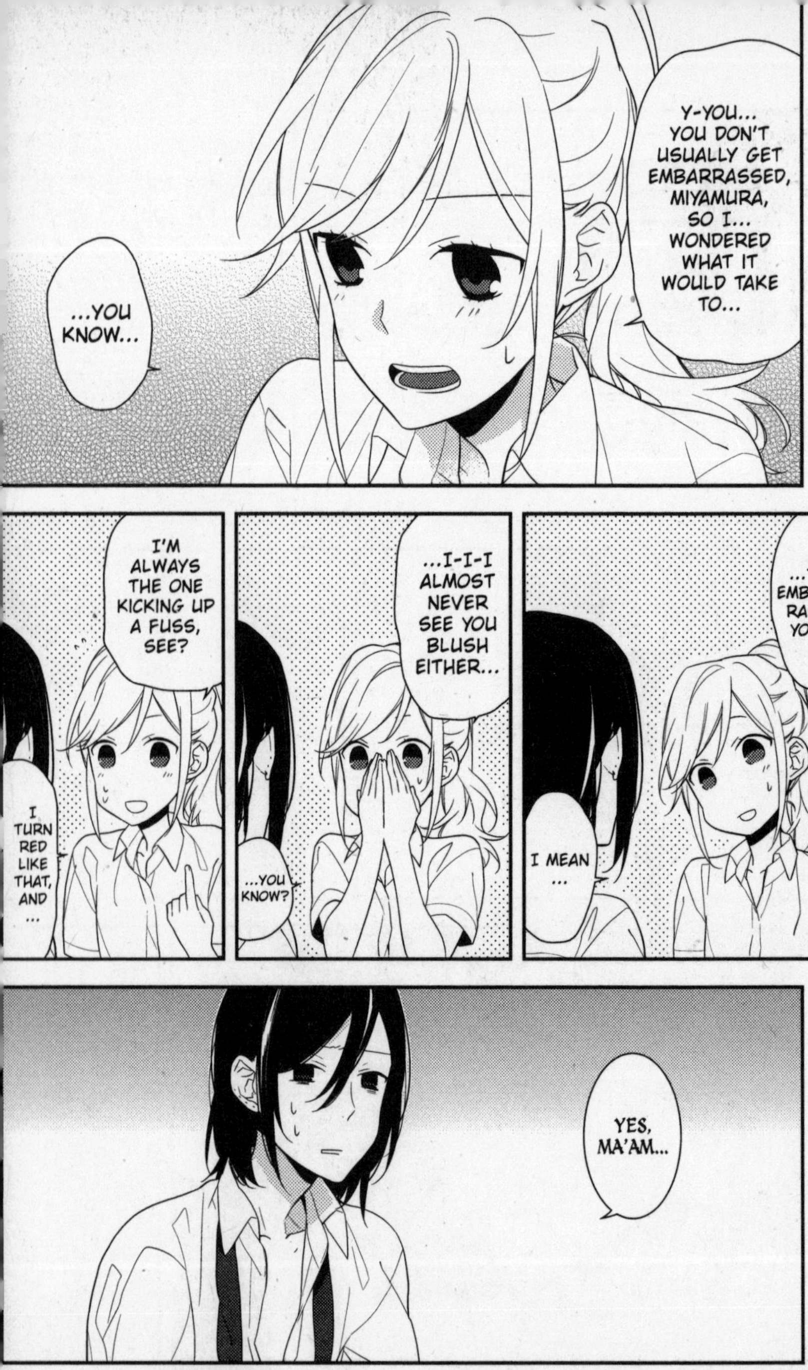
Y-YOU... YOU DON'T USUALLY GET EMBARRASSED, MIYAMURA, SO I... WONDERED WHAT IT WOULD TAKE TO...
...YOU KNOW...
...TO EMBARRASS YOU.
I MEAN ...
...I-I-I ALMOST NEVER SEE YOU BLUSH EITHER...
...YOU KNOW?
I'M ALWAYS THE ONE KICKING UP A FUSS, SEE?
I TURN RED LIKE THAT, AND ...
YES, MA'AM...

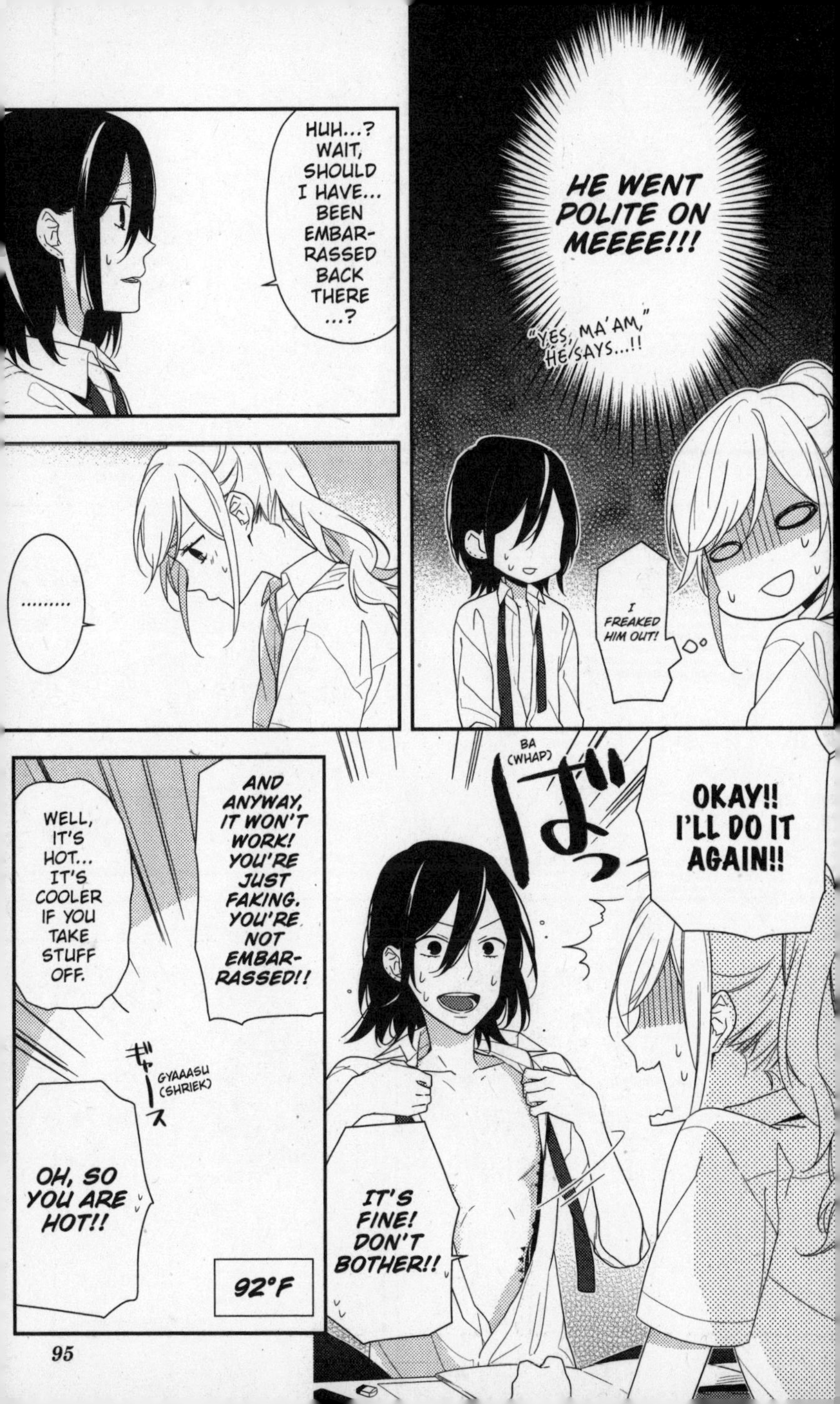
HE WENT POLITE ON MEEEE!!!
"YES, MA'AM," HE SAYS...!!
I FREAKED HIM OUT!
HUH...? WAIT, SHOULD I HAVE... BEEN EMBARRASSED BACK THERE ...?
....
OKAY!! I'LL DO IT AGAIN!!
BA (WHAP)
IT'S FINE! DON'T BOTHER!!
AND ANYWAY, IT WON'T WORK! YOU'RE JUST FAKING. YOU'RE NOT EMBARRASSED!!
WELL, IT'S HOT... IT'S COOLER IF YOU TAKE STUFF OFF.
GYAAASU (SHRIEK)
OH, SO YOU ARE HOT!!
92°F

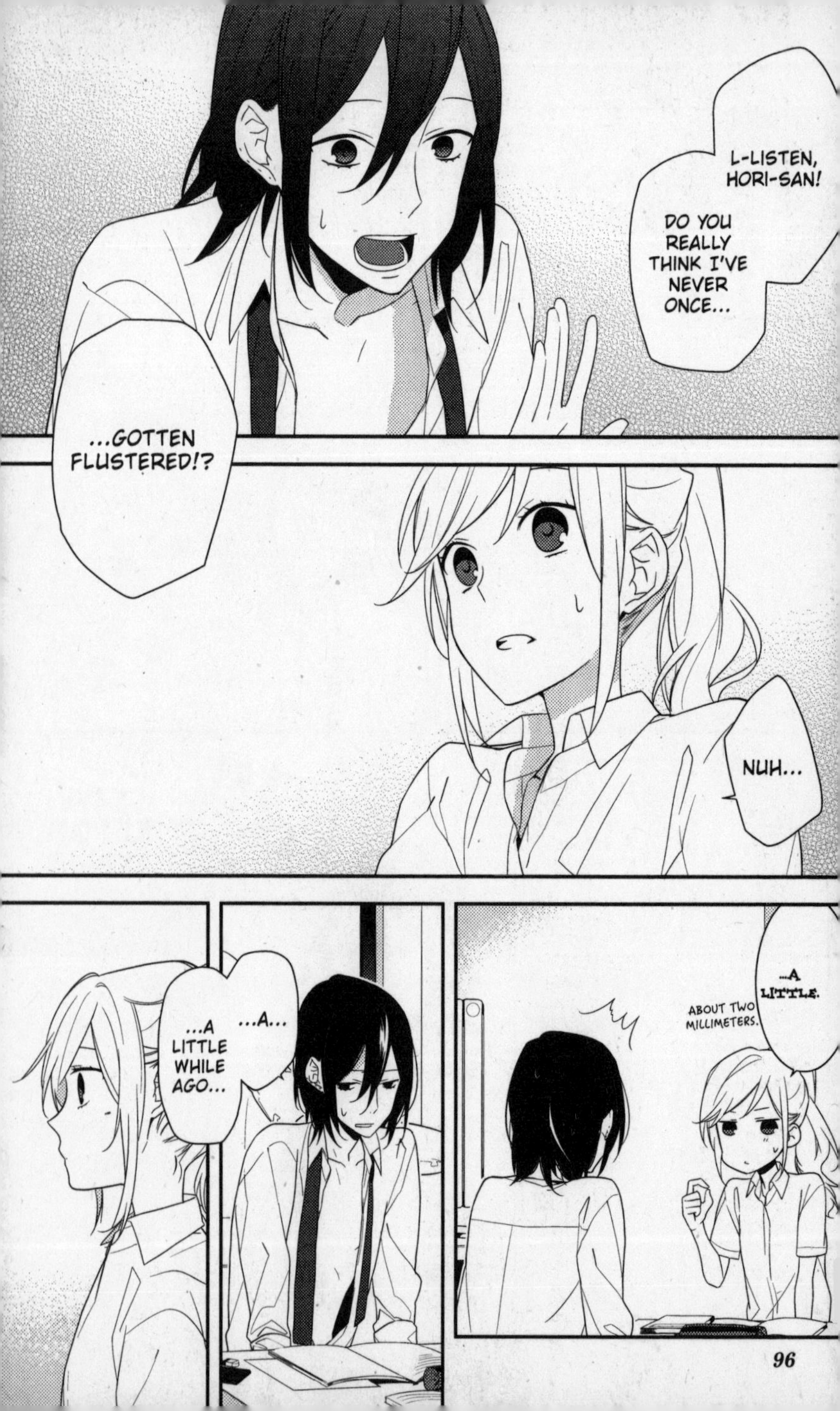
L-LISTEN, HORI-SAN!
DO YOU REALLY THINK I'VE NEVER ONCE...
...GOTTEN FLUSTERED!?
NUH...
...A LITTLE.
ABOUT TWO MILLIMETERS.
...A...
...A LITTLE WHILE AGO...

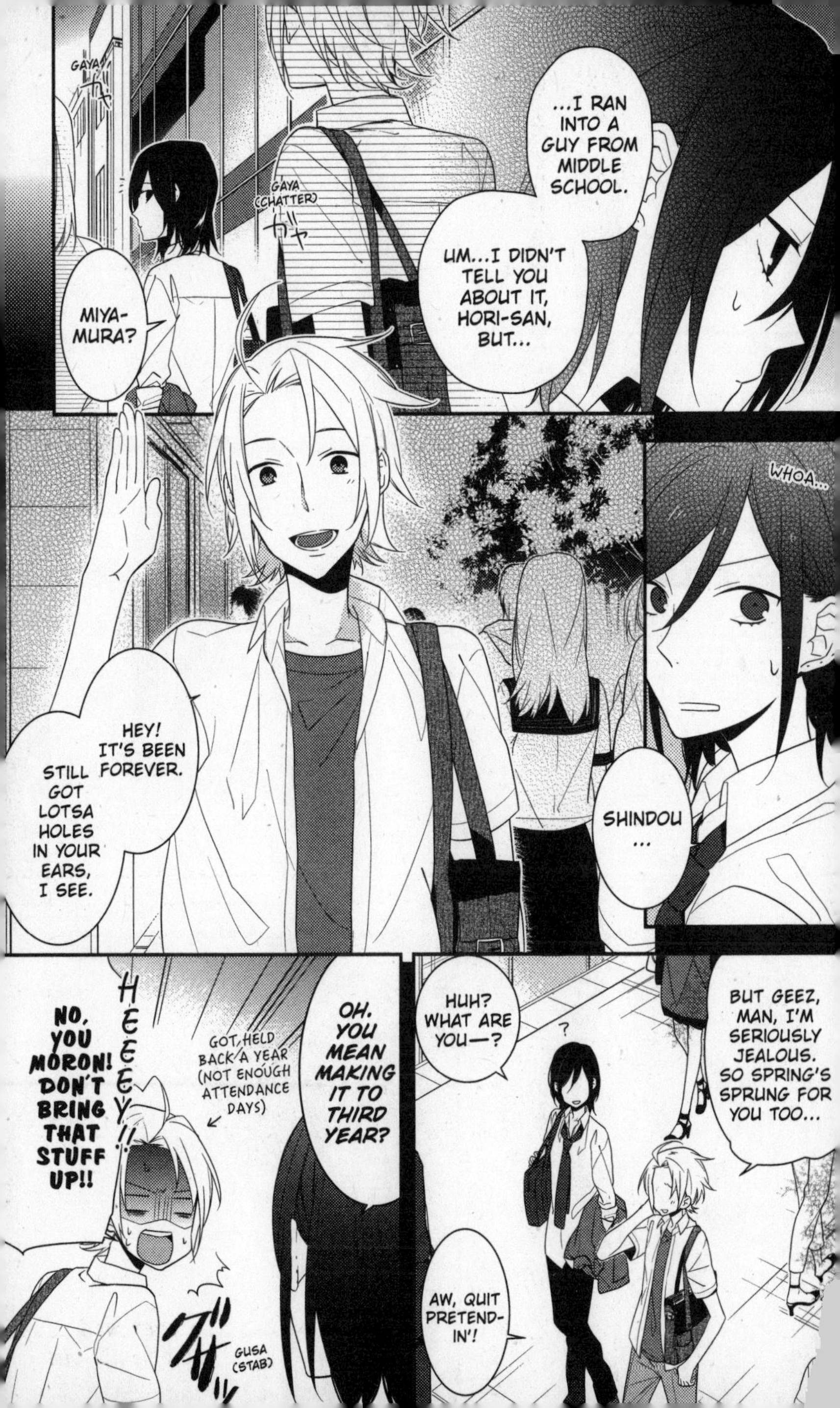
...I RAN INTO A GUY FROM MIDDLE SCHOOL.
UM...I DIDN'T TELL YOU ABOUT IT, HORI-SAN, BUT...
GAYA (CHATTER)
GAYA
MIYA-MURA?
WHOA...
SHINDOU ...
HEY! IT'S BEEN FOREVER.
STILL GOT LOTSA HOLES IN YOUR EARS, I SEE.
BUT GEEZ, MAN, I'M SERIOUSLY JEALOUS. SO SPRING'S SPRUNG FOR YOU TOO...
HUH? WHAT ARE YOU—?
AW, QUIT PRETENDIN'!
OH. YOU MEAN MAKING IT TO THIRD YEAR?
GOT HELD BACK A YEAR (NOT ENOUGH ATTENDANCE DAYS)
HEEEY!!
NO, YOU MORON! DON'T BRING THAT STUFF UP!!
GUSA (STAB)

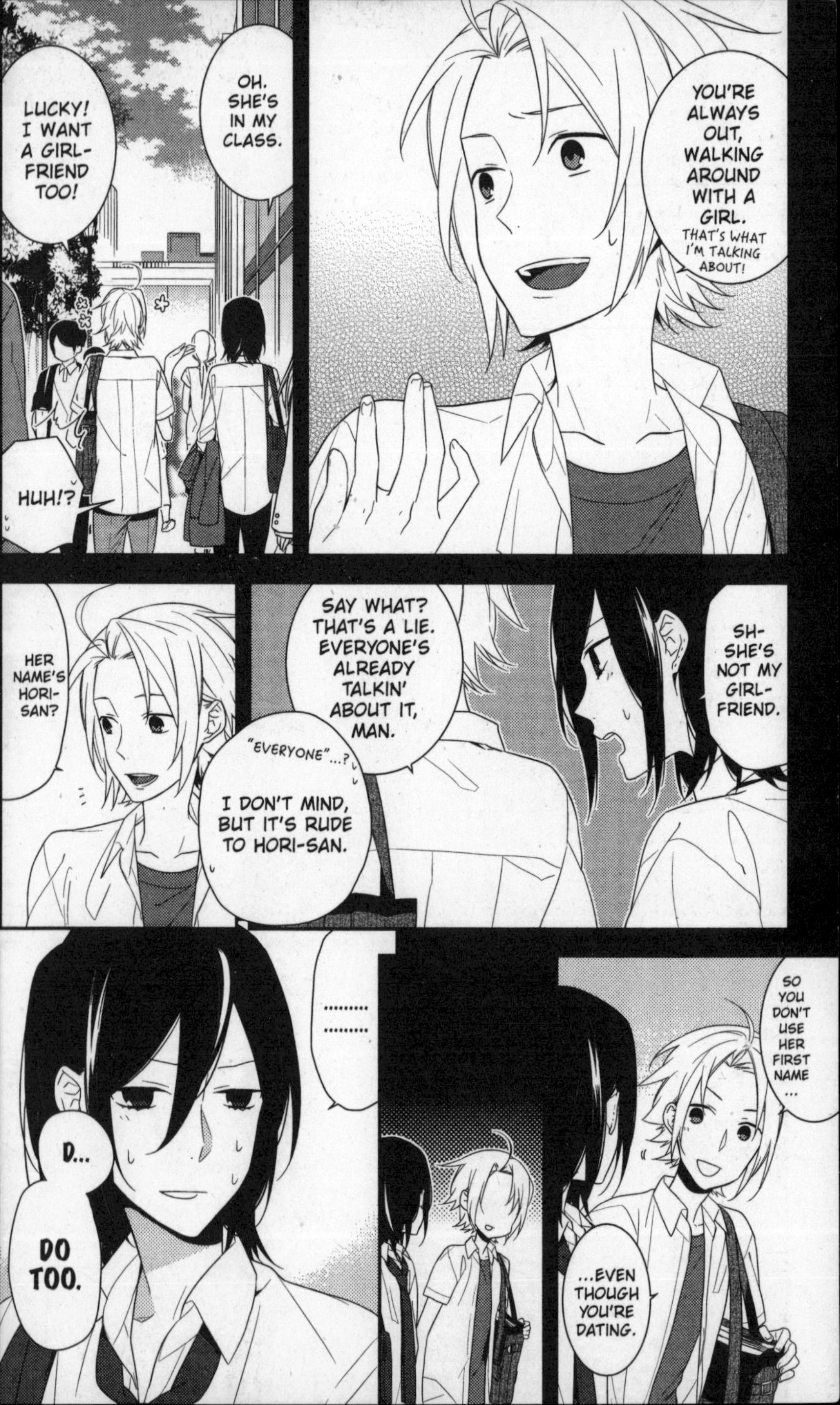
YOU'RE ALWAYS OUT, WALKING AROUND WITH A GIRL. THAT'S WHAT I'M TALKING ABOUT!
OH. SHE'S IN MY CLASS.
LUCKY! I WANT A GIRL-FRIEND TOO!
HUH!?
SH-SHE'S NOT MY GIRL-FRIEND.
SAY WHAT? THAT'S A LIE. EVERYONE'S ALREADY TALKIN' ABOUT IT, MAN.
"EVERYONE"...?
I DON'T MIND, BUT IT'S RUDE TO HORI-SAN.
HER NAME'S HORI-SAN?
SO YOU DON'T USE HER FIRST NAME...
...EVEN THOUGH YOU'RE DATING.
....
....
D...
DO TOO.

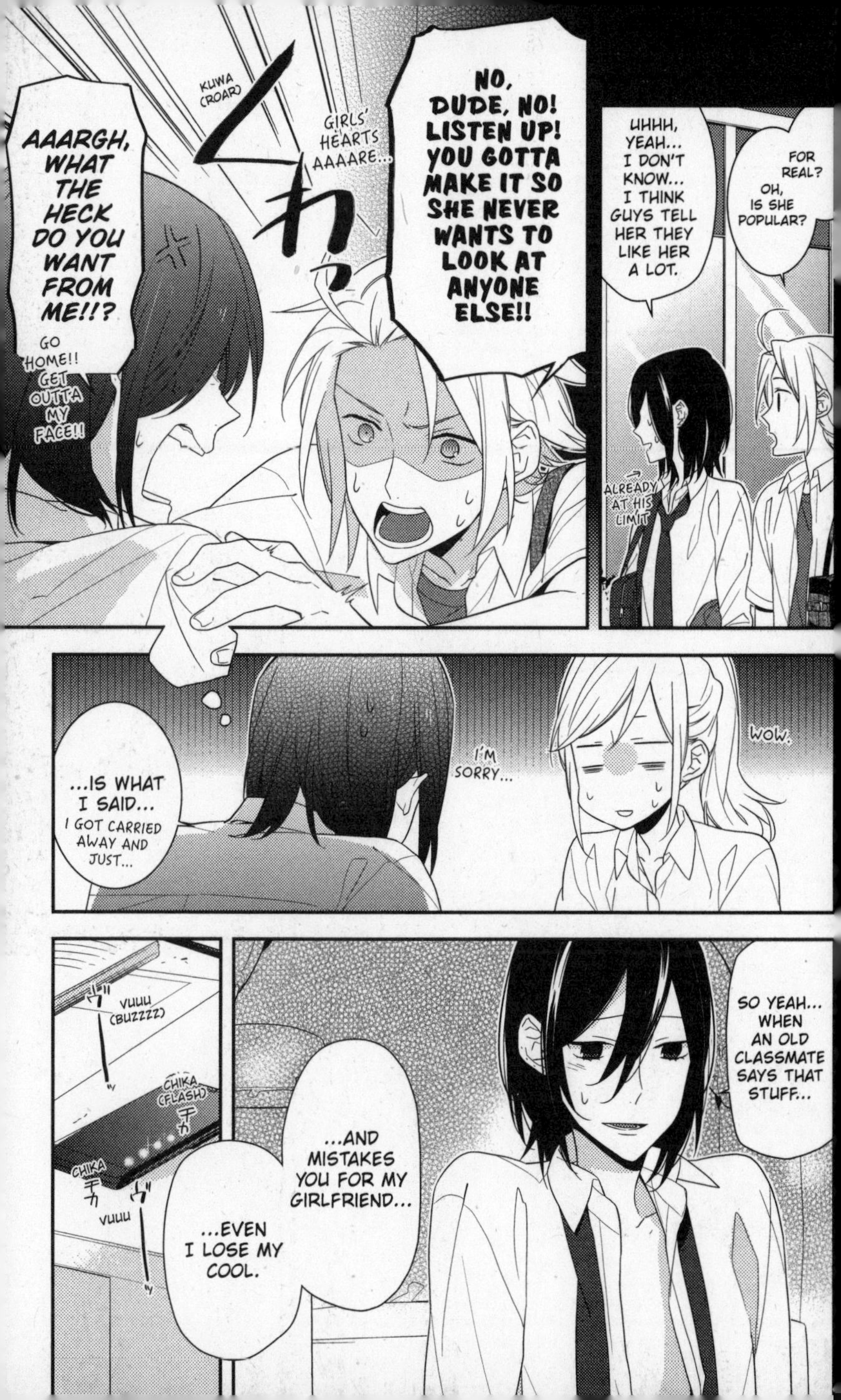
FOR REAL? OH, IS SHE POPULAR?
UHHH, YEAH... I DON'T KNOW... I THINK GUYS TELL HER THEY LIKE HER A LOT.
ALREADY AT HIS LIMIT
NO, DUDE, NO! LISTEN UP! YOU GOTTA MAKE IT SO SHE NEVER WANTS TO LOOK AT ANYONE ELSE!!
GIRLS' HEARTS AAAARE...
くわっ
KUWA (ROAR)
AAARGH, WHAT THE HECK DO YOU WANT FROM ME!!?
GO HOME!! GET OUTTA MY FACE!!
WOW.
I'M SORRY...
...IS WHAT I SAID... I GOT CARRIED AWAY AND JUST...
SO YEAH... WHEN AN OLD CLASSMATE SAYS THAT STUFF...
...AND MISTAKES YOU FOR MY GIRLFRIEND...
...EVEN I LOSE MY COOL.
VUUU (BUZZZZ)
CHIKA (FLASH)
CHIKA
VUUU

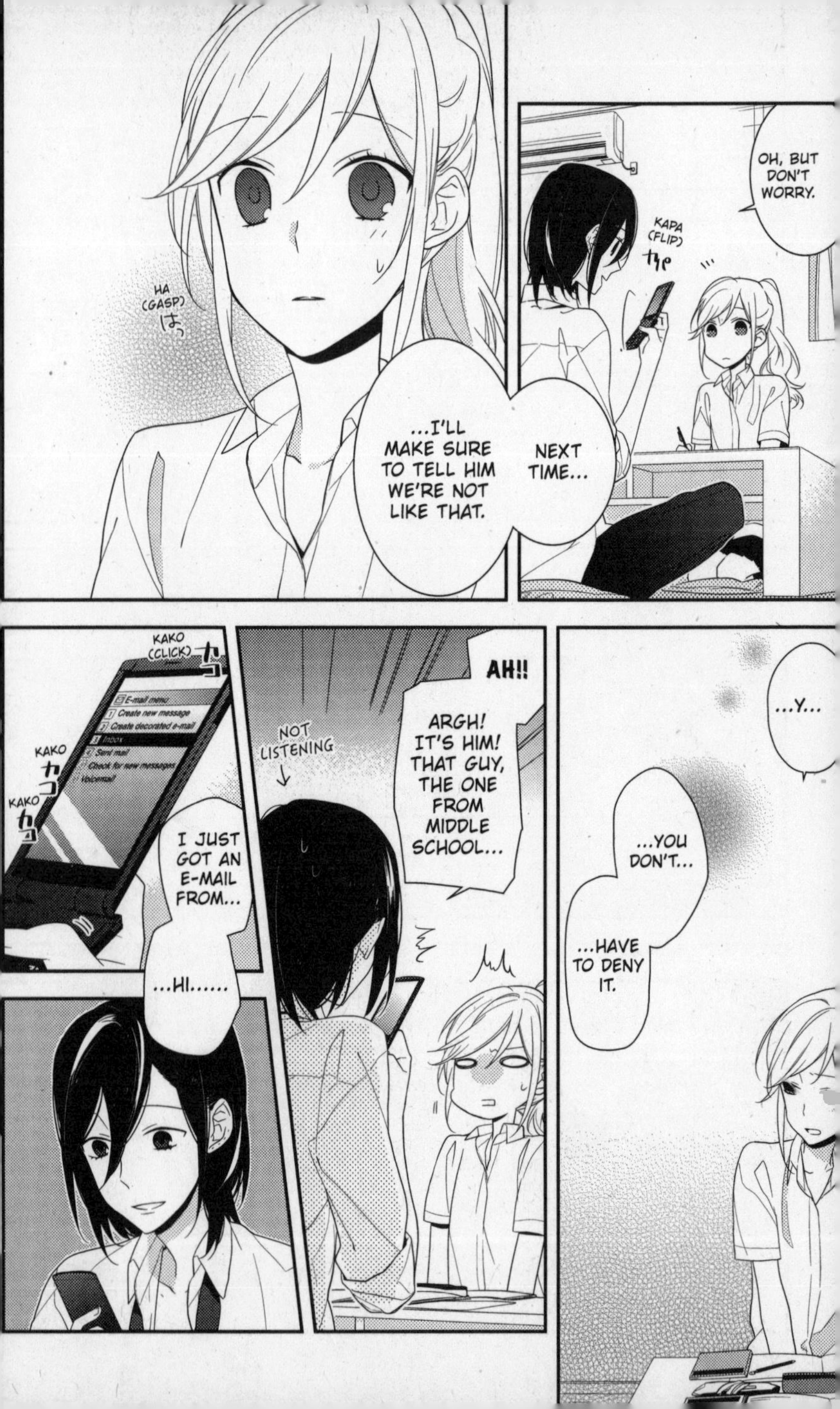
OH, BUT DON'T WORRY.
KAPA (FLIP)
NEXT TIME...
...I'LL MAKE SURE TO TELL HIM WE'RE NOT LIKE THAT.
HA (GASP)
...Y...
...YOU DON'T...
...HAVE TO DENY IT.
AH!!
ARGH! IT'S HIM! THAT GUY, THE ONE FROM MIDDLE SCHOOL...
NOT LISTENING
KAKO (CLICK)
KAKO
KAKO
E-mail menu
Create new message
Create decorated e-mail
Inbox
Sent mail
Check for new messages
Voicemail
I JUST GOT AN E-MAIL FROM...
...HI......

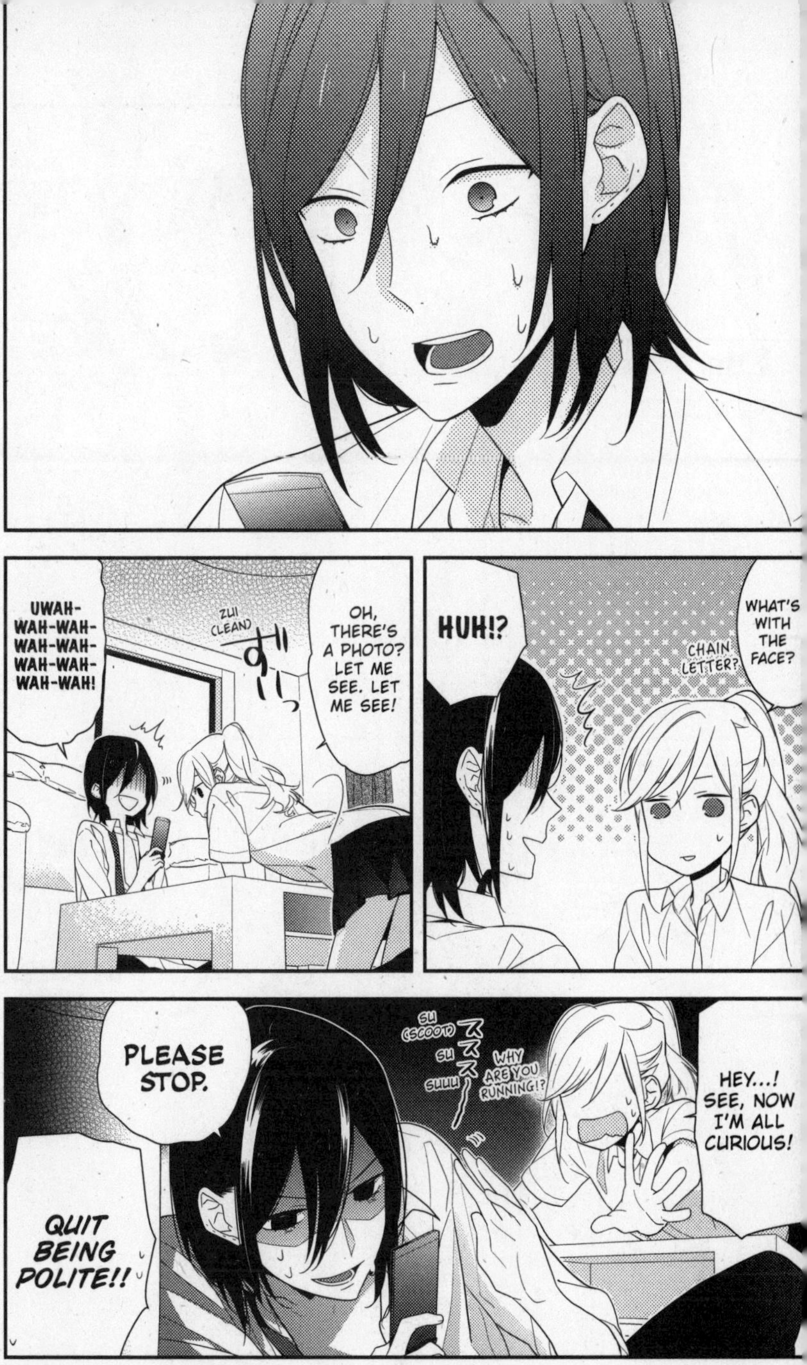

WHAT'S WITH THE FACE?
CHAIN LETTER?
HUH!?
OH, THERE'S A PHOTO? LET ME SEE. LET ME SEE!
ZUI (CLEAN)
ずいっ
UWAH-WAH-WAH-WAH-WAH-WAH-WAH-WAH-WAH!
HEY...! SEE, NOW I'M ALL CURIOUS!
WHY ARE YOU RUNNING!?
SU (SCOOT) SU SUUU
スススー
PLEASE STOP.
QUIT BEING POLITE!!

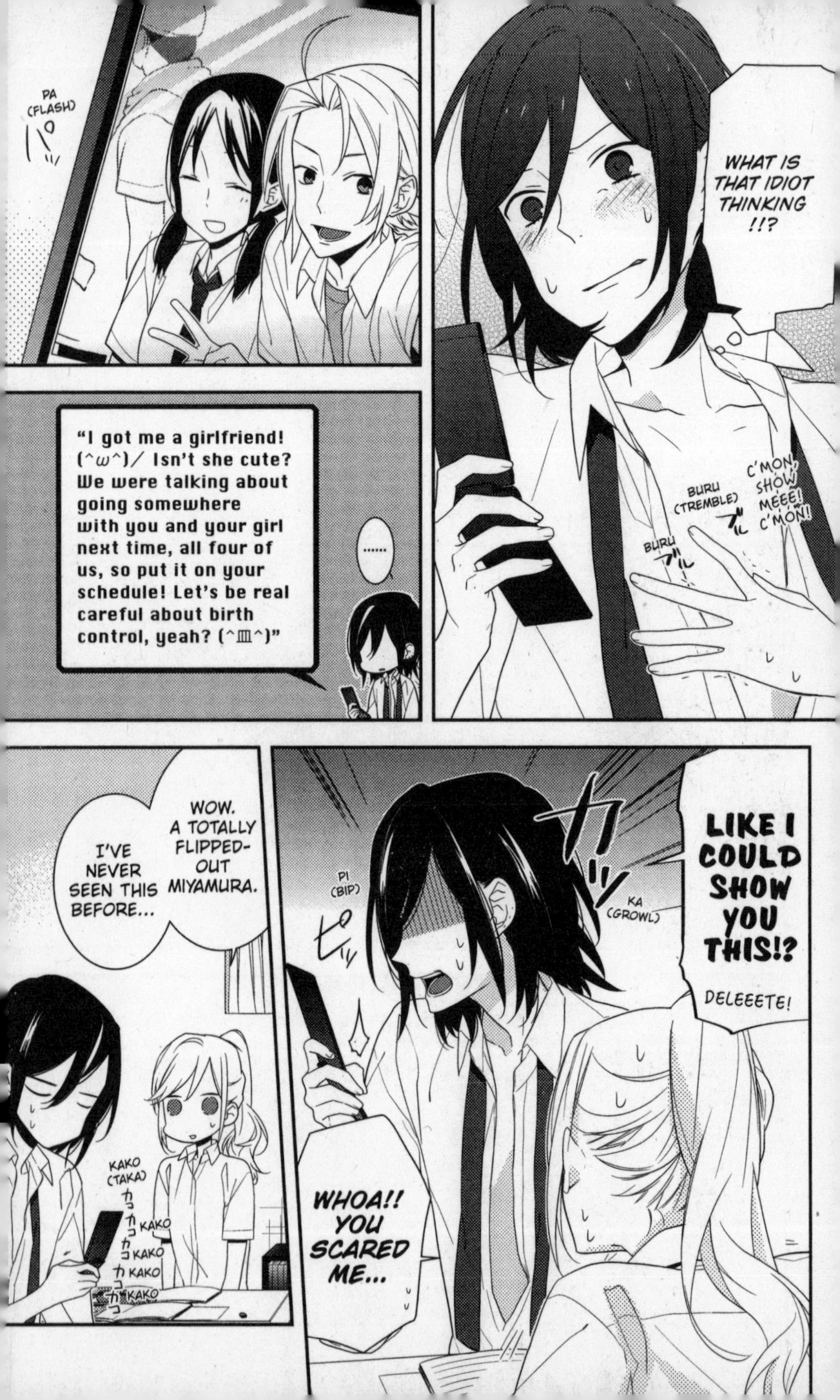
WHAT IS THAT IDIOT THINKING!!?
C'MON, SHOW MEEE! C'MON!
BURU (TREMBLE)
BURU
PA (FLASH)
"I got me a girlfriend! (^ω^)/ Isn't she cute? We were talking about going somewhere with you and your girl next time, all four of us, so put it on your schedule! Let's be real careful about birth control, yeah? (^皿^)"
......
LIKE I COULD SHOW YOU THIS!?
KA (GROWL)
PI (BIP)
DELEEETE!
WHOA!! YOU SCARED ME...
WOW. A TOTALLY FLIPPED-OUT MIYAMURA.
I'VE NEVER SEEN THIS BEFORE...
KAKO (TAKA)
KAKO
KAKO
KAKO
KAKO

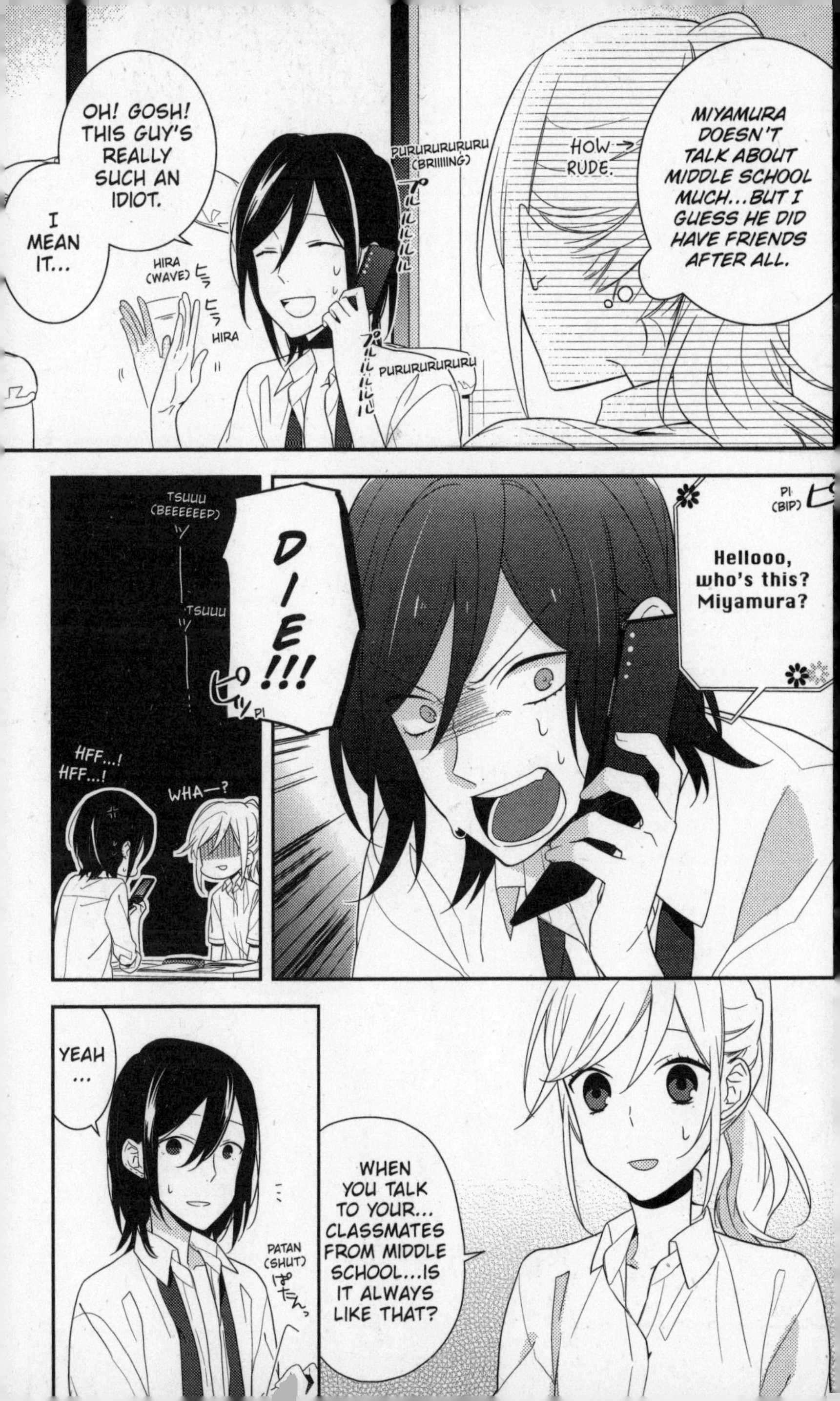
MIYAMURA DOESN'T TALK ABOUT MIDDLE SCHOOL MUCH...BUT I GUESS HE DID HAVE FRIENDS AFTER ALL.
HOW RUDE.
PURURURURURU (BRIIIIING)
PURURURURURU
OH! GOSH! THIS GUY'S REALLY SUCH AN IDIOT.
I MEAN IT...
HIRA (WAVE)
HIRA
PI (BIP)
Hellooo, who's this? Miyamura?
DIE!!!
PI
TSUUU (BEEEEEEP)
TSUUU
HFF...! HFF...!
WHA—?
WHEN YOU TALK TO YOUR... CLASSMATES FROM MIDDLE SCHOOL...IS IT ALWAYS LIKE THAT?
YEAH...
PATAN (SHUT)

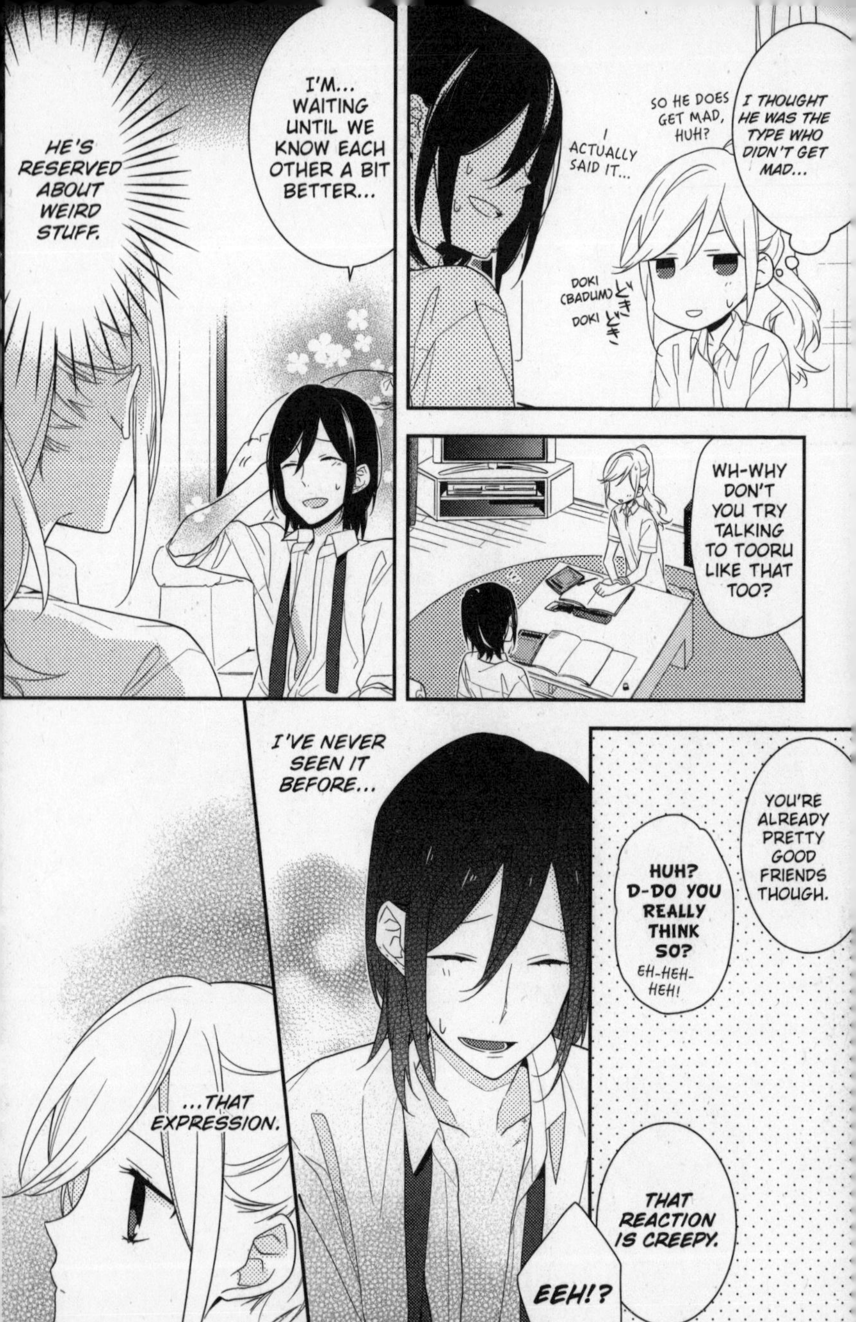
I THOUGHT HE WAS THE TYPE WHO DIDN'T GET MAD...
SO HE DOES GET MAD, HUH?
I ACTUALLY SAID IT...
DOKI (BADUMP) DOKI
WH-WHY DON'T YOU TRY TALKING TO TOORU LIKE THAT TOO?
I'M... WAITING UNTIL WE KNOW EACH OTHER A BIT BETTER...
HE'S RESERVED ABOUT WEIRD STUFF.
YOU'RE ALREADY PRETTY GOOD FRIENDS THOUGH.
HUH? D-DO YOU REALLY THINK SO?
EH-HEH-HEH!
THAT REACTION IS CREEPY.
EEH!?
I'VE NEVER SEEN IT BEFORE...
...THAT EXPRESSION.

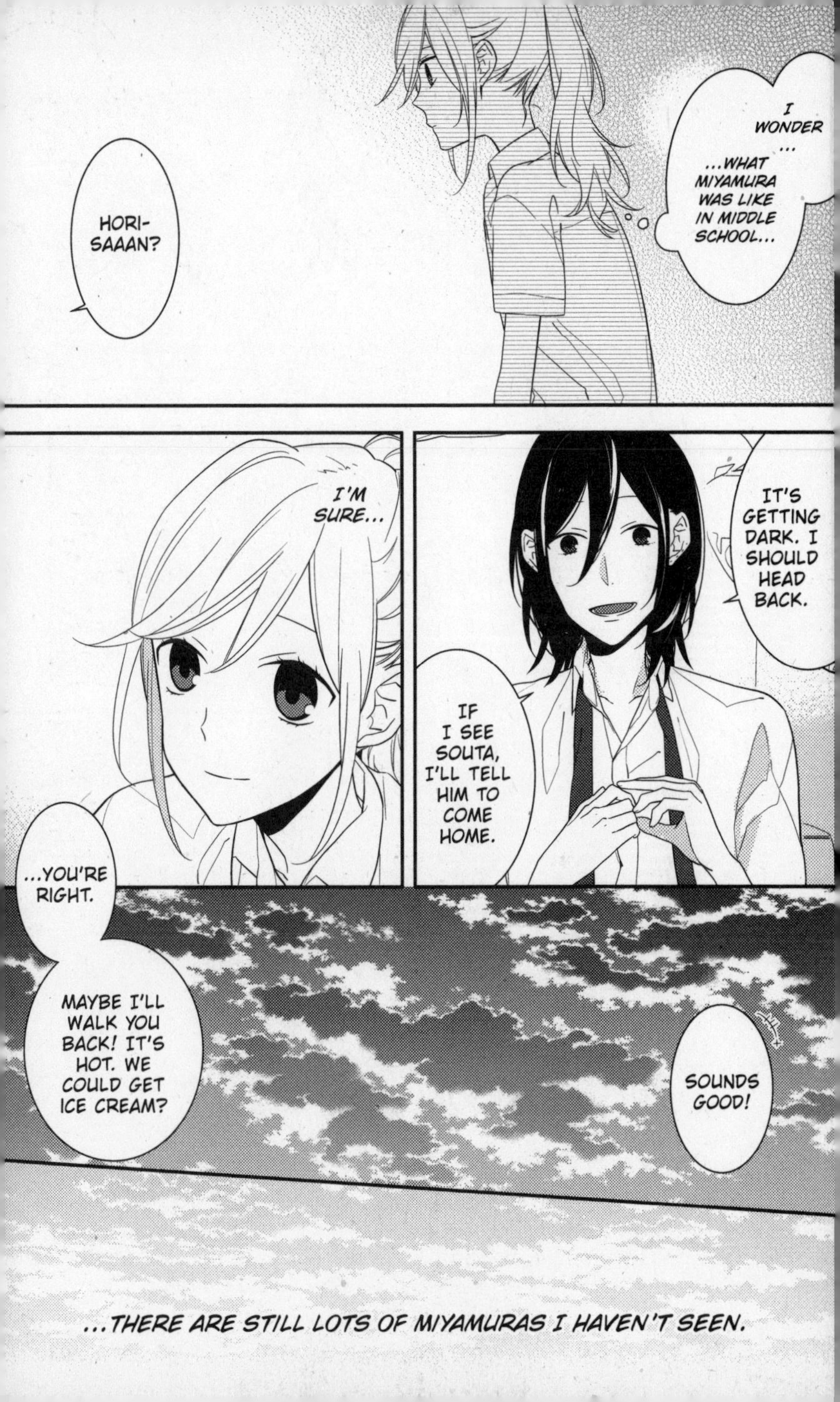
I WONDER ... ...WHAT MIYAMURA WAS LIKE IN MIDDLE SCHOOL...
HORI-SAAAN?
IT'S GETTING DARK. I SHOULD HEAD BACK.
IF I SEE SOUTA, I'LL TELL HIM TO COME HOME.
I'M SURE...
...YOU'RE RIGHT.
MAYBE I'LL WALK YOU BACK! IT'S HOT. WE COULD GET ICE CREAM?
SOUNDS GOOD!
...THERE ARE STILL LOTS OF MIYAMURAS I HAVEN'T SEEN.

HORIMIYA

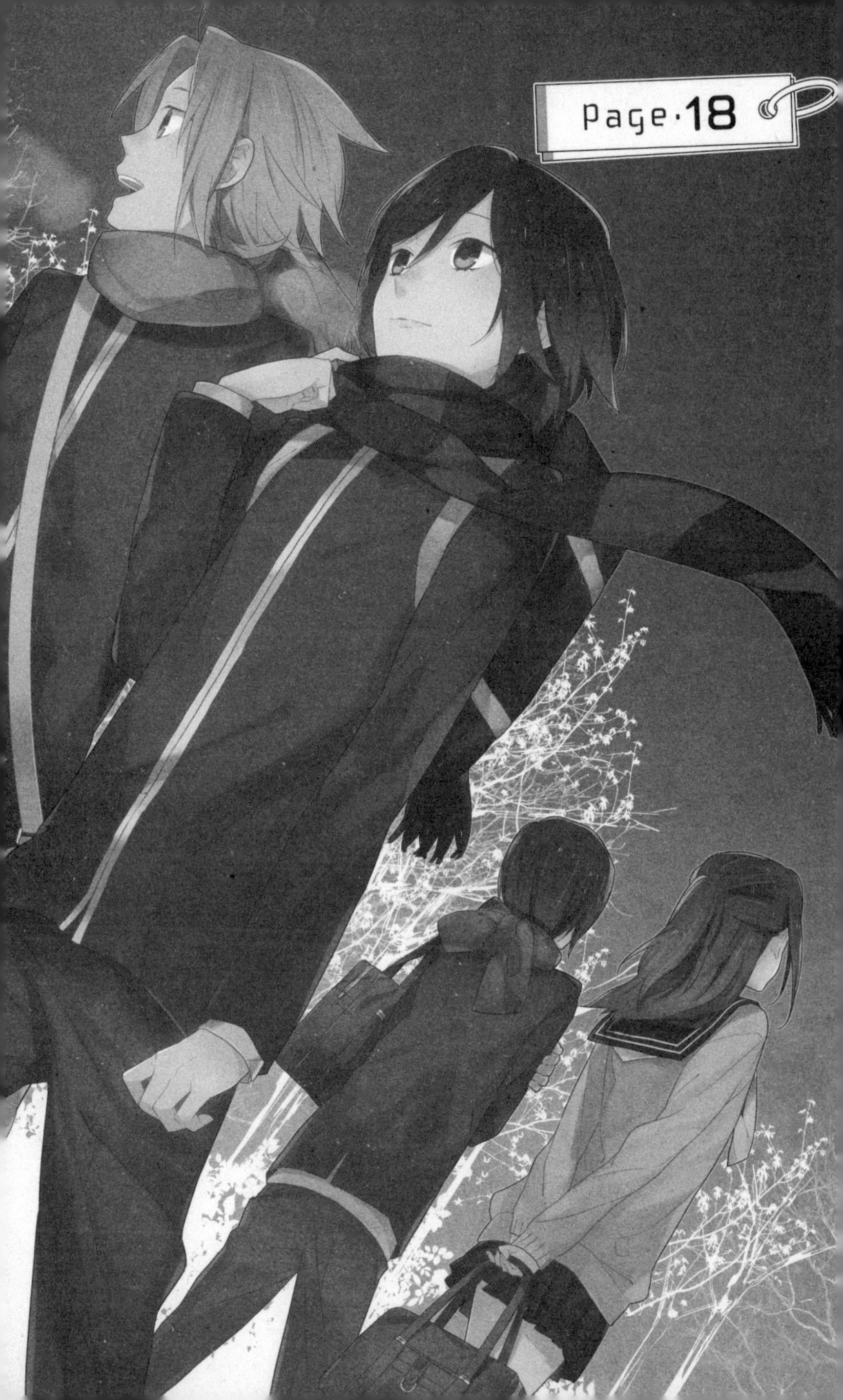
Page·18

HORIMIYA

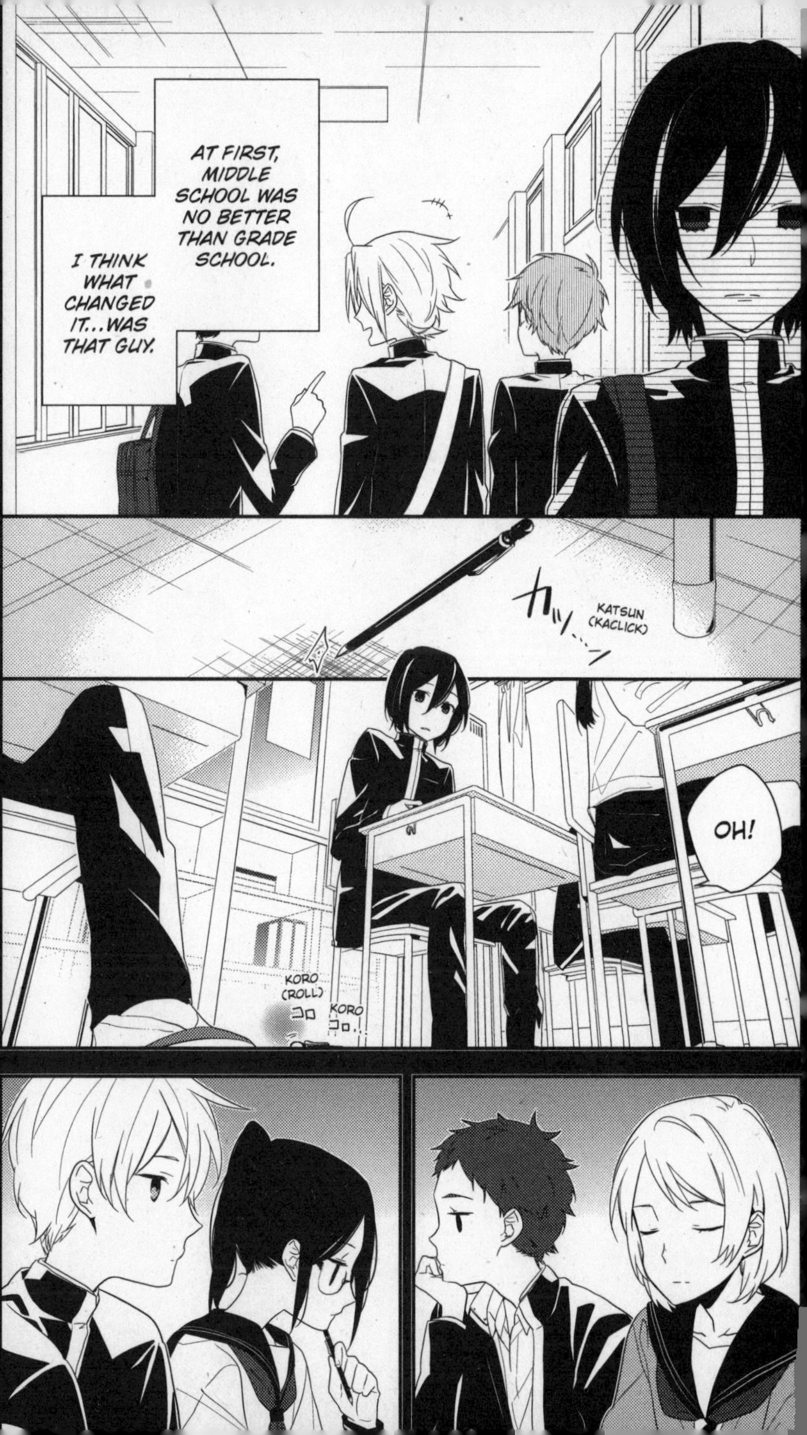
AT FIRST, MIDDLE SCHOOL WAS NO BETTER THAN GRADE SCHOOL.
I THINK WHAT CHANGED IT...WAS THAT GUY.
カッ…ッ
KATSUN (KACLICK)
OH!
KORO (ROLL)
コロ
KORO
コロ…!

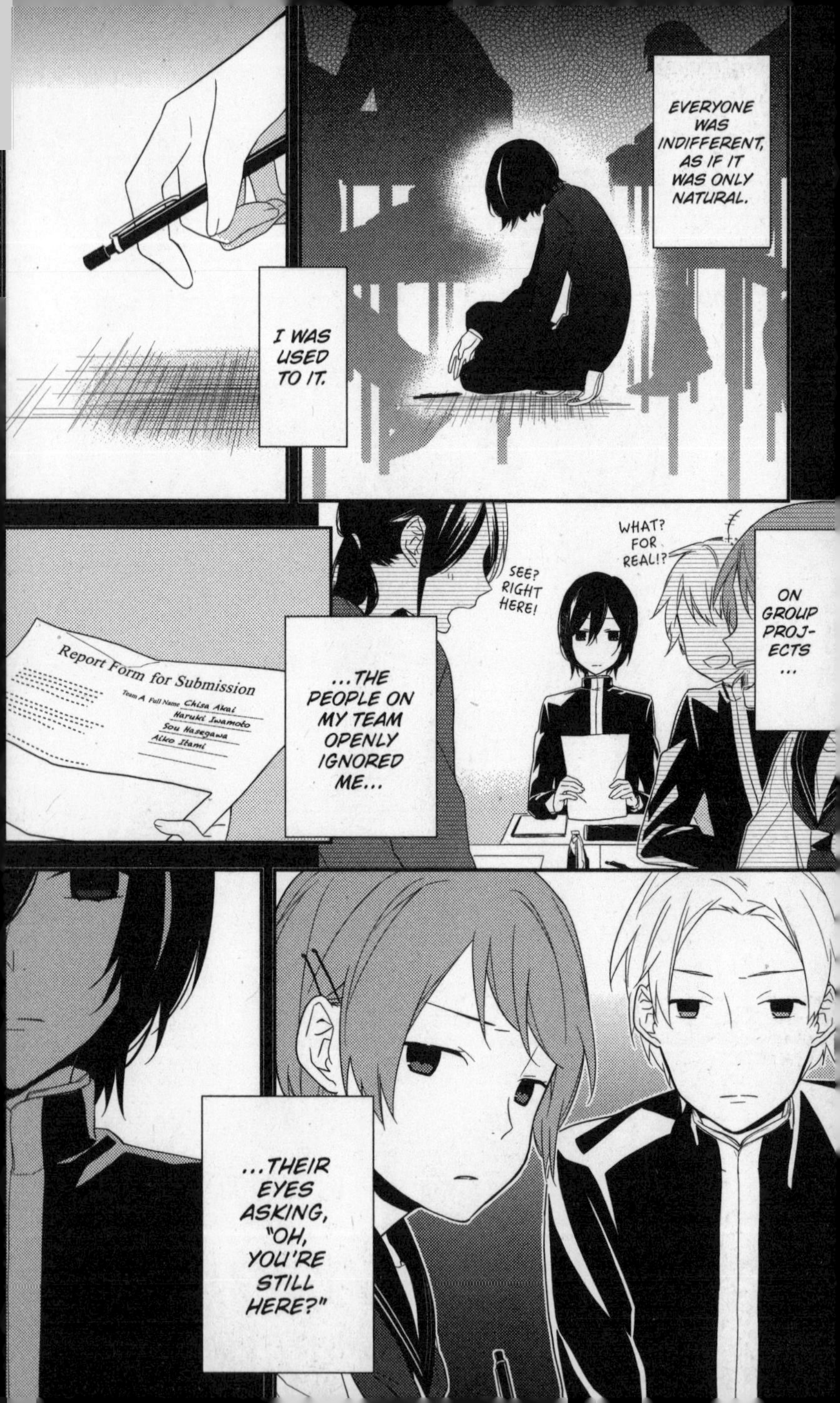

EVERYONE WAS INDIFFERENT, AS IF IT WAS ONLY NATURAL.
I WAS USED TO IT.
ON GROUP PROJ-ECTS...
WHAT? FOR REAL!?
SEE? RIGHT HERE!
...THE PEOPLE ON MY TEAM OPENLY IGNORED ME...
Report Form for Submission
Team A Full Name Chisa Akai
Haruki Iwamoto
Sou Hasegawa
Aiko Itami
...THEIR EYES ASKING, "OH, YOU'RE STILL HERE?"

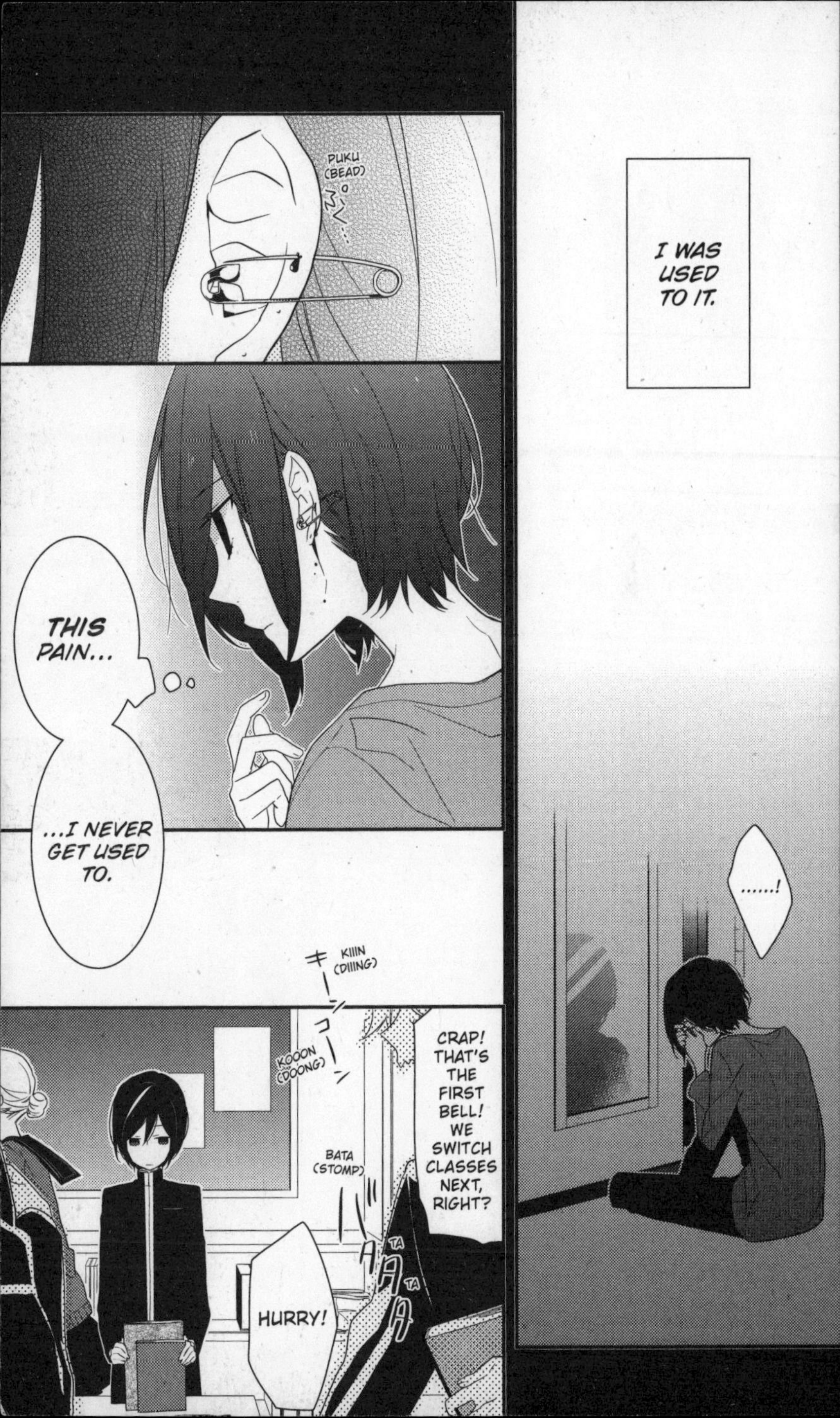
I WAS USED TO IT.
......!
PUKU (BEAD)
THIS PAIN...
...I NEVER GET USED TO.
KIIIN (DIIING)
KOOON (DOONG)
CRAP! THAT'S THE FIRST BELL! WE SWITCH CLASSES NEXT, RIGHT?
BATA (STOMP)
TA TA
HURRY!

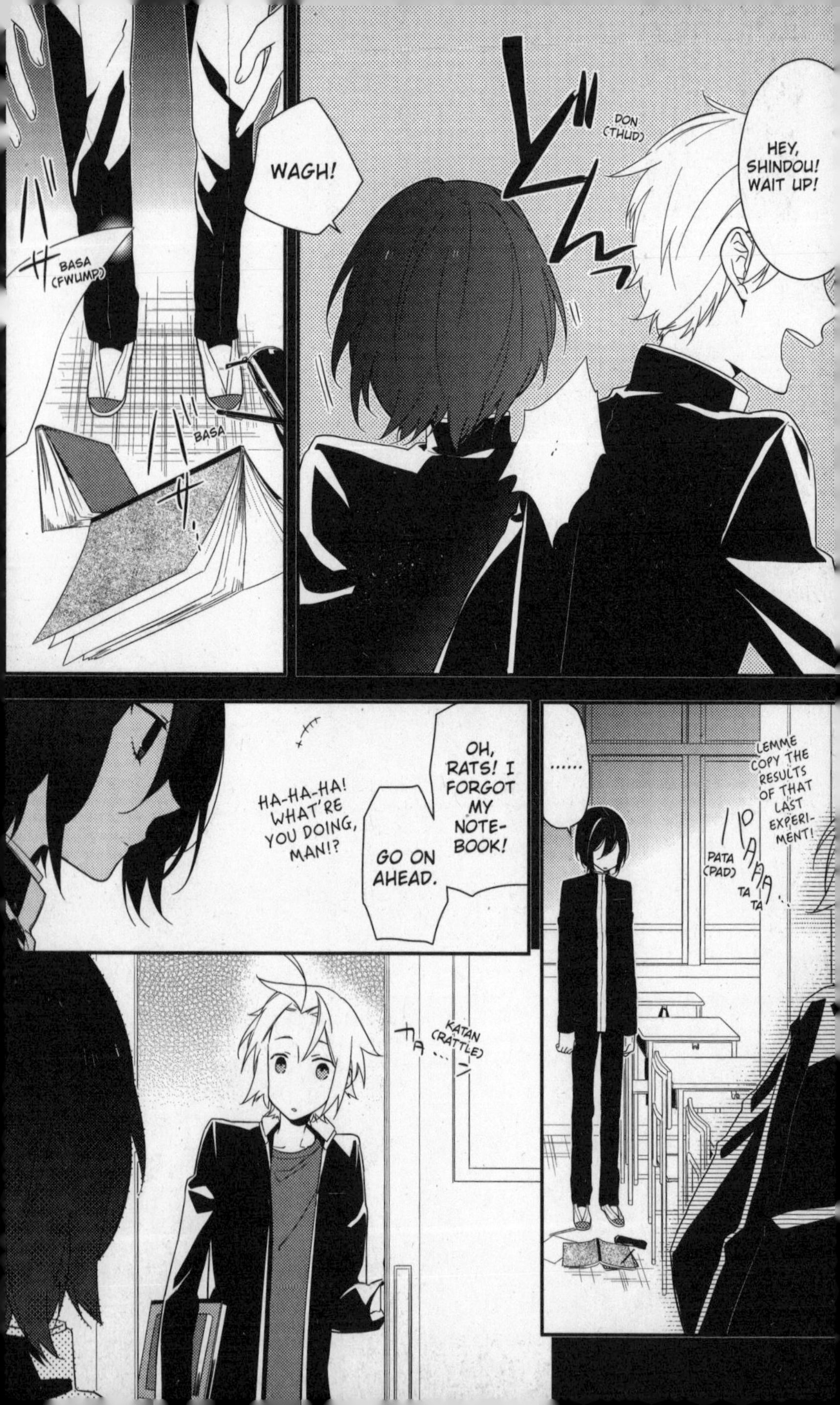

HEY, SHINDOU! WAIT UP!
DON (THUD)
WAGH!
BASA (FWUMP)
BASA
LEMME COPY THE RESULTS OF THAT LAST EXPERI-MENT!
......
PATA (PAD)
TA TA
OH, RATS! I FORGOT MY NOTE-BOOK!
GO ON AHEAD.
HA-HA-HA! WHAT'RE YOU DOING, MAN!?
KATAN (RATTLE)

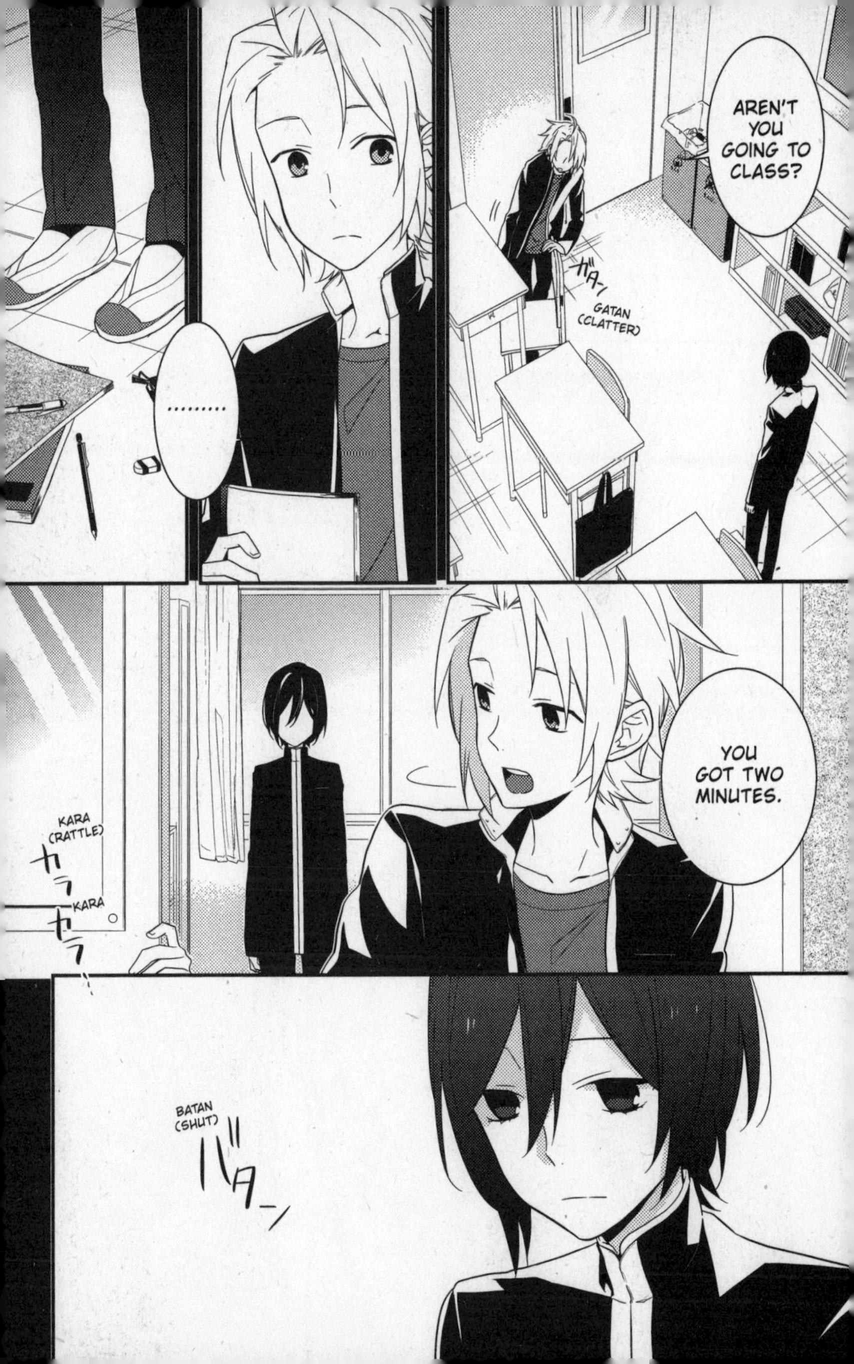
AREN'T YOU GOING TO CLASS?
ガターン
GATAN (CLATTER)
....
YOU GOT TWO MINUTES.
KARA (RATTLE)
カラ
KARA
カラ…
BATAN (SHUT)
バターン

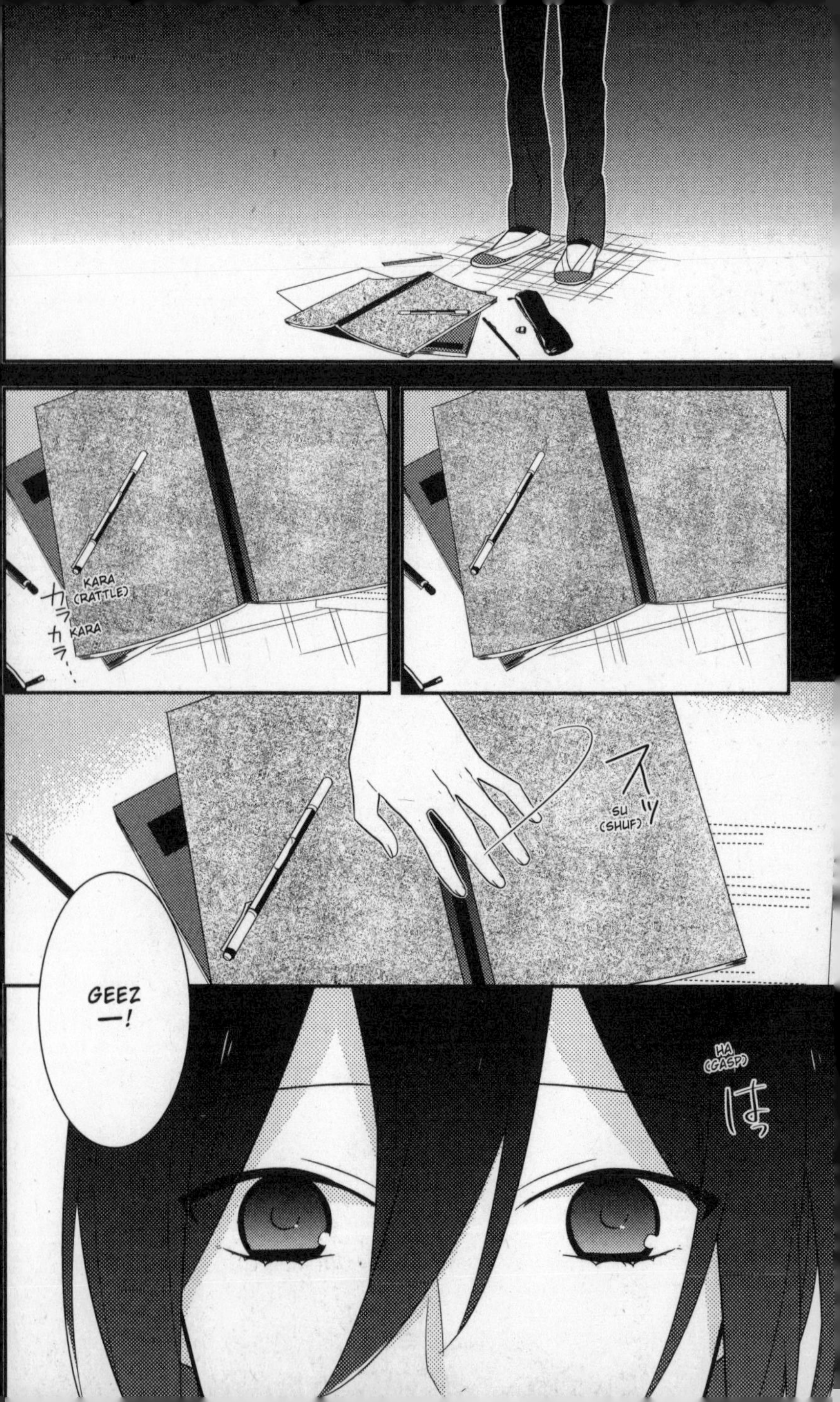
KARA (RATTLE)
カラ
KARA
カラ…
SU (SHUF)
スッ
GEEZ ー!
HA (GASP)
はっ

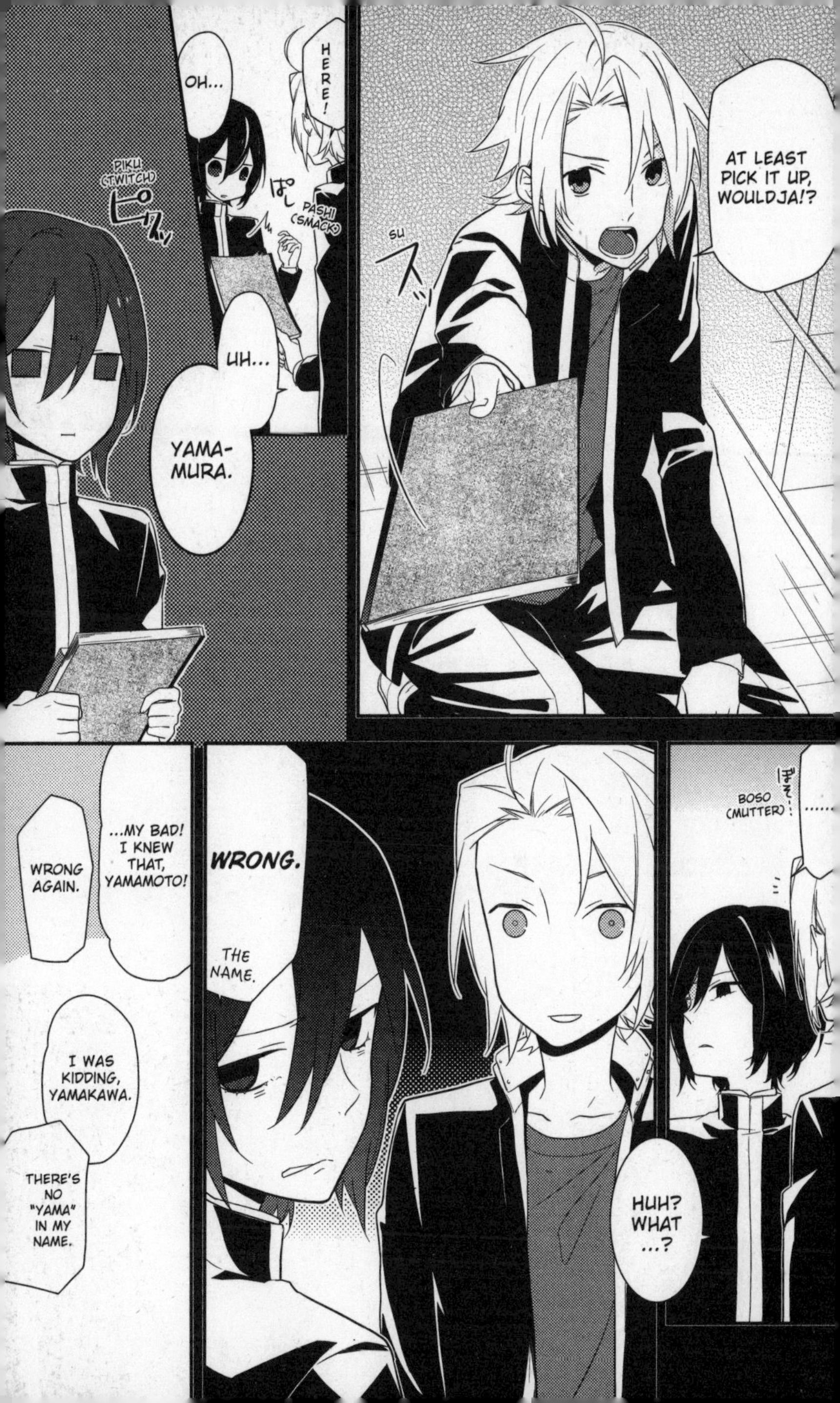
AT LEAST PICK IT UP, WOULDJA!?
SU
ス
HERE!
OH...
ぱし
PASHI (SMACK)
PIKU (TWITCH)
ピクッ
UH...
YAMA-MURA.
ぼそ
BOSO (MUTTER)
......
WRONG.
THE NAME.
HUH? WHAT ...?
...MY BAD! I KNEW THAT, YAMAMOTO!
WRONG AGAIN.
I WAS KIDDING, YAMAKAWA.
THERE'S NO "YAMA" IN MY NAME.

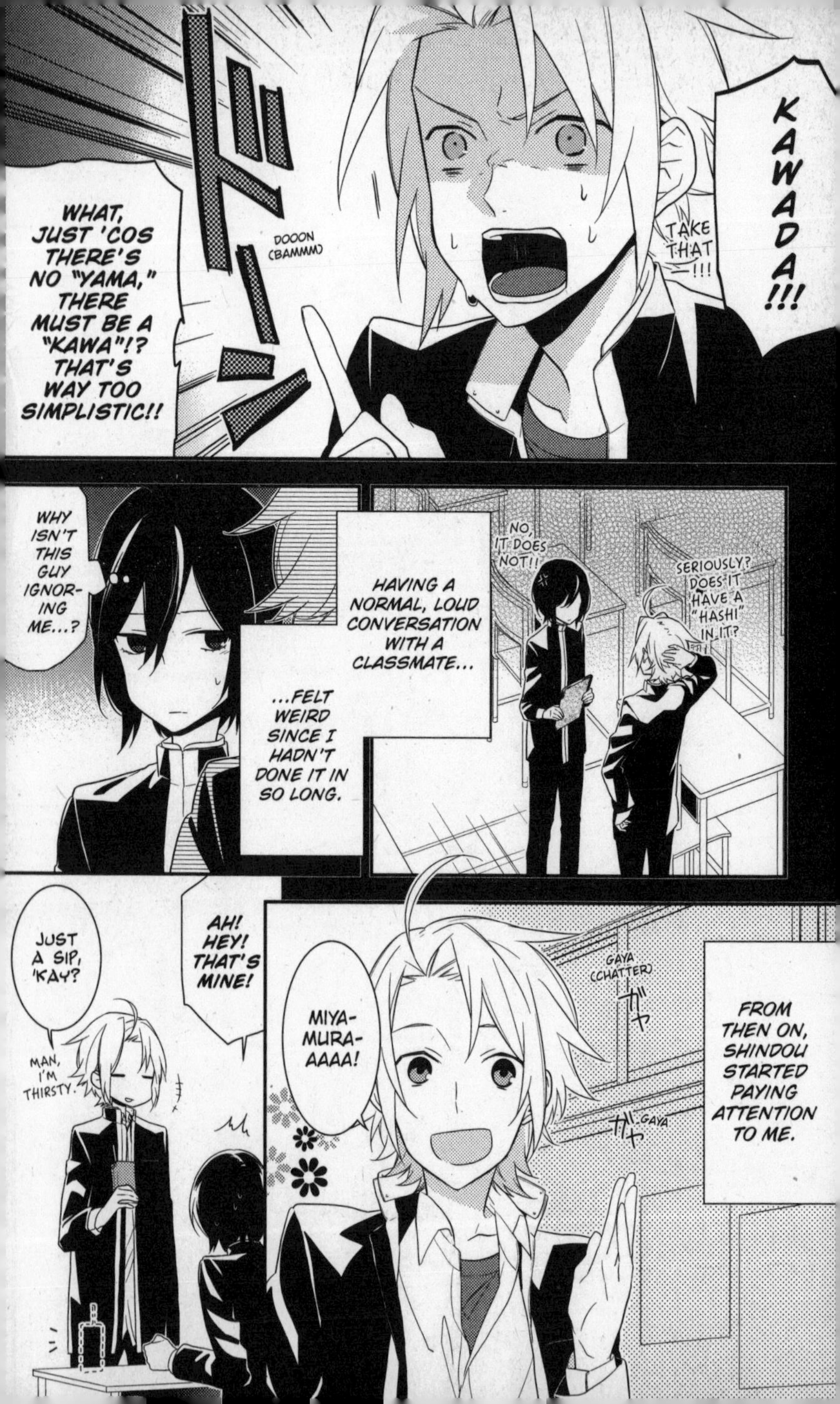
KAWADA!!!
TAKE THAT!!!
DOOON (BAMMM)
WHAT, JUST 'COS THERE'S NO "YAMA," THERE MUST BE A "KAWA"!? THAT'S WAY TOO SIMPLISTIC!!
SERIOUSLY? DOES IT HAVE A "HASHI" IN IT?
NO, IT DOES NOT!!
HAVING A NORMAL, LOUD CONVERSATION WITH A CLASSMATE...
...FELT WEIRD SINCE I HADN'T DONE IT IN SO LONG.
WHY ISN'T THIS GUY IGNORING ME...?
FROM THEN ON, SHINDOU STARTED PAYING ATTENTION TO ME.
GAYA (CHATTER)
GAYA
MIYA-MURA-AAAA!
AH! HEY! THAT'S MINE!
JUST A SIP, 'KAY?
MAN, I'M THIRSTY.

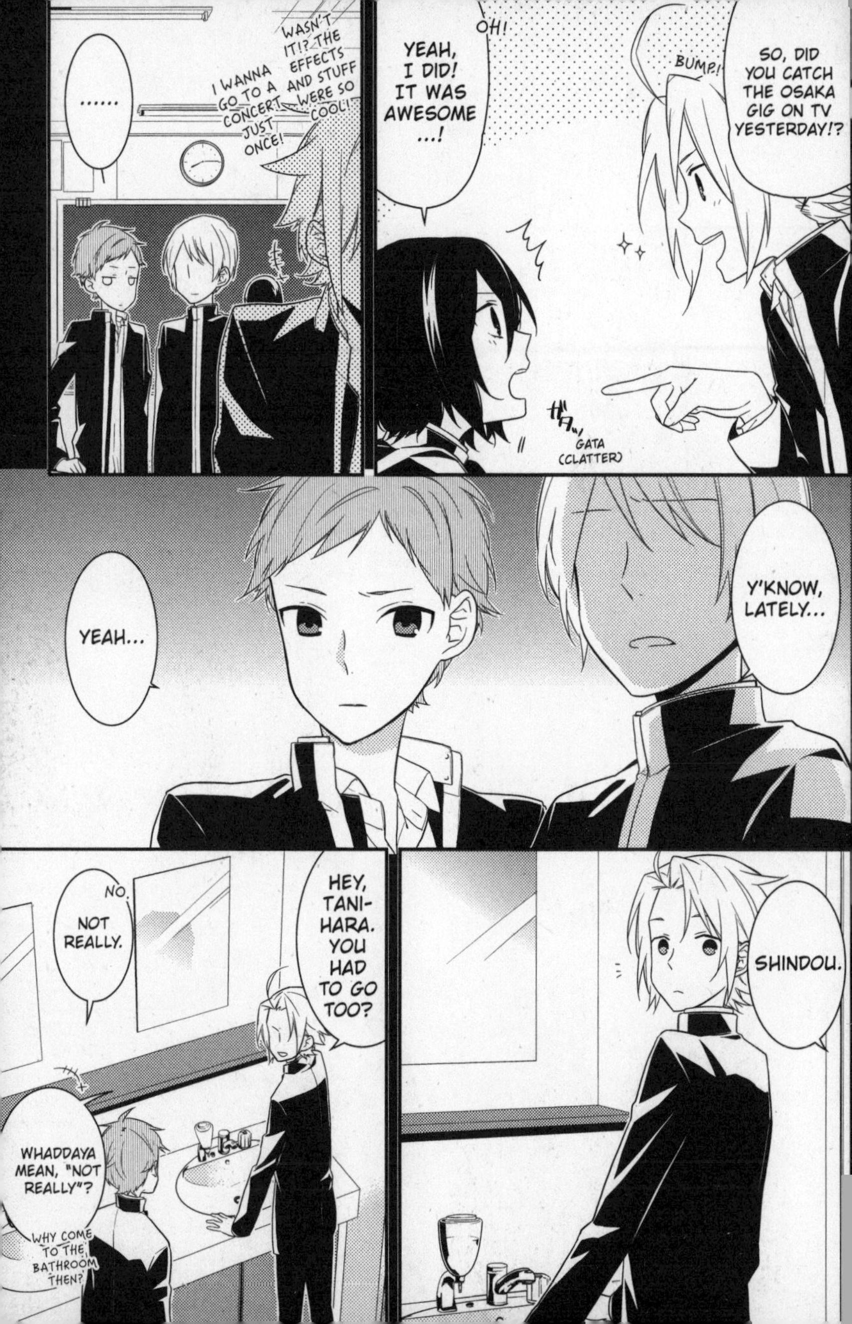
SO, DID YOU CATCH THE OSAKA GIG ON TV YESTERDAY!?
BUMP!
OH!
YEAH, I DID! IT WAS AWESOME ...!
ガタッ
GATA (CLATTER)
WASN'T IT!? THE EFFECTS AND STUFF WERE SO COOL!
I WANNA GO TO A CONCERT JUST ONCE!
......
Y'KNOW, LATELY...
YEAH...
SHINDOU.
HEY, TANI-HARA. YOU HAD TO GO TOO?
NO.
NOT REALLY.
WHADDAYA MEAN, "NOT REALLY"?
WHY COME TO THE BATHROOM THEN?

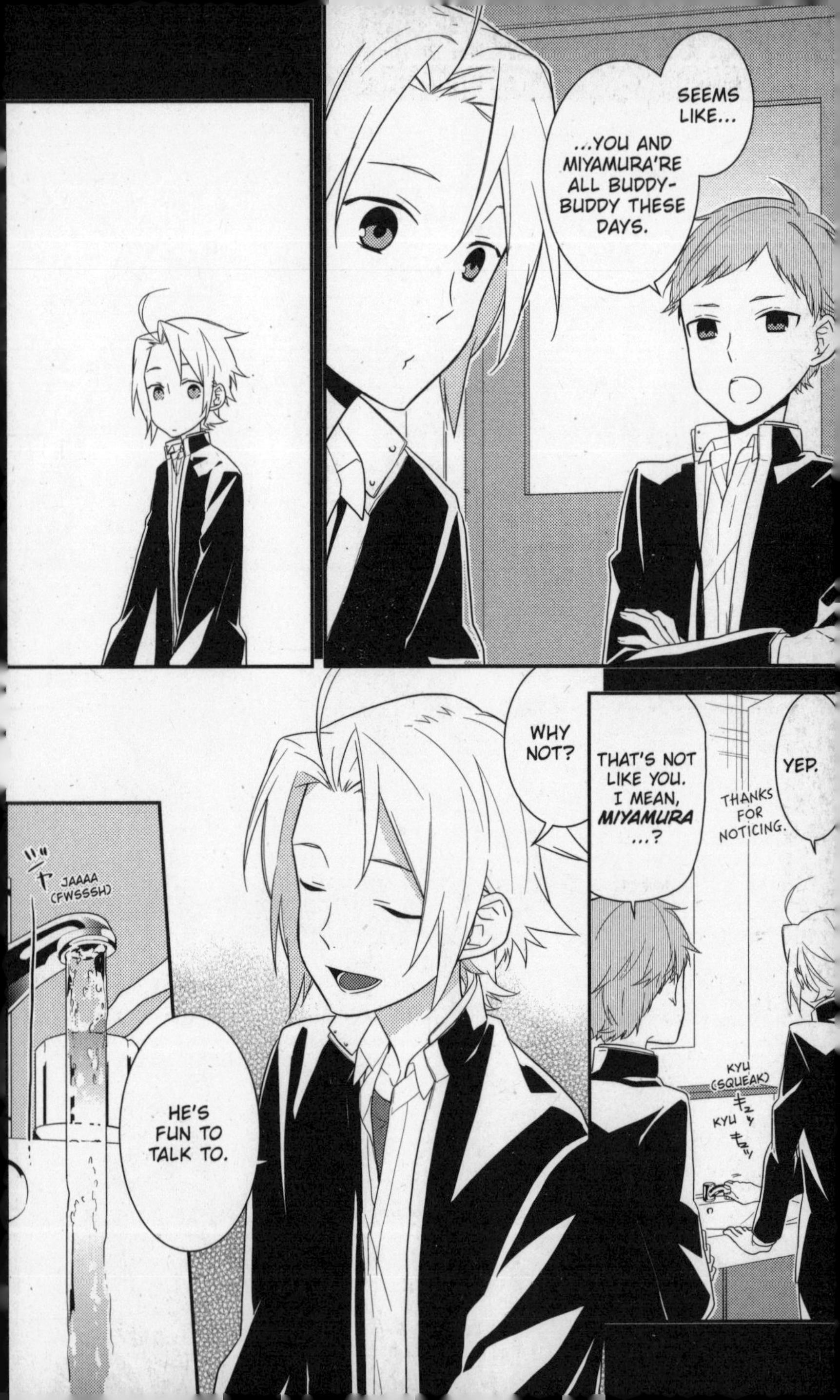
SEEMS LIKE...
...YOU AND MIYAMURA'RE ALL BUDDY-BUDDY THESE DAYS.
YEP.
THANKS FOR NOTICING.
THAT'S NOT LIKE YOU. I MEAN, *MIYAMURA* ...?
KYU (SQUEAK)
KYU
WHY NOT?
JAAAA (FWSSSH)
HE'S FUN TO TALK TO.

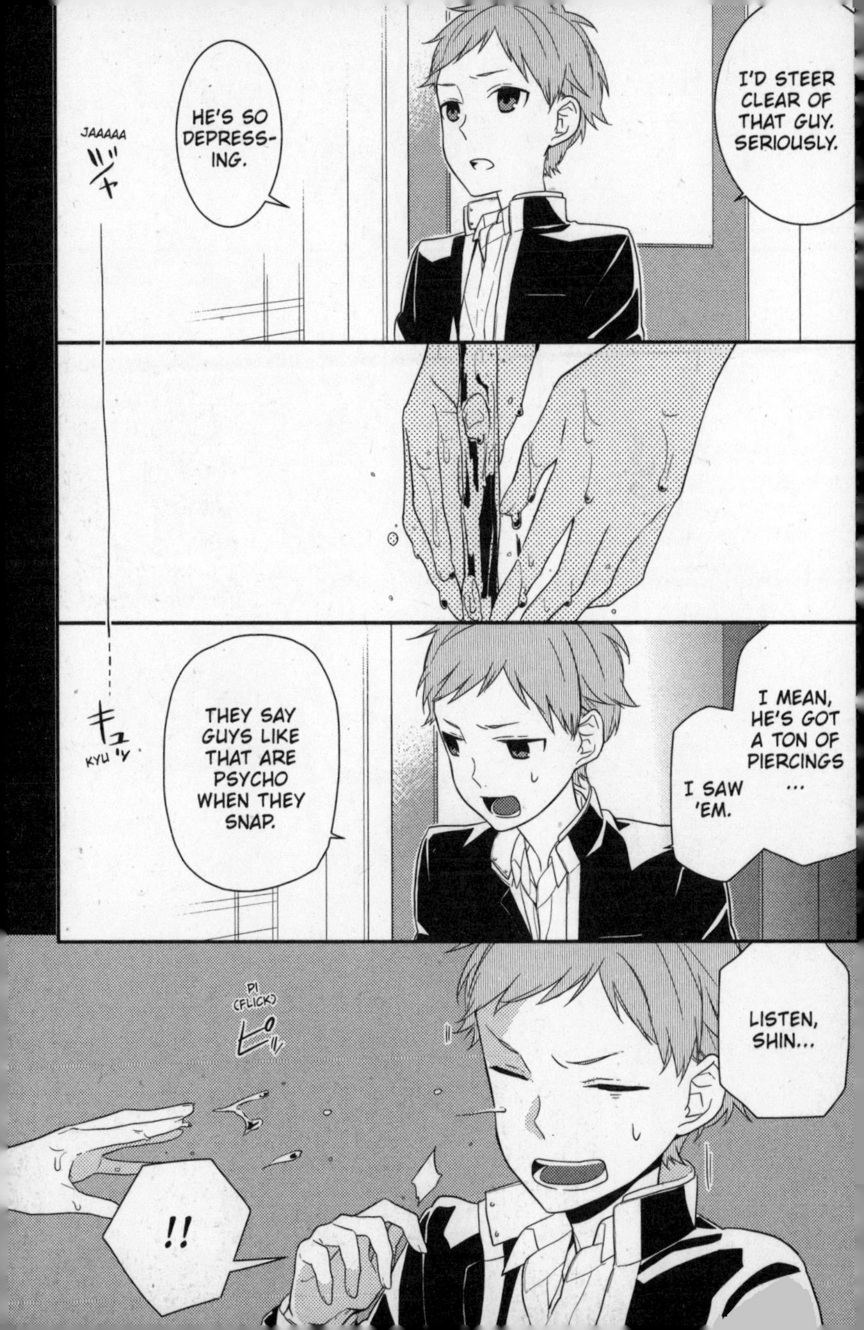

I'D STEER CLEAR OF THAT GUY. SERIOUSLY.
HE'S SO DEPRESS-ING.
JAAAAA
ジャ
I MEAN, HE'S GOT A TON OF PIERCINGS ...
I SAW 'EM.
THEY SAY GUYS LIKE THAT ARE PSYCHO WHEN THEY SNAP.
キュッ
KYU 'Y
LISTEN, SHIN...
PI (FLICK)
ピッ
!!

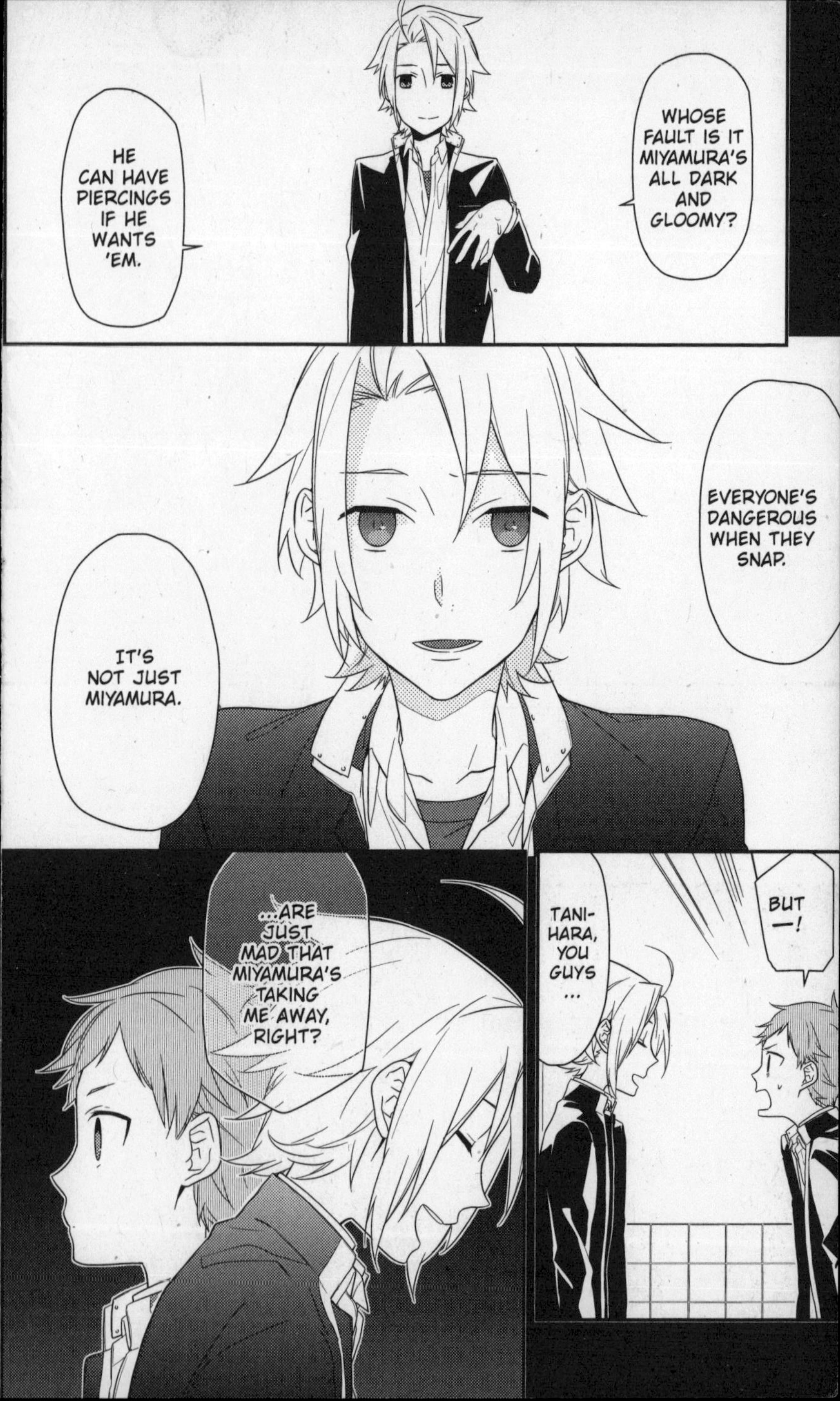
WHOSE FAULT IS IT MIYAMURA'S ALL DARK AND GLOOMY?
HE CAN HAVE PIERCINGS IF HE WANTS 'EM.
EVERYONE'S DANGEROUS WHEN THEY SNAP.
IT'S NOT JUST MIYAMURA.
BUT—!
TANI-HARA, YOU GUYS...
...ARE JUST MAD THAT MIYAMURA'S TAKING ME AWAY, RIGHT?

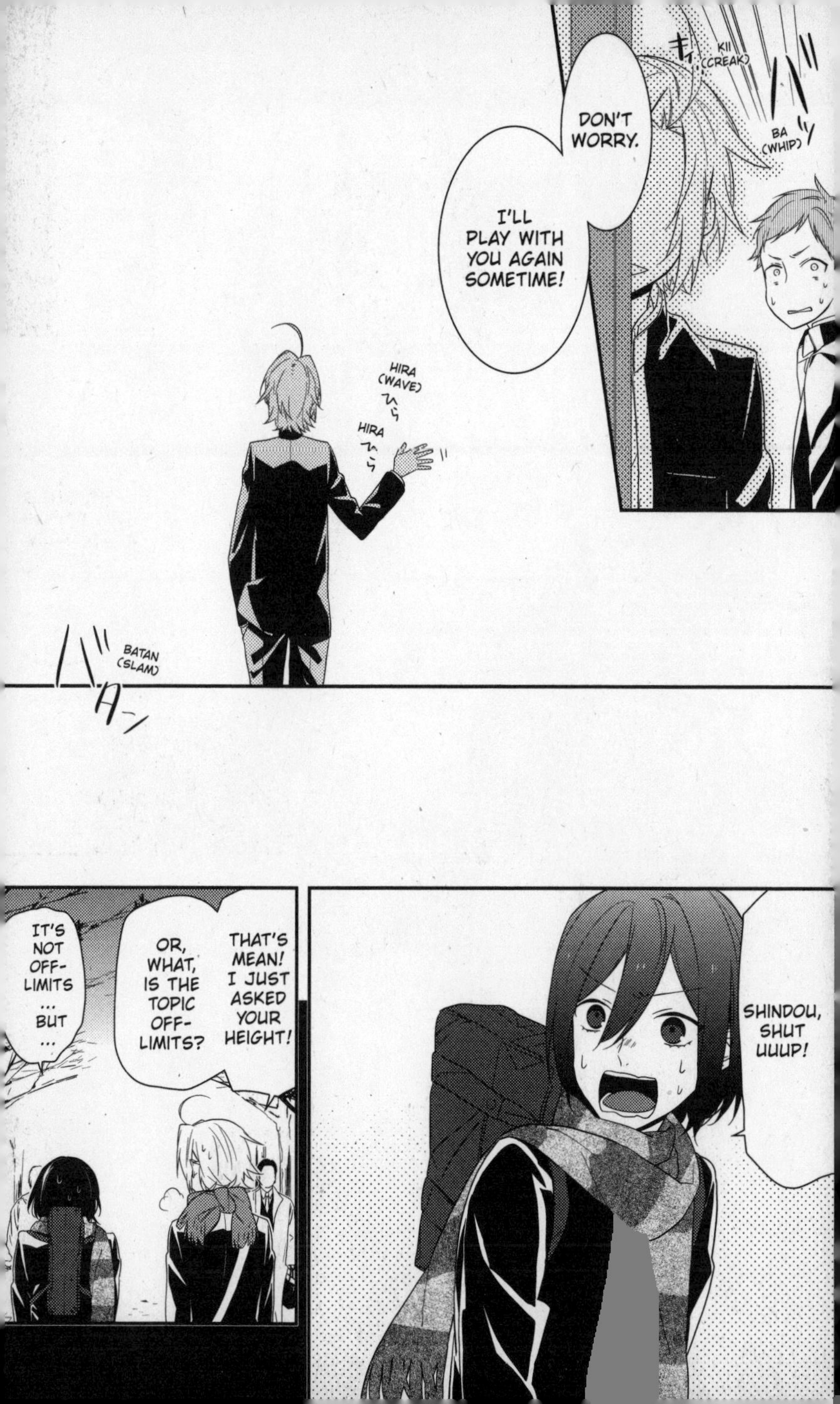
KII (CREAK)
BA (WHIP)
DON'T WORRY.
I'LL PLAY WITH YOU AGAIN SOMETIME!
HIRA (WAVE)
HIRA
BATAN (SLAM)
SHINDOU, SHUT UUUP!
THAT'S MEAN! I JUST ASKED YOUR HEIGHT!
OR, WHAT, IS THE TOPIC OFF-LIMITS?
IT'S NOT OFF-LIMITS ... BUT ...

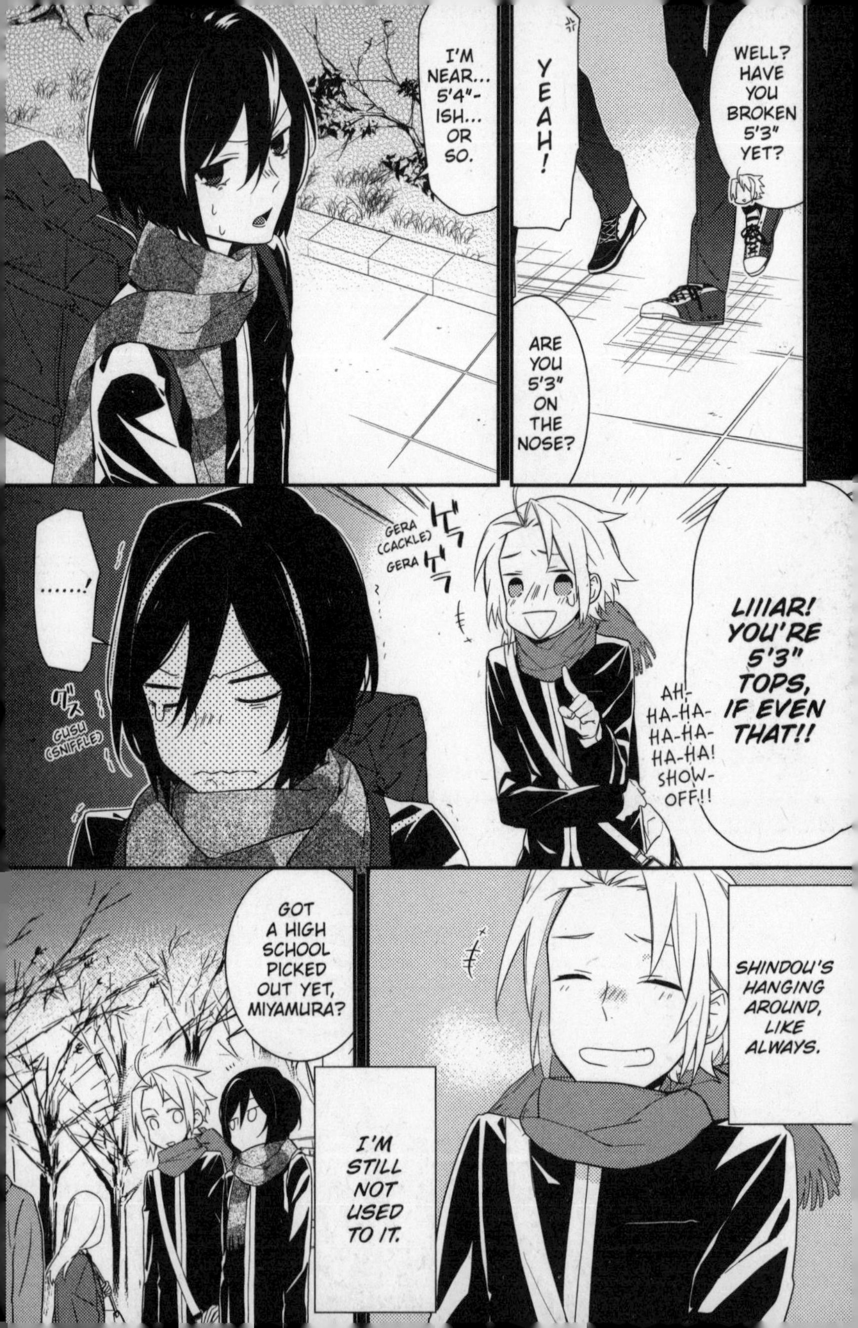
WELL? HAVE YOU BROKEN 5'3" YET?
YEAH!
ARE YOU 5'3" ON THE NOSE?
I'M NEAR... 5'4"-ISH... OR SO.
LIIIAR! YOU'RE 5'3" TOPS, IF EVEN THAT!!
AH-HA-HA-HA-HA-HA-HA! SHOW-OFF!!
ゲラ ゲラ
GERA (CACKLE) GERA
......!
グス
GUSU (SNIFFLE)
SHINDOU'S HANGING AROUND, LIKE ALWAYS.
GOT A HIGH SCHOOL PICKED OUT YET, MIYAMURA?
I'M STILL NOT USED TO IT.

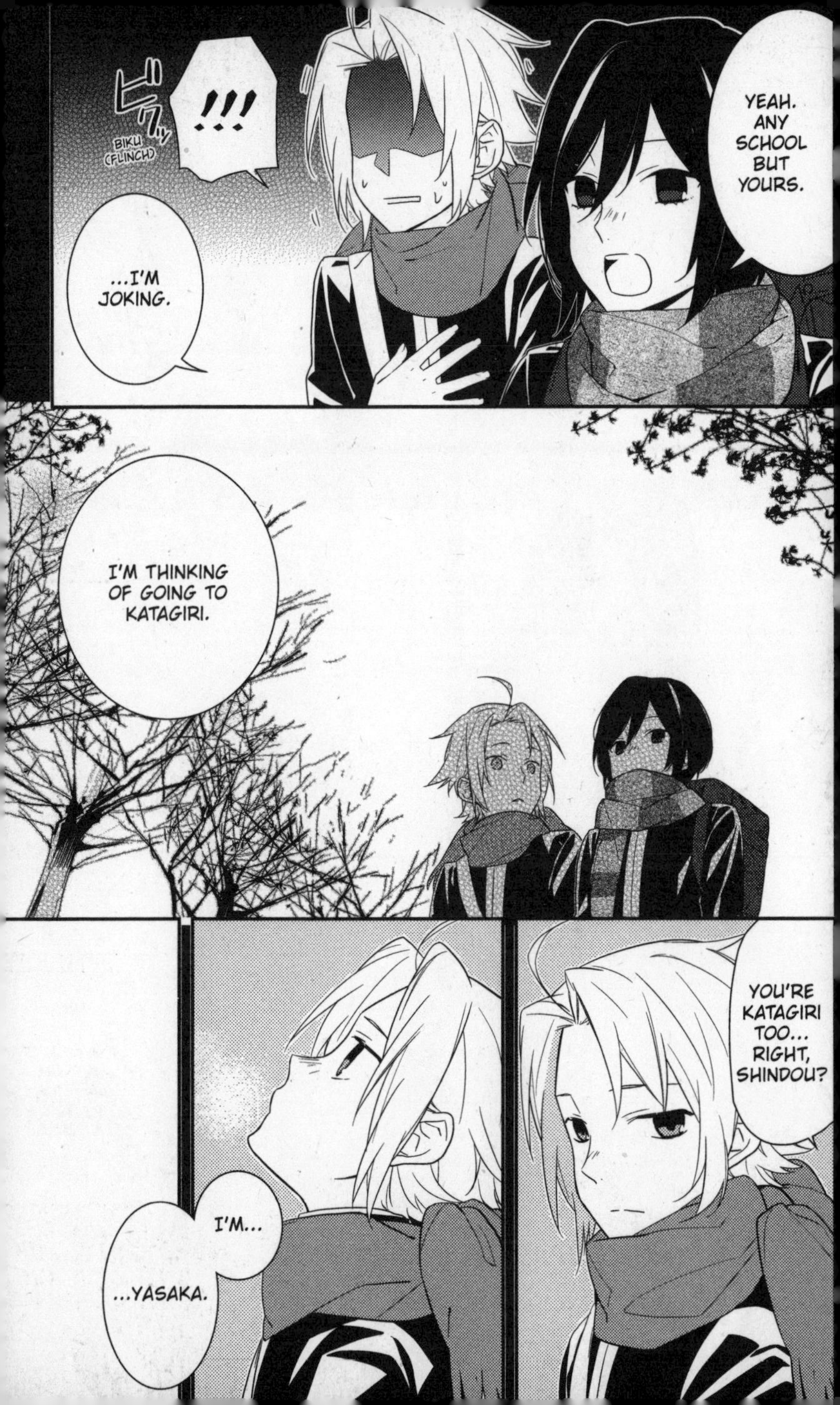
YEAH. ANY SCHOOL BUT YOURS.
BIKU (FLINCH)
!!!
...I'M JOKING.
I'M THINKING OF GOING TO KATAGIRI.
YOU'RE KATAGIRI TOO... RIGHT, SHINDOU?
I'M...
...YASAKA.

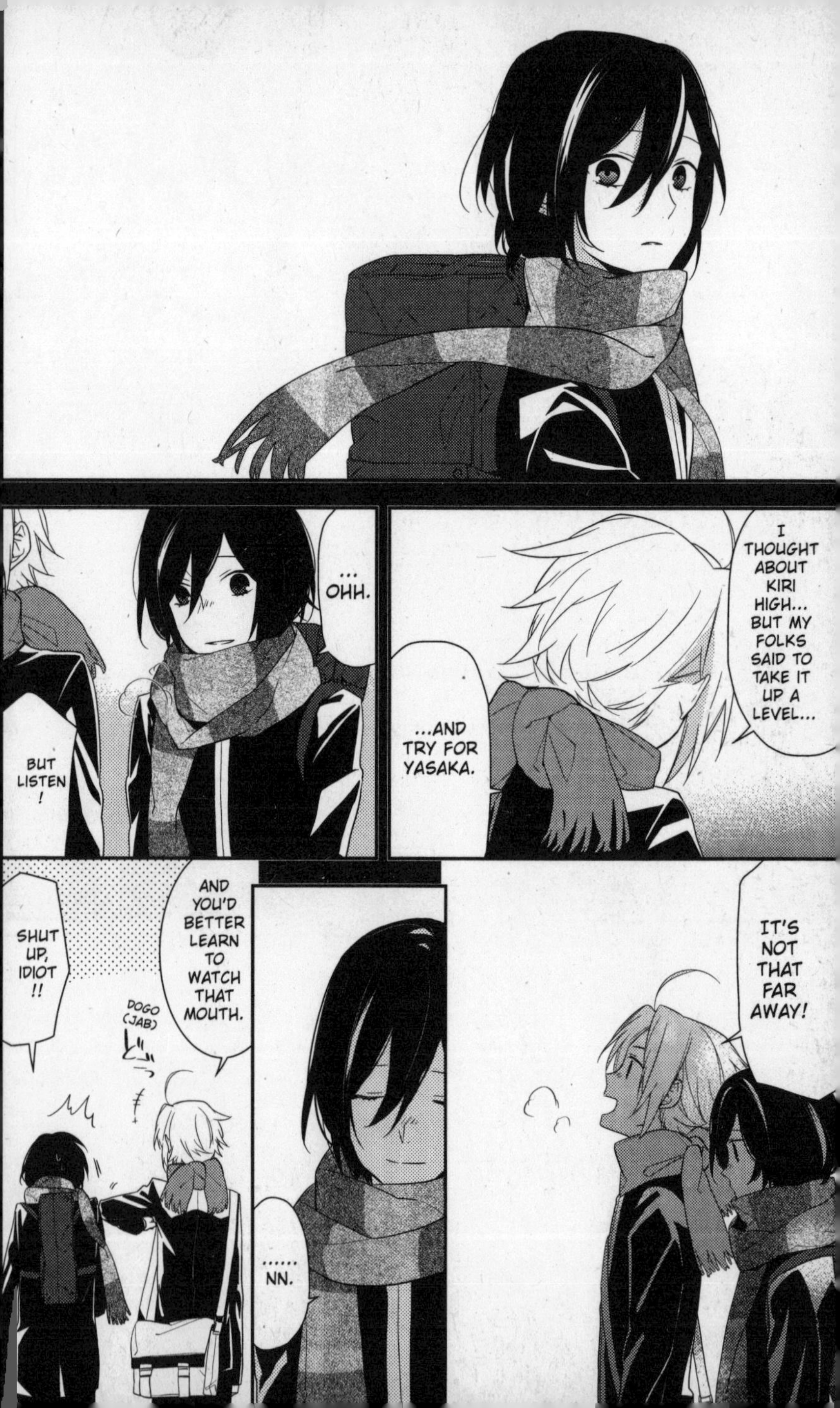
I THOUGHT ABOUT KIRI HIGH... BUT MY FOLKS SAID TO TAKE IT UP A LEVEL...
...AND TRY FOR YASAKA.
...OHH.
BUT LISTEN!
IT'S NOT THAT FAR AWAY!
......NN.
AND YOU'D BETTER LEARN TO WATCH THAT MOUTH.
SHUT UP, IDIOT!!
DOGO (JAB)

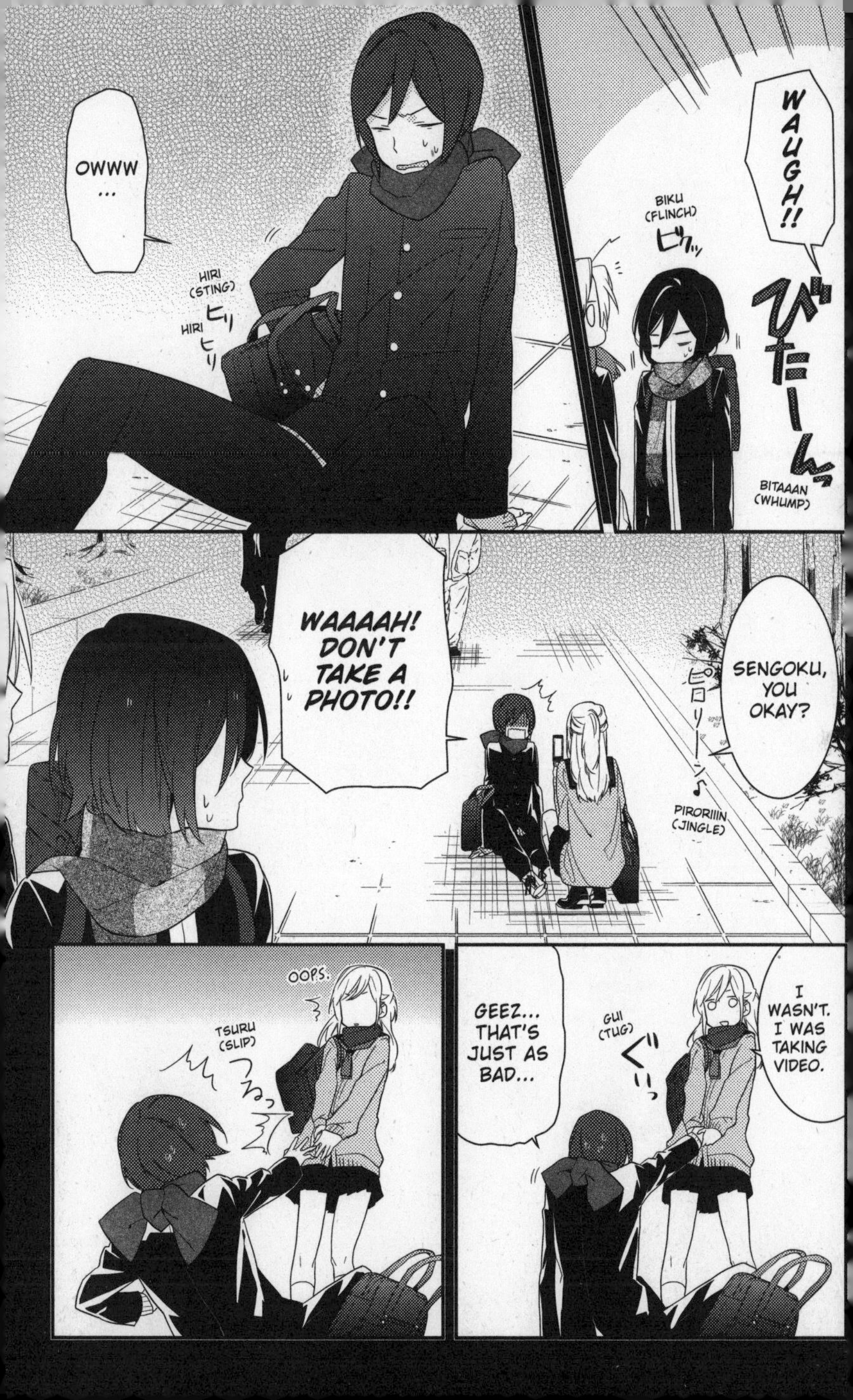
WAUGH!!
BIKU (FLINCH)
ビクッ
びたーん
BITAAAN (WHUMP)
OWWW...
HIRI (STING)
ヒリ
HIRI
ヒリ
SENGOKU, YOU OKAY?
ピロリーン♪
PIRORIIIN (JINGLE)
WAAAAH! DON'T TAKE A PHOTO!!
I WASN'T. I WAS TAKING VIDEO.
ぐいっ
GUI (TUG)
GEEZ... THAT'S JUST AS BAD...
OOPS.
TSURU (SLIP)
つるっ

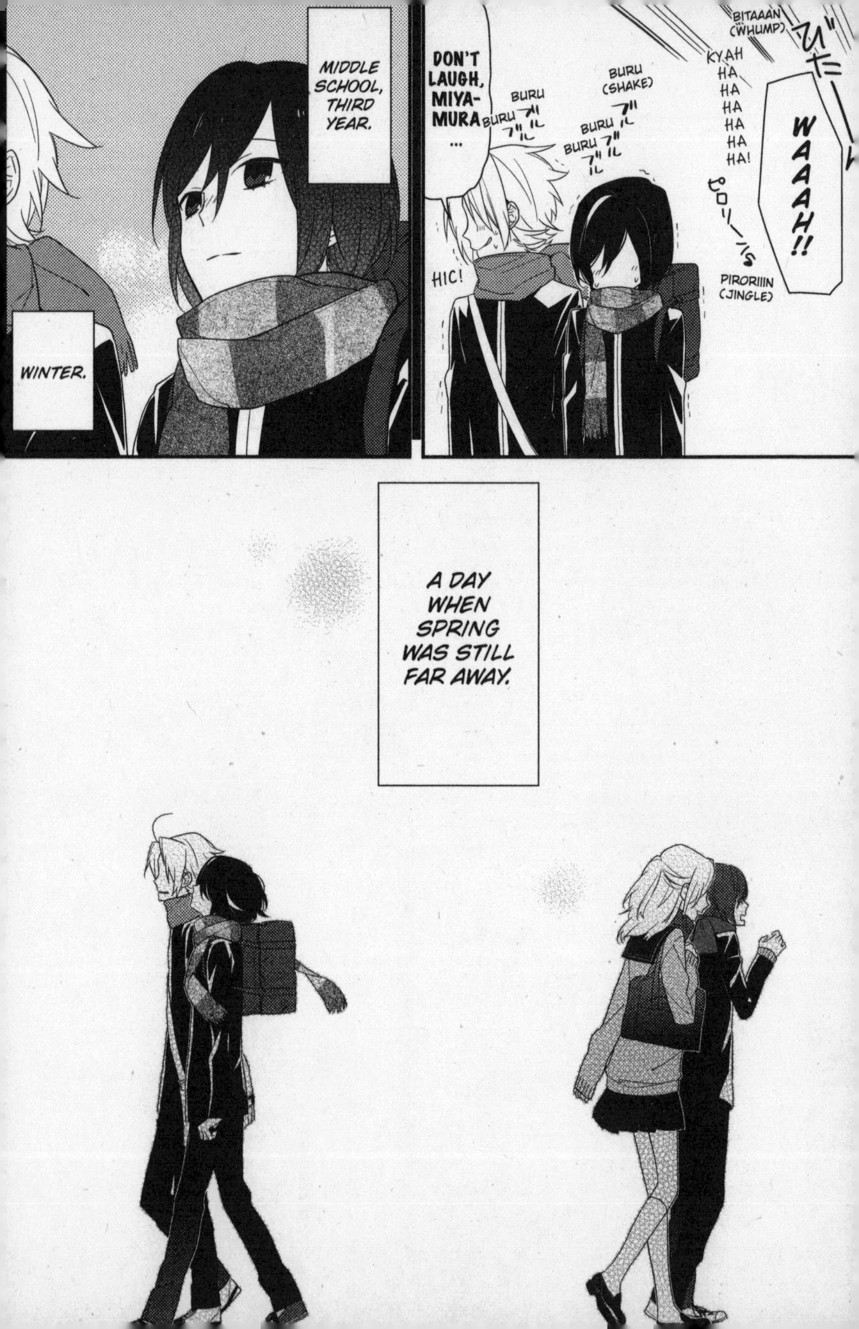
BITAAAN (WHUMP)
WAAAAH!!
KYAH HA HA HA HA HA HA!
PIRORIIIN (JINGLE)
BURU (SHAKE)
BURU BURU
BURU BURU
DON'T LAUGH, MIYAMURA...
HIC!
MIDDLE SCHOOL, THIRD YEAR.
WINTER.
A DAY WHEN SPRING WAS STILL FAR AWAY.

HORIMIYA

HORIMIYA

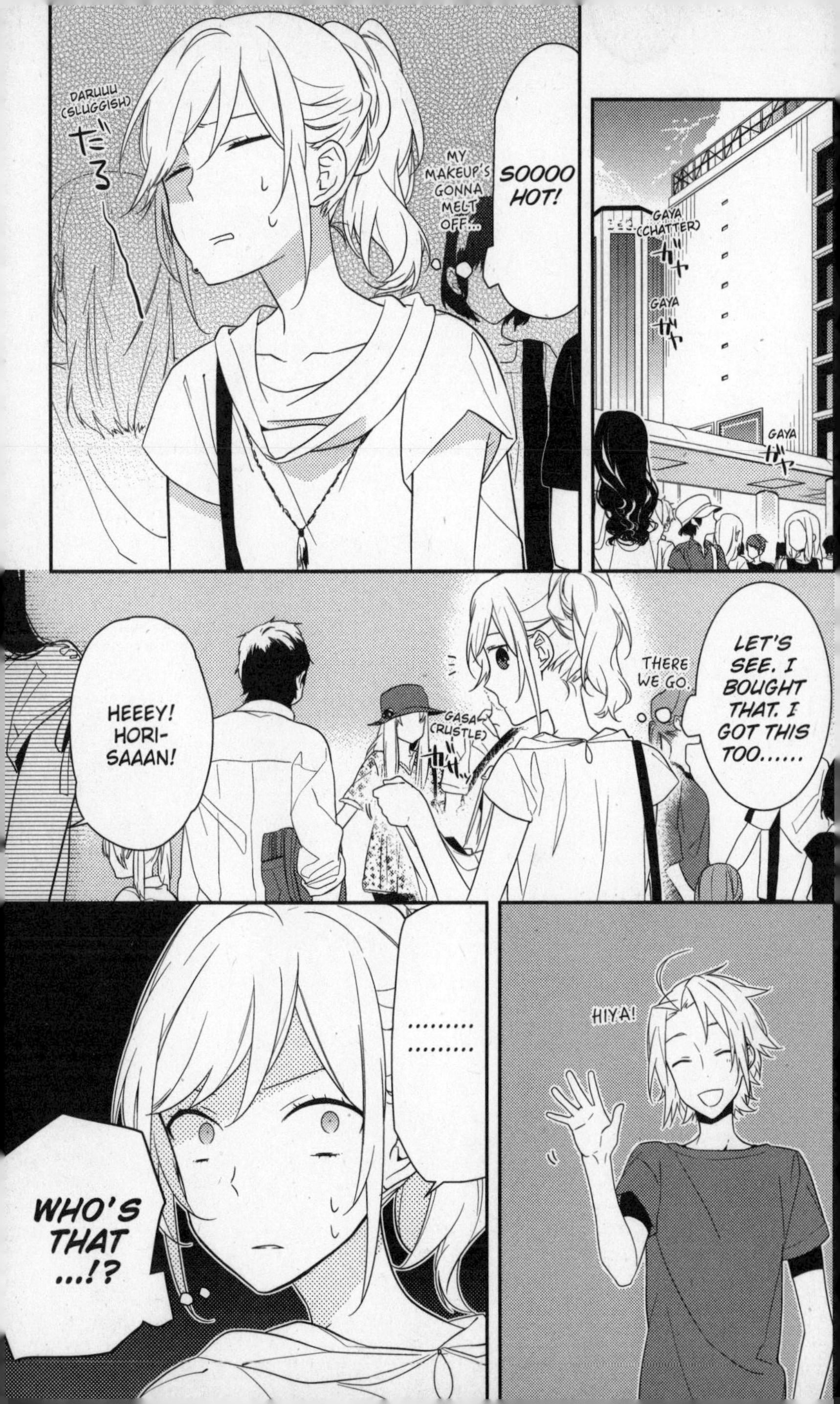
GAYA (CHATTER)
ガヤ
GAYA
ガヤ
GAYA
ガヤ
SOOOO HOT!
MY MAKEUP'S GONNA MELT OFF...
DARUUU (SLUGGISH)
だる
LET'S SEE. I BOUGHT THAT. I GOT THIS TOO......
THERE WE GO.
GASA (RUSTLE)
ガサ…
HEEEY! HORI-SAAAN!
HIYA!
....
....
WHO'S THAT ...!?

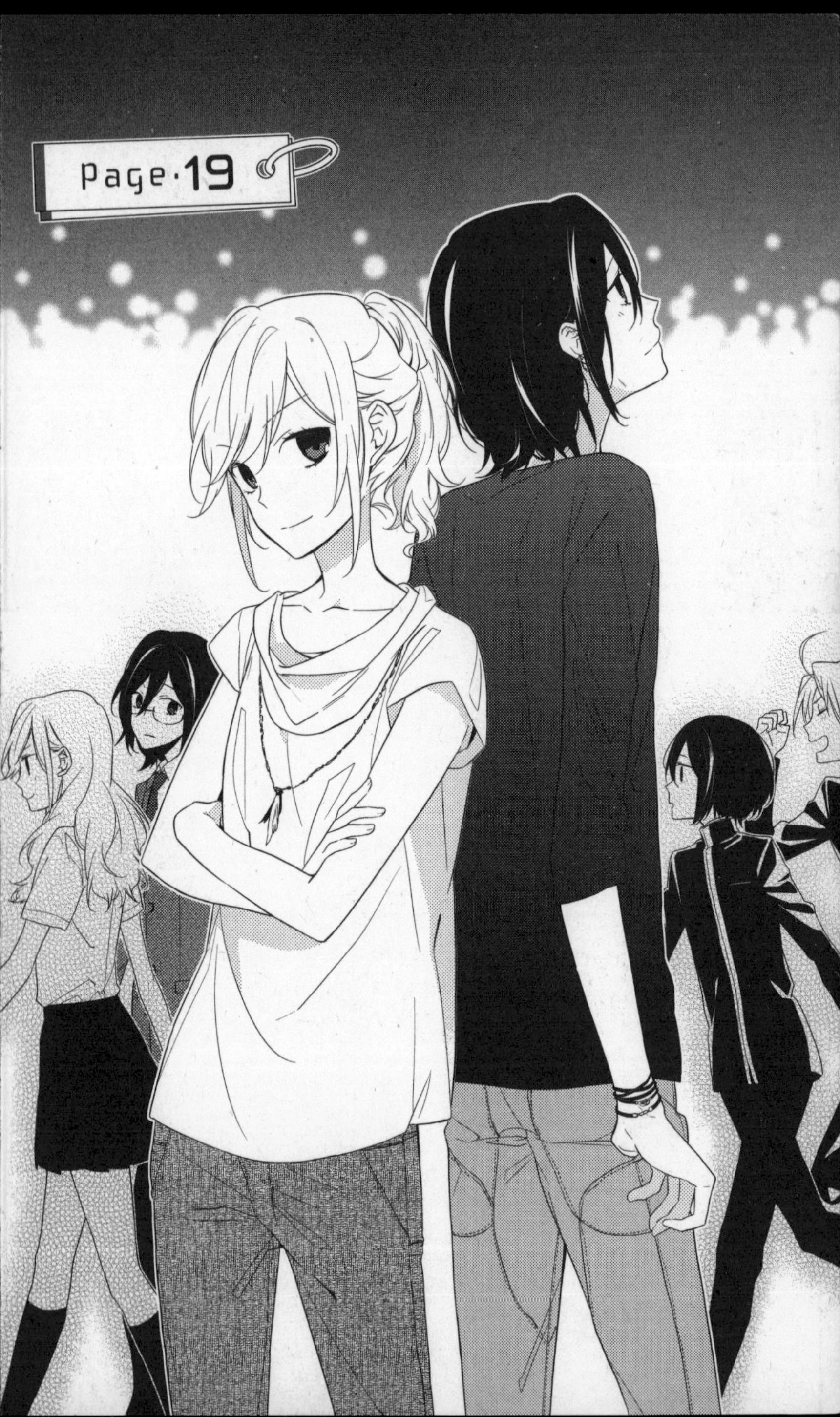
Page·19

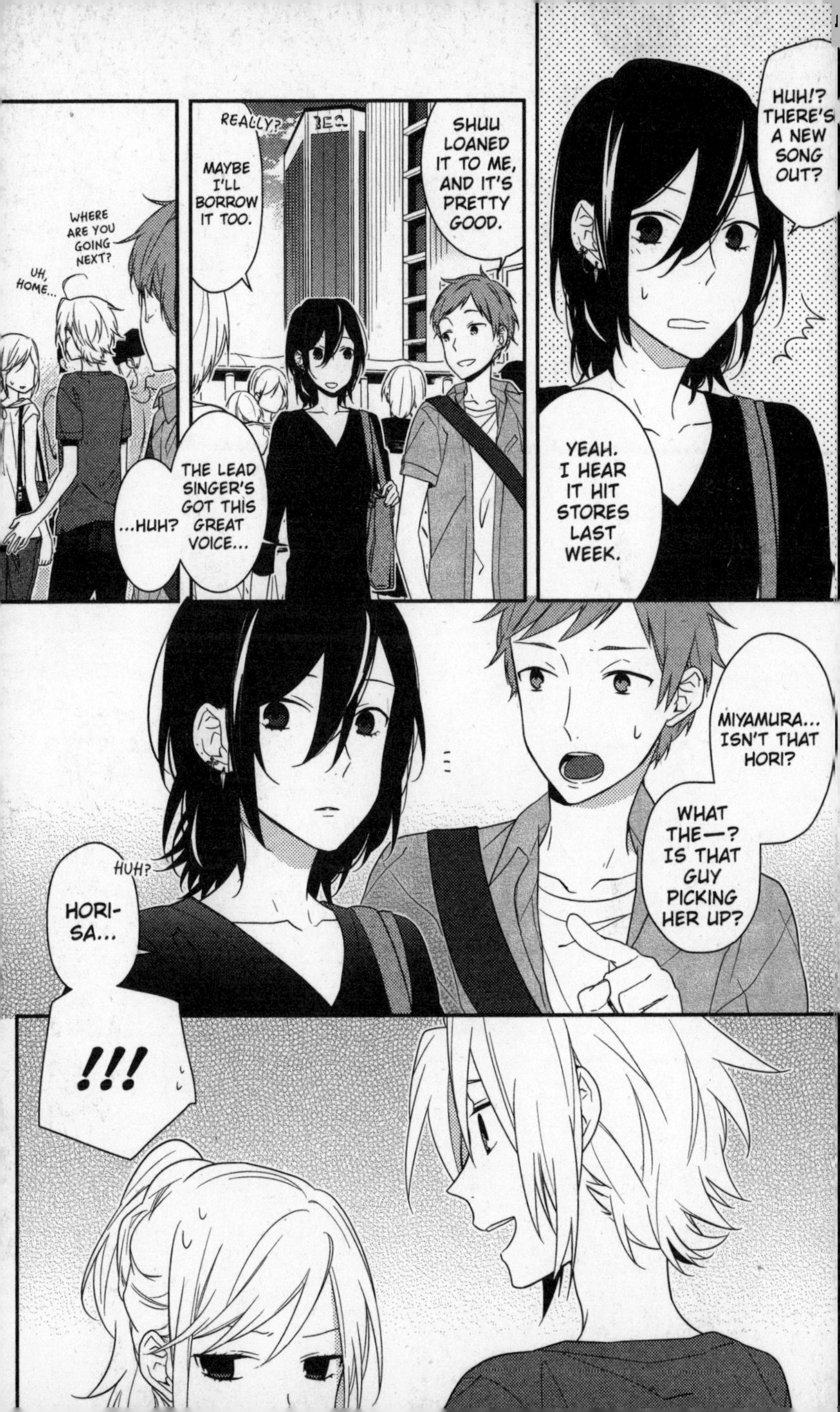
HUH!? THERE'S A NEW SONG OUT?
YEAH. I HEAR IT HIT STORES LAST WEEK.
SHUU LOANED IT TO ME, AND IT'S PRETTY GOOD.
REALLY?
MAYBE I'LL BORROW IT TOO.
THE LEAD SINGER'S GOT THIS GREAT VOICE...
...HUH?
WHERE ARE YOU GOING NEXT?
UH, HOME...
MIYAMURA... ISN'T THAT HORI?
WHAT THE—? IS THAT GUY PICKING HER UP?
HUH?
HORI-SA...
!!!

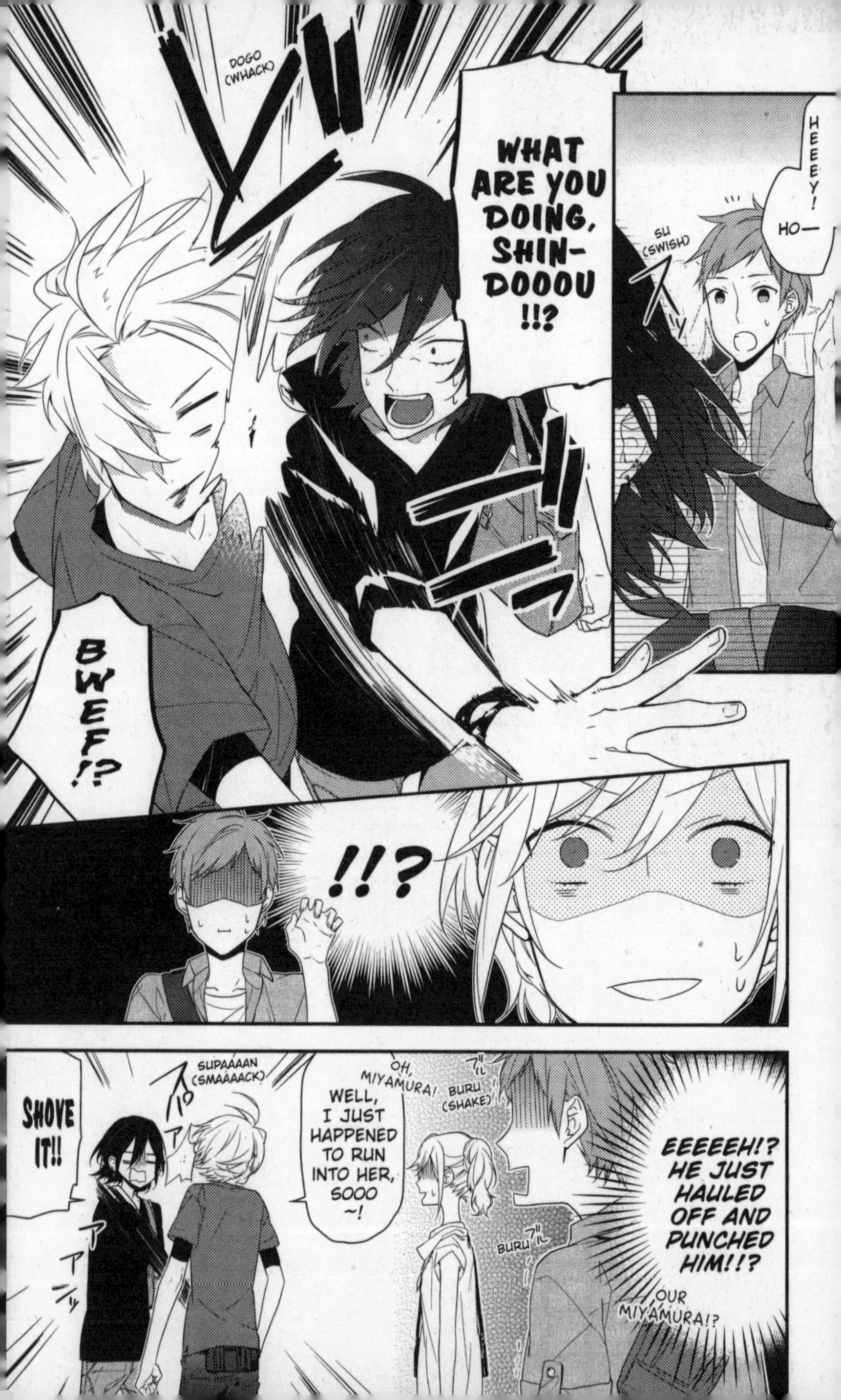
HEEEY! HO—
SU (SWISH)
WHAT ARE YOU DOING, SHIN-DOOOU!!?
DOGO (WHACK)
BWEF!?
!!?
EEEEEH!? HE JUST HAULED OFF AND PUNCHED HIM!!?
OUR MIYAMURA!?
BURU (SHAKE)
BURU
OH, MIYAMURA!
WELL, I JUST HAPPENED TO RUN INTO HER, SOOO ~!
SUPAAAAN (SMAAAACK)
SHOVE IT!!

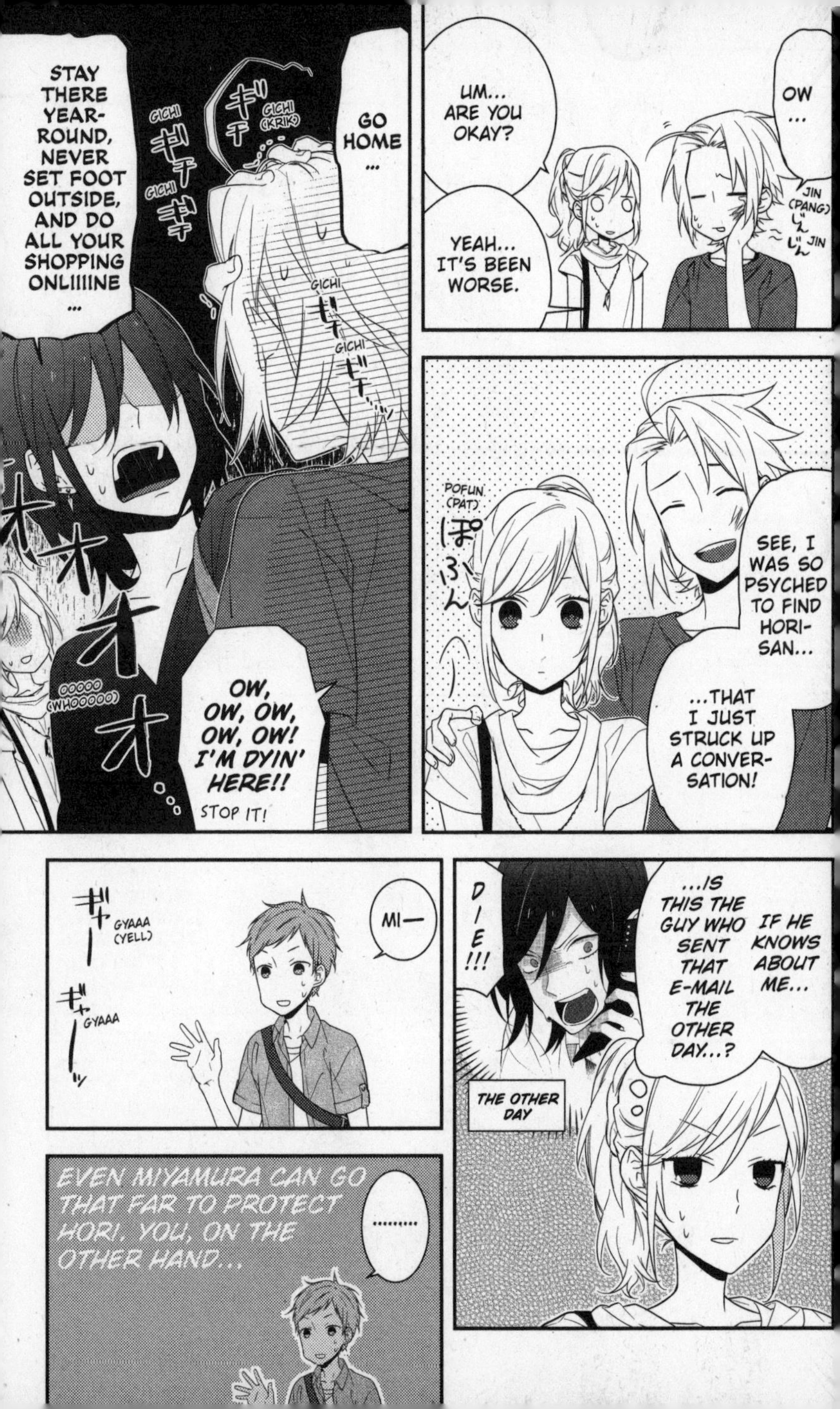
OW ...
JIN (PANG) じんじん JIN
UM... ARE YOU OKAY?
YEAH... IT'S BEEN WORSE.
SEE, I WAS SO PSYCHED TO FIND HORI-SAN...
POFUN (PAT) ぽふん
...THAT I JUST STRUCK UP A CONVERSATION!
GO HOME ...
GICHI (KRIK) ギチ
GICHI ギチ GICHI ギチ
STAY THERE YEAR-ROUND, NEVER SET FOOT OUTSIDE, AND DO ALL YOUR SHOPPING ONLIIIINE ...
GICHI GICHI
OW, OW, OW, OW, OW! I'M DYIN' HERE!!
OOOOO (WHOOOOO) オオオオ
STOP IT!
IF HE KNOWS ABOUT ME...
...IS THIS THE GUY WHO SENT THAT E-MAIL THE OTHER DAY...?
D-I-E!!!
THE OTHER DAY
MI—
GYAAA (YELL)
GYAAA
....
EVEN MIYAMURA CAN GO THAT FAR TO PROTECT HORI. YOU, ON THE OTHER HAND...

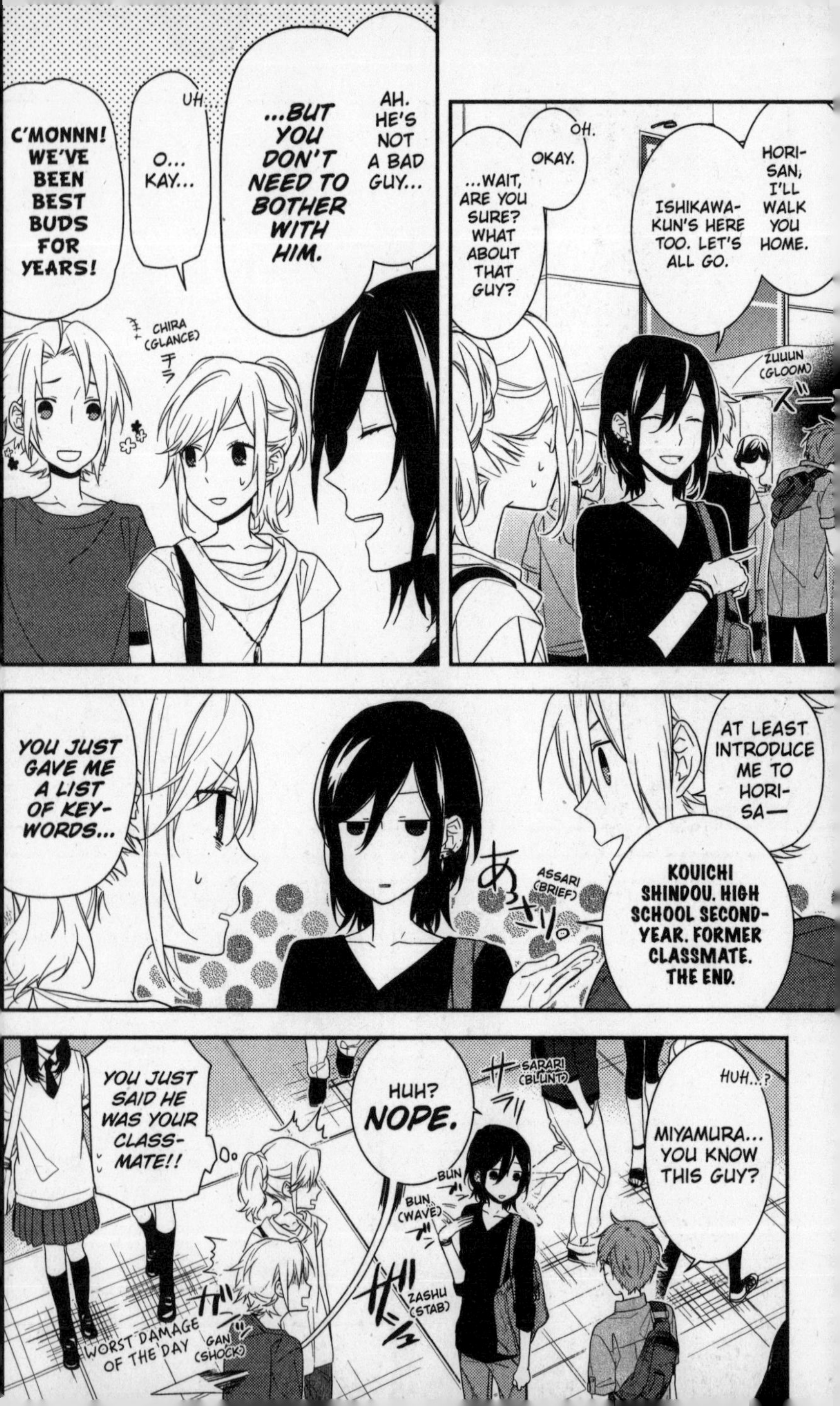
HORI-SAN, I'LL WALK YOU HOME.
ISHIKAWA-KUN'S HERE TOO. LET'S ALL GO.
ZUUUN (GLOOM)
OH.
OKAY.
...WAIT, ARE YOU SURE? WHAT ABOUT THAT GUY?
AH. HE'S NOT A BAD GUY...
...BUT YOU DON'T NEED TO BOTHER WITH HIM.
UH
O... KAY...
C'MONNN! WE'VE BEEN BEST BUDS FOR YEARS!
CHIRA (GLANCE)
AT LEAST INTRODUCE ME TO HORI-SA—
KOUICHI SHINDOU. HIGH SCHOOL SECOND-YEAR. FORMER CLASSMATE. THE END.
ASSARI (BRIEF)
YOU JUST GAVE ME A LIST OF KEY-WORDS...
HUH...?
MIYAMURA... YOU KNOW THIS GUY?
SARARI (BLUNT)
HUH? NOPE.
BUN BUN (WAVE)
ZASHU (STAB)
YOU JUST SAID HE WAS YOUR CLASS-MATE!!
GAN (SHOCK)
WORST DAMAGE OF THE DAY

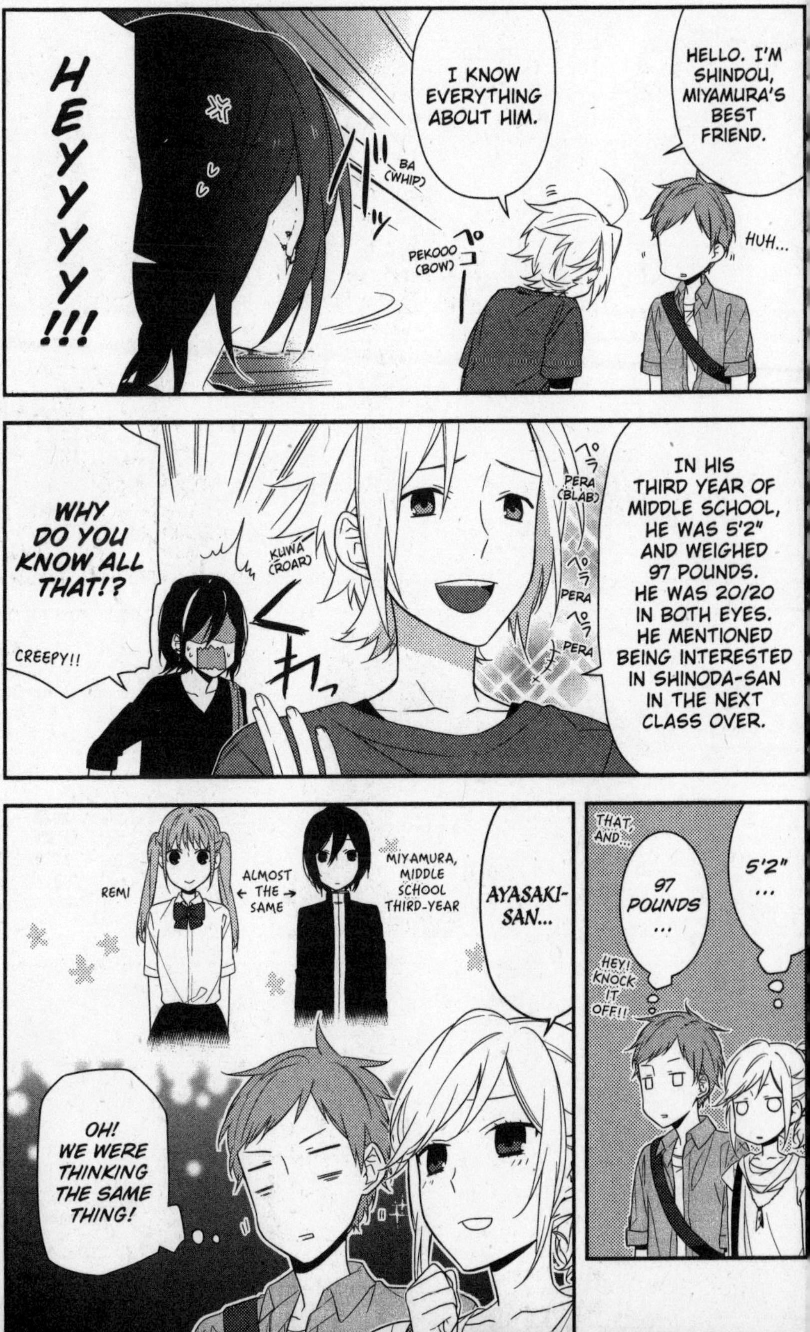
HELLO. I'M SHINDOU, MIYAMURA'S BEST FRIEND.
HUH...
I KNOW EVERYTHING ABOUT HIM.
PEKOOO (BOW)
BA (WHIP)
HEYYYY!!!
IN HIS THIRD YEAR OF MIDDLE SCHOOL, HE WAS 5'2" AND WEIGHED 97 POUNDS. HE WAS 20/20 IN BOTH EYES. HE MENTIONED BEING INTERESTED IN SHINODA-SAN IN THE NEXT CLASS OVER.
PERA (BLAB)
PERA
PERA
KUWA (ROAR)
WHY DO YOU KNOW ALL THAT!?
CREEPY!!
THAT, AND...
5'2"...
97 POUNDS...
HEY! KNOCK IT OFF!!
AYASAKI-SAN...
MIYAMURA, MIDDLE SCHOOL THIRD-YEAR
ALMOST THE SAME
REMI
OH! WE WERE THINKING THE SAME THING!

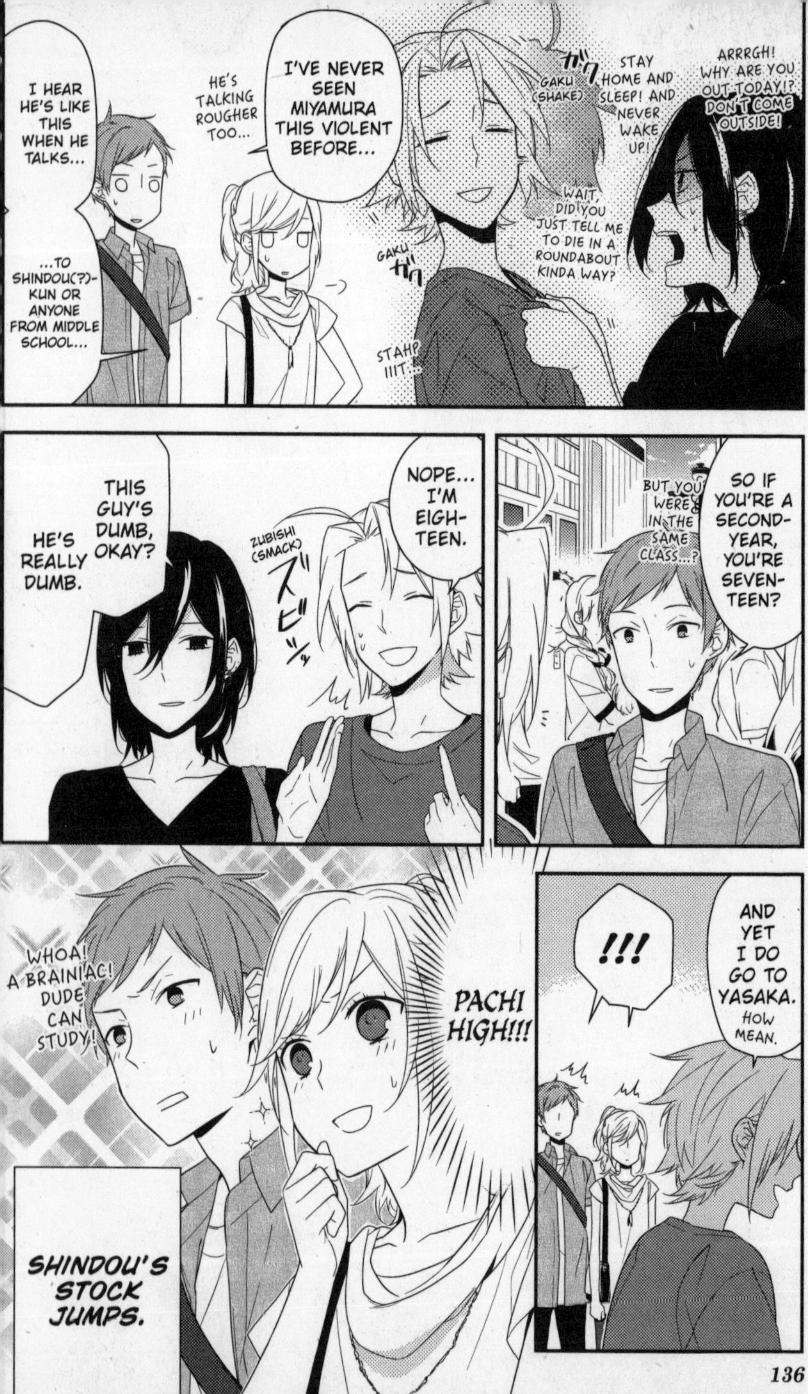
ARRRGH! WHY ARE YOU OUT TODAY!? DON'T COME OUTSIDE!
STAY HOME AND SLEEP! AND NEVER WAKE UP!
GAKU (SHAKE)
WAIT, DID YOU JUST TELL ME TO DIE IN A ROUNDABOUT KINDA WAY?
GAKU
STAHP IIIT...
I'VE NEVER SEEN MIYAMURA THIS VIOLENT BEFORE...
HE'S TALKING ROUGHER TOO...
I HEAR HE'S LIKE THIS WHEN HE TALKS...
...TO SHINDOU(?)-KUN OR ANYONE FROM MIDDLE SCHOOL...
SO IF YOU'RE A SECOND-YEAR, YOU'RE SEVENTEEN?
BUT YOU WERE IN THE SAME CLASS...?
NOPE... I'M EIGHTEEN.
ZUBISHI (SMACK)
THIS GUY'S DUMB, OKAY?
HE'S REALLY DUMB.
AND YET I DO GO TO YASAKA. HOW MEAN.
!!!
PACHI HIGH!!!
WHOA! A BRAINIAC! DUDE CAN STUDY!
SHINDOU'S STOCK JUMPS.

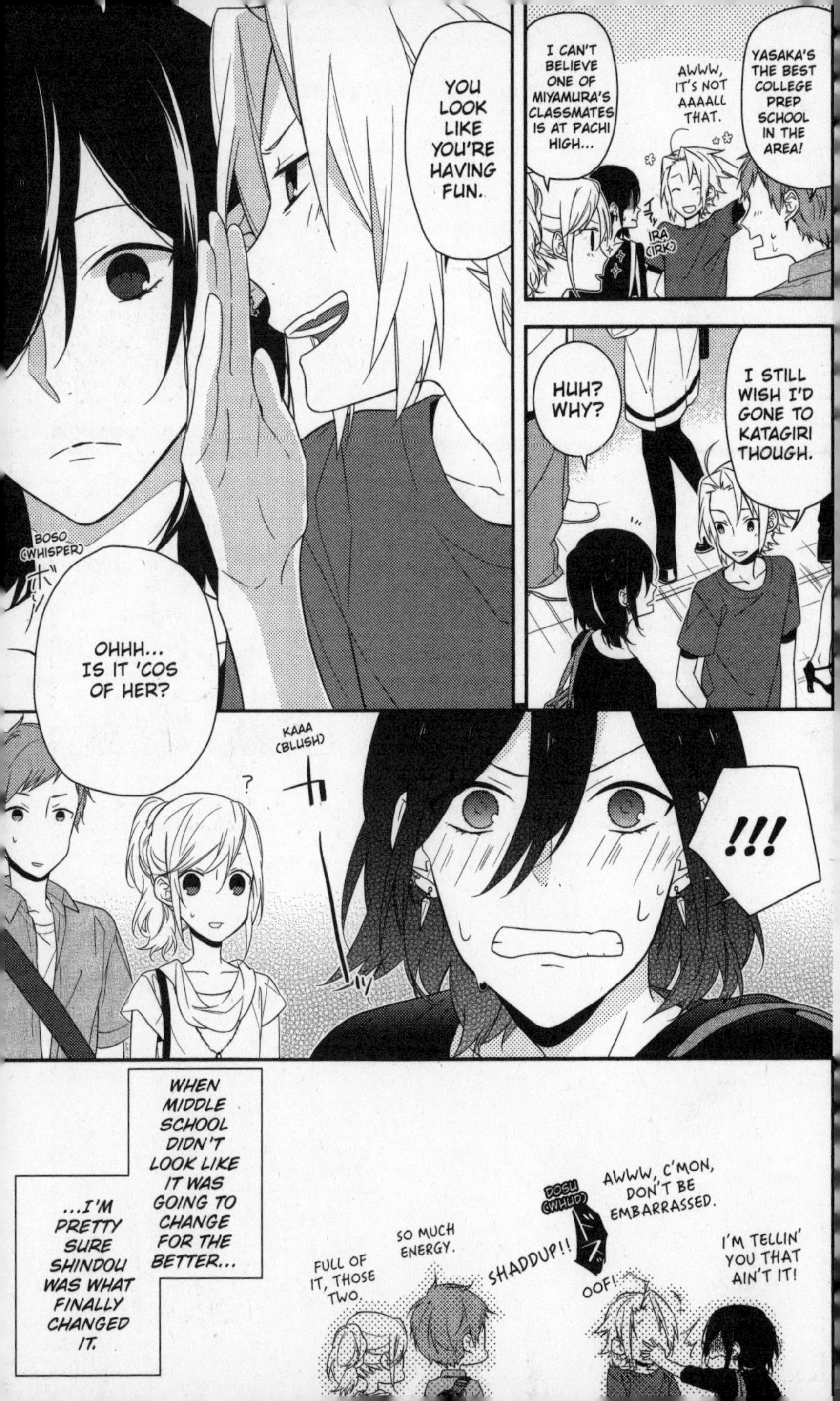
YASAKA'S THE BEST COLLEGE PREP SCHOOL IN THE AREA!
AWWW, IT'S NOT AAAALL THAT.
IRA (IRK)
I CAN'T BELIEVE ONE OF MIYAMURA'S CLASSMATES IS AT PACHI HIGH...
I STILL WISH I'D GONE TO KATAGIRI THOUGH.
HUH? WHY?
YOU LOOK LIKE YOU'RE HAVING FUN.
BOSO (WHISPER)
OHHH... IS IT 'COS OF HER?
!!!
KAAA (BLUSH)
?
AWWW, C'MON, DON'T BE EMBARRASSED.
I'M TELLIN' YOU THAT AIN'T IT!
DOSU (WHUD)
OOF!
SHADDUP!!
SO MUCH ENERGY.
FULL OF IT, THOSE TWO.
WHEN MIDDLE SCHOOL DIDN'T LOOK LIKE IT WAS GOING TO CHANGE FOR THE BETTER...
...I'M PRETTY SURE SHINDOU WAS WHAT FINALLY CHANGED IT.

"YOU LOOK LIKE YOU'RE HAVING FUN."

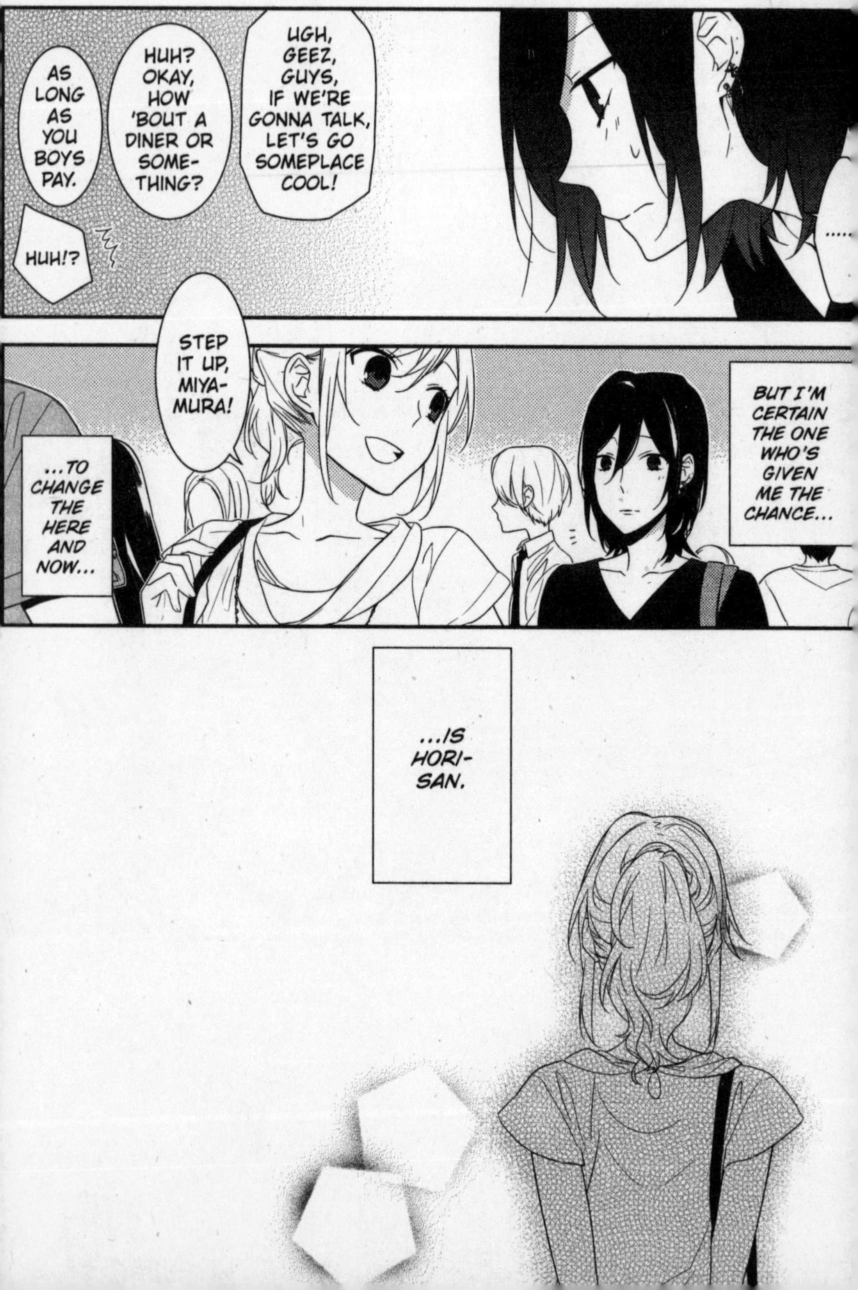
.....
UGH, GEEZ, GUYS, IF WE'RE GONNA TALK, LET'S GO SOMEPLACE COOL!
HUH? OKAY, HOW 'BOUT A DINER OR SOME-THING?
AS LONG AS YOU BOYS PAY.
HUH!?
BUT I'M CERTAIN THE ONE WHO'S GIVEN ME THE CHANCE...
STEP IT UP, MIYA-MURA!
...TO CHANGE THE HERE AND NOW...
...IS HORI-SAN.

HORIMIYA

HORIMIYA

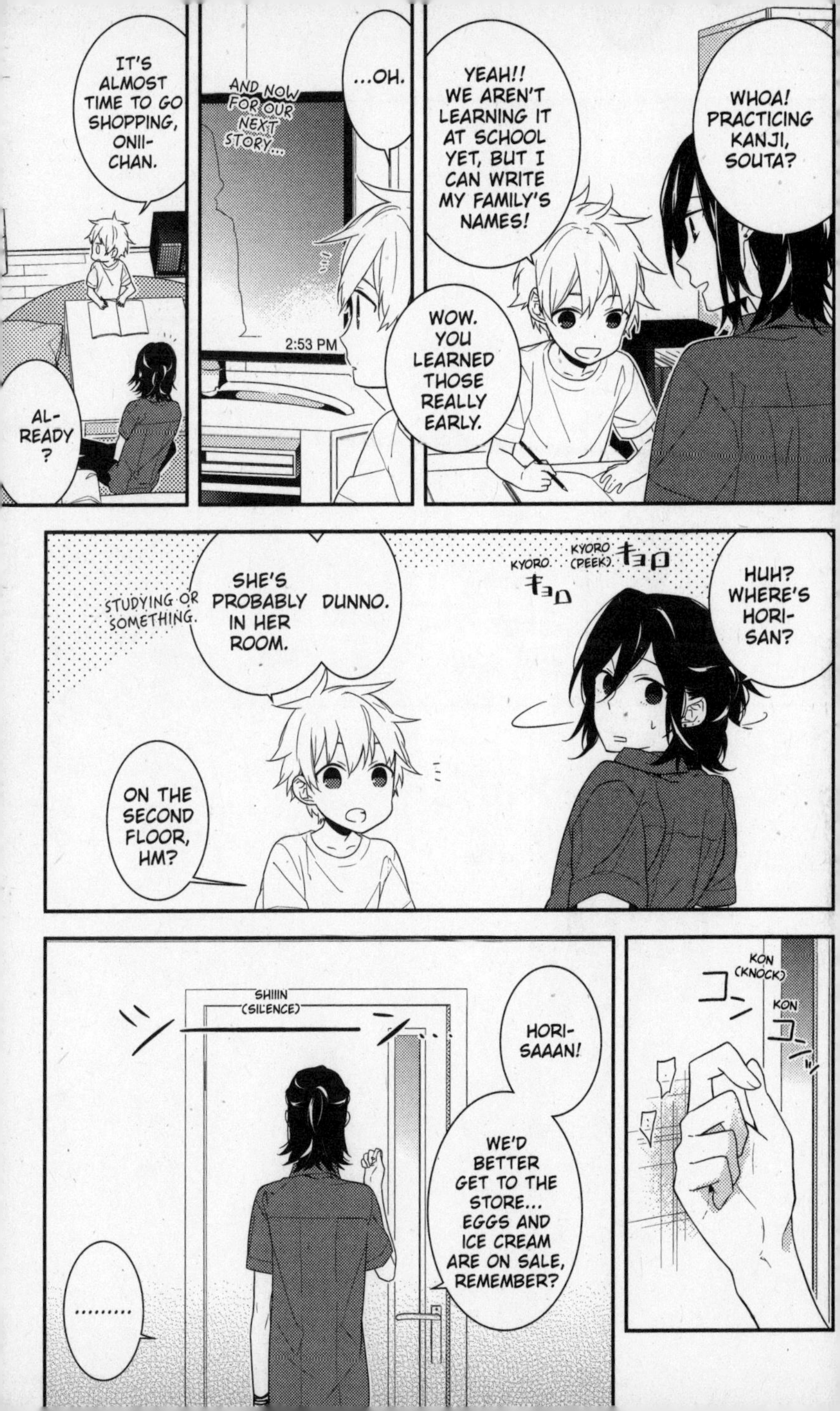
WHOA! PRACTICING KANJI, SOUTA?
YEAH!! WE AREN'T LEARNING IT AT SCHOOL YET, BUT I CAN WRITE MY FAMILY'S NAMES!
WOW. YOU LEARNED THOSE REALLY EARLY.
...OH.
AND NOW FOR OUR NEXT STORY...
2:53 PM
IT'S ALMOST TIME TO GO SHOPPING, ONII-CHAN.
AL-READY?
HUH? WHERE'S HORI-SAN?
KYORO (PEEK) キョロ
KYORO キョロ
DUNNO.
SHE'S PROBABLY IN HER ROOM.
STUDYING OR SOMETHING.
ON THE SECOND FLOOR, HM?
KON (KNOCK) コン
KON コン
HORI-SAAAN!
WE'D BETTER GET TO THE STORE... EGGS AND ICE CREAM ARE ON SALE, REMEMBER?
SHIIIN (SILENCE)
....

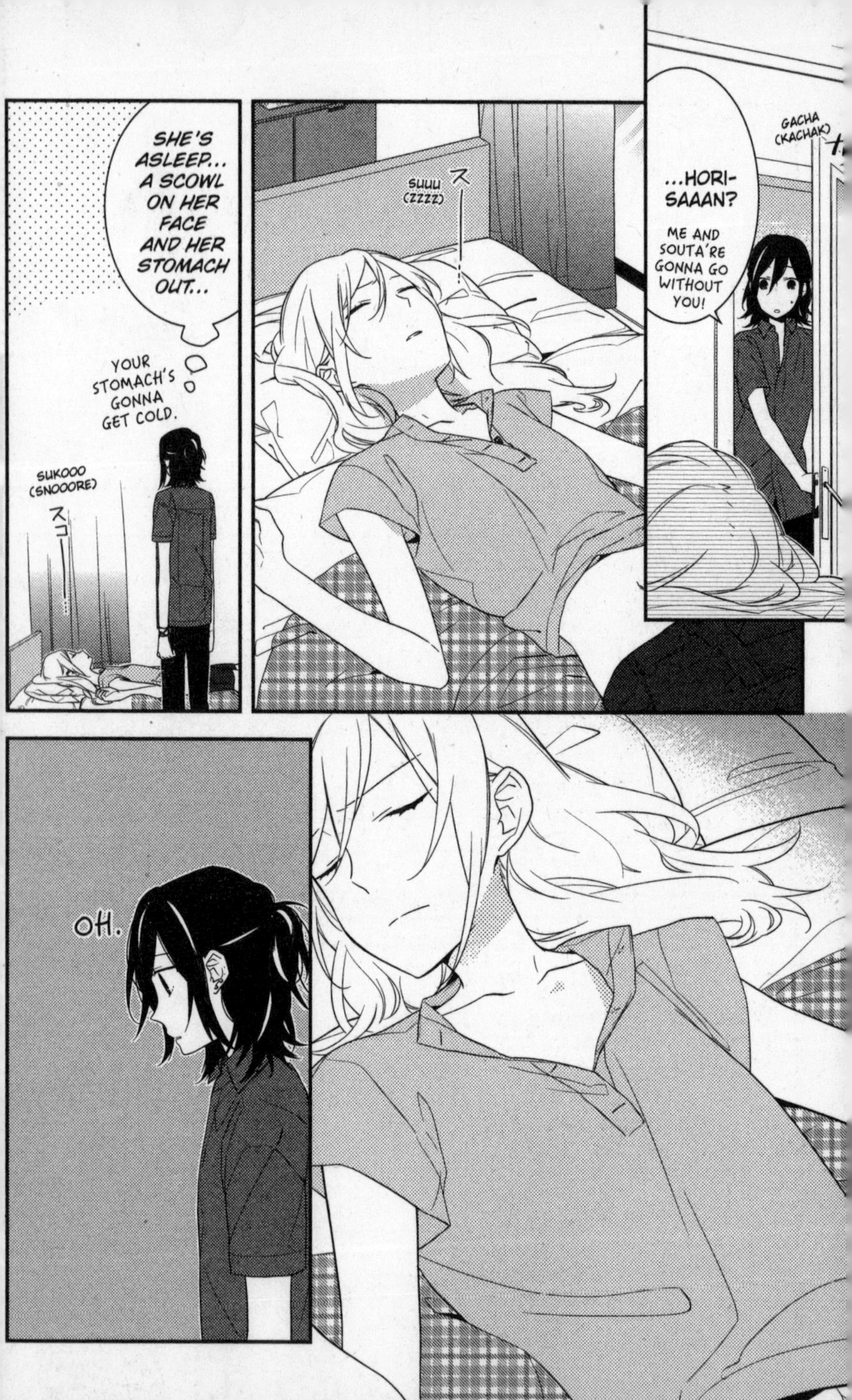
GACHA (KACHAK)
ガチャ
...HORI-SAAAN?
ME AND SOUTA'RE GONNA GO WITHOUT YOU!
SUUU (ZZZZ)
ス…
SHE'S ASLEEP... A SCOWL ON HER FACE AND HER STOMACH OUT...
YOUR STOMACH'S GONNA GET COLD.
SUKOOO (SNOOORE)
スコー…
OH.

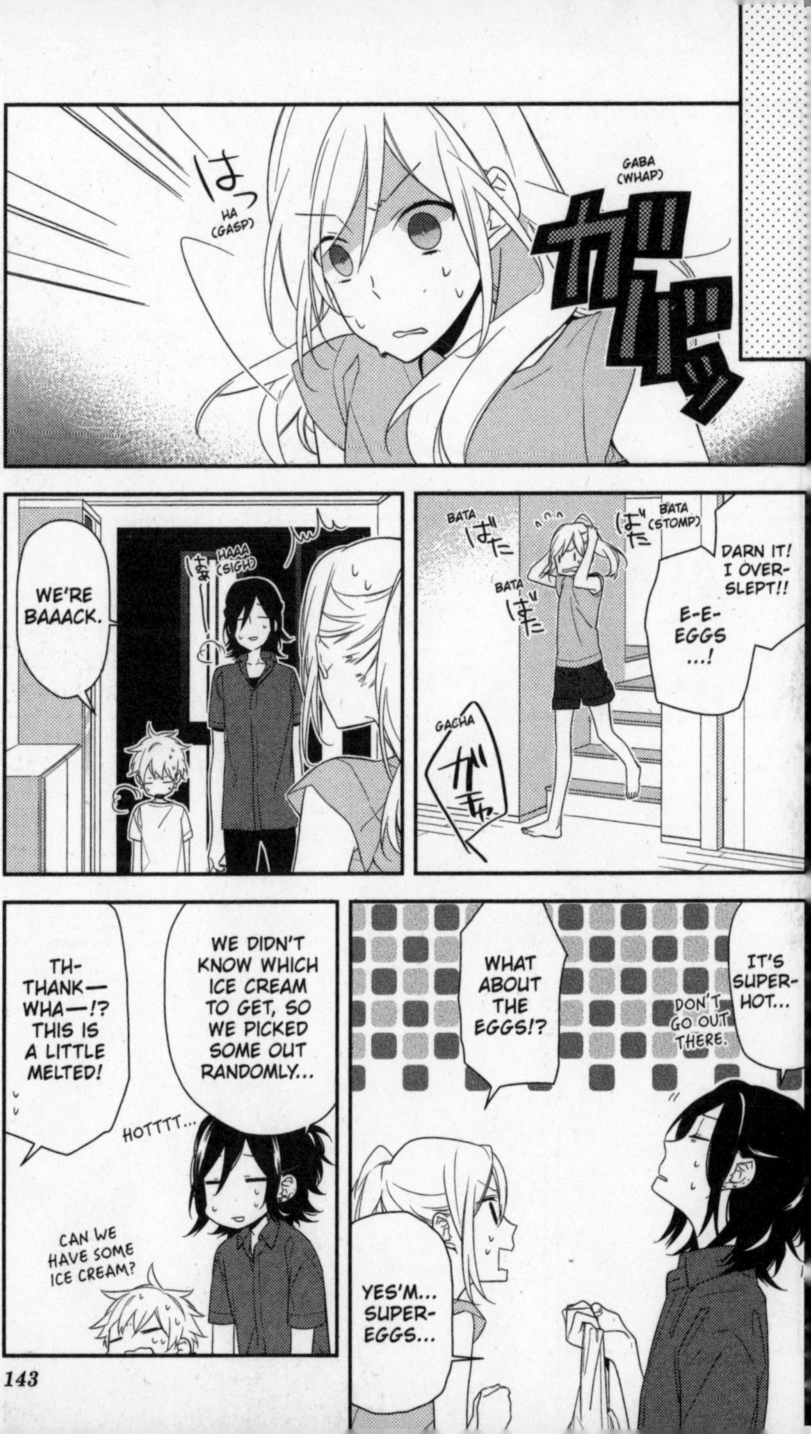

GABA (WHAP)
はっ
HA (GASP)
BATA (STOMP)
DARN IT! I OVERSLEPT!!
E-E-EGGS ...!
BATA
BATA
GACHA
HAAA (SIGH)
WE'RE BAAACK.
IT'S SUPER-HOT...
DON'T GO OUT THERE.
WHAT ABOUT THE EGGS!?
YES'M... SUPER-EGGS...
WE DIDN'T KNOW WHICH ICE CREAM TO GET, SO WE PICKED SOME OUT RANDOMLY...
TH-THANK— WHA—!? THIS IS A LITTLE MELTED!
HOTTTT...
CAN WE HAVE SOME ICE CREAM?

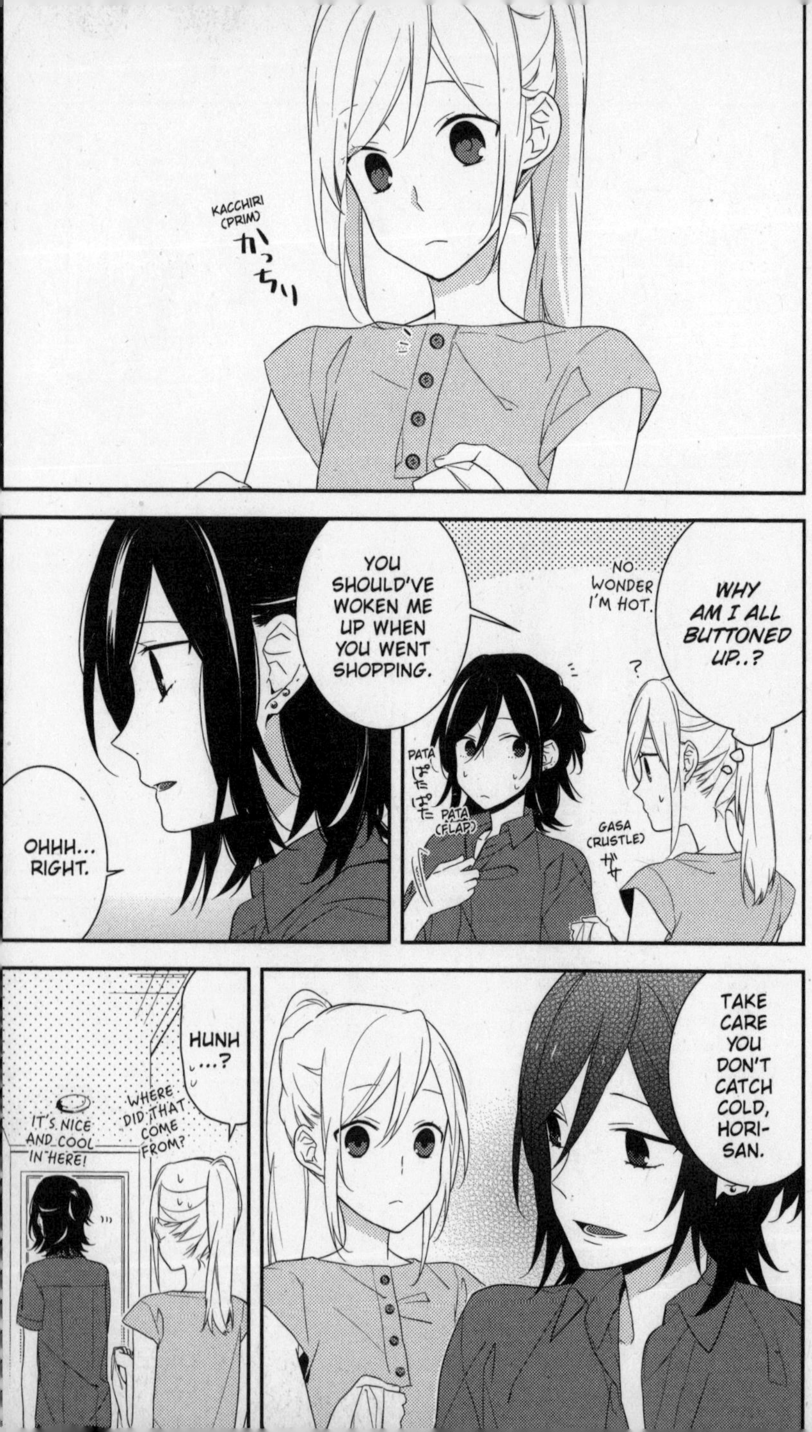
KACCHIRI (PRIM)
かっちり
WHY AM I ALL BUTTONED UP..?
?
NO WONDER I'M HOT.
YOU SHOULD'VE WOKEN ME UP WHEN YOU WENT SHOPPING.
PATA ぱた
PATA ぱた (FLAP)
GASA (RUSTLE) ガサ
OHHH... RIGHT.
TAKE CARE YOU DON'T CATCH COLD, HORI-SAN.
HUNH ...?
WHERE DID THAT COME FROM?
IT'S NICE AND COOL IN HERE!

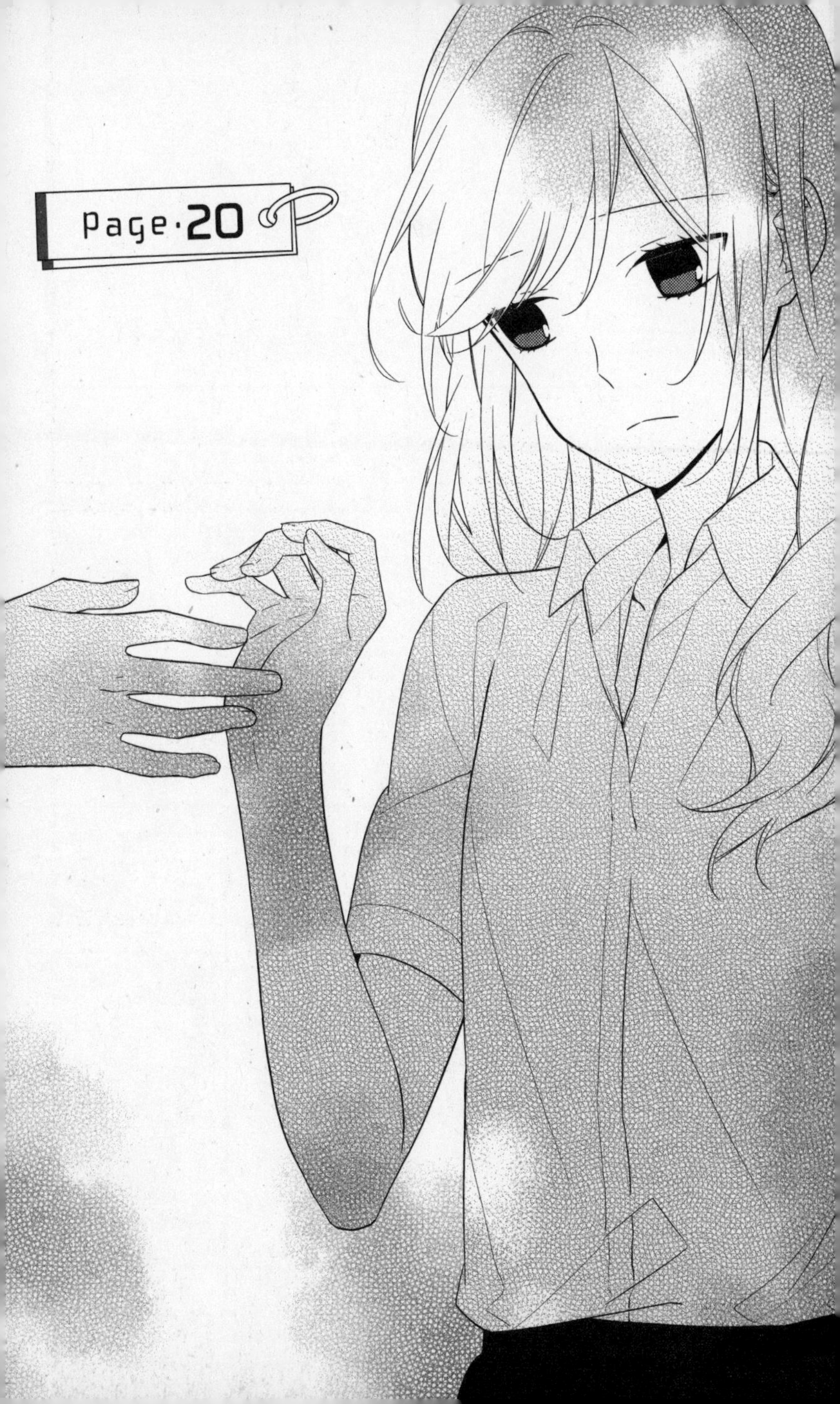
page·20

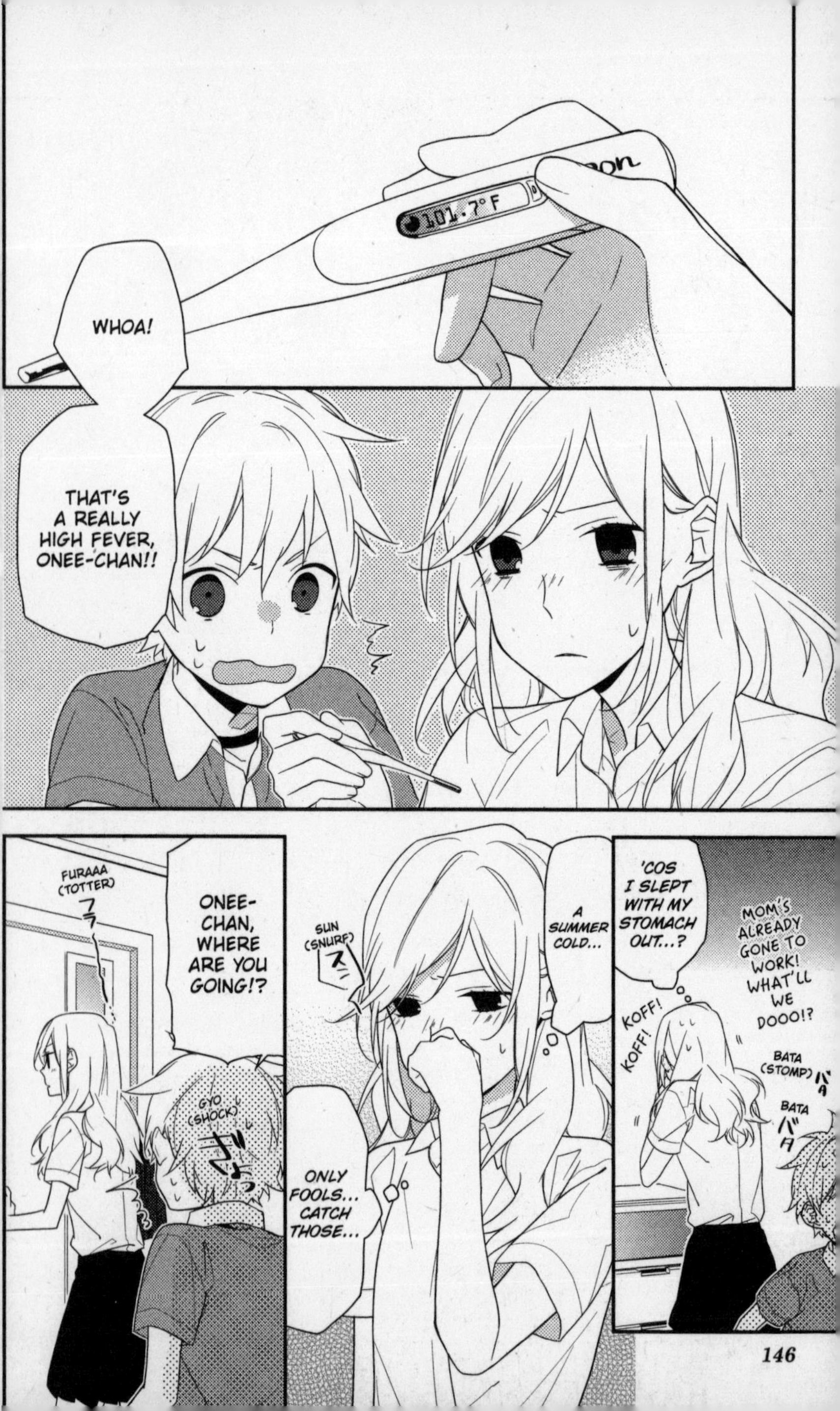
101.7° F
WHOA!
THAT'S A REALLY HIGH FEVER, ONEE-CHAN!!
'COS I SLEPT WITH MY STOMACH OUT...?
MOM'S ALREADY GONE TO WORK! WHAT'LL WE DOOO!?
KOFF! KOFF!
BATA (STOMP)
BATA
A SUMMER COLD...
SUN (SNURF)
ONLY FOOLS... CATCH THOSE...
ONEE-CHAN, WHERE ARE YOU GOING!?
FURAAA (TOTTER)
GYO (SHOCK)

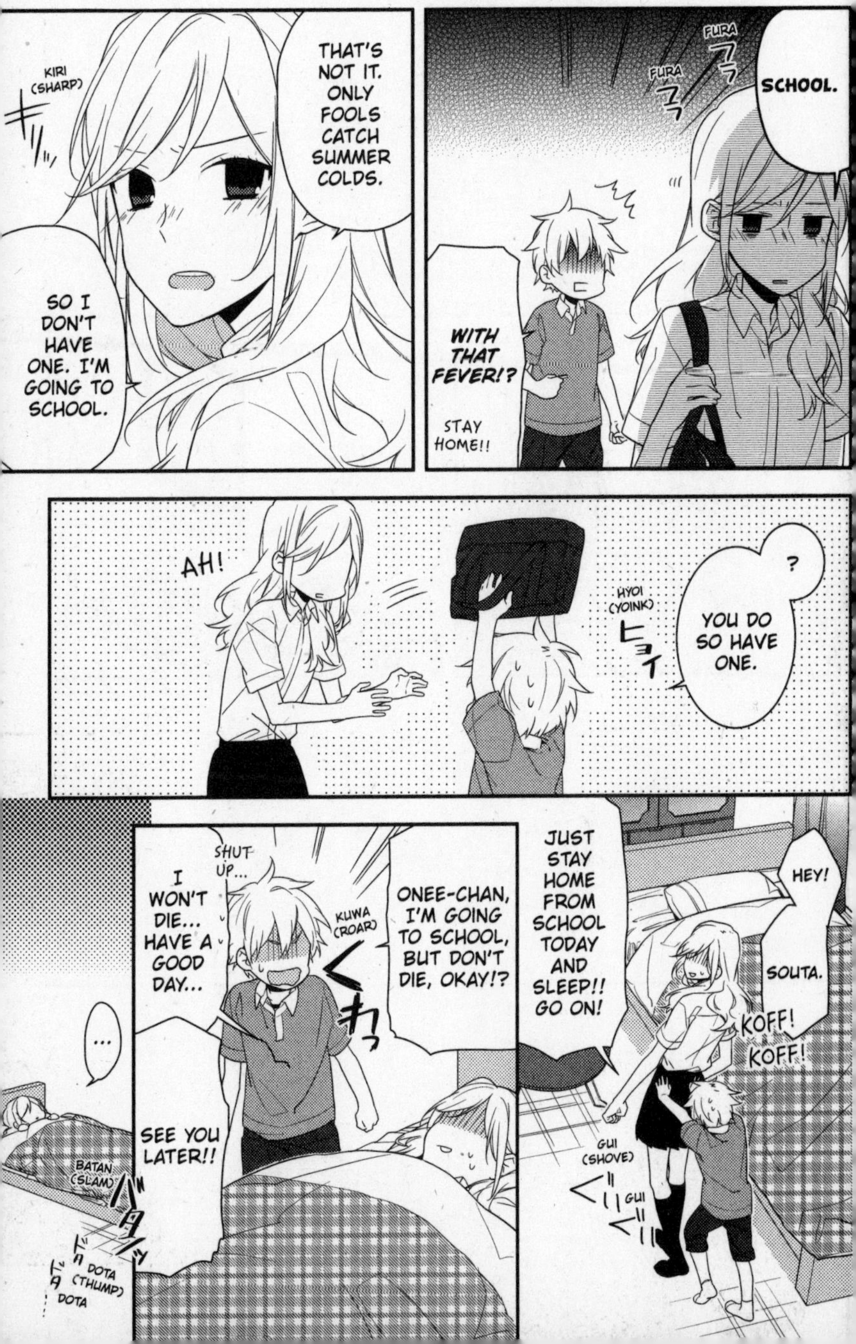
FURA
FURA
SCHOOL.
WITH THAT FEVER!?
STAY HOME!!
KIRI (SHARP)
THAT'S NOT IT. ONLY FOOLS CATCH SUMMER COLDS.
SO I DON'T HAVE ONE. I'M GOING TO SCHOOL.
?
YOU DO SO HAVE ONE.
HYOI (YOINK)
AH!
HEY!
SOUTA.
KOFF! KOFF!
JUST STAY HOME FROM SCHOOL TODAY AND SLEEP!! GO ON!
GUI (SHOVE)
GUI
KUWA (ROAR)
ONEE-CHAN, I'M GOING TO SCHOOL, BUT DON'T DIE, OKAY!?
SHUT UP...
I WON'T DIE... HAVE A GOOD DAY...
SEE YOU LATER!!
...
BATAN (SLAM)
DOTA (THUMP)
DOTA

SOUTA'S GOTTEN REALLY RESPONSIBLE. WHEN DID THAT HAPPEN...?

HAA (SIGH)

KACHI

KACHI

KACHI (TICK)

KACHI

KACHI

UTO (DOZE)

KACHI

KACHI !

"—KYOUKO.

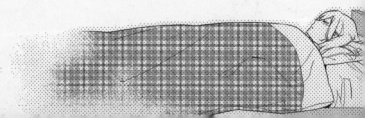

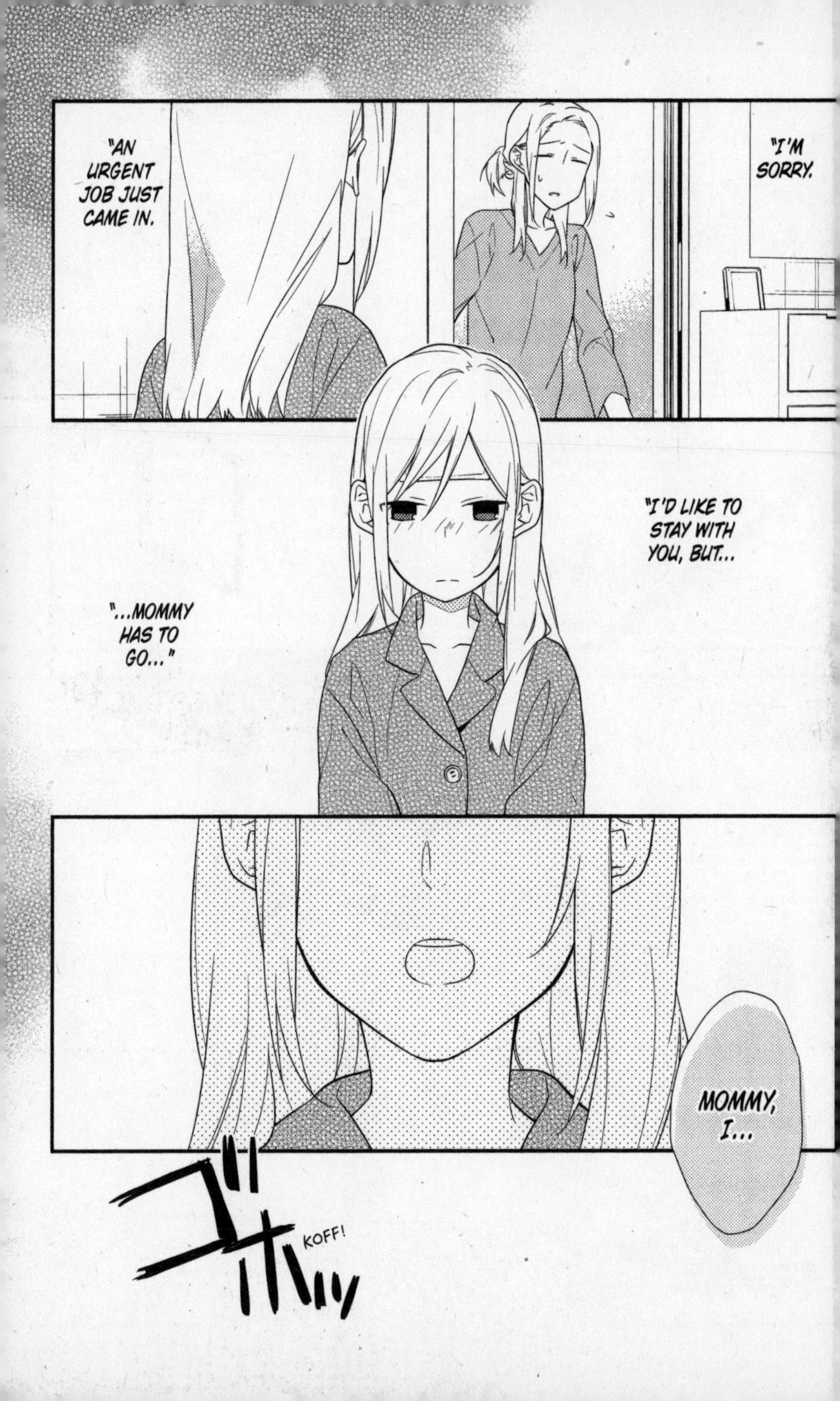
"I'M SORRY.
"AN URGENT JOB JUST CAME IN.
"I'D LIKE TO STAY WITH YOU, BUT...
"...MOMMY HAS TO GO..."
MOMMY, I...
ゴホッ
KOFF!

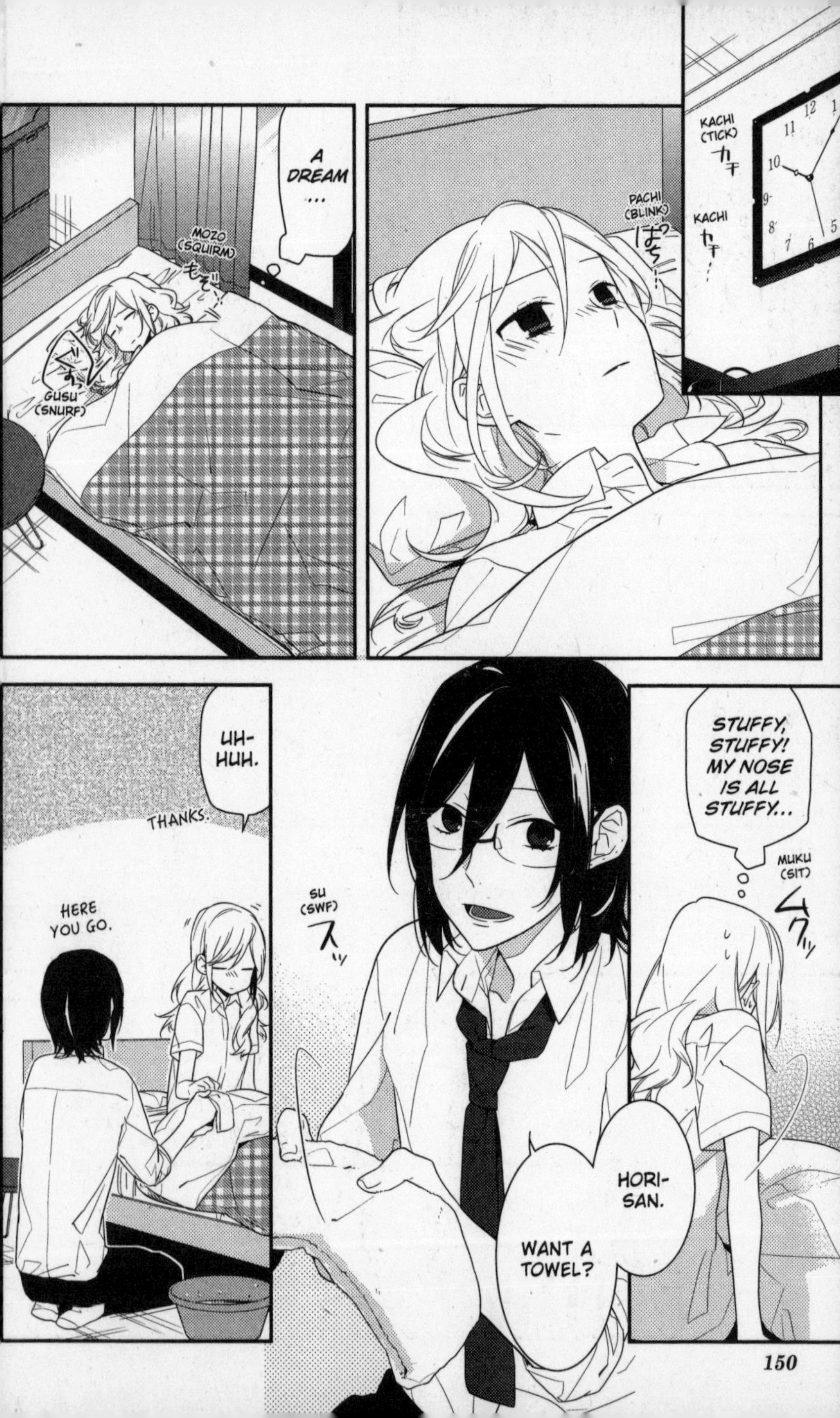
KACHI (TICK)
カチ
KACHI
カチ…
PACHI (BLINK)
ぱち…
A DREAM…
MOZO (SQUIRM)
もぞ…
GUSU (SNURF)
STUFFY, STUFFY! MY NOSE IS ALL STUFFY…
MUKU (SIT)
ムクッ
SU (SWF)
スッ
HORI-SAN.
WANT A TOWEL?
UH-HUH.
THANKS.
HERE YOU GO.

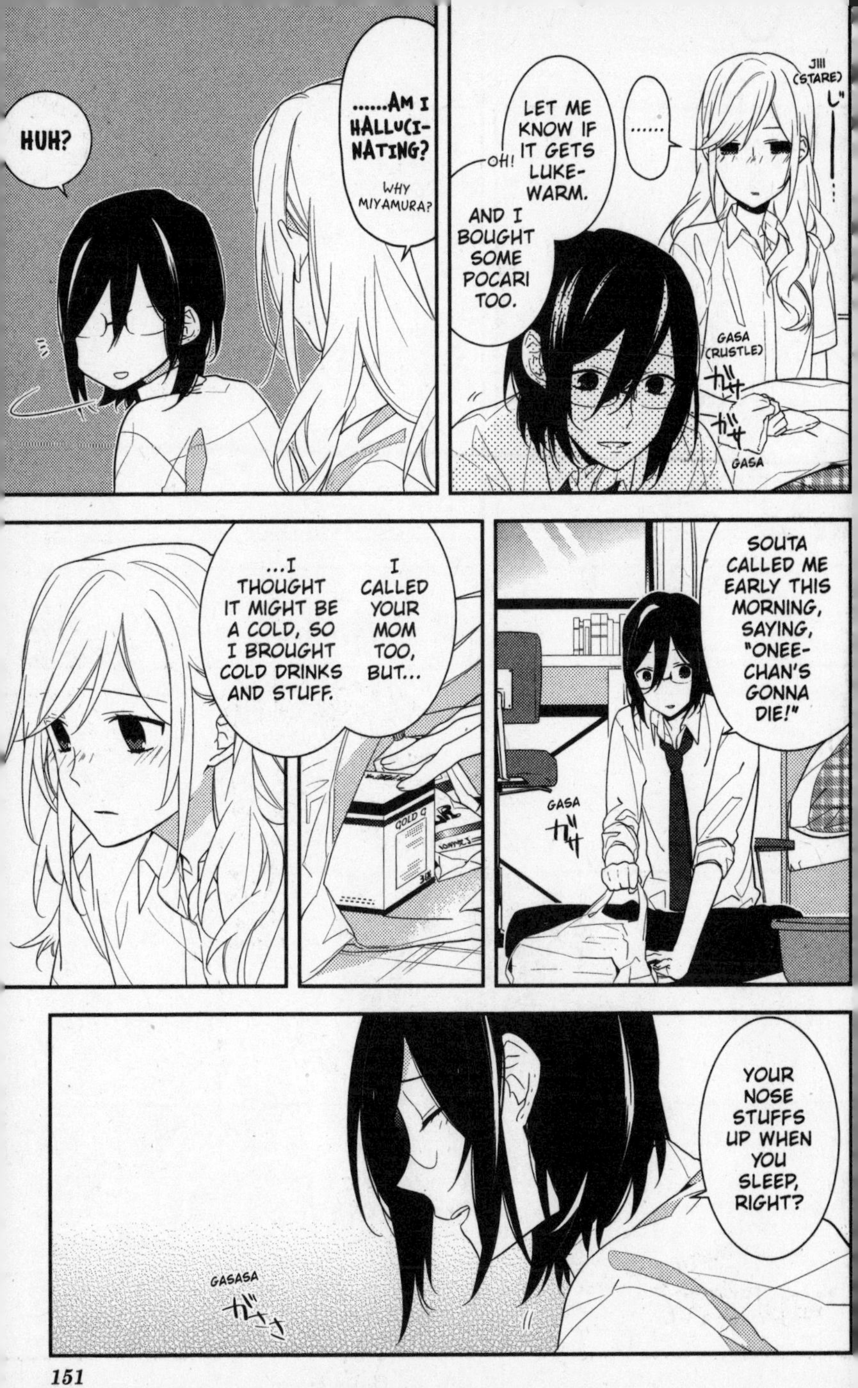

JIII (STARE)
......
LET ME KNOW IF IT GETS LUKE-WARM.
OH!
AND I BOUGHT SOME POCARI TOO.
GASA (RUSTLE)
GASA
......AM I HALLUCI-NATING?
WHY MIYAMURA?
HUH?
SOUTA CALLED ME EARLY THIS MORNING, SAYING, "ONEE-CHAN'S GONNA DIE!"
GASA
I CALLED YOUR MOM TOO, BUT...
...I THOUGHT IT MIGHT BE A COLD, SO I BROUGHT COLD DRINKS AND STUFF.
YOUR NOSE STUFFS UP WHEN YOU SLEEP, RIGHT?
GASASA

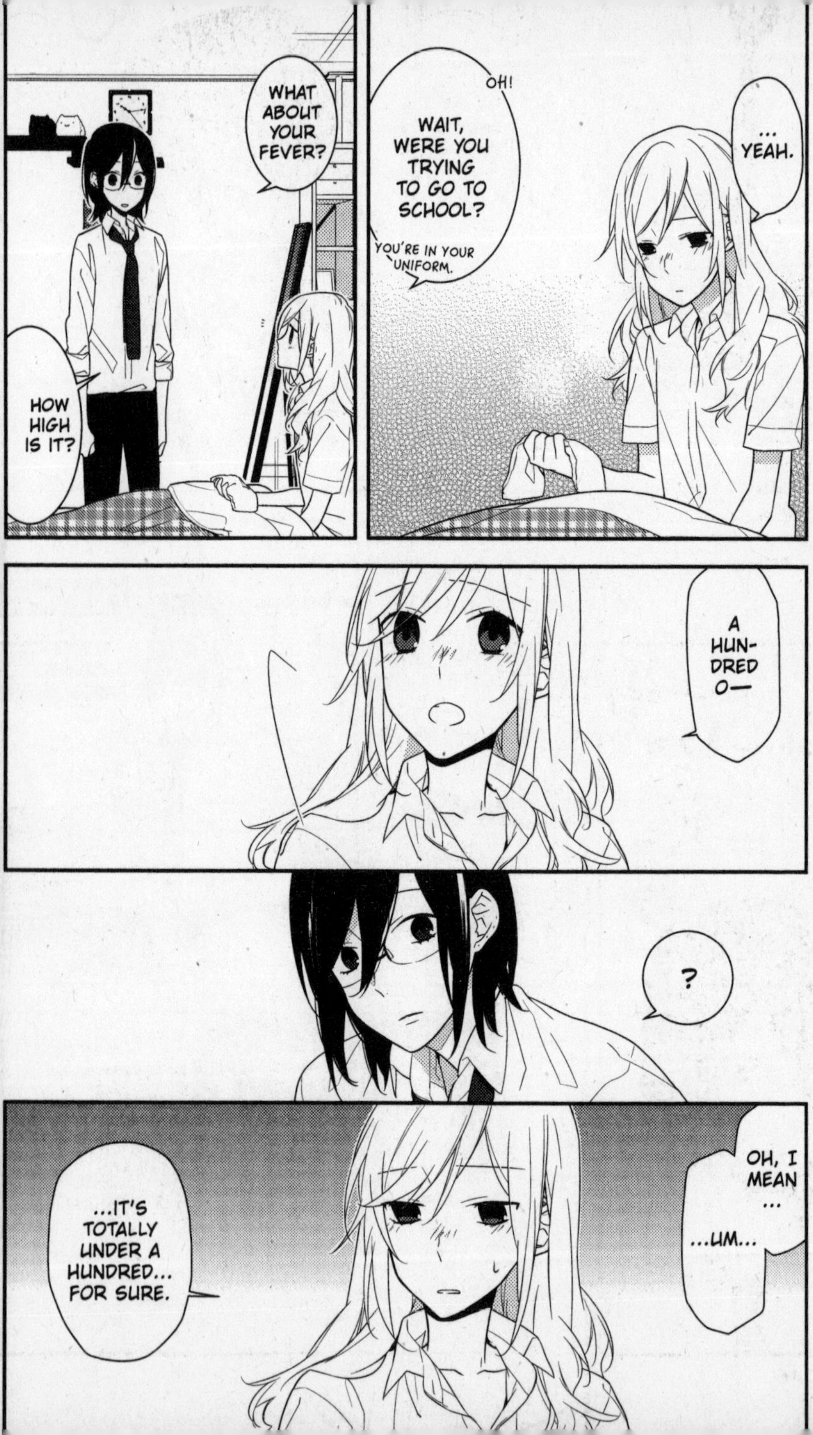
...YEAH.
OH!
WAIT, WERE YOU TRYING TO GO TO SCHOOL?
YOU'RE IN YOUR UNIFORM.
WHAT ABOUT YOUR FEVER?
HOW HIGH IS IT?
A HUN-DRED O—
?
OH, I MEAN...
...UM...
...IT'S TOTALLY UNDER A HUNDRED... FOR SURE.

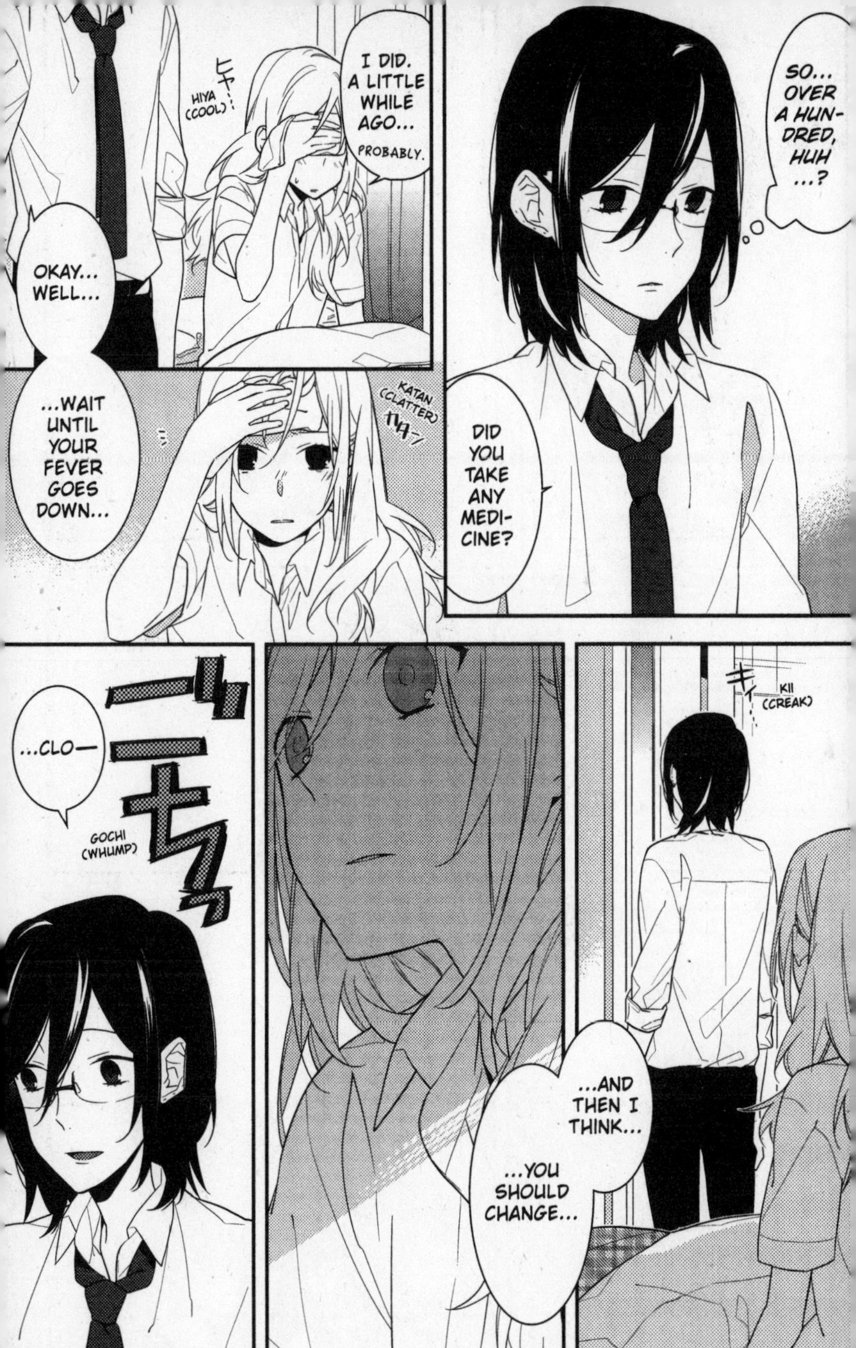
SO... OVER A HUNDRED, HUH...?
DID YOU TAKE ANY MEDICINE?
I DID. A LITTLE WHILE AGO...
PROBABLY.
HIYA (COOL)
OKAY... WELL...
...WAIT UNTIL YOUR FEVER GOES DOWN...
KATAN (CLATTER)
KII (CREAK)
...AND THEN I THINK...
...YOU SHOULD CHANGE...
...CLO—
GOCHI (WHUMP)

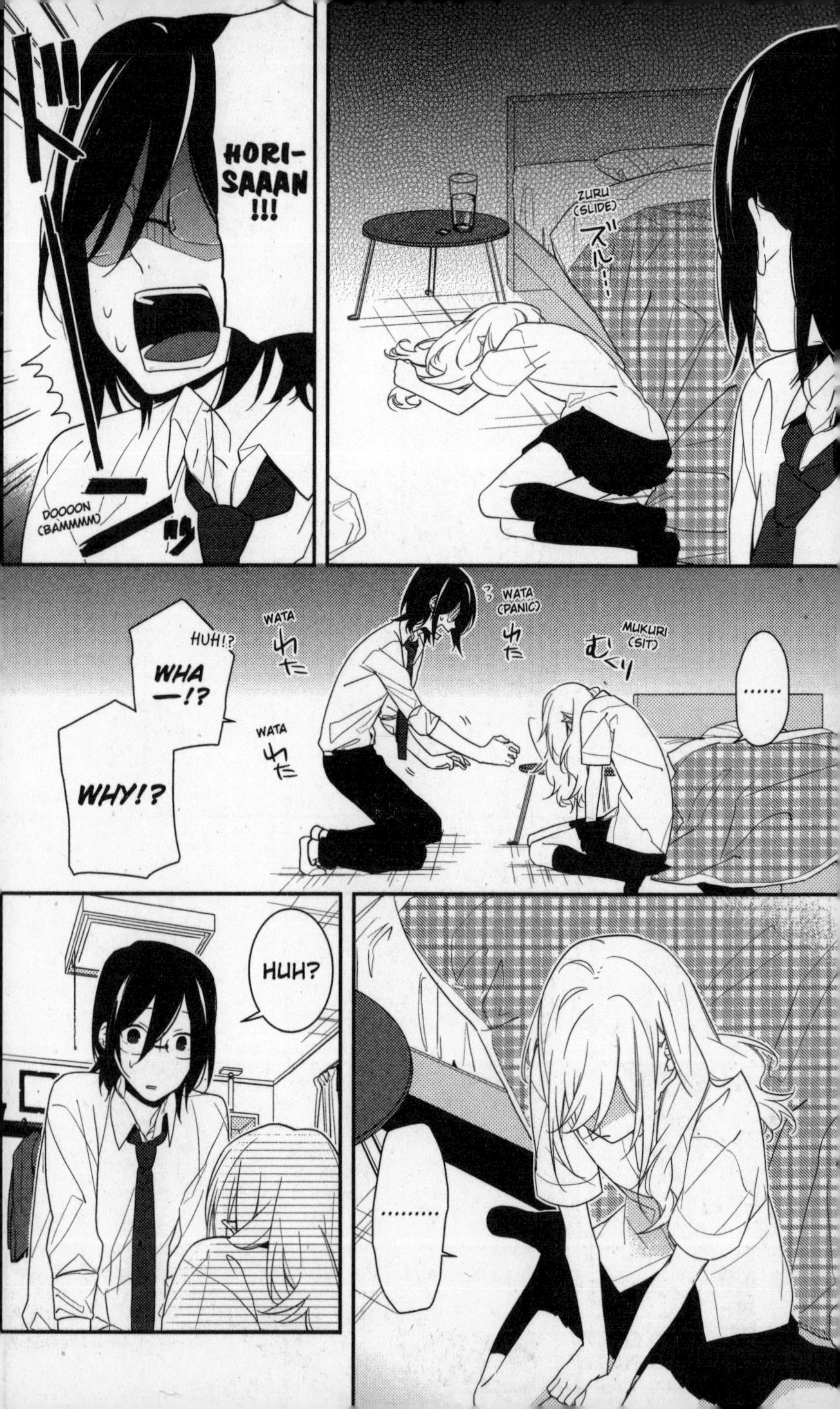
ZURU (SLIDE)
ズル…
HORI-SAAAN!!!
DOOOON (BAMMMM)
ドーン
......
MUKURI (SIT)
むくり
WATA (PANIC)
わた
WATA
わた
WATA
わた
HUH!? WHA—!? WHY!?
....
HUH?

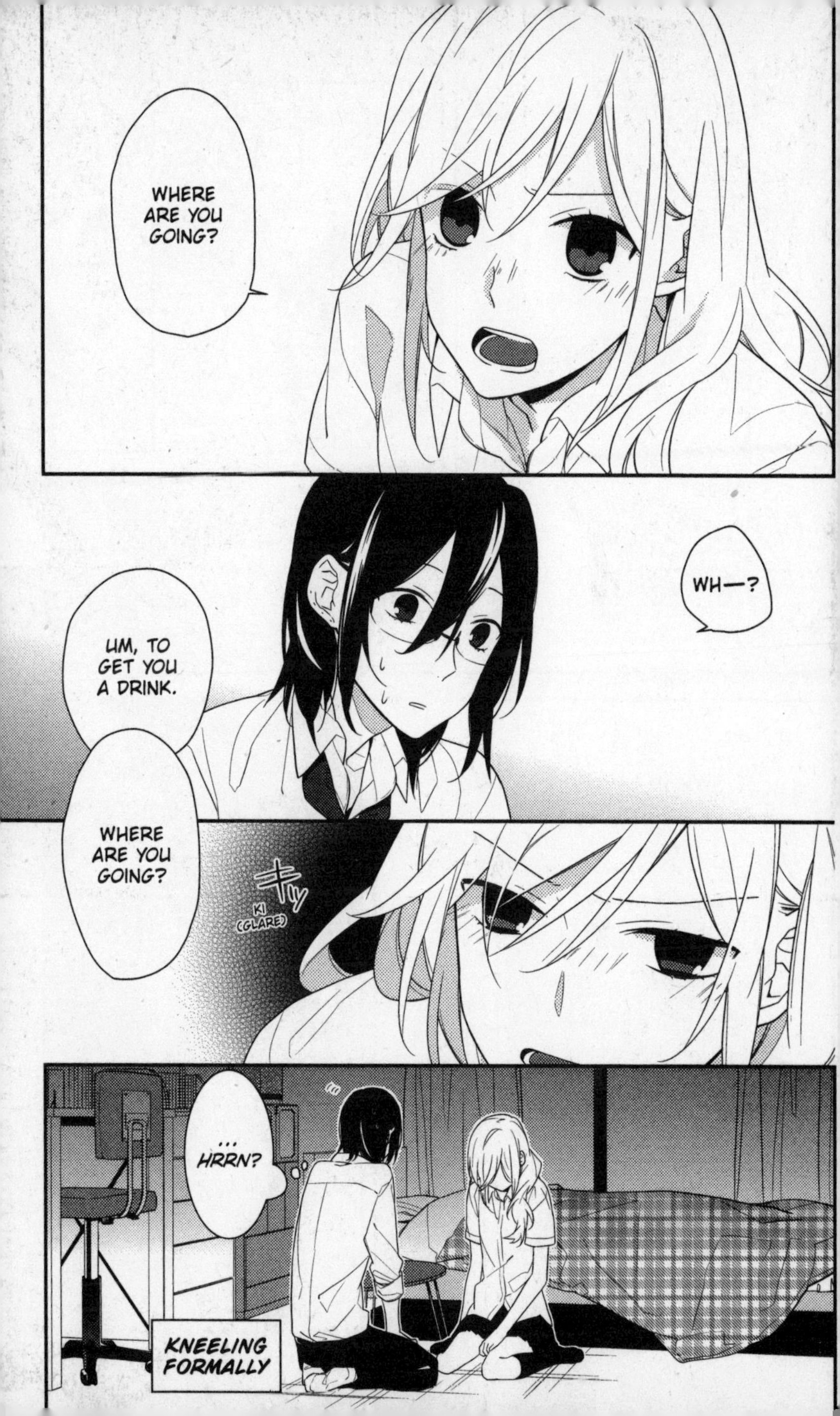
WHERE ARE YOU GOING?
WH—?
UM, TO GET YOU A DRINK.
WHERE ARE YOU GOING?
キッ
KI (GLARE)
... HRRN?
KNEELING FORMALLY

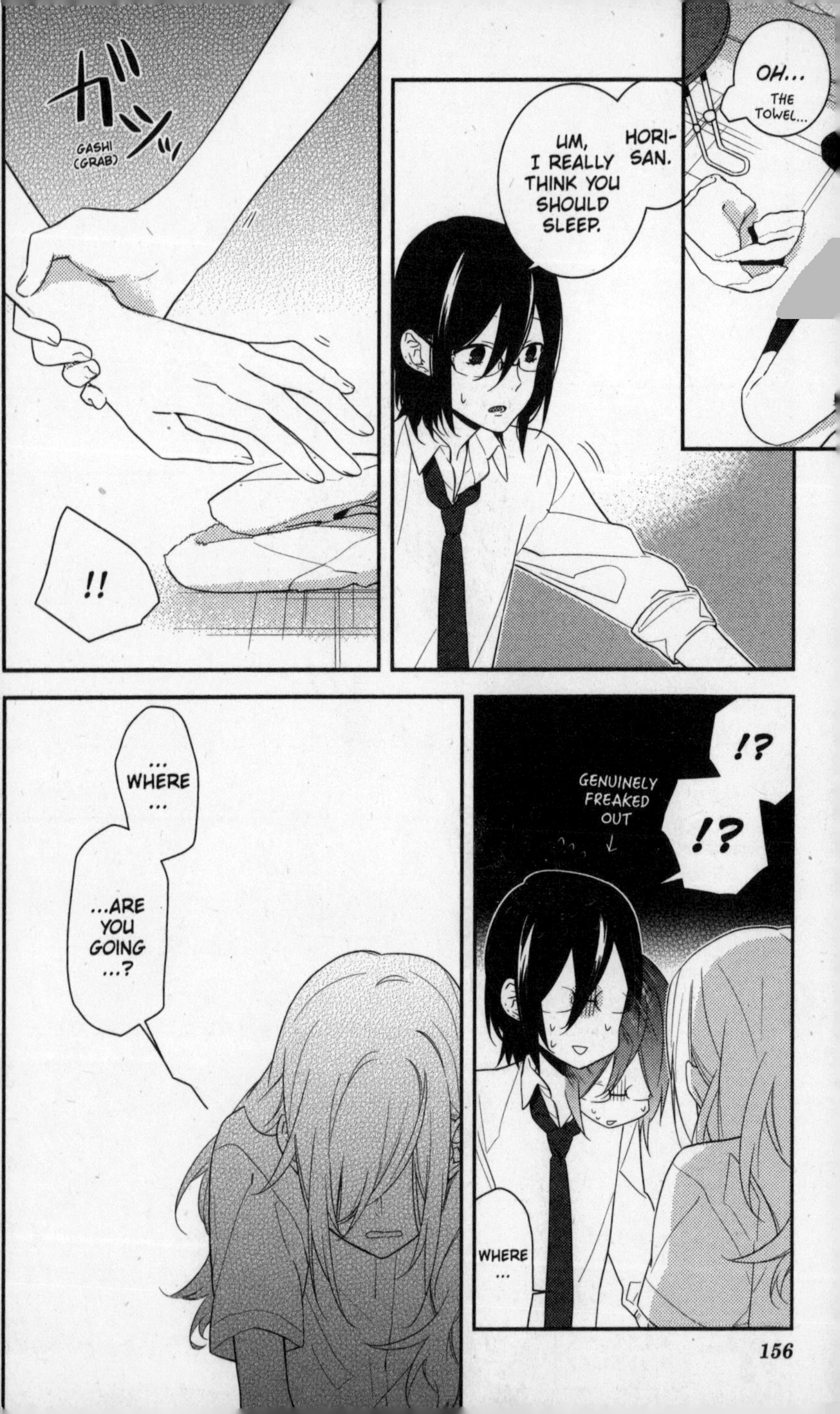
OH... THE TOWEL...
HORI-SAN.
UM, I REALLY THINK YOU SHOULD SLEEP.
ガッ
GASHI (GRAB)
!!
!?
!?
GENUINELY FREAKED OUT
WHERE ...
... WHERE ...
...ARE YOU GOING ...?

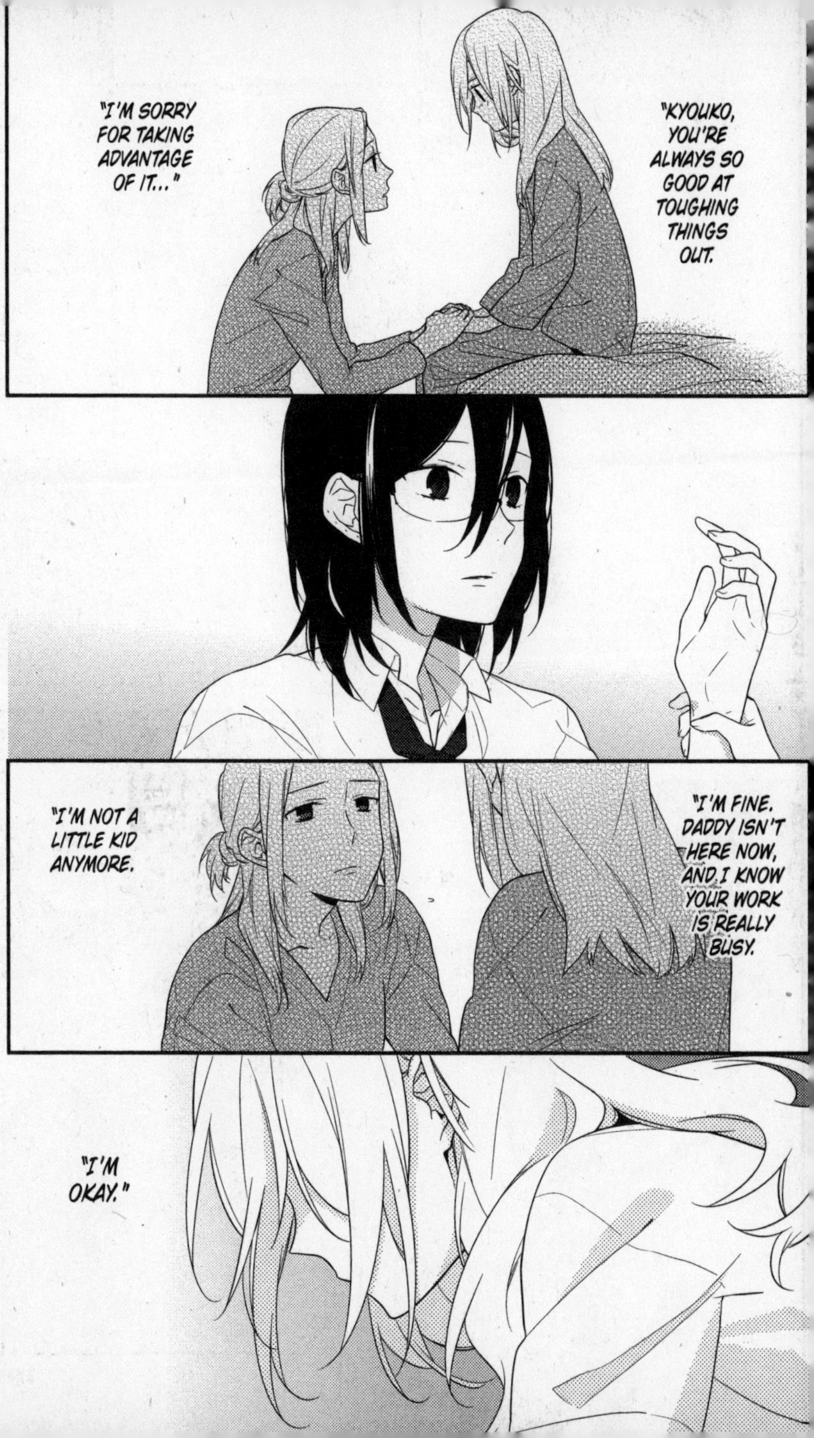
"KYOUKO, YOU'RE ALWAYS SO GOOD AT TOUGHING THINGS OUT.
"I'M SORRY FOR TAKING ADVANTAGE OF IT..."
"I'M FINE. DADDY ISN'T HERE NOW, AND I KNOW YOUR WORK IS REALLY BUSY.
"I'M NOT A LITTLE KID ANYMORE.
"I'M OKAY."

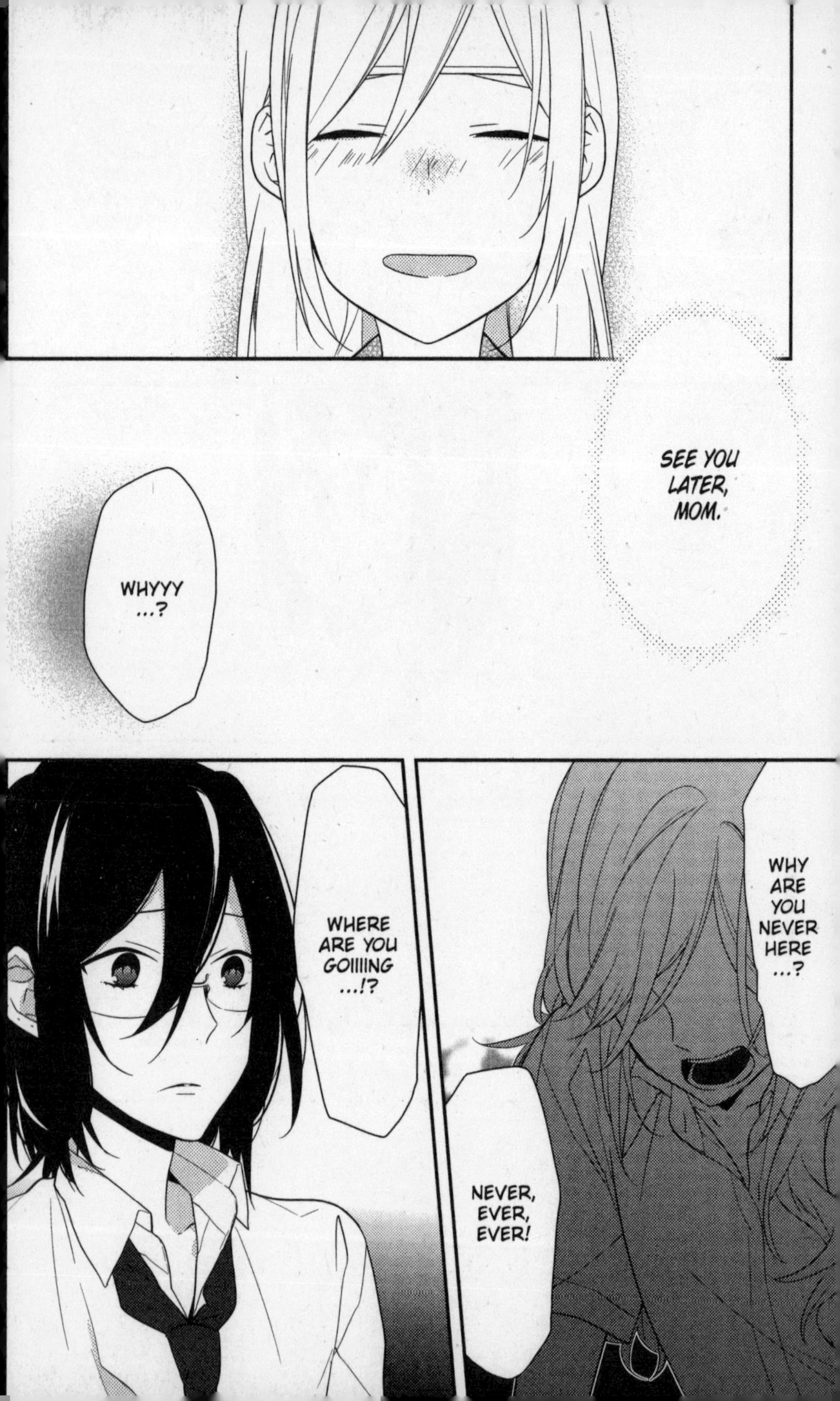
SEE YOU LATER, MOM.
WHYYY ...?
WHY ARE YOU NEVER HERE ...?
NEVER, EVER, EVER!
WHERE ARE YOU GOIIIING ...!?

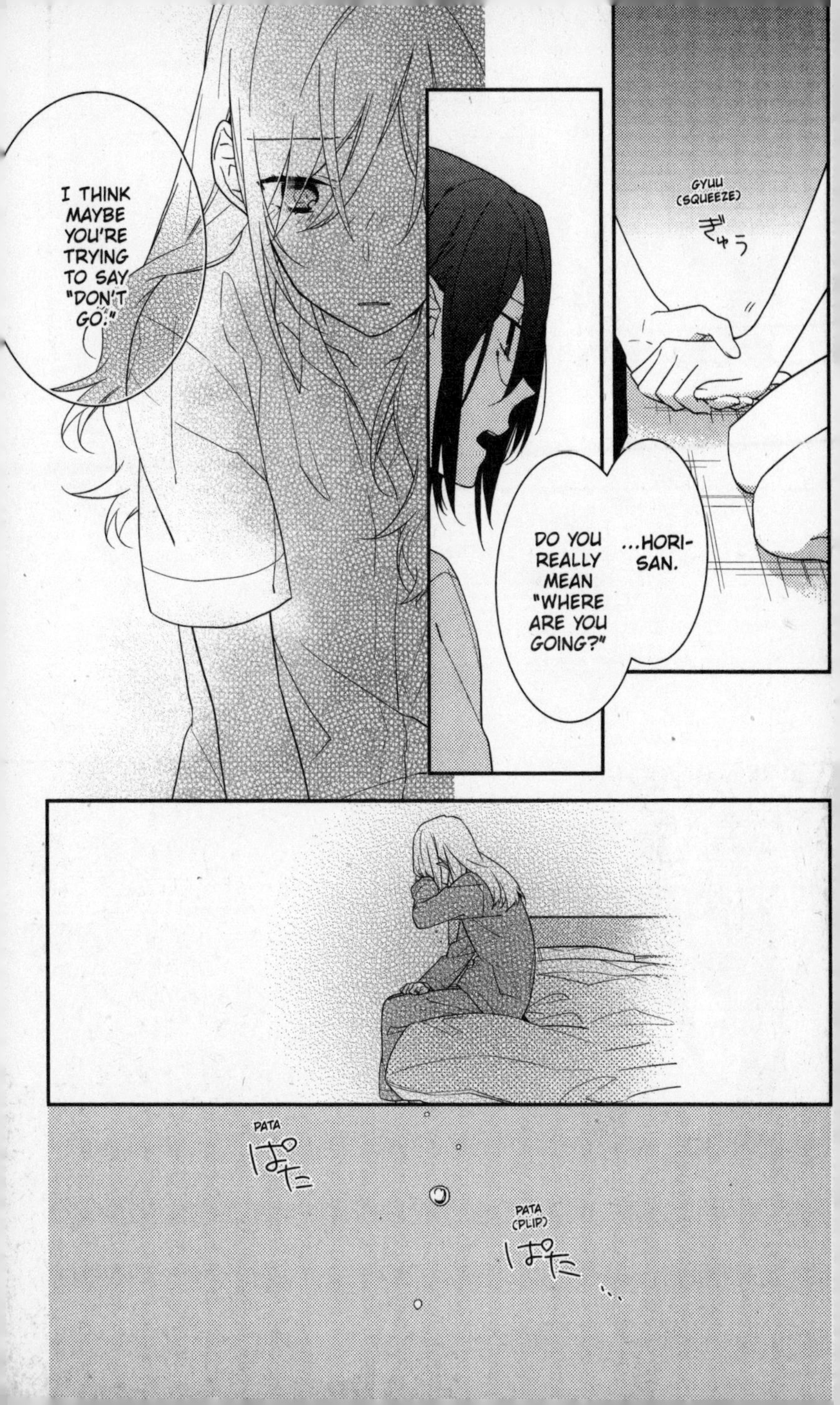
GYUU (SQUEEZE)
ぎゅう
...HORI-SAN.
DO YOU REALLY MEAN "WHERE ARE YOU GOING?"
I THINK MAYBE YOU'RE TRYING TO SAY "DON'T GO."
PATA
ぱた
PATA (PLIP)
ぱた…

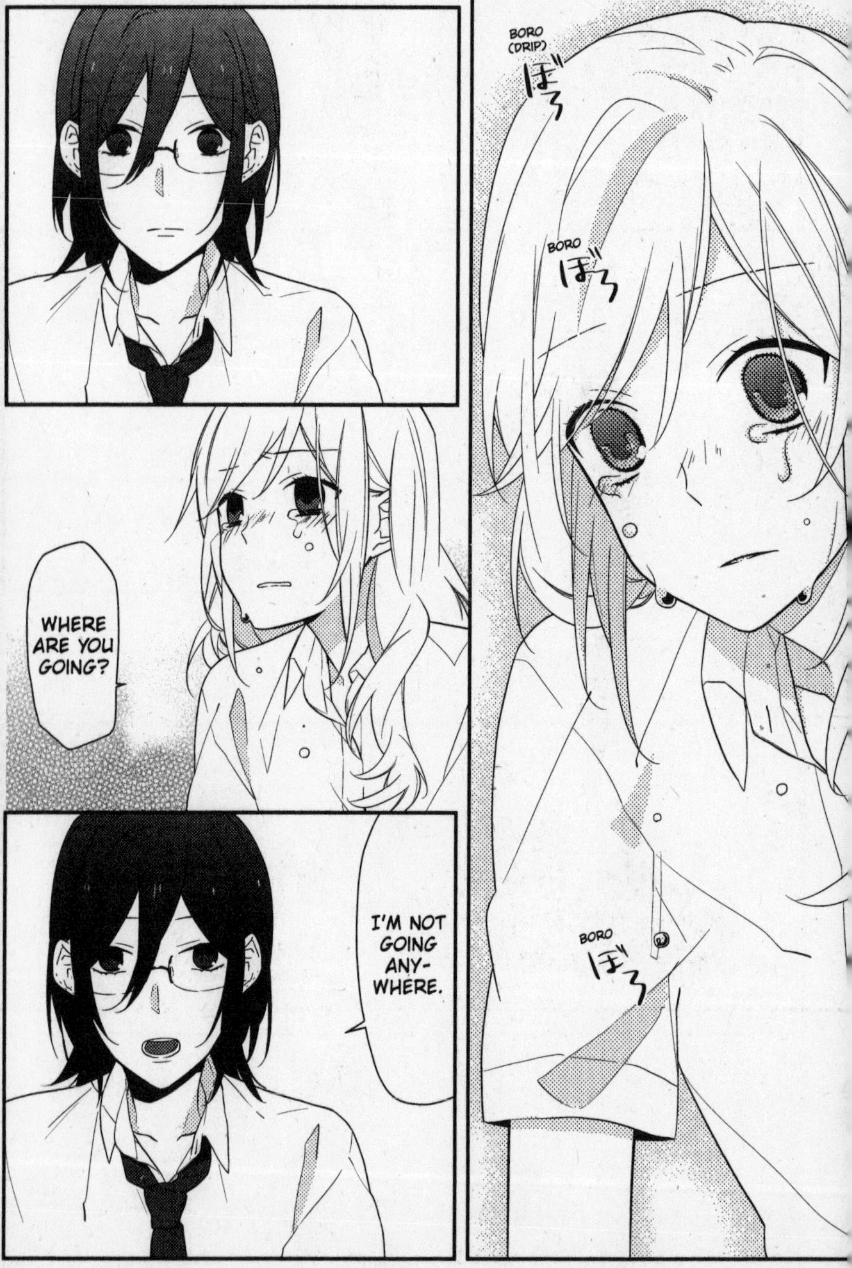
BORO (DRIP)
ぼろ
BORO
ぼろ
BORO
ぼろ
WHERE ARE YOU GOING?
I'M NOT GOING ANY-WHERE.

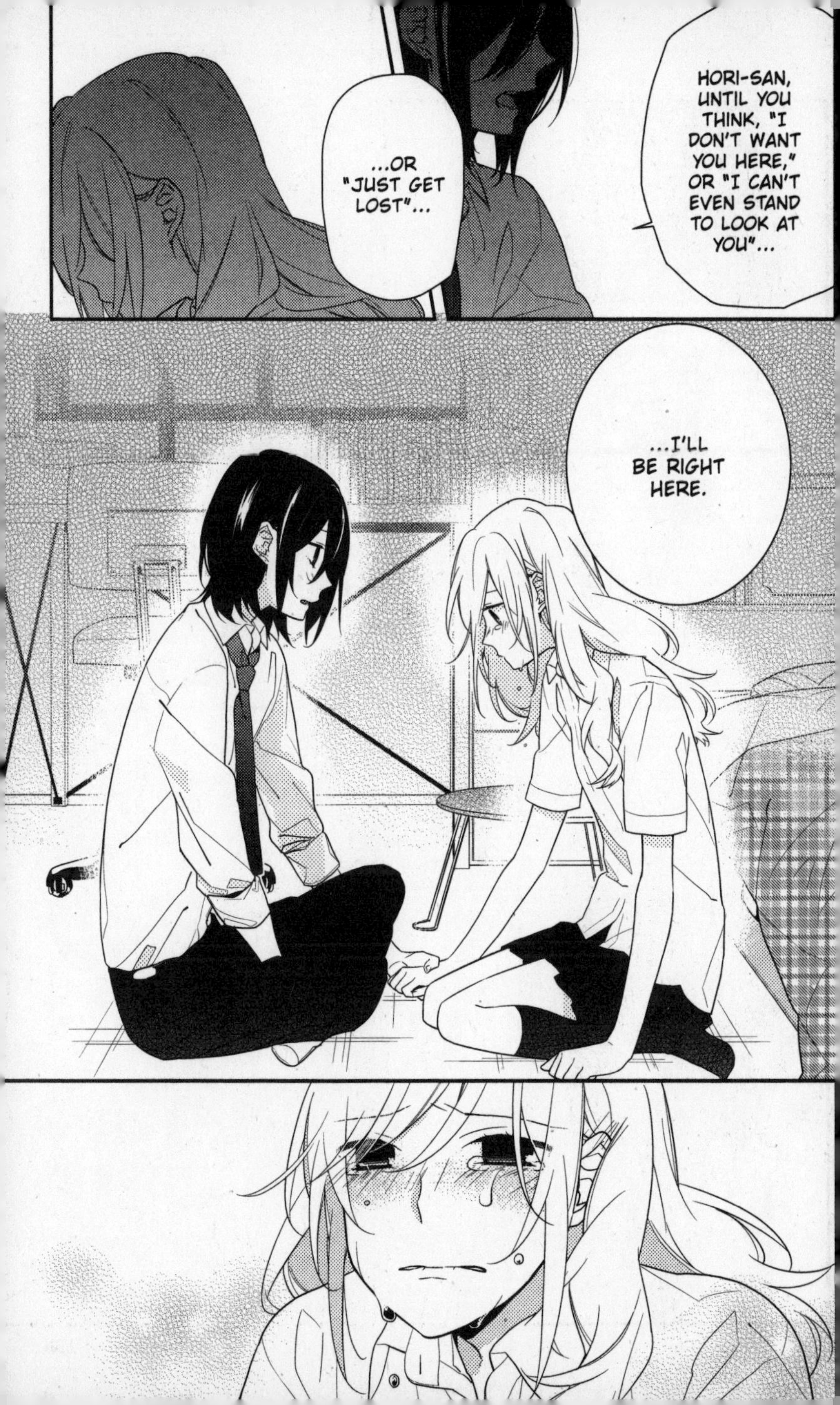
HORI-SAN, UNTIL YOU THINK, "I DON'T WANT YOU HERE," OR "I CAN'T EVEN STAND TO LOOK AT YOU"...
...OR "JUST GET LOST"...
...I'LL BE RIGHT HERE.

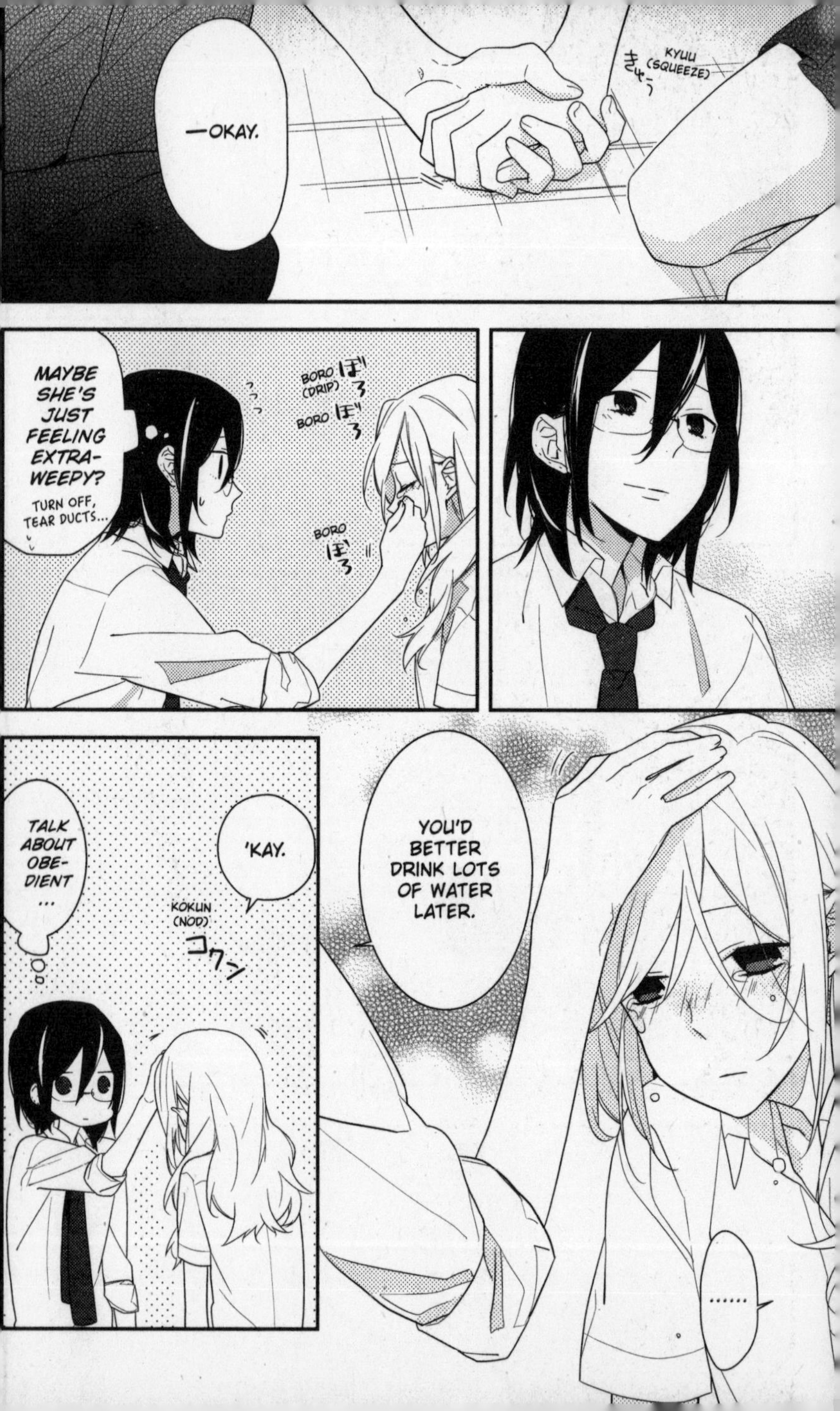
KYUU (SQUEEZE)
きゅう
—OKAY.
BORO (DRIP)
ぼろ
BORO
ぼろ
MAYBE SHE'S JUST FEELING EXTRA-WEEPY?
TURN OFF, TEAR DUCTS...
BORO
ぼろ
YOU'D BETTER DRINK LOTS OF WATER LATER.
......
'KAY.
KOKUN (NOD)
コクン
TALK ABOUT OBEDIENT...

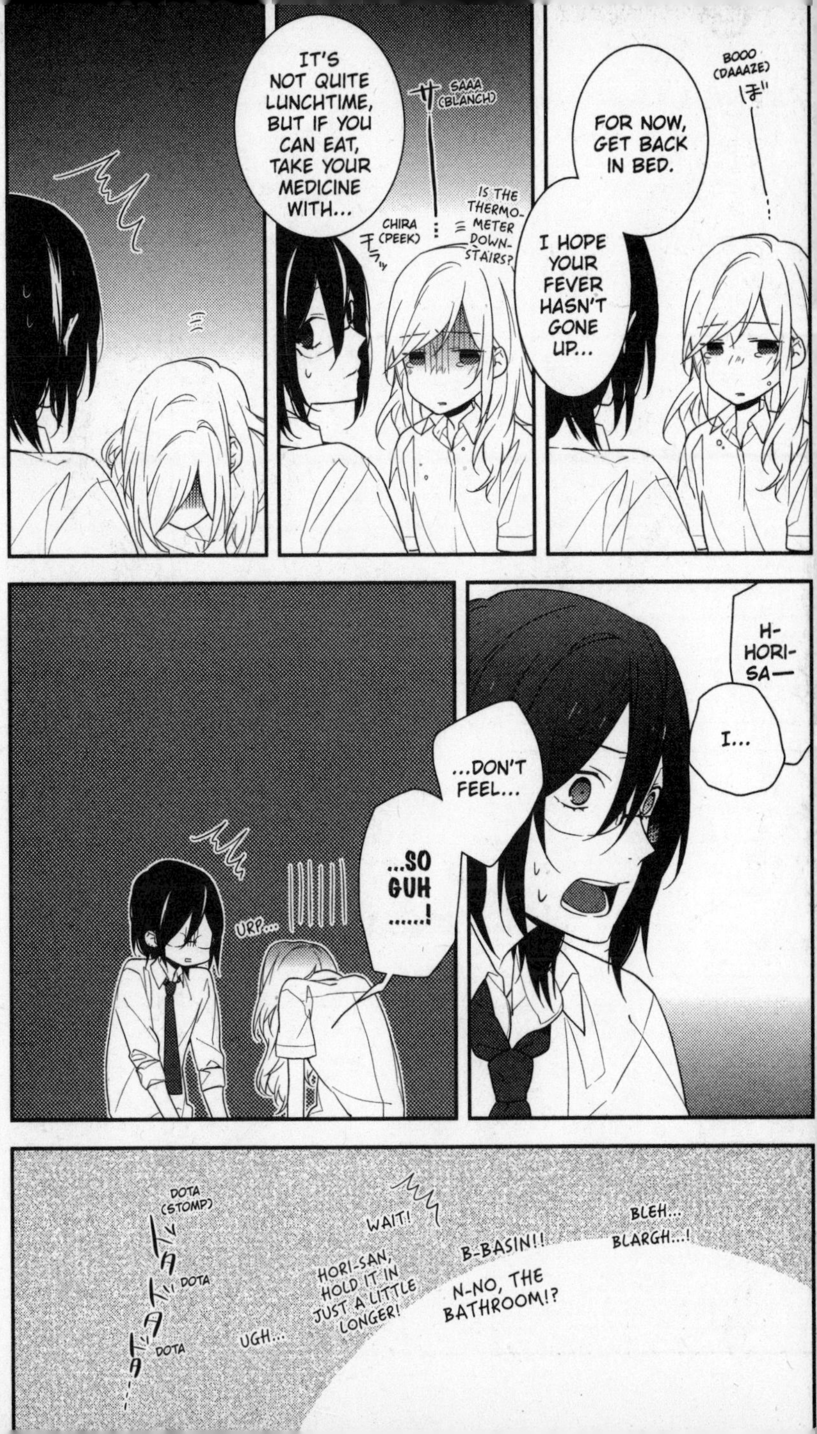
BOOO (DAAAZE)
ぼ
FOR NOW, GET BACK IN BED.
I HOPE YOUR FEVER HASN'T GONE UP...
SAAA (BLANCH)
サ
IT'S NOT QUITE LUNCHTIME, BUT IF YOU CAN EAT, TAKE YOUR MEDICINE WITH...
IS THE THERMOMETER DOWNSTAIRS?
CHIRA (PEEK)
H-HORI-SA—
I...
...DON'T FEEL...
...SO GUH......!
URP...
BLEH... BLARGH...!
N-NO, THE BATHROOM!?
B-BASIN!!
WAIT!
HORI-SAN, HOLD IT IN JUST A LITTLE LONGER!
UGH...
DOTA (STOMP)
DOTA
DOTA

A HUNDRED POINT FOUR...

PI (BIP)

PI
PI
PI

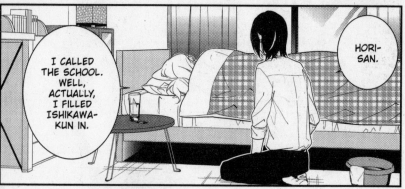

I CALLED THE SCHOOL. WELL, ACTUALLY, I FILLED ISHIKAWA-KUN IN.

HORI-SAN.

SHIIIN (SILENCE)

IS SHE ASLEEP?

164

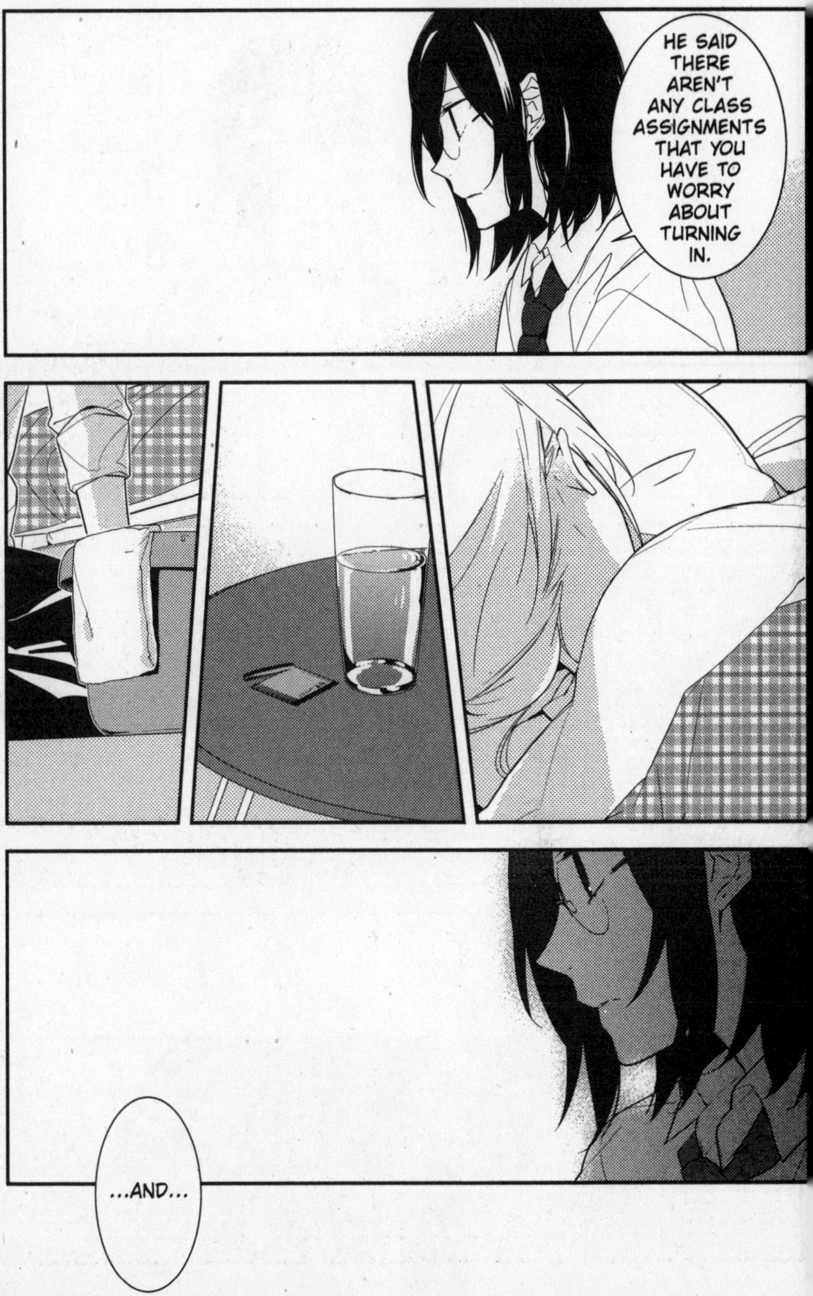
HE SAID THERE AREN'T ANY CLASS ASSIGNMENTS THAT YOU HAVE TO WORRY ABOUT TURNING IN.
...AND...

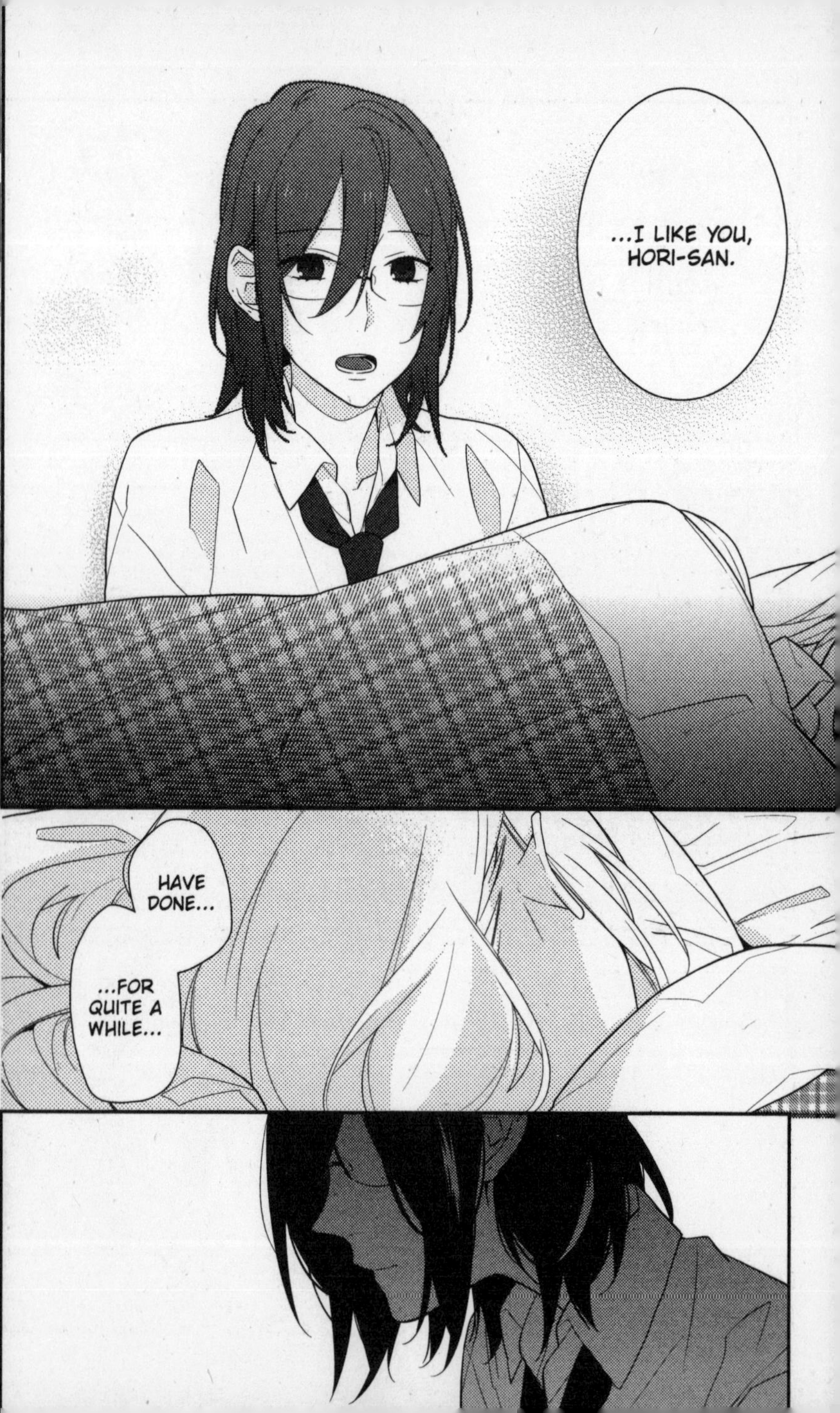
...I LIKE YOU, HORI-SAN.
HAVE DONE...
...FOR QUITE A WHILE...

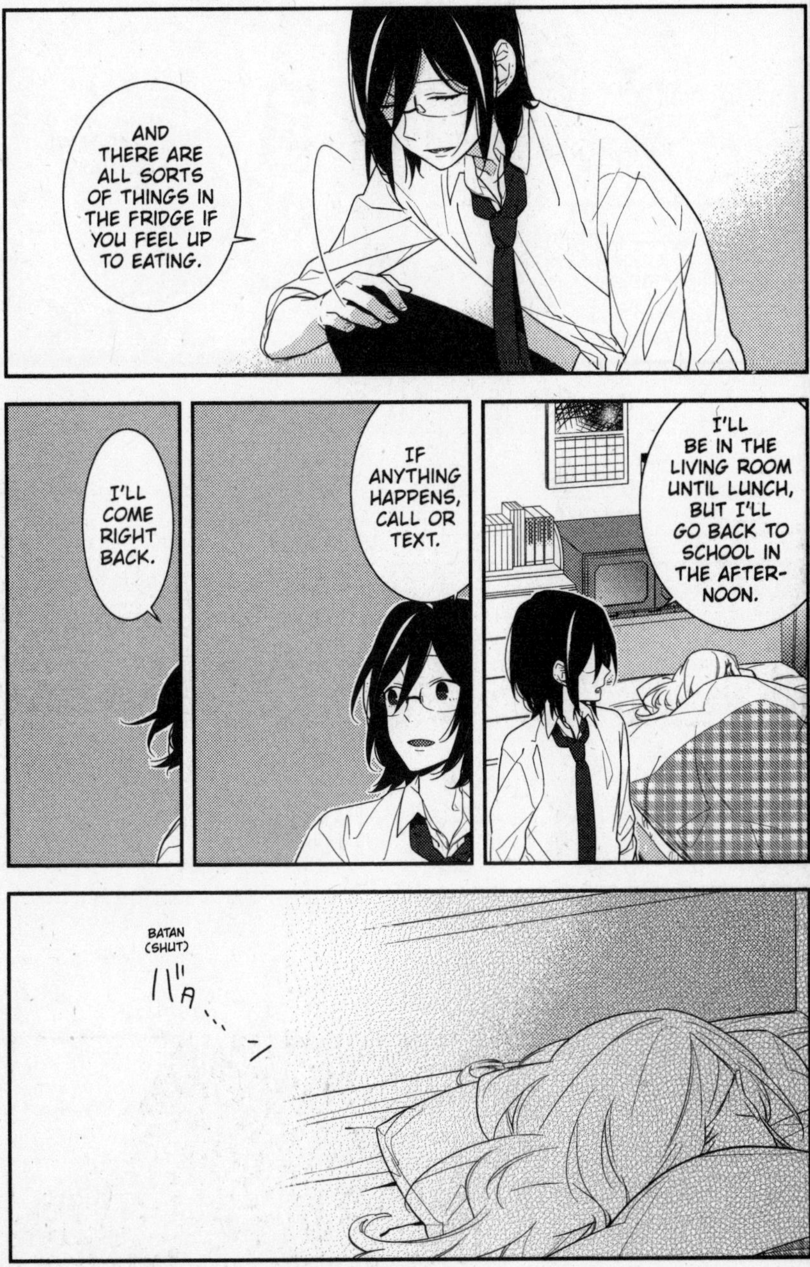
AND THERE ARE ALL SORTS OF THINGS IN THE FRIDGE IF YOU FEEL UP TO EATING.
I'LL BE IN THE LIVING ROOM UNTIL LUNCH, BUT I'LL GO BACK TO SCHOOL IN THE AFTERNOON.
IF ANYTHING HAPPENS, CALL OR TEXT.
I'LL COME RIGHT BACK.
BATAN (SHUT)

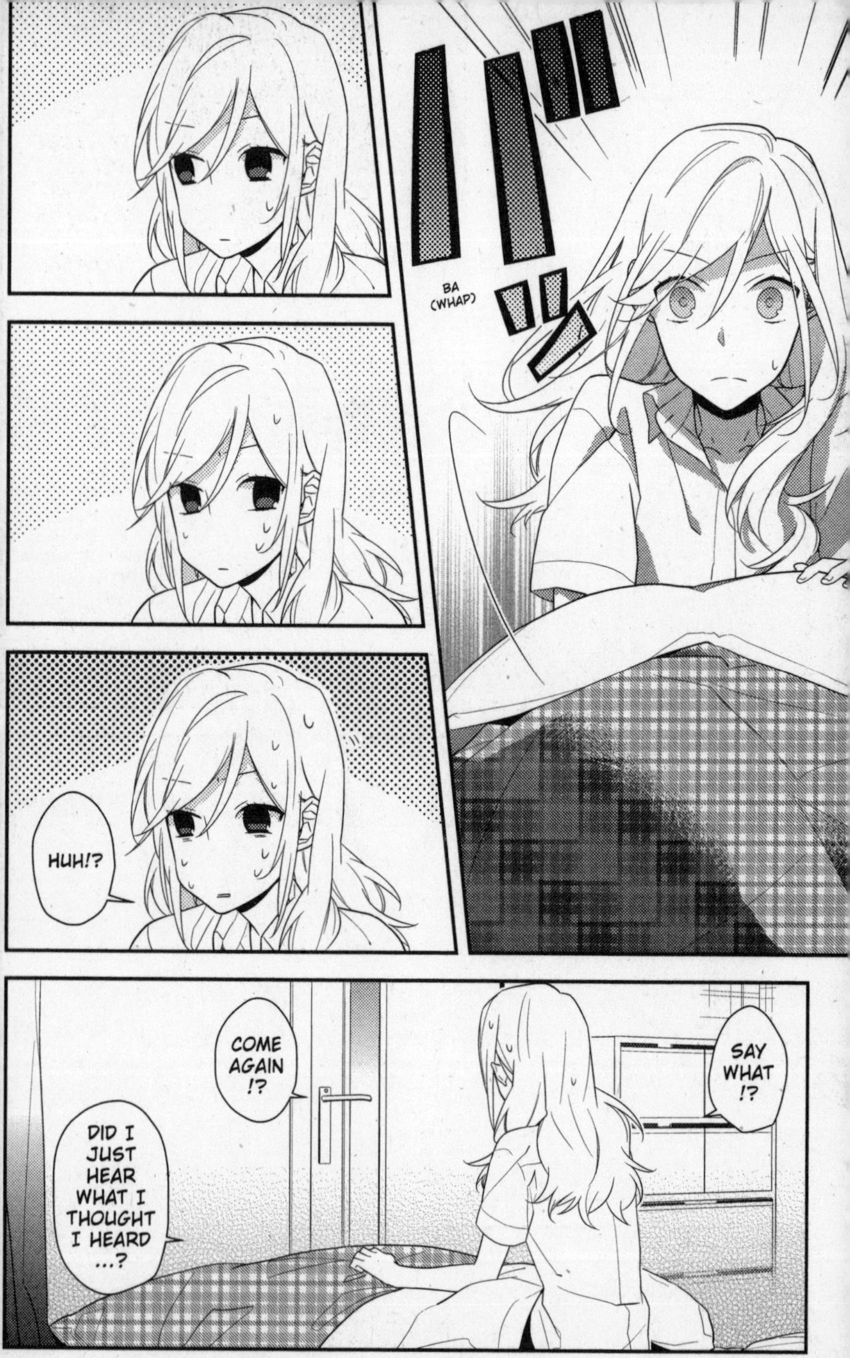
BA (WHAP)
HUH!?
SAY WHAT !?
COME AGAIN !?
DID I JUST HEAR WHAT I THOUGHT I HEARD ...?

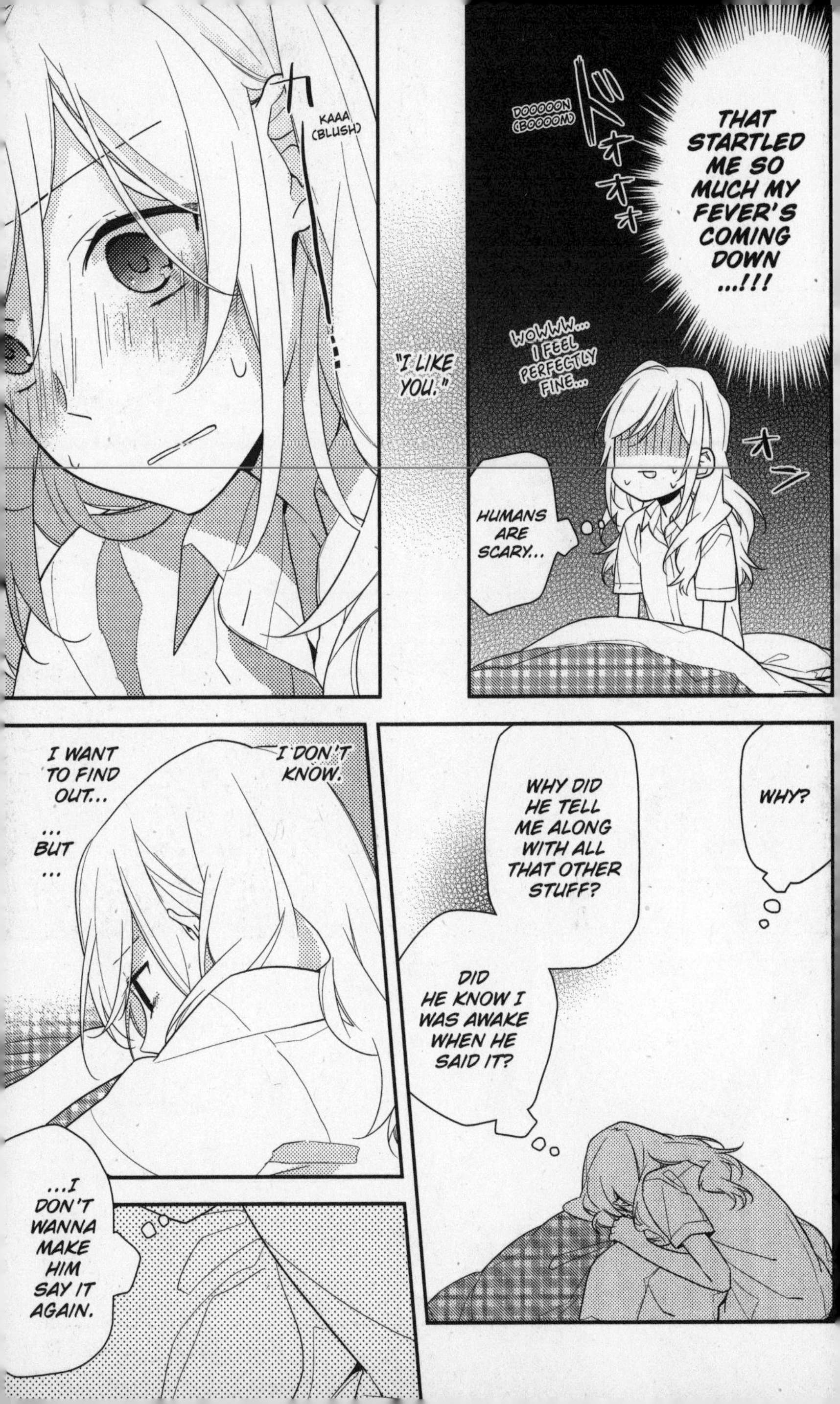
DOOOOON (BOOOOM)
THAT STARTLED ME SO MUCH MY FEVER'S COMING DOWN ...!!!
WOWWW... I FEEL PERFECTLY FINE...
HUMANS ARE SCARY...
"I LIKE YOU."
KAAA (BLUSH)
WHY?
WHY DID HE TELL ME ALONG WITH ALL THAT OTHER STUFF?
DID HE KNOW I WAS AWAKE WHEN HE SAID IT?
I DON'T KNOW.
I WANT TO FIND OUT...
... BUT ...
...I DON'T WANNA MAKE HIM SAY IT AGAIN.

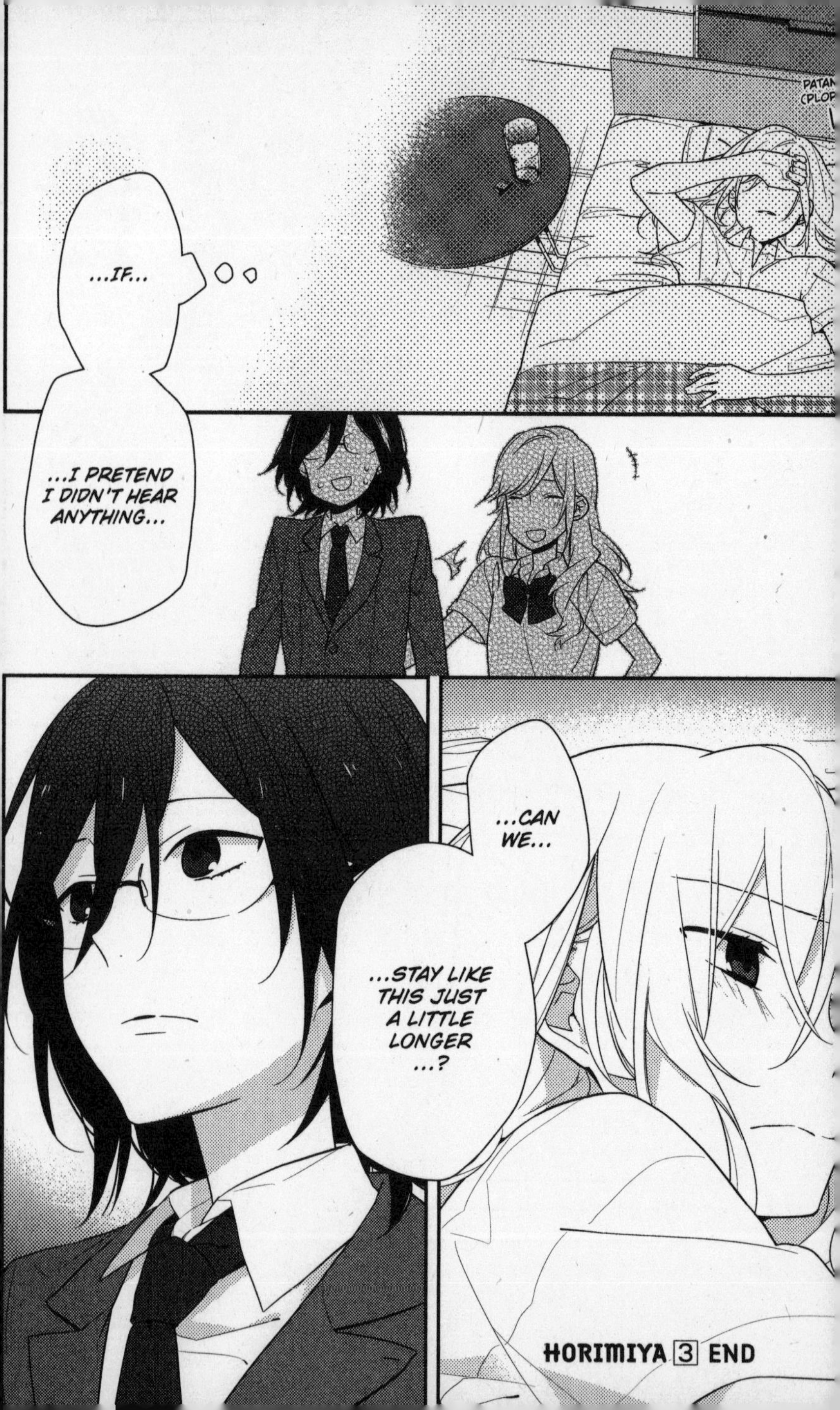
PATAN (PLOP
...IF...
...I PRETEND I DIDN'T HEAR ANYTHING...
...CAN WE...
...STAY LIKE THIS JUST A LITTLE LONGER ...?
HORIMIYA 3 END

To Be Continued...

Translation Notes

Page 33 – Stew
Going by the color, the stew Miyamura likes is probably cream stew, a Western-style Japanese dish of meat and vegetables simmered in a thick creamy white soup.

Page 115-116 – Yama, Kawa, Hashi
Each of Shindou's name guesses incorporates one of these three kanji, which are relatively common in Japanese surnames. *Yama* means "mountain," *kawa* means "river," and *hashi* means "bridge."

Page 117 – Bump
This is most likely a reference to Bump of Chicken, an extremely popular J-rock band formed in 1994.

Page 136 – Pachi High
The first kanji character in *Yasaka* can also be read *pachi*.

Page 146 – Summer colds
Hori is referring to the Japanese proverb that says "Idiots catch cold in summertime." ("*Natsukaze wa baka ga hiku.*")

Page 151 – Pocari
Pocari Sweat is a Japanese sports drink designed mainly to replenish electrolytes.

BONUS MANGA: MYAMURA ②

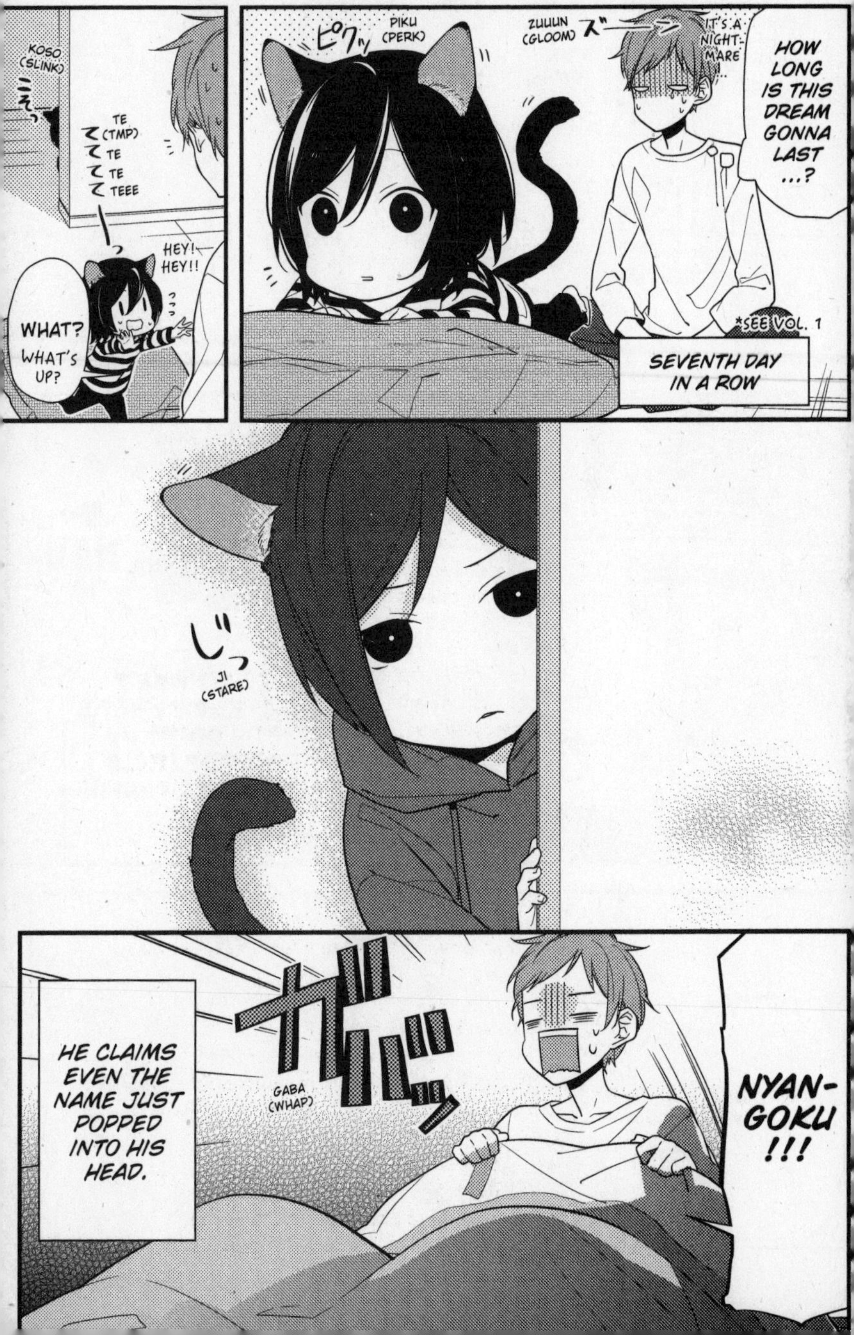

HOW LONG IS THIS DREAM GONNA LAST ...?
IT'S A NIGHTMARE ...
ZUUUN (GLOOM)
PIKU (PERK)
*SEE VOL. 1
SEVENTH DAY IN A ROW
KOSO (SLINK)
TE (TMP) TE TE TEEE
HEY! HEY!!
WHAT? WHAT'S UP?
じっ
JI (STARE)
NYAN-GOKU!!!
GABA (WHAP)
HE CLAIMS EVEN THE NAME JUST POPPED INTO HIS HEAD.

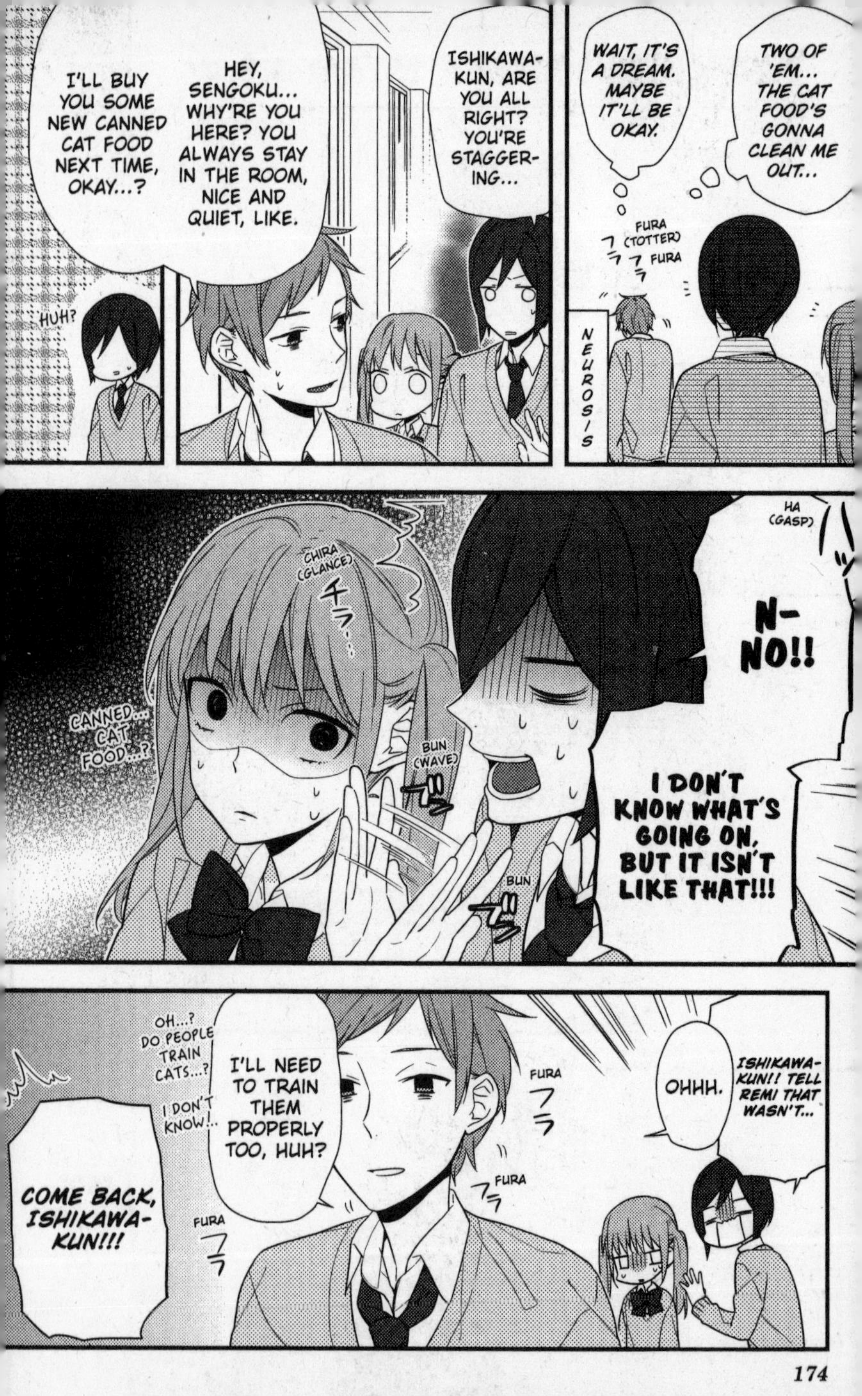
TWO OF 'EM... THE CAT FOOD'S GONNA CLEAN ME OUT...
WAIT, IT'S A DREAM. MAYBE IT'LL BE OKAY.
FURA (TOTTER) FURA
NEUROSIS
ISHIKAWA-KUN, ARE YOU ALL RIGHT? YOU'RE STAGGERING...
HEY, SENGOKU... WHY'RE YOU HERE? YOU ALWAYS STAY IN THE ROOM, NICE AND QUIET, LIKE.
I'LL BUY YOU SOME NEW CANNED CAT FOOD NEXT TIME, OKAY...?
HUH?
HA (GASP)
N-NO!!
I DON'T KNOW WHAT'S GOING ON, BUT IT ISN'T LIKE THAT!!!
CHIRA (GLANCE)
BUN (WAVE)
BUN
CANNED... CAT FOOD...?
ISHIKAWA-KUN!! TELL REMI THAT WASN'T...
OHHH.
FURA
FURA
I'LL NEED TO TRAIN THEM PROPERLY TOO, HUH?
OH...? DO PEOPLE TRAIN CATS...?
I DON'T KNOW!...
FURA
COME BACK, ISHIKAWA-KUN!!!

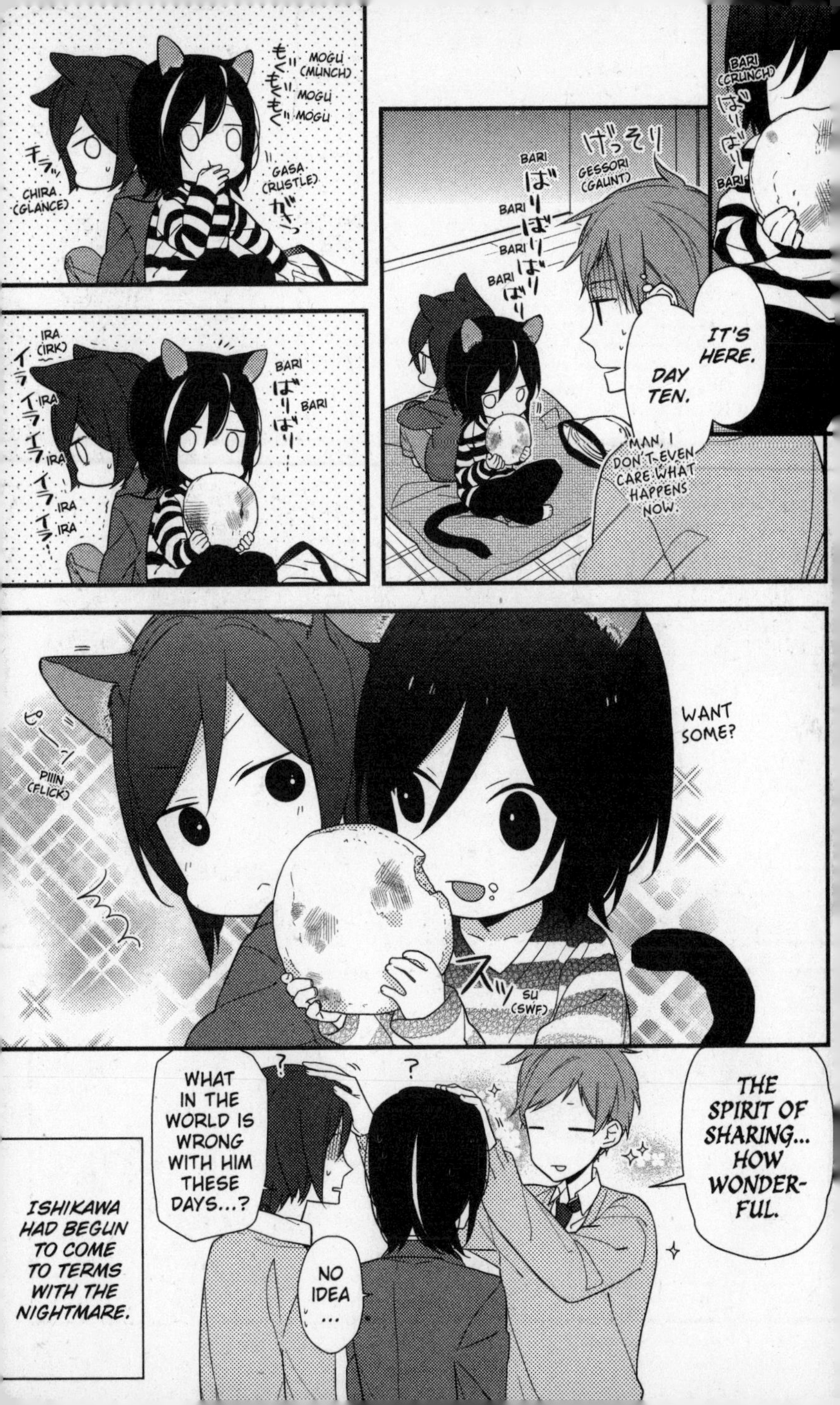

BARI (CRUNCH)
ばりばり
BARI
げっそり
GESSORI (GAUNT)
ばりばりばりばり
BARI
BARI
BARI
BARI
IT'S HERE.
DAY TEN.
MAN, I DON'T EVEN CARE WHAT HAPPENS NOW.
もぐもぐもぐ
MOGU (MUNCH)
MOGU
MOGU
チラッ
CHIRA (GLANCE)
ガサッ
GASA (RUSTLE)
ばりばり
BARI
BARI
イライライラ
IRA (IRK)
IRA
IRA
IRA
IRA
WANT SOME?
ピーン
PIIIN (FLICK)
スッ
SU (SWF)
THE SPIRIT OF SHARING... HOW WONDERFUL.
WHAT IN THE WORLD IS WRONG WITH HIM THESE DAYS...?
NO IDEA...
ISHIKAWA HAD BEGUN TO COME TO TERMS WITH THE NIGHTMARE.

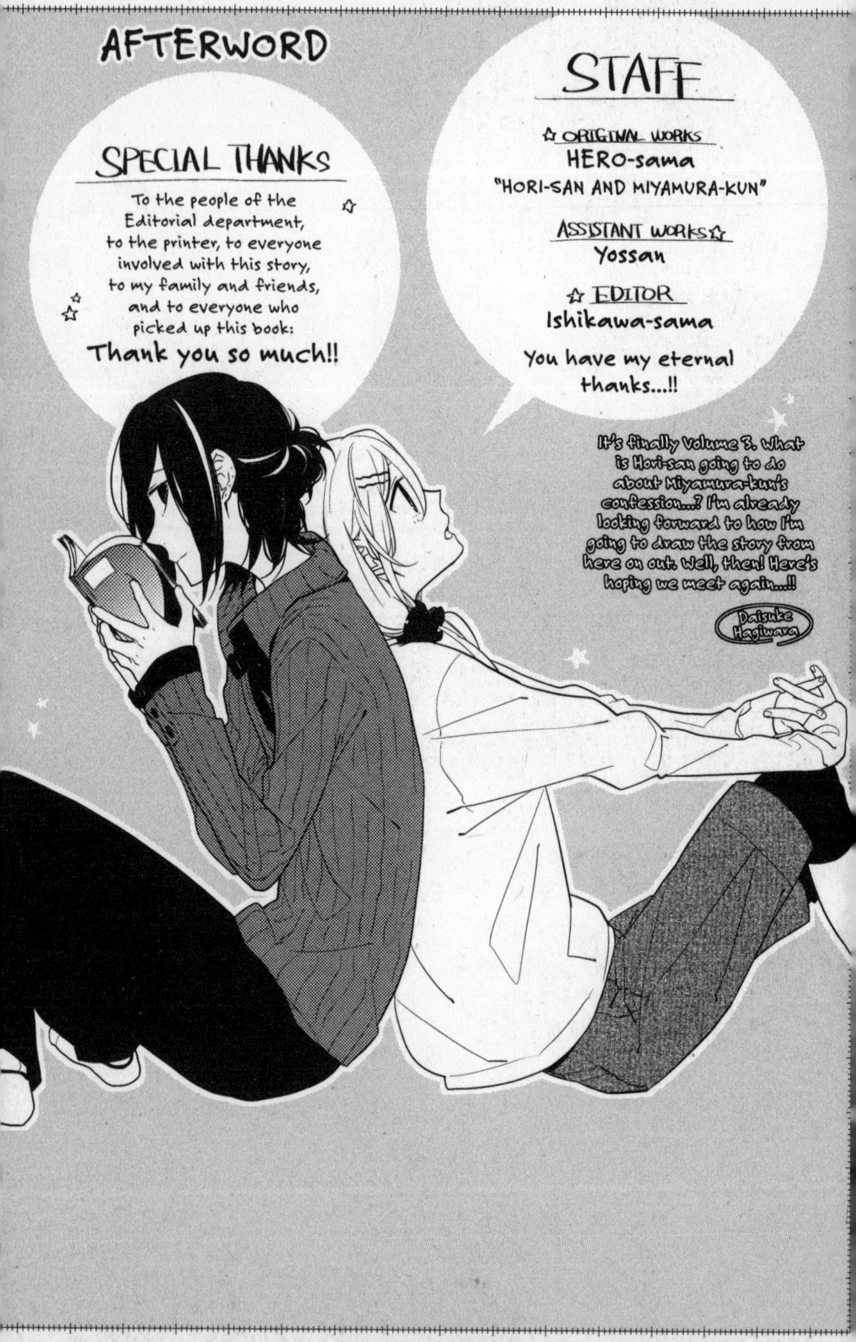
AFTERWORD
STAFF
☆ ORIGINAL WORKS
HERO-sama
"HORI-SAN AND MIYAMURA-KUN"
ASSISTANT WORKS ☆
Yossan
☆ EDITOR
Ishikawa-sama
You have my eternal thanks...!!
SPECIAL THANKS
To the people of the Editorial department, to the printer, to everyone involved with this story, to my family and friends, and to everyone who picked up this book:
Thank you so much!!
It's finally Volume 3. What is Hori-san going to do about Miyamura-kun's confession...? I'm already looking forward to how I'm going to draw the story from here on out. Well, then! Here's hoping we meet again...!!
Daisuke Hagiwara

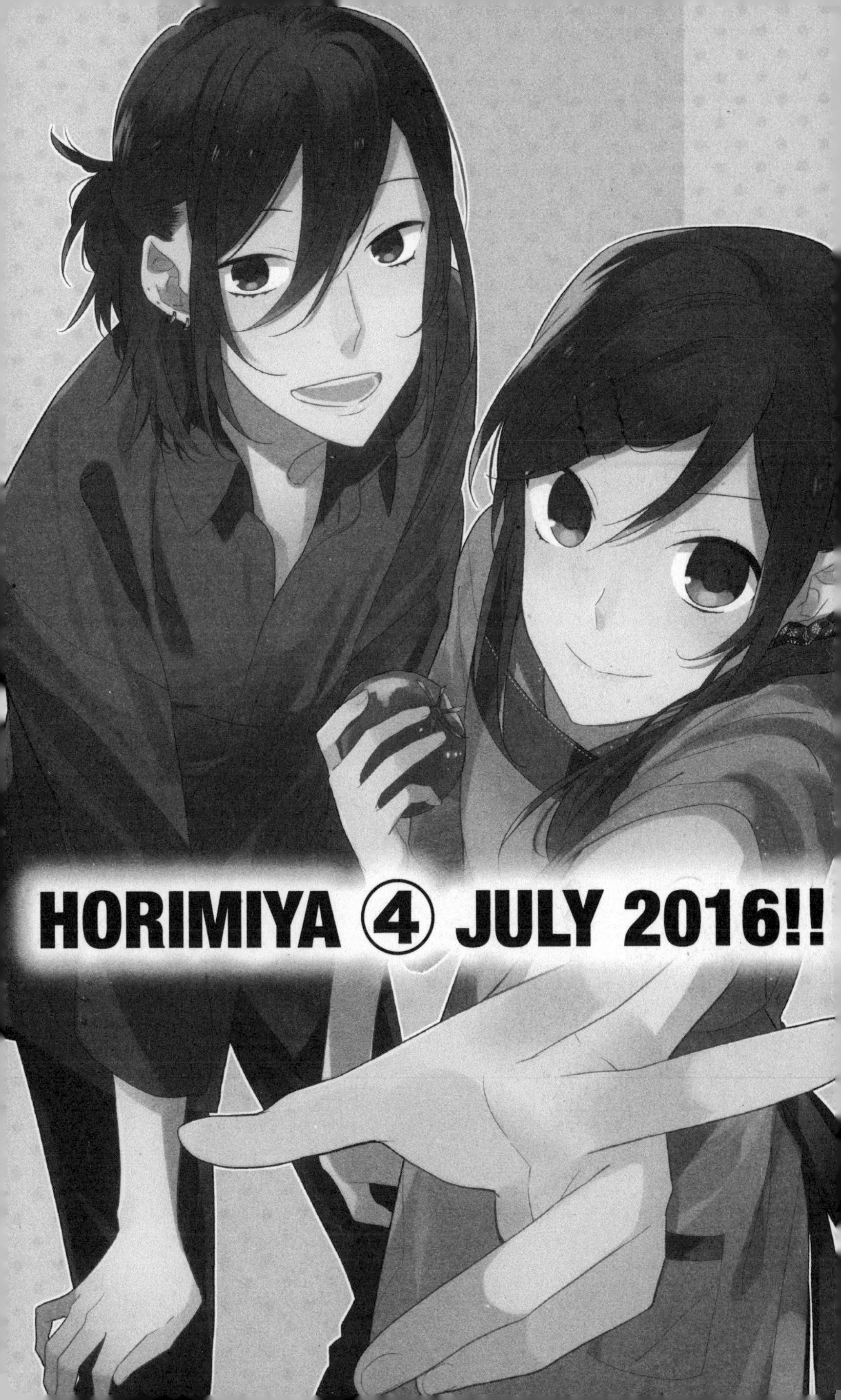
HORIMIYA ④ JULY 2016!!

HORIMIYA

HERO × DAISUKE HAGIWARA

Translation: Taylor Engel
Lettering: Alexis Eckerman

HORIMIYA vol. 3
© HERO • OOZ
© 2013 Daisuke Hagiwara / SQUARE ENIX CO., LTD. First published in Japan in 2013 by SQUARE ENIX CO., LTD. English translation rights arranged with SQUARE ENIX CO., LTD. and Yen Press, LLC through Tuttle-Mori Agency, Inc.

English translation © 2016 by SQUARE ENIX CO., LTD.

Yen Press
1290 Avenue of the Americas
New York, NY 10104

Visit us at yenpress.com • facebook.com/yenpress • twitter.com/yenpress • yenpress.tumblr.com

First Yen Press Edition: April 2016

Yen Press is an imprint of Yen Press, LLC. The Yen Press name and logo are trademarks of Yen Press, LLC.

The publisher is not responsible for websites (or their content) that are not owned by the publisher.

Library of Congress Control Number: 2015960115

ISBNs: 978-0-316-27010-6 (paperback)
978-0-316-35662-6 (ebook)
978-0-316-35663-3 (app)

10 9 8 7 6 5

WOR

Printed in the United States of America